THE IDEA OF LIBERTY IN CANADA
DURING THE AGE
OF ATLANTIC REVOLUTIONS,
1776–1838

McGill-Queen's Studies in the History of Ideas
Series Editor: Philip J. Cercone

THE IDEA OF LIBERTY
IN CANADA DURING THE AGE
OF ATLANTIC REVOLUTIONS,
1776–1838

Michel Ducharme

Translated by Peter Feldstein

McGill-Queen's University Press
Montreal & Kingston • London • Ithaca

© McGill-Queen's University Press 2014
ISBN 978-0-7735-4400-0 (cloth)
ISBN 978-0-7735-4401-7 (paper)
ISBN 978-0-7735-9625-2 (ePDF)
ISBN 978-0-7735-9626-9 (ePUB)

Legal deposit third quarter 2014
Bibliothèque nationale du Québec

Printed in Canada on acid-free paper that is 100% ancient forest free
(100% post-consumer recycled), processed chlorine free

This book has been published with the help of a grant from the Canadian
Federation for the Humanities and Social Sciences, through the Awards to
Scholarly Publications Program, using funds provided by the Social Sciences
and Humanities Research Council of Canada. We acknowledge the financial
support of the Government of Canada, through the National Translation
Program for Book Publishing, for our translation activities.

McGill-Queen's University Press acknowledges the support of the Canada
Council for the Arts for our publishing program. We also acknowledge the
financial support of the Government of Canada through the Canada Book
Fund for our publishing activities.

Library and Archives Canada Cataloguing in Publication

Ducharme, Michel, 1975
      [Concept de liberté au Canada à l'époque des révolutions atlantiques,
      1776–1838. English]
      The idea of liberty in Canada during the age of Atlantic revolutions,
      1776–1838 / Michel Ducharme; translated by Peter Feldstein.

      (McGill-Queen's studies in the history of ideas; 62)
      Translation of: Le concept de liberté au Canada à l'époque
      des révolutions atlantiques, 1776–1838.
      Includes bibliographical references and index.
      Issued in print and electronic formats.
      ISBN 978-0-7735-4400-0 (bound). – ISBN 978-0-7735-4401-7 (pbk.). –
      ISBN 978-0-7735-9625-2 (ePDF). – ISBN 978-0-7735-9626-9 (ePUB)

      1. Canada – History – 18th century. 2. Canada – History – 19th century.
      3. Canada – Social conditions – 18th century. 4. Canada – Social conditions –
      19th century. 5. Canada – Intellectual life – 18th century. 6. Canada –
      Intellectual life – 19th century. 7. Canada – Politics and government –
      Philosophy. I. Feldstein, Peter, 1962–, translator II. Title. III. Title: Concept
      de liberté au Canada à l'époque des révolutions atlantiques, 1776–1838.
      English. IV. Series: McGill-Queen's studies in the history of ideas; 62

      FC95.3.D8313 2014   971.03   C2014-902250-6
                                                         C2014-902251-4

This book was typeset by Interscript in 10/12 New Baskerville.

Contents

British North America under the Quebec Act (1774)

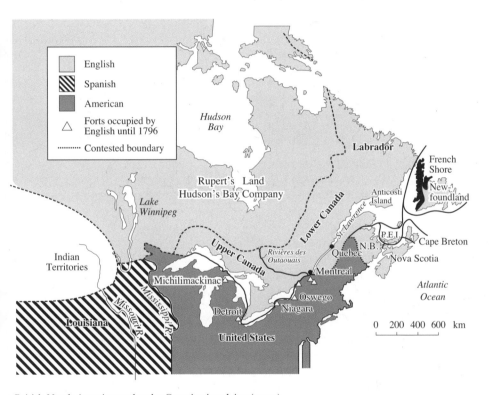

English

Spanish

American

△ Forts occupied by English until 1796

...... Contested boundary

Hudson Bay

Labrador

French Shore

New-foundland

Rupert's Land
Hudson's Bay Company

Anticosti Island

Lake Winnipeg

Lower Canada

St-Lawrence

P.E.I.

Cape Breton

Indian Territories

Upper Canada

Rivières des Outaouais

Quebec

N.B.

Nova Scotia

Michilimackinac

Montreal

Atlantic Ocean

Detroit

Oswego

Niagara

Mississippi R.

Missouri R.

0   200 400 600 km

Louisiana

United States

British North America under the Constitutional Act (1791)

THE IDEA OF LIBERTY IN CANADA
DURING THE AGE
OF ATLANTIC REVOLUTIONS,
1776–1838

Introduction

ON 4 JULY 1776, thirteen of the sixteen British colonies of North America declared their independence. The Province of Quebec (1763–91), along with Nova Scotia and Saint John's Island (renamed Prince Edward Island in 1798), did not join the rebel colonies. This decision had profound implications for its development and would colour subsequent interpretations of that development. The American, French, European, and South American revolutionaries of the late eighteenth and early nineteenth centuries had waved the banner of liberty; as a result of the loyalist outcome in Quebec, its history has long been interpreted as one of having been untouched by Enlightenment ideas and left out of the struggles that characterized the Atlantic world. Indeed, the province has traditionally been considered the embodiment of counterrevolutionary ideals: loyalty and order, not liberty.[1]

While these ideals were present in colonial Quebec, they were not the only ones at play.[2] This book considers the role played by the concept of liberty in the development of the Canadian state between the American Revolution (1776) and the Upper and Lower Canadian rebellions (1837–38). I will situate Quebec's history within the Atlantic framework, presenting a kind of "cis-Atlantic history" or local history told as part of a broader Atlantic history.[3] Few historians of the Atlantic world have devoted much attention to the Canadian experience;[4] conversely, only a few Canadianists have attempted to set their work within the Atlantic context.[5] Quebec historians in particular have tended to look at Quebec through the lens of "Americanness" (*américanité*),[6] or of new societies, or instead have compared Quebec's history with that of the small European nationalities of the nineteenth century.[7] English Canadian historians, for their part, have generally opted for a continental (American) or imperial (British) perspective.[8] While these various perspectives have shed light on important aspects of the Canadian experience and are still useful today, the Atlantic framework – at the crossroads of French, British, and American history – has the advantage of conjoining them. It allows one to revisit Canadian history in the light of these three spheres of influence.[9]

I intend this book primarily as a contribution to intellectual history: the history of ideas, prejudices, principles, values, concepts, and ideologies as they influence the lives of individuals and the development of societies. The ability to think is what enables human beings to make choices, justify decisions, choose courses of action, structure and legitimize complex sociopolitical systems; it is what allows us to give meaning to our existence. The ability to think contributes to the shaping of human societies and guides their development. Ideas, as British historian Michael Braddick put it, "sketch the boundaries of what can and cannot be done." They constitute "limits on the sphere of action that can plausibly be justified with reference to certain particular values."[10] Concepts are thus essential to life in society in that each "establishes a particular horizon for potential experience and conceivable theory,"[11] in the words of the German historian Reinhart Koselleck. Obviously, the relationship between ideas and the horizon of possibilities in a society is not unidirectional. While ideas circumscribe this horizon, they are in turn being adapted and reinvented as a function of historical circumstances, and this horizon is continually opening, transforming, and closing accordingly. Thus, to truly grasp the meanings of ideas and concepts, their evolution over time must be studied.

Of all the ideas at play in the eighteenth-century Atlantic world, liberty is certainly one of the most important and subversive. Not only did the idea of liberty undermine the foundations of the ancien régime in Europe and pose a threat to colonial ties between European empires and American colonies, but it also boded a reconceptualization of the workings of society. The Province of Quebec, and later Upper and Lower Canada (1791–1841), belonged to this world; yet the manner in which liberty influenced their development has remained somewhat obscure.[12] My analysis in this book is an attempt to shed light on the different meanings assigned to liberty and freedom in this historical context.[13] It will discuss the political implications of these conceptions, how they evolved over time, and how they influenced Canadian history in the late eighteenth and early nineteenth centuries, when the Atlantic revolutions were in full swing.

It would be invalid, in my view, to adopt an arbitrary present-day definition of liberty at the outset as a kind of standard against which historical conceptions either do or do not measure up. Instead, I will postulate that all definitions of liberty are, a priori, equally valid. Liberty, for my purposes, is a subjective perception formed by individuals of themselves and the society in which they live. It is a way of conceiving of the roles, responsibilities, and rights of individuals vis-à-vis one another, society, and the state. This perception is influenced by one's education, culture, membership in a particular community (ethnicity, class, gender, etc.), particular circumstances, and personal thought processes. Put another way, I start from the postulate that an individual is free if and only if he believes himself to be free within an existing context, political system, or social hierarchy.

TWO CONCEPTS OF LIBERTY

Without question, the revolutionaries of the late eighteenth century waged their struggles under the banner of liberty. Their definition of this concept, inspired by the English, American, and French republicans and radicals, was encapsulated in the phrase "liberty, equality, fraternity (community)." Founded, as we shall see, on popular sovereignty, political participation, and the omnipotence of the legislative branch, it was conceptualized around an ethic of civic virtue and an agrarian ideal.[14]

But despite its pervasive influence, the republican conception of liberty was not the only one in play. Facing off against it was another form of liberty that I shall term "modern liberty." The term derives from the fact that the concept originated in the modern era, in conjunction with the appearance of the modern conception of the individual. Termed "the liberty of the moderns" by Benjamin Constant in 1819, this form of liberty is today simply called "modern liberty."[15] Modern liberty originated in the late seventeenth century, was institutionalized in England following the Glorious Revolution (1688), and spread throughout Europe in the century that followed. It was the work of first-generation Enlightenment philosophers, English Whigs, a few Scottish philosophers, American federalists, and others. It gave primacy to a group of individual rights that have often been encapsulated in the phrase "liberty, property, security." Less concerned with equality than individual autonomy, the partisans of modern liberty conceived of the state in such a way that it could not, as they saw it, violate these rights. Such a state allowed for private interests to compete for influence within the general framework marked out by political institutions. It gave impetus to commerce and wealth accumulation.

If we are to deepen our understanding of the Atlantic world in general, and British North America in particular, it will be necessary to elucidate the differences between these two competing conceptions of liberty. I will begin by challenging the conventional wisdom that all eighteenth-century thinkers largely shared the same conception of liberty, and hence the same ideal of society. As a preliminary remark, I would note that revolutionary ideas did not simply spring from the Enlightenment as the night follows the day. Historians have often struggled to explain the relationship between these ideas, probably because their roots in the Enlightenment are much shallower than is generally assumed.[16] There was in fact an abrupt shift between the ideas developed by philosophers from 1700 to 1750 and those developed by republicans and revolutionaries after 1760. Both attacked the foundations of the state; but while the philosophers launched their attack from the modern conception of liberty, the republicans and revolutionaries launched theirs from the republican conception. These two conceptions of liberty produce very different understandings of the state and the social order. Likewise, they produce different understandings of the individual and of his rights, duties, and responsibilities (to himself and others).

This analytical framework sheds light on the intellectual foundations of the Canadian experience. It suggests that the Province of Quebec's refusal to join the ranks of the rebel colonies did not necessarily consign it to the margins of the Atlantic world, to a place where the idea of liberty never took root. In fact, liberty was a matter for debate there in the last decades of the Enlightenment century and the first decades of the next. On the one hand, the colonial elites freely borrowed, used, and reinterpreted prevailing Atlantic ideas during this period. On the other hand, when the British Parliament passed the Constitutional Act of 1791, it reconceptualized political power and social relations in the Province of Quebec (thenceforth Upper and Lower Canada) based on a certain conception of liberty – namely, modern liberty – forcing the colonial elites to adjust their understanding to the new political reality. The ideal embodied in the new constitution was different from the one that undergirded the Atlantic Revolutions, yet still proceeded directly from the Enlightenment. I cannot go along with a Manichean view in which the British colonists, in rejecting the revolution, ipso facto opted for reaction or counterrevolution. It is fairer to say that they rejected one form of liberty in the interests of preserving and promoting another.

A close analysis of the concepts of liberty that existed in the Canadas also provides an opportunity to revisit the Canadian crisis of the 1830s. Until now, this crisis has been set down to economic, social, and political causes, particularly as a result of the vexed relationship between the Canadas and the empire. All this is true and has been amply demonstrated. Not enough attention has been devoted, however, to the irreducible ideological clash that took place between two visions of social relations and power dynamics. The political impasse that gripped Lower

Canada as of 1836, giving way to the rebellions of 1837–38, can be ascribed in large part to a clash between the defenders of the constitution, who subscribed to the ideals of modern liberty, and the forces demanding a reconfiguration of power in the colonies, who subscribed to republican liberty. If this clash had not occurred, a peaceful solution to the crisis might have been easier to find. This reinterpretation of early Canadian intellectual history is also useful in reincorporating the rebellions into the ideological framework of the revolutions that shook the Atlantic world in the late eighteenth century, as Allan Greer has suggested they should be.[17] From this perspective, the 1837–38 rebellions emerge as the final chapter of the Atlantic revolutions.[18]

And finally, by clarifying the underlying principles of the pre-rebellion colonial state, I will try to shed light on the foundations of the modern Canadian liberal state. Historians have examined in detail how Canada's governmental apparatus began to modernize in the 1840s with the revision of many laws and the creation of new institutions and functions, including police, municipalities, schools, responsible government, a professional bureaucracy, prisons, and statistics.[19] More recently, Ian McKay and Jean-Marie Fecteau have described what took place at this time as the inception of a new liberal order.[20] But the antecedents of this new order are less well known, a lacuna this study seeks to rectify in the wake of recent work on Whiggism and liberalism.[21]

Note, however, that while modern liberty is indeed fundamental to the liberalism that developed in Canada after 1840, I prefer the term "constitutionalism" to describe its predecessor ideology. "Commercialism," the term preferred by intellectual historians of the Atlantic world, is less well suited to a reconceptualization of this ideology as the political equal of republicanism. As for the term "liberalism," its usage in this context would be largely anachronistic.[22] In British North America prior to 1840, "liberal" mainly meant "generous"; "liberalism," referring to an ideology based on individual rights, was largely unknown. Furthermore, most eighteenth-century theorists of modern liberty could hardly be classed as ideological liberals in today's sense. Many of them advocated a social order whose economic, social, and hierarchical underpinnings emanated directly from the ancien régime, a regime with which later liberals would be perpetually at odds. "Whiggism" is another alternative for describing the ideology in question, but this term had too many different and contradictory meanings in the eighteenth and nineteenth centuries to be truly useful here.[23] Moreover, the use of this term would focus attention on the intellectual and political divide between the Whig and Tory politicians of the time, ignoring their shared adherence to a certain conception of liberty. On an ideological plane, then, this study deals with the historical opposition between republicanism and constitutionalism. The former would, in the nineteenth century, give rise to democracy (political equality) and socialism (economic equality) while the latter would engender British and Canadian liberalism and conservatism.[24]

METHODOLOGICAL APPROACH

I have chosen in this study to re-examine the histories of both Upper and Lower Canada. My purpose in doing so is to bring English Canadian and Quebec historiography out of their mutual isolation. There is nothing problematic or illegitimate about viewing history within a national/nationalist framework, but it is unfortunate that this framework has led the two solitudes to develop two almost entirely separate historiographies since the nineteenth century. Apart from textbooks and a few works published in English Canada in the 1960s,[25] the two Canadian historiographies have been practically deaf to each other, as if the histories of English Canada and French Canada (Quebec) have not been intimately linked for two centuries; as if the experience of each of these groups had nothing to teach the other.

My book, then, takes up Jocelyn Létourneau's suggestion that the nationalist framework within which Quebec historiography has developed since 1845 is due for revision. It is time, says Létourneau, to transcend Quebec nationalist historiography by reincorporating Quebec history into the Canadian framework. Canadianness (*canadianité*), his term for this approach, seeks neither to deny the internal conflicts existing in Canadian society nor the specificity of Quebec, but rather to see them as part and parcel of a broader Canadian experience.[26] A discussion of liberty lends itself well to such an approach, since the two Canadas were characterized by a single constitution, similar political institutions, a shared preindustrial framework, and the existence of political ferment during the 1830s. This is not to deny the problems that cultural diversity has caused in the development of the Canadas, nor the contempt in which certain colonial or British anglophones held the French Canadians, nor the desire of the former to minimize the power of the latter in Lower Canada. The point is that the national or colonial framework is not necessarily the best suited to a study of liberty, state legitimacy, and power dynamics in the late eighteenth and early nineteenth centuries. Therefore, I make no attempt in this book to study state legitimacy with reference to the national question; rather, I integrate the issue of cultural diversity, where useful, into the analysis of liberty as an important source of state legitimacy in Canada.

My approach is elite-centred: it concerns itself only with the leaders of the groups in question. Obviously, I make no claim that the relationship between the elites and the general public was unidirectional, with the former simply manipulating the latter. Still, before examining the interactions between these two groups, it is necessary to understand the principles, ideals, and values specific to each. In *The Patriots and the People,* Allan Greer dwells on popular republicanism in Lower Canada during the 1830s and the ways in which it was autonomous with respect to the ideology of the elites. But elite discourse itself has yet to be subjected to an equally meticulous analysis. While certain groups – the Patriotes, for example – have received a great deal of attention from historians,[27] others, such as the Lower Canadian anglophone elite, have been practically ignored. What is more, there is no existing general framework of interpretation applicable to the intellectual history of the period. This book aims to sketch an outline of such a framework.

In attempting to discover how liberty was variously defined in the Canadas and how these definitions influenced the development of the state, I opted for the method of discourse analysis. When a member of the colonial elite spoke in public, he was conscious of the political and social issues facing the colonies as well as the implications of his particular conception of liberty for colonial development. My analysis, then, is intended to reconstruct the ways in which state legitimacy and power relations were constructed (unilaterally) by the metropolitan authorities in 1791, as well as the manner in which the colonists proceeded to either recognize or contest this legitimacy.

Any discourse, need it be said, contains an element of propaganda and manipulation – not to mention that discourse often veils as much as it reveals. But discourse was nonetheless central to the legitimation of power dynamics and social relations in the eighteenth-century Atlantic world. Societal order was preserved not mainly by a strong military but by the articulation of a discourse distinguishing legitimate from illegitimate conduct. Physical force was used only to compel holdouts and deviants to obey laws that were, all things considered, just a formal recitation of the rules of society.

While I understand that pointed personal interests can lurk behind words and ideologies,[28] it is, I think, valuable to focus on the internal logic of colonial political speech and its evolution from 1776 to 1838, not on the reasons why various individuals spoke as they did. It is conceivable that the two concepts of liberty are reducible to mere tools used by people wishing to hold onto power (e.g., bureaucrats and members of the Family Compact) and by people wishing to wrest it away from them (e.g., the reformers, radicals, and Patriotes). But while I make occasional allusion to these actors' personal interests, a thorough study of those interests goes beyond the bounds of this study.

As a related point, the approach taken here focuses more on intellectual constructs than on institutions. Institutions, inasmuch as I give consideration to them, are studied with reference to their intellectual underpinnings. This approach facilitates our understanding of the organizational logic of the colonies, since their political institutions rested, as they do everywhere, on (frequently fictitious) premises whose purpose was to keep them running smoothly. To understand the nature of the colonial state, it is not sufficient to determine who had the power to do what; what is needed is to understand the grounds on which certain institutions and/or people were asserted to possess certain powers and not others. This intellectual approach is likewise useful in elucidating the nature and importance of the colonial protest movements. Most pertinently, such a movement is more threatening if it attacks the foundations of the state than if it merely calls for institutional reform.

The two concepts of liberty that I have reconstructed based on contemporaneous discourse represent ideal types *sensu* Weber – analytical categories useful for finding meaning in Canadian political history at the time of the Atlantic revolutions. This categorization, I think, affords a fair rendering of the fundamental opposition existing between well-defined groups in society at that time; yet, for all it illuminates, it does have its limitations. It does not fully do justice to the malleability of these concepts, the ways in which they were adapted and remade by politicians and intellectuals as the context required. For some examples, it makes no attempt to illuminate the tensions that existed within the republican and modern ranks, whether regional (Montreal versus Quebec, York/Toronto versus Kingston), linguistic (French Canadian versus English Canadian), or political (conservatives versus reformers among the advocates of modern liberty); nor does it account for the positions taken by more moderate intellectuals and politicians, or the peculiarities of each colony's experience.

Another point of qualification: since this study deals with liberty as the anchor of state legitimacy, it does not concern itself with the individual rights and freedoms that existed in the colonies, such as habeas corpus, freedom of religion, freedom of the press, freedom of association, and suffrage. Nor is the religious question considered. To begin with, Catholics and Protestants of all denominations enjoyed the same rights in the Province of Quebec as of 1774. The question of freedom of conscience and religion was not much debated from then until the rebellions, except as regards the rights of Jews. Still, the religious question did find itself central to several conflicts in both Upper and Lower Canada, though these often involved rather temporal issues.

For example, English-speaking Lower Canadian constitutionalists complained of the power of the Catholic Church in the colonies, whereas Catholics in Britain and Ireland were not yet emancipated, at least not before 1829. Their position found its roots in the British anti-Catholicism that provoked violent episodes ranging from the Gordon Riots of 1780 to the violence surrounding the creation of a Catholic hierarchy in Great Britain in the early 1850s. Similarly, a struggle for power and influence pitted the clergy against the Assembly in Lower Canada after 1791.[29] In Upper Canada, the two main bones of contention between the Anglican elite and the other groups were the distribution of clergy reserves among the various churches and the privileged status of the Church of England.[30] Despite the importance of these issues during and after the period in question, they did not relate to liberty or state legitimacy so much as to the relationship between church and state, between temporal power and spiritual power.

It would certainly be interesting to delve deeper into various aspects of the intellectual nexus between the colonial churches and the political scene in which they evolved. What specific concept of liberty did each subscribe to? What were the religious affiliations of the era's prominent intellectuals and politicians, and to what extent did those affiliations influence their public discourse? Conversely, what was the political position of these figures on the contentious issues surrounding Church-state relations and the official recognition of churches at the time of the Atlantic revolutions? Unfortunately, I did not have space here to focus on these issues, which would be fruitful subjects for further research.

Given the nature of my object of study, I relied heavily upon official documents and minutes of debate. The parliamentary system in which the two Canadas evolved after 1791 provided ample opportunities for both defence and criticism of the colonial order; indeed, competition between political ideas and agendas was a cornerstone of Canadian political life in that era. The formal documents of the period, including resolutions, petitions, addresses, and laws, reflect this vibrancy. Resolutions, along with the petitions and addresses stemming from them, generally gave a clear and concise expression of the overarching principles to which their partisans subscribed, while legislative texts must surely have reflected the principles shared by a good number of the members sitting at the time of their passage. British documents, such as laws (including the Canadian constitution), dispatches from British ministers, correspondence between London and the colonial governors, and reports of commissions of inquiry were also consulted. Since London made the key decisions concerning the nature of the Canadian state, a study of these sources is essential to an understanding of how state legitimacy was constructed.

While some of the principles in question transpire from these official documents, these principles were frequently elucidated or made explicit during colonial and imperial parliamentary debate; hence the minutes of these debates have been another important documentary resource for this study. The British debates are contained in the Parliamentary Register and the Hansard, while for the colonial debates several newspapers were searched. All these speeches constitute vitally important sources of contemporaneous opinion on the concept of liberty. These documents are complemented by extraparliamentary sources including polemical books and pamphlets published in the colonies between 1776 and 1841, but especially after 1828. Since these documents are few in number, they were given exhaustive consideration. I also consulted newspapers of the time for polemical writings and international news that help situate the Canadian experience within the Atlantic framework.

The outline of the book is as follows. In Chapter 1, I discuss the relationship between liberty and revolution. I situate pre-rebellion Canadian history within the Atlantic world and discuss the two conceptions of liberty that were then prevalent. In Chapter 2, I discuss the influence of the American and French revolutions on the colonies and the nature of the liberty that formed the basis for the Constitutional Act of 1791. Here I demonstrate that the Canadian state, while it came under the influence of revolutionary movements, developed from this period onward in accordance with the modern ideal of liberty. In Chapter 3, I analyze the principles according to which protest movements took shape in the Canadas after 1805, explaining how the colonial reformers came to abandon the modern concept of liberty during the 1820s and to gravitate towards the republican concept.

Chapters 4, 5, and 6 deal with the crisis of the 1830s from the standpoint of ideology. The discourses of the Lower Canadian Patriotes, the Upper Canadian radicals, and the defenders of the constitution (constitutionalists) are reconstructed with reference to their basic principles, their preferred institutional arrangements, and the principles of exclusion they articulated. This discourse analysis is important in that it allows for a comparison of the two major ideologies present in the colonies. It sheds light on the ideological aspects of the crisis of the 1830s, when the partisans of republican liberty (Patriotes and radicals) and the advocates of modern liberty (constitutionalists) came head to head. Chapter 6 illustrates the extent to which Lower Canadian politics found itself at an impasse in 1837; it explains the ideological nature of the opposition between the two groups, which made it increasingly difficult for them to cooperate within the existing political institutions. This impasse drove the two camps towards an extraparliamentary clash. With the military defeat of the Patriotes and radicals in 1837–38, the British succeeded not only in liquidating the republican opposition in the colonies but also in putting an end to the cycle of the Atlantic revolutions begun with the empire's own defeat in 1783.

Liberty and Revolution
in the Atlantic World

IN THE LATE EIGHTEENTH CENTURY, Europe and the Atlantic world underwent profound political, economic, social, and religious upheavals, representing the culmination of a hundred years of vibrant intellectual debate. Throughout the Enlightenment century, philosophers had challenged the social and political order of the ancien régime, questioning the power relations that existed in society. This led them ultimately to call for the abolition of privilege, the recognition of freedom of religion, freedom of the press, and freedom of association, and even at times to defend the right of subjects to political participation. That these philosophers demanded certain reforms was not in itself threatening; that they questioned the established order by rejecting its traditional justifications – divine right, dynastic right, and right of conquest – certainly was. In essence, they demanded that power relations and the social order be reconfigured to accord with the principle of liberty. Liberty was the necessary foundation of state legitimacy and the social order; its protection and promotion was the yardstick by which acts of authority must be measured. In the latter half of the eighteenth century, these philosophers were joined by polemicists, pamphleteers, and politicians in both Europe and the Thirteen Colonies. By century's end, this contrarian tendency had turned into a wave of revolution that shook the Atlantic world to its foundations.

According to Robert R. Palmer and Jacques Godechot, all these individual revolutions, notwithstanding each one's peculiar features, constituted a single movement, in essence a single "Atlantic revolution" taking place at the end of the eighteenth century.[1] While there were troubles in Geneva during the 1760s, it was the American Revolution (1775–83) that inaugurated nearly a half-century of revolutionary agitation. The success of the American Revolution not only robbed Great Britain of its best colonies but forced it to concede some autonomy to Ireland and to reorganize its remaining North American colonies. The revolution also inspired radicals in the home country, and the American influence was soon felt throughout all of Europe.[2] Next to be seriously shaken by revolts were the United Provinces (the patriots' revolt of 1783–87) and the Austrian Netherlands (1787–90). Then it was France's turn. The Revolution of 1789 was pivotal not only because it fundamentally transformed one of Europe's most important kingdoms but also because, from 1792 on, France's foreign policy gave impetus to other revolutions and attempted revolutions in Europe.[3]

As ambitious as it might be, this first attempt by Palmer and Godechot to integrate the revolutions of the late eighteenth century into a broad interpretive framework was somewhat limited in time and space. The putative Atlantic revolution only encompassed the United States and Europe during the period from 1776 to 1800, to the exclusion of the rest of the Americas (e.g., the Saint-Domingue slave revolts leading to the independence of Haiti in 1804). More recently, the Haitian experience has been integrated into this Atlantic framework, as has that of the Spanish and Portuguese empires, where revolutions swept across Central and South America in the early nineteenth century.[4] In view of the diversity of these experiences, it is more accurate at this point to speak of not one but several Atlantic revolutions.

Despite its limitations, the Palmer and Godechot framework bolsters two important arguments about these late eighteenth-century events. First, it shows up the inadequacy of the thesis of American or French exceptionalism, reminding us that these were not the only Atlantic nations shaken by revolutions after 1776. Second, it highlights the common ideological thread running through these revolutions, regardless of their peculiarities and final outcomes, since most of the revolutionaries were inspired by similar ideals. Palmer uses the word "democratic" to describe these revolutions.[5] While this word was indeed extant in that era, its several meanings were quite far from the meaning it has today.[6] Nevertheless, the democrats of the revolutionary era agreed on the need for equality among citizens and had no use for any hereditary privileges, whether of the monarchic or aristocratic variety. While describing these revolutions as "democratic" was initially useful for their integration into a new analytical framework, the term ultimately leads to confusion in view of the very different definition of democracy now in common use.

Beginning in the 1960s, intellectual historians such as Bernard Bailyn, J.G.A. Pocock, Quentin Skinner, and Gordon Wood began giving closer study to the ideological nature of protest movements in the Anglo-American world, including those that led to the English Commonwealth in the seventeenth century and the American Revolution in the eighteenth century. Reacting to the liberalism and individualism then dominant in the West, these historians sought to put the historical importance of liberalism as an oppositional ideology in England and the United States into perspective.[7] Drawing upon the work of Zera Fink and Caroline Robbins, who had rediscovered republicanism in seventeenth- and eighteenth-century English political thought,[8] they minimized liberalism's role as a reformist and emancipatory ideology in the eighteenth century by relativizing the intellectual influence of John Locke before 1750.[9] For these historians, classical republicanism, not liberalism, was the true emancipatory ideology of the eighteenth century.

Republicanism's roots, they argued, stretched back to antiquity. Rediscovered by Machiavelli in the sixteenth century, it was asserted to have been imported into England by James Harrington (1611–77) and reprised by the seventeenth-century Commonwealthmen as well as by the American rebels.[10] Its partisans believed that society should be organized around independent and virtuous small landholders who were resistant to corruption (or, put another way, untouched by clientelism) and capable of putting the common interest or "commonwealth" before their own when participating in the political affairs of the republic.[11]

While the work of Bailyn, Pocock, Skinner, and Wood initially focused on the Anglo-American landscape, it spawned similar studies by historians focusing on other countries. This new analytical framework helped revitalize the intellectual history of the Atlantic world and Europe in general,[12] as well as of England and Ireland, the United States, France, and the United Provinces in particular.[13] Many historians now acknowledge the republican ideological kinship of several eighteenth-century revolutions. The nineteenth-century Latin American revolutions stand apart in that they were not fundamentally inspired by this kind of republicanism (even though they did lead to the creation of new republics).[14] Thus, republicanism fundamentally and durably changed the conception of the state and the social order in the northern Atlantic world. It set legitimate authority, power, and social relations on new foundations, pitting liberty and equality against privileges and hereditary rights.

The history of these Atlantic revolutions now covers, to varying degrees, essentially the entirety of Europe and the Americas from 1760 to 1826. But Canada has yet to be integrated into this framework in any systematic way;[15] to date, only Jean-Pierre Wallot (focusing on Lower Canada) has made any attempt to accomplish this. Other historians working on the late eighteenth and early nineteenth centuries have devoted more attention to the direct or indirect effects of the American and French revolutions on Canada and to the arrival of the Loyalists.[16]

If Atlantic and Canadian historiography is our guide, the North American colonies that stayed with the empire must have remained aloof from all this Atlantic ideological ferment. Yet the colonial population (except of course for the First Peoples) was composed of European and American immigrants of relatively recent provenance. They brought with them their political, intellectual, and cultural references. In economic terms, the colonies were part of a mercantile empire. Constitutionally, they were subordinate to the British government. And intellectually, the Canadian elites were well aware of the issues being debated in Europe and America from the 1780s on. There was, in short, no reason why these colonies would have developed at the margins of the Atlantic world, or why their inhabitants would not have participated in or been influenced by the great debates of the epoch in one way or another.

INTELLECTUAL LIFE IN THE ATLANTIC WORLD
DURING THE ENLIGHTENMENT

It is of course undeniable that the Province of Quebec did not join the ranks of the rebel colonies in 1775–76, and that a revolution did not take place there in the 1790s. Republican revolutionary principles did not triumph in Canada. How, then, can this experience be integrated into the framework of the Atlantic revolutions? An answer to this question begins with the observation that the intellectual history of the eighteenth-century Atlantic world is not exhausted by republicanism. This is clearly true for the Latin American revolutionaries, who drew their inspiration from other sources. But it is also true for the British world, whose intellectual historians now consider republicanism to be only one strand of a more sophisticated analytical framework.

In their view, the modern history of the British Empire is not correctly characterized by the traditional opposition between conservatives favourable to the status quo and reformist liberals. It is better viewed as an opposition between partisans of commercialism and classical republicanism. Commercialism, a conservative ideology grounded in the works of Thomas Hobbes (1588–1679), David Hume (1711–1776), and Adam Smith (1723–1790), posited a definition of life in society based on individual rights and autonomy vis-à-vis the state. Its partisans, often depicted in the historical literature as liberals, insisted on the inviolability of private property, the benefits of wealth accumulation and concentration, and the necessity of patronage. Classical republicanism was a reformist, emancipatory, communitarian ideology that advocated for the right of political participation by all citizens. If the history of the Province

of Quebec and the Canadas is difficult to analyze in terms of republicanism alone, it makes better sense when interpreted in the context of an
opposition between republicanism and commercialism.

A number of Canadian and Quebec historians, political scientists, and
sociologists have drawn upon this analytical framework in recent years.
Apart from David Milobar, however, who focused on the influence of
republicanism (also known as the Country ideology) in the discourse of
English-speaking merchants in the Province of Quebec,[17] all of these
scholars have used this analytical framework to study the nineteenth century. Gordon T. Stewart, the first Canadian scholar to do so, in *The Origins
of Canadian Politics*, argued that nineteenth-century Canadian history was
characterized by the triumph of the commercialists (the Court ideology). In 1995, political scientists Peter J. Smith and Janet Ajzenstat took
this approach further, contending that an opposition between republicanism and liberalism has driven Canada's history since the nineteenth
century. The book they edited, *Canada's Origins*, constituted the first
genuine effort to recast Canadian history in the mould developed by intellectual historians of the Atlantic world.[18]

Louis-Georges Harvey used a similar framework to study the roots of
reformist discourse in Lower Canada. He found that while Canadian republicanism did not triumph in parallel with the revolutions in the
United States and Europe, it did provide inspiration to the Lower
Canadian reform movement from 1805 to 1837. Attempting to reconcile republicanism with the thesis of Americanness, Harvey presented
the 1837–38 rebellions as inspired by republicanism and therefore similar in nature to the American Revolution.[19] Allan Greer made the same
point, arguing that republicanism characterized political activity down
to the local level.[20] The sociologist Stéphane Kelly, in *La petite loterie*,
paired the Atlantic framework with the pariah theory developed by
Hannah Arendt. He sought to demonstrate that the history of Canada
East in the era 1837–67 was in essence that of the Court party's victory
over the Country party due to the corruption of Étienne Parent, Louis-
Hippolyte La Fontaine, and George-Étienne Cartier.[21]

While interesting, the general interpretive framework pitting commercialism against republicanism poses some problems. First, these ideologies are not generally given equal consideration in the academic literature,
and it is republicanism that has tended to dominate. Quebec historians in
particular have tended to address the question from a pro-republican
standpoint, either by focusing on the Patriotes' republican discourse
(Harvey) or by presenting the proponents of the Court ideology in a particularly negative light (Kelly). Meanwhile, scholars in English Canada
(e.g., Ajzenstat) have tended to look favourably on commercialism, which

they liken to liberalism. Such reciprocal bias has made it difficult to gain a true picture of this crucial ideological clash. What is needed in order to revitalize the analytical framework is to put the study of both ideologies on an equal footing.

Second, the classic works taking this approach have exaggeratedly polarized the opposition between republicanism and commercialism, obscuring or ignoring many subtleties. Pocock's *The Machiavellian Moment* and Wood's *The Creation of the American Republic*, to name two, greatly minimized the importance accorded to individual rights in republican discourse, particularly around the time of American independence. This bias began to be rectified in the early 1980s with works by Isaac Kramnick, Joyce Appleby, and Lance Banning, who maintained that republicanism and liberalism were not as antithetical as once believed. In this they followed in the footsteps of Bailyn, who argued that both these ideologies were in evidence during the American Revolution.[22] Others, including Paul A. Rahe and Vickie B. Sullivan, have shed light on the liberal features of English republicanism.[23] Still others have attempted to elucidate the many factors that distanced American republicanism from forms of republicanism that have little regard for individual liberties. According to Rahe, Thomas Pangle, and Jean M. Yarbrough, the "republicanism" in play during the American Revolution was not classical in nature but modern, and thus accepting of individual liberty.[24] Similarly, Mark Hulliung and Lee Ward have presented the United States as being the product of both republicanism and liberalism.[25]

Nothing about this debate negates the relevance of the analytical framework in which republicanism and commercialism (liberalism) are presented as two distinct ideologies. The point here is to underscore the ambiguity surrounding their definition as ideologies. If ideology is defined as a hierarchy of principles allowing an individual to face the world and give it meaning, to comprehend the organization of the society in which he lives or wishes to live, and to justify his political actions,[26] it becomes clear that republicanism and commercialism constitute two different ideologies, two distinct ways of conceiving of society and the state. It can certainly be said that people in the eighteenth century were either ideologically republican or ideologically commercialist. The republicans structured their thinking around the idea of popular sovereignty and the political participation of the virtuous citizen; the commercialists, around individual autonomy with respect to the state. The republicans were interested primarily in the nature of sovereign authority, liberals in the limits to its power over the individual. Still, these ideologies shared certain principles. For example, republicans could acknowledge, as their adversaries did, that individuals possess numerous and extensive civil rights.

Commercialists (liberals) could at times acknowledge popular sovereignty and advocate for political participation if these were perceived as useful for the protection of civil liberties. Given this overlap, it is not sufficient to study the specific rights held dear by each side; one must also determine the priority accorded to each.

Third, this framework is not readily applicable to Canada without modification, for it was originally designed to be applied to a specific spatiotemporal context. Jean-Marie Fecteau has, moreover, expressed doubts about the possibility that such an ideological conflict could have existed in the colonies in the 1830s. He writes that this approach "would appear to pose enormous analytical problems, if only because it postulates the continuity and stability of this ideological rivalry beyond the great revolutions of the turn of the nineteenth century."[27] All ideologies are indeed born out of particular contexts, but nothing prevents other people and thinkers from borrowing them, reworking them, or adapting them to new contexts, which explains why ideologies typically survive, in some form, the context in which they emerged. By revisiting the foundations of the republican and commercialist ideologies, one can discover how they were adapted to new contexts.

THE CONCEPT OF LIBERTY DURING THE ENLIGHTENMENT

In my view, the analytical framework used by Anglo-American intellectual historians of the Atlantic world can be liberated from the context in which it was devised, and thereby adapted to the Canadian context (without denaturing it completely), by recentring it around the concept of liberty. Liberty was certainly one of the most important values of the time. It did not refer solely to the exercise of certain rights but was also construed as the foundation of state legitimacy.

An apparent obstacle to this approach arises in that the Atlantic revolutions have always seemed to go hand in hand with liberty, as if the rise of liberty in the eighteenth century necessarily had revolution as its consequence. The opponents of revolution have thus been portrayed as the enemies of liberty: as conservatives, counterrevolutionaries, or reactionaries. While there was certainly a link between revolution and liberty in the European and South American nations, this connection is more problematic to establish for the British Empire. The British authorities, it is true, did move to crush protest movements and radical groups as the ancien régime was being toppled in Europe.[28] These measures were often reactionary and counterrevolutionary in nature. But this does not mean that the British constitution was itself counterrevolutionary. The Whig constitution of the 1790s was, after all, based on fundamental principles arising out of a much earlier revolution: the Glorious Revolution of 1688.[29]

This association between liberty and revolution is also predicated on the idea that liberty meant the same thing for all of its eighteenth-century partisans. Not so.[30] While they all considered liberty fundamental to the state and the social order, their consensus extended to only two other points. First, they considered liberty to be proper to "individuals," not social groups. (No matter that only a small minority of individuals could at that time claim to possess individual liberty: many years would pass before slaves, women, the poor, and foreigners would enjoy it.) It was a different concept from medieval liberty, which was synonymous with privileges granted to either groups or persons.[31] It was also different from the liberty of nations or of social classes, two categories developed in the late eighteenth or early nineteenth century.

Even though eighteenth-century liberty was a matter of individual rights, it had collective implications. Its advocates strove for compatibility between the potentially conflicting dictates of individual autonomy and societal coexistence. Liberty went beyond the individual to encompass the dynamics of power and submission within society. It marked out the rights, duties, and responsibilities of individuals to one another as well as the nature of the relationship between individuals and the state.

Second, all proponents of liberty considered it tantamount to law. Based on this fact, historian John Phillip Reid has contended that there was only a single, unambiguous concept of liberty at play in the eighteenth-century Anglo-American world.[32] But that was not the case: these thinkers did not agree on what constituted a legitimate law, much less on what constituted legitimate legislative institutions.

The fact is that seventeenth- and eighteenth-century thinkers in the Atlantic world recognized the existence of at least two forms of liberty. Thomas Hobbes, in *Leviathan* (1651), was among the first to distinguish between "[the] Libertie of Particular men" and the liberty of the "Common-wealth." The first was proper to men as individuals or subjects. The second, derived from classical Greek and Latin writings, concerned the social body created by individuals when they banded together out of a need for security: the Commonwealth.[33] This opposition between individual and collective forms of liberty was reprised in different forms throughout the Enlightenment century. Jean-Louis de Lolme (1740–1806) reiterated it in his commentary on the English constitution. Jean-Jacques Rousseau (1712–1778) continually appealed to the example of the ancients (liberty of the Commonwealth). Madame de Staël (1766–1817) discussed it in a 1798 essay on how to put an end to the excesses of the revolution. Finally, Charles-Louis de Secondat, Baron de Montesquieu (1689–1755) studied the governmental structures that would allow these two types of liberty to be institutionalized.[34]

But it was Benjamin Constant (1767–1830) who gave the best presentation of this opposition in a speech titled "De la liberté des anciens comparée à celle des modernes" (Of the Liberty of the Ancients Compared to That of the Moderns), which he delivered at the Athénée royale de Paris in 1819.[35] A devotee of liberty, Constant had nonetheless been disgusted by the excesses of the revolution. He strove to demonstrate a fundamental contradiction between two distinct forms of liberty, one of which could be condemned without invalidating the idea of liberty itself. For him, all the ills that had afflicted Europe in the preceding thirty years – the revolutions, the Jacobins' crimes, and what came after – had been caused by the rediscovery of the "liberty of the ancients," which could be summarized as the "sharing of social power among the citizens of the fatherland."[36] This form of collective freedom required citizens to accept "the complete subjection of the individual to the authority of the community."[37] Individuals enjoyed no independence but were subsumed within the body politic.

Constant espoused instead a seventeenth- and eighteenth-century invention, the "liberty of the moderns," that involved individual autonomy and could be summarized as the enjoyment of individual rights. For a modern, liberty was

the right to be subjected only to the laws, and to be neither arrested, detained, put to death or maltreated in any way by the arbitrary will of one or more individuals. It is the right of everyone to express their opinion, choose a profession and practice it, to dispose of property, and even to abuse it; to come and go without permission, and without having to account for their motives and undertakings. It is everyone's right to associate with other individuals, either to discuss their interests, or to profess the religion which they and their associates prefer, or even simply to occupy their days or hours in a way which is most compatible with their inclinations or whims.[38]

An individual was free in the modern sense if he could act within society as he saw fit, in keeping with his own tastes and interests. For Constant, this type of liberty was better suited to the state of the world in the nineteenth century. Modern citizens, unlike the citizens of the ancient republics, could not enjoy the sensation of wielding influence over the state because nation-states were now much bigger. In compensation, they could enjoy private rights: "Our freedom must consist of peaceful enjoyment and private independence."[39] It is not that Constant disapproved of political participation – on the contrary, he considered it a right of all citizens – but that he believed it needed to be subordinated to the enjoyment of the individual rights it made possible.

After 1850, many writers came to believe that the advent of "liberal democracy" had resolved the opposition between the liberty of the ancients and the liberty of the moderns. Democracy and individual autonomy now seemed inseparable. To be free meant both to participate in politics and to enjoy autonomy with respect to other citizens. While this idea never gained unanimous approval, it was and still is influential in the West.

At his 1958 inaugural lecture in Oxford, the philosopher Isaiah Berlin revived the old distinction between two forms of liberty, which he termed "negative" and "positive" liberty, claiming that both still existed in the West. The first concerned the autonomy permitted to individuals in society, or "freedom from"; the second, the capacity of individuals to be guided by their own lights, or "freedom to."[40] Berlin's distinction remains controversial, as does his definition of these two concepts; still, it restored currency to the idea that liberty in the West has been a polysemous idea since the seventeenth century.[41]

REPUBLICAN LIBERTY VERSUS MODERN LIBERTY

Constant's distinction between the liberty of the ancients and that of the moderns is a good starting point from which to rethink the ideologies of the eighteenth century. When the opposition between republicanism and commercialism is recast as a struggle over the meaning of liberty, the result is a flexible interpretive framework for Atlantic intellectual history that is freed from the context in which it emerged. This framework is useful in explicating, at least in part, a number of late eighteenth-century disputes between different advocates of liberty – between Rousseau and Voltaire, between British Whigs and Radicals at the time of the American and French revolutions, between *anglomanes* and *américanistes* in 1780s' France, and between Jeffersonian republicans and Hamiltonian federalists in the United States (1787–1815), for some examples.[42] In all these disputes, the partisans of two concurrent and frequently contradictory conceptions of liberty – republican and modern – squared off.

Among the republicans were various thinkers who made political participation the central feature of their definition of liberty. They included seventeenth-century Commonwealthmen such as John Milton (1608–1674), James Harrington (1611–1677), Marchamont Needham (1620–1678), Henry Neville (1620–1694), and Algernon Sydney (1622–1683); the advocate of "country" ideas Henry Saint John, 1st Viscount Bolingbroke (1678–1751); the English radicals Richard Price (1723–1791), Joseph Priestley (1733–1804), Thomas Paine (1737–1809), James Mackintosh (1765–1832), and Mary Wollstonecraft (1759–1797); the French pamphleteer and politician Emmanuel-Joseph Sièyes (1748-1836); the French Girondists Jacques-Pierre Brissot (1754–1793), Antoine Nicolas de Condorcet (1743-1794), and Olympe de Gouges (1748–1793); and the American Thomas Jefferson (1743–1826). More radical in their conception of the world, the French and francophone republicans, including Gabriel Bonnot de Mably (1709–1785), Jean-Jacques Rousseau, Jean-Paul Marat (1743–1793), and Maximilien Robespierre (1743–1794), pushed this conception to its outer bounds.

While they shared a single idea of liberty, these people did not all concur on its political and practical implications. Some were moderate and open to compromise, others were extremist. Differences between republican currents at times became so extreme that they degenerated into a fight to the death, viz. the confrontation between the Girondists (led by Jacques-Pierre Brissot) and the Montagnards (including the Jacobins led by Robespierre) that ended with the former's liquidation in October 1793. The context in which republican discourse was articulated also influenced the overall shape of institutions and the manner in which politics were practised. To see this, one need only compare the divergent outcomes of the American and French Revolutions, both stemming from republican agitation. Republican rhetoric and policy were unavoidably adapted to suit the form of the preexisting state, the prevailing political culture, and the existence of an internal or external enemy (whether real or perceived). Still, all republicans shared a common ideal: to live in a republic composed of virtuous citizens.

As to the modern conception of liberty first appearing in seventeenth-century England, it held that there are certain inalienable rights – variously termed natural rights, absolute rights, sacred rights, or birth rights – that exist among humans in a state of nature. Among the theorists of modern liberty were the first Enlightenment generation, including John Locke (1632–1704),[43] Voltaire (1694–1778), Charles-Louis de Secondat, Baron de Montesquieu (1689–1755), and Louis de Jaucourt (1704–1780); admirers of the British constitution such as William Blackstone (1723–1780) and Jean-Louis de Lolme; Scottish thinkers such as Adam Smith; the Physiocrats, including François Quesnay (1694–1774), Jacques Turgot (1727–1781), and Mercier de la Rivière (1719–1801);[44] the English Whigs, including Charles James Fox (1749–1806), Edmund Burke (1729–1797), and their conservative disciples; the French *anglomanes*, including Jean-Joseph Mounier (1758–1806), Stanislas de Clermont-Tonnerre (1757–1792), and Trophime-Gérard de Lally-Tolendal (1751–1830); and American Federalists such as Alexander Hamilton (1755–1804) and John Adams (1735–1826). Since Great Britain was the only eighteenth-century nation built upon this notion of liberty, the partisans of modern liberty generally admired the British constitution (excepting the French Physiocrats who for many years leaned towards legal despotism before, in the case of Turgot and others, falling into the republican camp).

Like the republicans, the moderns had internal conflicts. They were not always political allies, as shown in Britain by the opposition between Fox and Burke during the French Revolution or between the Whigs and Tories in the nineteenth century. Nor did they shrink from alliances with those whose conception of liberty differed – one thinks of the *anglomane-américaniste* collaboration in the initial months of the French Revolution, or the Whig-Radical alliance in 1830s' Britain. But such cohabitation was infrequent. It was generally provoked by the presence of a common enemy, whose eventual defeat or victory obviated the need for the lesser evil of further collaboration.

Liberty and Equality

In terms of its principles, republican liberty was closely tied to the concept of civic equality, a form of equality that had moral, legal, social, and economic components.[45] To begin with, equality was considered the natural state of individuals – an essential postulate, since only equals could participate in politics and, in so doing, be free. Republican equality was also a legal construct. Individuals could only be free if they enjoyed the same rights and were subjected to the same laws. Finally, republican equality was economic and social. It was based on the idea that the concentration of wealth in a small number of hands undermined political freedom and thereby threatened the very foundations of society. While the advocates of this form of liberty did not reject private property, they considered it a civil and not a natural right: "The very idea of property, or right of any kind, is founded upon a regard to the general good of the society, under whose protection it is enjoyed; and nothing is properly *a man's own*, but what general rules, which have for their object the good of the whole, give to him."[46] On this premise, property had to be subordinated to the will of the whole. Rousseau wrote,

My thought ... is not to destroy private property absolutely, because that is impossible, but to restrict it within the narrowest limits; to give a measure, a rule, a brake that restrains it, that directs it, that subjugates it, and keeps it always subordinated to the public good. In a word, I want the property of the state to be as great, as strong and that of the citizens as small, as weak as possible.[47]

As this quote illustrates, republicans did not seek to abolish private property but only to rein in economic inequality to the greatest extent possible.

The partisans of modern liberty, for their part, did not reject the idea of equality but gave it a legal definition that did not have social leveling as a necessary consequence. This is evident from an *Encyclopédie* passage written by Louis de Jaucourt, whose vision was representative of the moderns:

Let no one do me the injustice of supposing that with a sense of fanaticism I approve in a state that chimera, absolute *equality*, which could hardly give birth to an ideal republic. I am only speaking here of the *natural equality* of men. I know too well the necessity of different ranks, grades, honors, distinctions, prerogatives, subordinations that must prevail in all governments. And I would even state that *natural* or *moral equality* are not contrary to this.[48]

Against republican equality, which they regarded as inimical to the foundations of society, the moderns pitted two putatively natural rights: property and security.[49] All free human beings, they argued, should be able to enjoy and possess the fruits of their labour. As Adam Smith wrote, "the property which every man has in his own labour, as it is the original foundation of all other property ... is the most sacred and inviolable."[50] Freedom thus implied the protection of persons and property. De facto inequality among individuals would result from their putting different amounts of effort into personal enrichment. Inequality, though anathema to the republicans, was perfectly acceptable to the moderns. What is more, unequal wealth was not only the result of well-employed freedom but also a condition for the prosperity and progress of society as a whole.

Wealth accumulation being (for the moderns) a natural fact, it followed that people were entitled to the security of their person and property.[51] Indeed, the moderns considered the relationship among liberty, property, and security so strong and fundamental that they were prone to conflating the three. Montesquieu wrote, "The political liberty of the subject is a tranquillity of mind arising from the opinion each person has of his safety."[52] He added, "Political liberty consists in security, or, at least, in the opinion that we enjoy security."[53] The role of guaranteeing the security of persons and property fell to the state.

Virtue versus Wealth

Not only did the two concepts of liberty differ at the level of principles but they were predicated on two different conceptions of the social order. The republicans articulated an ethic of virtue that they derived from the seventeenth-century Commonwealthmen, in which notions of equality and independence were paramount. To be free, it was not enough for individuals to be equal: they also had to be mutually independent, both economically and politically. This was the essence of republican virtue.

On a practical level, independence meant that no person could be under the control of another; and for this to be the case, the partisans of republican liberty believed that society, and the state governing it, should be fundamentally agrarian, made up of small, mutually independent landholders. Property was generally presented as a sacred natural right, but the term referred to the agrarian smallholdings that formed the basis for equality among citizens. It did not mean the unbridled accumulation of wealth, which led to social inequality. In a republic, agriculture ought to be the economic activity par excellence. It guaranteed people's equality and independence while encouraging farmers to embody simplicity and frugality, two values integral to the republican concept of virtue. Members of an agrarian society were independent if they owned land and contented themselves with the simple life it afforded. Republican virtue thus was inseparable from an agrarian ideal. As Rousseau put it, "It is better ... to live in abundance than in opulence; be better than pecunious, be rich. Cultivate your fields well, without worrying about the rest, soon you will harvest gold."[54] Because this economic system allowed for independence, encouraged frugality, and maintained equality among citizens, it was the only one compatible with liberty. The republicans did not necessarily oppose commerce but they generally subordinated it to agriculture.

The independence in question was a political concept as well as an economic one. It was essential to their independence that individuals remain uncorrupt, free of undue influence. They must never sell their allegiance to the highest bidder but always hold the general interest above their private interests where these two were at odds. As Priestley wrote, "the happiness of the whole community is the ultimate end of government ... and all claims of individuals inconsistent with the public good are absolutely null and void."[55] Robespierre expressed the same sentiment in different terms: "the long convulsions that tear states apart are only the combat of prejudice against principle, egoism against the general interest."[56] In sum, republican virtue was synonymous with both economic and political independence. Its corollary was patriotism – citizens were expected to put the general interest before their own.

The moderns, on the contrary, espoused an ethic of personal enrichment. Accumulation of property was the visible sign of the proper use of liberty. The most extreme example of this ethic is found in *The Fable of the Bees, or, Private Vices, Public Benefits* (1723–28) by Bernard Mandeville (1670–1733). Mandeville contended that while luxury might be considered a vice from a moral standpoint, society still prospered from its enjoyment by the rich. Not everyone took such an extreme position. Nevertheless, the moderns saw no reason to adopt the republican opposition between the public and the private interest. On the contrary: for them, the public interest was merely the sum of legitimate private interests.

It was still necessary to ensure that all these private interests encountering one another in society could be harmoniously accommodated. The moderns understood that there would have to be limits on individual liberty – which, to repeat, they regarded as a natural right – so that individuals could not harm each other. What could impose such limits? For the moderns, the answer was reason. Reason is what enables individuals to know the scope and limits of their own liberty. It is the brake on excess that renders private interests compatible. As such, it is the faculty that the moderns set up against republican virtue.

Republican Popular Sovereignty

The differences between republican and modern ideals had major implications for the organization of the state, and in particular, for the definition of sovereignty. Any discussion of liberty must grapple with this issue; the degree of autonomy enjoyed by individuals in society and the nature of their relationship to power depends on it. While the word *sovereignty* has other meanings,[57] I will use it here primarily to refer to the source of supreme authority in a state.

Since republicans structured life in society around civic equality, independence, and political participation, they all agreed that sovereignty could not belong to anyone in particular: only to the people, the nation, as a totality.[58] This was the central concept of popular sovereignty. Rousseau went as far as to contend that the social contract could be summed up in a single fact: "the total alienation of each associate with all of his rights to the whole community." On these grounds he argued that "each of us puts his person and his full power in common under the supreme direction of the general will; and in a body we receive each member as an indivisible part of the whole."[59] While not all republicans were as categorical as the Citizen of Geneva, they all believed that the people were the sole source of legitimate authority.[60] In a republic, the people's will was law. This form of sovereignty was the foundation of both the US constitution (1787) and the *Declaration of the Rights of Man and of the Citizen* (1789).

Caution is called for, however, in interpreting the republican concept of the "people." It does not refer to the sum of the individuals living in a republic; rather, it is an intellectual construct, a metaphysical reality, a legal fiction whose purpose is to legitimize power and to structure the relations among political institutions in a republic.[61] To quote Edmund S. Morgan, "the success of government ... requires the acceptance of fictions, requires the willing suspension of disbelief, requires us to believe that the emperor is clothed even though we can see that he is not."[62] The fiction of the people was central to the discourse of republican liberty in that it constituted the primary organizing principle of the republic. The people were to the republic what God was to absolute monarchies: the legal fiction through which power was conferred on those who held it.

Thus, there was no necessary correlation between the sum total of electors and the "people," between the will of the majority (a sum of individual interests) and the general will (the people's interest). As Rousseau wrote, "There is often a considerable difference between the will of all and the general will: the latter looks only to the common interest, the former looks to private interest, and is nothing but a sum of particular wills."[63] The popular will might even contradict the will of the majority. In such cases, Rousseau contended, the guidance of a legislator – for example, Lycurgus in Sparta – was needed. Robespierre presented himself as such a legislator, invoking the general will and the good of the nation in his justification of the Jacobin dictatorship and the Terror.

Such was a republic: an enactment of popular sovereignty whose purpose was to preserve the common good. Its citizens were free when they had their say in the making of laws. Republican liberty was in this way a form of civic liberty. But modern republics were too large to allow for the direct expression of all members of society. Representation was the only way for all citizens' political voices to be heard. For such representation to be genuine, it had to conform to certain rules:

First, the representation must be complete. No state, a part of which only is represented in the Legislature that governs it, is self-governed ... Secondly, the representatives of a free state must be freely chosen ... Thirdly, after being freely chosen they must be themselves free ... Fourthly, they must be chosen for short terms and, in all their acts, be accountable to their constituents ... With respect, in particular, to a government by representation, it is evident that it deviates more or less from liberty in proportion as the representation is more or less imperfect.[64]

It was thus a matter of "subject[ing] the representatives to following their instructions exactly and to giving a strict account to their constituents of their conduct at the Diet."[65] In this way, the representatives became the ambassadors of their constituents.[66]

In our day, republic and monarchy are routinely considered the antithesis of one another. A republic is theoretically based on popular sovereignty while a monarchy is based on the sovereignty of a king. It is true that eighteenth-century republican principles had no room for the kind of monarchical sovereignty to which Louis XV alluded during the Séance de la flagellation held in the Paris Parliament on 3 March 1766: "It is in my person alone that sovereign power resides ... It is to me alone that legislative power belongs, without dependence and without sharing."[67] But what really posed a problem for republicans was monarchic absolutism. As long as the king's power was limited to the executive sphere, he could be tolerated or even defended. Indeed, as Rousseau put it, a republic could have any "form of administration" or executive power.[68] But it could not be a republic without popular sovereignty being embodied in the legislature. Indeed, seventeenth- and eighteenth-century republicans such as Rousseau, Harrington, and the American rebels appealed to Polybius's theory of mixed government, in which monarchy, aristocracy, and democracy complement one another.[69] But for all these thinkers, the role of the aristocracy and the monarchy was either consultative or strictly tied to executive power. The French republicans and revolutionaries, for their part, tried to restructure French political institutions after 1789 in such a manner as to reconcile their principles with the existence of the Capetian monarch, which created all sorts of problems.[70] It was not long before they abandoned this idea of republican mixed government or monarchy, and from the nineteenth century on this idea was taken up exclusively by the moderns.

Parliamentary Sovereignty

Mixed government entailed an entirely different conception of sovereignty and the state. Rather than entrust sovereignty to a one-dimensional fiction – the "people" – that was equated with the state, the moderns entrusted it to an entity whose constitution was based on an internal division of power. They did this because their main interest was to guarantee the natural rights and autonomy of individuals, whereas they believed a sovereign people would threaten these rights. In contrast, mixed government would put a check on any tendency for the state to become too tyrannical. In the British case, sovereignty was vested in Parliament, which was in turn composed of the House of Lords (aristocracy), the House of Commons (democracy), and a monarch. Each of these entities derived its legitimacy from a different source and had different interests, and it was practically inconceivable for them to conspire against individual liberty. The "people" represented by Parliament was thus a different sort of fiction. It was not an indivisible entity speaking with a single voice but a composite of monarchy, aristocracy, and democracy. The representatives of the general public only accounted for one-third of Parliament. Put another way, the modern state was organized around a balance of power and forces within the sovereign power: a mixed government.

As we have seen, the republicans structured the state around the legislative branch as the sovereign people's legitimate voice. The moderns, by contrast, put executive and legislative power on a more equal footing. Their system of government established balance between these two branches of government, even though it was the legislative branch – Parliament – that was theoretically sovereign. In practice, the moderns made the executive branch the guardian of liberty, autonomy, and security as well as the promoter of societal development. As they saw it, no other body was capable of fulfilling this role. To prevent the executive branch from interpreting its powers too broadly and thereby encroaching on individual rights, it was enough to subordinate its power to the legislative branch in certain respects. The judicial branch played a similar role. As Montesquieu put it, "To prevent this abuse [of power], it is necessary from the very nature of things that power should be a check to power."[71]

Since sovereignty and legislative power rested with Parliament, it followed that the moderns based their state not on popular sovereignty but on the rule of law. For a republican, the unambiguous will of the people found expression in the laws enacted by one sovereign body. Nothing in theory restrained the exercise of republican law, other than a belief that the legislative branch would not act so as to tread recklessly upon individual liberty. But the moderns were suspicious of an all-powerful sovereign legislative power, and because of that suspicion they entrusted sovereignty to a parliament composed of divergent interests. They claimed on several grounds that this approach would protect liberty. First, as we have seen, it would take an unlikely conspiracy between three conflicting sets of interests (monarchy, aristocracy, democracy) to pass a repressive law. Second, since individual liberty was reasonable, laws were regarded as the collective expression of reason, which made liberty possible in society. Moreover, Locke and Blackstone both associated liberty with law, arguing that "where there is no law there is no freedom."[72] It was to guarantee the reasonability of law that the majority of moderns appealed to representation. This was what enabled the moderns to transpose the idea of individual liberty into the societal framework. Collective self-government guaranteed society that laws would be based on reason and not on the prejudices of a few individuals. Third, if Parliament did manage to pass a repressive law, the judiciary could strike it down. This check on legislative power did not exist in Great Britain, where Parliament was all-powerful, but the American Federalists gave the Supreme Court the role of guaranteeing the constitutionality of laws passed by the legislative branch.[73]

Since the moderns did not regard political participation as the fundamental component of liberty, they conceived of representation in a very
different way from the republicans. Elected representatives were not and
need not be beholden to the will of their constituents. They were more
like trustees:

It ought to be the happiness and glory of a Representative, to live in the strictest
union, the closest correspondence, and the most unreserved communication
with his constituents ... But, his unbiased opinion, his mature judgment, his enlightened conscience, he ought not to sacrifice to you; to any man, or any sett
[sic] of men living ... Your Representative owes you, not his industry only, but his
judgement; and he betrays, instead of serving you, if he sacrifices it to your opinion ... Parliament is not a *Congress* of Ambassadors from different and hostile
interests ... but Parliament is a *deliberative* Assembly of *one* Nation, with *one*
Interest, that of the whole; where, not local Purposes, not local Prejudices ought
to guide, but the general Good, resulting from the general Reason of the whole.
You chuse a Member indeed; but when you have chosen him, he is not Member
of Bristol, but he is a Member of *Parliament*.[74]

Thus, a member was not elected to represent the opinion of his electors but to think and make decisions on their behalf.

Civil Rights and Political Rights

A final fundamental difference between republicans and moderns concerns the relationship each perceived between civil rights and political
rights. To begin with, we must dispense with a simplistic equation of republican liberty with political freedom and modern liberty with civil liberties. For both camps, the relationship between these freedoms was
much more complex.

This complexity, as regards the republicans, relates to the fact that
they did not form a homogeneous group in terms of the degree of importance they accorded to civil liberties. Rousseau and de Mably, for example, paid little attention to civil liberties, while Price and Priestley at
times used rhetoric that all but erased the distinction between civil liberties and political freedom. Generally speaking, the complementarity
between the two was central to the republican discourse in the Anglo-
American world. All republicans agreed, however, that the people's will
had to trump individual rights, or else it would not be sovereign. It followed that individual rights were conventional, since they were granted
to citizens at the behest of the "people." It was not that the citizens of a
republic could not enjoy natural rights but that political freedom

prevailed where the two were in conflict. Thus, Price wrote that "a distinction should be made between the liberty of a state, and its not suffering oppression, or between a free government and a government under which freedom is enjoyed. Under the most despotic government liberty may happen to be enjoyed."[75]

On a similar note, Tom Paine situated the question of civil liberties within a historical framework. Human beings, he claimed, had certainly enjoyed rights when they lived in a state of nature. It was clear that "man [had not entered] into society to become *worse* then he was before, not to have fewer rights than he had before, but to have those rights better secured."[76] But the essence of those natural rights had been altered when human beings joined together in society. Once sacred and inviolable – as they still were for the moderns – these rights were now to republicans a matter of convention, existing at the pleasure of the sovereign people.

Finally, the *Declaration of the Rights of Man and of the Citizen* affirmed the right to equality (Article 1) and the right to liberty, property, security, and resistance to oppression (Article 2); but it should be noted that these rights were recognized by virtue of the *Declaration*'s adoption by the National Constituent Assembly of France. At the same time, the *Declaration* provided that all sovereignty resided with the nation (Article 3) and affirmed that law was "the expression of the general will" (Article 6).

For the moderns, the primacy was reversed: individual rights (civil liberties) trumped political freedom. Some, such as Voltaire, were as comfortable with the French monarchy and Prussian absolutism as with the English constitutional regime. Or consider the Physiocrats, for whom freedom of commerce was the ultimate societal good and who defended legal despotism until 1776, when Louis XVI dismissed Turgot from his position as controller-general. De Lolme, Denis Diderot, Jean le Rond d'Alembert, and other philosophers likewise made no bones about their admiration for enlightened despots such as Catherine II and Frederick II.[77] There were even some nineteenth-century French thinkers who adopted an aristocratic liberal discourse that rejected the importance accorded to the political participation of French subjects.[78]

Nevertheless, most moderns regarded civil liberties and political freedom as far from incompatible. Benjamin Constant wrote, "It is not political liberty which I wish to renounce; it is civil liberty which I claim, along with other forms of political liberty." There was no need to choose between the two forms of liberty since it was participation that guaranteed individual rights: "Individual liberty ... is the true modern liberty. Political liberty is its guarantee, consequently political liberty is indispensable." Constant believed that to renounce political freedom "would be a folly like that of a man who, because he only lives on the first floor, does not care if the house itself is built on sand." He thus concluded his 1819 speech to the Athénée royal de Paris by stating, "Therefore, Sirs, far from renouncing either of the two sorts of freedom which I have described to you, it is necessary, as I have shown, to learn to combine the two together."[79] Specifically, that combination consisted of the protection of civil liberties by the state *through the agency of* political freedom.[80]

Let us be clear: what differentiated the republicans from the moderns was not that the first defended political freedom alone while the second defended individual rights alone, for both groups generally attempted to reconcile the two. It was the primacy accorded to the two concepts: the republicans put political freedom first, while the modernists put civil rights first. On the whole, it may be said that republican liberty and modern liberty were in a dialogue of sorts, as summarized in Table 1.1.

*Republican Liberty and Modern Liberty
in the Atlantic Framework*

These two conceptions of liberty, entailing two different models for the state, inspired the philosophers and politicians of the seventeenth- and eighteenth-century Atlantic world. Republican freedom was deeply subversive since it considered the popular will to be the foundation of the state. It transferred sovereignty from an individual (the king) or an institution (parliament) to an intellectual fiction (the people) speaking through the voice of those who identified with it. The people, being necessarily sovereign, could alter at will the institutions by which they were governed. Republican liberty thus gave ready legitimacy to the opponents of any regime that did not explicitly appeal to popular sovereignty. It was this idea of the sovereign people that was invoked in support of the Commonwealth of England in the seventeenth century. Furthermore, republican liberty and republicanism provided the intellectual underpinnings of the American and European revolutions of the eighteenth century. In intellectual terms, all these revolutions drank from a single source, and it is apposite to group them together as the "Atlantic revolutions," even if the application of these principles varied greatly from one revolution to another.

In contrast, modern liberty did not directly threaten the established political order and could scarcely be appealed to as a justification for revolution, since it situated freedom essentially outside the political arena.[81] As long as the powers that be did not unduly restrict civil liberties (and there was no strict definition of such liberties, apart from a few rights seen as "natural"), revolution seemed unjustifiable. Modern liberty, then, did

Table 1.1
Comparison between republican liberty and modern liberty (principles and institutions)

Basic principles	Republican liberty	Modern liberty
Thinkers / philosophers	Commonwealthmen (Harrington, Milton, Sidney) English Radicals (Price, Priestley, Wollstonecraft, Paine, Mackintosh) American republicans (Jefferson) French Girondists (Condorcet) French republicans (Rousseau, de Mably, Sieyès, Robespierre)	First Enlightenment generation (Locke, Voltaire, Montesquieu) English constitutionalists or Anglophiles (Blackstone, De Lolme) English Whigs (Fox, Burke, Russell) Scottish thinkers (Smith) American Federalists (Hamilton, Adams) French liberals (Constant)
Basic definition of liberty	Political participation (political freedom)	Individual rights (civil liberties)
Relationship between political freedom (participation) and civil liberties (individual rights).	By means of political freedom, citizens grant themselves civil liberties	Political freedom guarantees civil liberties
Two values associated with liberty	Equality and community (fraternity)	Property and security
Organization of political power	The legislative power is central to political affairs because liberty is first and foremost a matter of political participation	The executive power is very powerful and highly autonomous because it is the only power that can protect individual liberty
Sovereignty	The "people"	Parliament
Members of Parliament represent ...	The electors	The nation
Economic basis of society	Agriculture	Commerce
Ethic based on ...	Independence of citizens	Accumulation of wealth
International relations	Independence of peoples	Not inconsistent with empire
Relationship to preexisting state	Subversive and revolutionary form of liberty	Non-subversive form of liberty

not present very effective oppositional arguments. Here was its fundamental limitation: it was a conception that allowed for reforms from within the political establishment itself. If it triumphed in eighteenth-century
Great Britain it was because it could offer an a posteriori justification for
the Glorious Revolution of 1688 and the establishment of the Whig system.[82] It legitimized the existing political system, not those who protested
against it.

It was modern liberty that inspired the first Enlightenment generation
in France. However, its effectiveness as an oppositional idea was more or
less nil. It did not allow the adepts of modern liberty to make significant
gains during the first half of the century. Religious tolerance was not acquired in France until 1787, almost a century after it had been instituted
in England. In the Thirteen Colonies, modern liberty was of no use to the
colonists who were opposing British policies from 1765 on, because
Parliament's sovereignty over the colonies was the very basis of their political system. Indeed, it was partially because modern liberty had no significant influence over politics during the first two-thirds of the Enlightenment
century that republican liberty took its place as the principal ideology of
protest. It was this latter form of liberty that proceeded to shake the
Atlantic world to its foundations. It provided the impetus, the explanation, and the justification for the Atlantic revolutions.

2

Liberty in the Province of Quebec, 1776–1805

CANADA'S HISTORY has been inscribed within the framework of Atlantic history from the very beginning of European colonization. Acadia and New France, which became Nova Scotia and the Province of Quebec, were outposts of empire – France followed by Great Britain. They were managed for the benefit of the mother country and administered and populated by its subjects. The relationship between centre and periphery was not merely political and economic in nature; it was also cultural and intellectual. Administrators and colonists brought with them their value system, their understanding of power and social relations, and their cultural practices. These were perpetuated in part thanks to administrators who imposed or saw to the application of edicts, ordinances, proclamations, and laws imported from across the Atlantic. Meanwhile, the clergy laboured to keep Christian values alive among the faithful.

These and other factors kept the colonial elites intellectually in touch with the other colonies and Europe on the eve of the Atlantic revolutions, and particularly with debates raging over ideas of freedom, power, state legitimacy, and social relations. One was the increasing availability of newspapers and books, both local and foreign. Starting in June 1764 with the bilingual *Quebec Gazette/Gazette de Québec*, newspapers made their appearance in the Saint Lawrence valley.[1] American and French writings circulated as well. The province's borders were, in a word, permeable to revolutionary ideas, to rhetoric that threatened to topple kings and upset the established order in the name of freedom.[2] Another factor was that as a British colony in North America, Quebec's fate was inevitably tied to that of the empire, which, until 1783, included the thirteen American rebel colonies. And finally, France, the former parent state, was Britain's main rival during this period.

The Province of Quebec, succeeded by Upper and Lower Canada after 1791, did not ultimately join the revolutionary movement. Nor is the

Constitution of 1791 influenced by the underlying principles of the American and French Revolutions. But this does not mean that it was reactionary, the enemy of liberty. The concept of liberty was just as fundamental to the development of the colony as it was to the republics. Even as the idea of liberty was invoked in defence of the new republican states, it played a central role in the legitimation of the Canadian state. However, the particular concept of liberty in play was very different.

REPUBLICAN LIBERTY
IN THE PROVINCE OF QUEBEC (1775–1791)

The Province of Quebec was directly affected by the American Revolution from the outset. In fact, it had contact with the American insurgents before the publication of Thomas Paine's *Common Sense* (January 1776) – the republican work that inflamed the Thirteen Colonies and thrust them towards independence – and before the Declaration of Independence (4 July 1776).[3] In October 1774 and again in May 1775, the Continental Congress meeting in Philadelphia invited the French Canadians to join their revolt. Faced with the latter's inaction, the rebels invaded the southern region of the colony in the fall of 1775, demanding that the French Canadians join forces with them. They sent two letters, one of them signed by George Washington. The rebels were defeated in December at the Battle of Quebec and retreated in the new year as British reinforcements arrived. But the Congress sent another appeal to the French Canadians in January 1776.[4] Emissaries including Benjamin Franklin visited the colony in April and May. While the American invasion ended in failure, the ideas behind the American Revolution were certainly making themselves felt in the colony.

The official launch of the war of independence was met by a hardening of the British authorities' stance: the governor of Quebec, Frederick Haldimand (1778–86), was no friend of dissent and acted to curtail the circulation of republican ideas, the presence of French printer Fleury Mesplet in the colony notwithstanding. Mesplet had come in the spring of 1775 to promote the principles of the American insurgents and did not return to the Thirteen Colonies with the rebels. He instead set up shop in Montreal, where he published various newspapers until his death in 1794. Despite his republican principles, his first newspaper, the *Gazette du commerce et littéraire de Montréal* (1778–79), avoided discussion of the political situation in the colonies.[5] He and his journalist Valentin Jautard did, however, engage in a philosophical polemic around questions of tolerance and education,[6] as well as venturing criticism of certain judges. Their writings got them arrested and imprisoned without trial in 1779, and they spent several years behind bars. That put an end to discussions of liberty in the colony since the only other newspaper, the *Quebec Gazette*, was under the government's control.

The French Revolution, when it came, also found its way into the public consciousness. The news of the Revolution was generally well received by the Canadian elites.[7] There is nothing surprising about this: even the British were initially pleased by the tribulations of the Capetian monarchy. The *Quebec Gazette* and the *Gazette de Montréal*, the bilingual weekly founded by Mesplet in 1785, covered the events. The reportage went beyond factual accounts to include detailed descriptions of debates taking place in the French National Assembly and documents relating to the proposed constitutional reform. The result was to disseminate the ideas underlying the political and social transformations underway in France. The republican conception of liberty had reappeared in the colony, and would circulate quite freely from then on.

Newspaper coverage of the French Revolution was largely positive, particularly in the case of the *Gazette de Montréal*. Mesplet still adhered to republican principles and seized the opportunity to promote them. The general tone of the newspaper was decidedly republican, with its references to the life and writings of Benjamin Franklin, a pivotal figure of the American Revolution; Thomas Paine, Richard Price, and Joseph Priestley, the leading lights of English Radicalism; and Gabriel Bonnot de Mably and Emmanuel-Joseph Sièyes, two of the most important French republican intellectuals.[8] The paper published an essay by Paine and two other essays attacking Edmund Burke's writings on the French Revolution.[9] It also contained indirect references to republican theorists. Louis XVI was lampooned as the "Patriot King" in reference to Bolingbroke's *The Idea of a Patriot King* (1738).[10] On 11 February 1790, Mesplet published an article titled "Extrait d'une lettre de Paris à un Monsieur de New Haven" (Excerpt of a letter from Paris to a Gentleman of New Haven). The allusion to Condorcet's *Lettres d'un bourgeois de New-Haven à un citoyen de Virginie, sur l'inutilité de partager le pouvoir législatif entre plusieurs corps* (1788) is hard to miss. The correspondent, for whom the right "to participate in the legislative process" was "the first and most essential of all these privileges," wrote under the pseudonym of "Sidney," an allusion to the English Commonwealthman Algernon Sidney who died on the scaffold in 1685.[11] While there can be no doubt about Mesplet's intellectual leanings, it must be realized that he was not explicitly advancing a revolutionary agenda. The paper did not have an editorial section. Insofar as it disseminated republican ideals, this resulted from the choice of news stories, speeches, and documents printed.

The *Quebec Gazette* also, to a degree, promoted republicanism. It published articles approving of the French Revolution and similar movements, including a revolt in Catalonia described as the "Spanish Revolution" (21 January 1790), the rebellion in the Austrian Netherlands (11 March 1790), the agitation in the Papal States (3 June 1790), and the political upheavals in Poland (28 July 1791). Its coverage was more ambiguous, however, than that of the *Gazette de Montréal*. Its publisher, Samuel Neilson, was careful not to report only the revolutionaries' successes; he also informed Canadians of the problems France was having. Neilson's less partisan stance was due to the fact that he was not himself a republican: he believed in the modern conception of liberty. While he did promote republicanism to some extent, this was largely not deliberate. Like the majority of his contemporaries, Neilson made no distinction between republican liberty and modern liberty. Freedom from despotism was all that mattered, and the Revolution embodied that freedom. Therefore, the partisans of modern liberty initially rallied to the revolutions. Neilson's stance, similar to that of the French *anglomanes*, was typical. However, when his newspapers defined liberty and how it should be enshrined in a constitution, this discussion was generally couched in terms of modern liberty. For example, on 3 and 24 February 1791 he published two essays on the nature and organization of governments. These were taken from a reputedly counterrevolutionary royalist newspaper running from November 1789 to October 1791, *Les Actes des Apôtres*, which opposed the "democratic" French Revolution and espoused modern liberty. Both essays argued for the separation of powers in a mixed constitutional government. The first was a near-verbatim version of the section on the English constitution in Montesquieu's *The Spirit of Laws*.

Lower Canadian subjects, whether loyal or republican, were not the only ones deliberately or implicitly promoting republican principles in the colonies. In June 1793 Edmond-Charles Genêt, the French ambassador to the United States, sent out an appeal to the French Canadians titled *Les Français libres à leurs frères les Canadiens*.[12] It was based on a memorial by Henri-Antoine Mézière, a former *Gazette de Montréal* contributor who had just expatriated to the United States. The memorial, *Observations sur l'état actuel du Canada et sur les dispositions politiques de ses habitants,* explained that the province was not well-defended and that the French Canadians could not be counted on to defend it. French Canadians, it argued, were ready to throw over the English regime and accept the freedom offered by France. They were ready to replace the sovereignty of the king with national sovereignty.[13] Pursuing Mézière's thrust, Genêt exhorted the French Canadians to join the French in their fight for freedom. He reminded them that "men have the right to govern themselves, [that] laws must reflect the will manifested by the organ of their representatives, [and that] no one is entitled to oppose their enforcement." He went on to explain the benefits that the French Canadians would derive from throwing off the English yoke. They would "choose themselves a government, appoint the members of the legislative body and the executive power themselves." With the abolition of the executive veto, the legislative branch would achieve full sovereignty. The revolution would lead to the independence of the colony; equality among citizens, with universal access to employment and the abolition of hereditary title; freedom of commerce and an end to trade privileges; the abolition of the seigneurial system, corvées, and tithes; freedom of religion, and a new educational system.

THE CONSTITUTIONAL ACT
AND THE ATLANTIC REVOLUTIONS

As we have just seen, the ideas underlying the American and French Revolutions had currency in contemporaneous Quebec (and then in Lower Canada). But while these ideas did threaten the colonial state, they did not bequeath any republican legacy. Some have even maintained that the principles that triumphed in Canada were counterrevolutionary, since the parliamentary institutions granted to the colony in 1791 were designed to prevent the republican wave from carrying off the colony. This certainly was the aim of the Constitutional Act; still, it is not clear that the adjective *counterrevolutionary* is appropriate, at least from a Canadian perspective. As Jean-Pierre Wallot has noted, "the Constitution of 1791 actually came as a political revolution." It was not, on its face, an attempt to shore up despotism. It was based on an ideal of liberty that included the right of subjects to a degree of political participation through the election of a legislative assembly. The passage of the Constitutional Act was revolutionary inasmuch as it altered the entire structure of the colonial state under the influence of a particular conception of liberty. However, Wallot is perhaps too enthusiastic when he states that the Constitutional Act "instituted, at least theoretically, a movement of popular participation in government that is clearly consistent with R.R. Palmer's 'democratic revolution.'"[14] The Constitutional Act does not fit within the framework of the Atlantic revolutions since it clearly derives from the principles of modern liberty. It is much closer in spirit to the Whig settlement of 1688. While the Atlantic revolutions were overturning Europe and America, Canadians received a constitution that had nothing to do with republican liberty – yet was still founded on liberty.

British policy on the North American colonies between 1783 and 1791 was not made in a vacuum. The British government paid heed to both local conditions, including the colonists' demands, and the international situation, including the American and French Revolutions. Facing the government were at least two British constituencies: British-American subjects who had immigrated to the colony between 1760 and 1776, and loyalists who had arrived between 1776 and 1784. But all the colonists agreed that the institutions created by the Quebec Act of 1774 were unacceptable. No one had left his original colony and, in the case of the loyalists, his possessions and former life for a place where habeas corpus and trial by jury did not exist, where French civil and commercial law applied, where land was divided according to seigneurial tenure, and where subjects enjoyed no political rights. The British colonists and the loyalists rapidly coalesced around a demand for full integration into the empire, the creation of a house of assembly, and repeal of the Quebec Act.[15] Certain loyalists would ultimately limit their demands to the division of the province so that the colonists living west of Lake Saint Francis would no longer be subjected to French laws and institutions.[16]

While the movement for representative institutions remained essentially Anglo-Protestant,[17] some French Canadians could be found among its members.[18] On 24 November 1784, old and new subjects signed a petition for an assembly.[19] That same year, Pierre du Calvet sued for reparations in London after he, like Mesplet and Jautard, had spent nearly three years in prison without trial. He published a work, *Appel à la justice de l'État*, arguing for colonial reforms including habeas corpus, recognition of the rule of law over the governor's arbitrary discretion, the right to send Canadian members to Parliament, and freedom of the press.[20] He also demanded a colonial house of assembly. Du Calvet died in a shipwreck en route to Great Britain in 1786, but not before his appeal reached London's ears.

The demand for representation vexed Governor Haldimand, who doubted the French Canadians' loyalty. Nor could he understand why the loyalists would want representative institutions that had served them so badly in the past. He wrote to the prime minister, Lord North, on 6 November 1783: "These unfortunate People have Suffered too Much by Committees and Houses of Assembly, to have retained any prepossession in favour of that Mode of Government, and that they have no Reluctance to Live under the Constitution established by Law for this Country."[21] The governor's displeasure with the reformers, who did indeed demand such institutions, was exacerbated by his perception that their activities constituted a republican threat.[22] It did not: all the petitioners and submitters calling for an assembly between 1775 and 1790 based their demand on the principles of modern liberty. They never presented political participation as being equivalent to liberty but as a means for individuals to secure guarantees of their rights, freedoms, security, and property.[23]

As it pondered a new constitution for the colonies during the 1780s, the British government inevitably had to contemplate the outright loss of the empire. The last thing it wanted was a repetition of the American Revolution in the Province of Quebec. Adding to these concerns was the French Revolution and its repercussions in Great Britain, which was itself caught up in the revolutionary ferment. The republican Richard Price gave a speech on 4 November 1789 titled "A Discourse on the Love of Our Country" in which he asserted that the principles of the French Revolution were in fact foundational to the English constitution. He reinterpreted the Glorious Revolution in the light of republican liberty, asserting that the English had claimed "the right to chuse [their] own governors, to cashier them for misconduct, and to frame a government for [themselves]."[24] Edmund Burke, a modern who had kept his silence on the Revolution, came out against it in February 1790. His *Reflections on the Revolution in France* denied that the Glorious Revolution had been inspired by "the rights of man," which, for him, were destroying the institutions of France. Three Radicals responded to Burke in defence of Price's theses: Mary Wollstonecraft with *A Vindication of the Rights of Man* (1790), James Mackintosh with *Vindiciæ Gallicæ* (1791), and Thomas Paine with *The Rights of Man* (1791). These authors espoused the principles at the heart of the French Revolution and wrote in defence of them. In addition, the epoch saw the founding of clubs and societies in support of the Revolution. In short, the French Revolution and its underlying principles were an influential force in Britain at the time of the Constitutional Act.

Claude Galarneau has thus correctly maintained that the Constitution of 1791 was "one of the clearest outcomes of the revolutionary impact," since "London granted [it] to its colony in large part for fear of seeing the Canadians wake up to the implications of the triumphant French Revolution."[25] But though the French Revolution certainly alerted Britain to the need for Canadian reform, the Constitution was first and foremost a response to the American Revolution and the loyalists' demands.[26] After all, the first two constitutional reform bills date from 1786 and 1788, before the French Revolution, while a third bill was tabled in the House of Lords in February 1791.[27]

The Constitutional Act divided the Province of Quebec into two sections – Upper and Lower Canada – and gave each of them parliamentary institutions. Legislative power belonged to a provincial legislature composed of an appointed governor, an appointed legislative council, and an elected legislative assembly. Executive power belonged to a colonial governor. While an executive council was created, the governor was under no obligation to consult with it; nor could its members be held responsible for their advice. The hand of the British authorities had been forced, as well they knew. They had had no choice but to include elected assemblies in the new constitution. So, to place a check on the assemblies' power, they also included the monarchic and aristocratic institutions (governor and legislative council). It should be realized that there was nothing reactionary or counterrevolutionary about this decision. The government was simply applying to the Canadas the rules of mixed government inherent in its own constitution. The republican liberty that had inspired the rebels in the Thirteen Colonies had to be combated, and London's response was to grant a form of government partaking of modern liberty.

In a Commons debate over the bill, Prime Minister William Pitt (among others) spoke for the government; Edmund Burke and Charles James Fox spoke for the opposition. On 6 May 1791, the debate degenerated into open conflict. The session was to have dealt with the Canadian question by passing the government's bill, but Burke embarked on a long disquisition on constitutional principles, taking the opportunity to lambaste the French Revolution. A point of order was raised as to the pertinence of his remarks, and Burke's colleague Fox supported a motion to censure him. Burke took offence and loudly broke with his associate. The nature of the disagreement became evident as the debate turned increasingly bitter and polarized. This debate over the French Revolution is in fact a pivotal moment in Canadian history, since what was at stake was the nature of the liberty enshrined in the new constitution. The fault lines over the bill did not form between the government and the opposition but within the ranks of the opposition itself. The dispute caused a schism in the Whig party.[28] When Burke found himself isolated, Pitt extended his hand, stating that he was willing to cooperate "to preserve [the constitution], and deliver it down to posterity, as the best security for the prosperity, freedom, and happiness of the British people."[29] It was after this schism that Burke published *An Appeal from the New to the Old Whigs* (1791). Thus, a reconfiguration of British politics began with a debate around the Constitutional Act for Canada.

The interesting thing is that this debate took place solely within the bounds of modern liberty. Burke did set his principles up against those of the Revolution and simultaneously accused Fox of supporting the republicans and "the rights of man" (a favourite republican expression). But despite his efforts to couch the debate in terms of a clash between modern and republican liberty, both camps were actually arguing within the framework of modern liberty. For the bill's supporters (Pitt and Burke), this fact was obvious. There was no need to consult the population: the authorities "knew of their sentiments already."[30] Sovereignty was exercised by Parliament, not the people. While Pitt made clear reference to liberty by asserting that the reform "was intended to give a free constitution to Canada, according to British ideas of freedom,"[31] it was Burke who best articulated the discourse of modern liberty. It was clear, he declared, that Britain should give Canada a free constitution because "the people of Canada should have nothing to envy in the constitution of a country so near to their own [the United States]."[32] But he rejected the notion that the Revolution had brought freedom to France and that those who denounced the "anarchy and confusion that had taken place in France" should be considered "enemies to liberty."[33]

Fox, for his part, did not hide his sympathies for the Revolution, which he saw as "one of the most glorious events in the history of mankind."[34] He stated,

The rights of man, which [Burke] had ridiculed as chimerical and visionary, were in fact the basis and foundation of every rational constitution, and even of the British constitution itself, as our statute proved: since, if [Fox] knew anything of the original compact between the people of England and its government, as stated in that volume, it was a recognition of the original inherent rights of the people as men, which no prescription could supersede, no accident remove or obliterate.[35]

A man of principle and a polemicist, Fox went further to explain that he was "so far a republican, that he approved all Governments where the *res publica* was the universal principle, and the people, as under our constitution, had considerable weight in the Government."[36] While these statements might seem to imply that Burke's accusations were justified, they should not be given inordinate weight. Unlike Price, who reinterpreted the Glorious Revolution as an expression of republican principles and maintained that it had given rise to a republican monarchy, Fox analyzed the French Revolution according to modern principles and maintained that it had brought about a constitutional monarchy. Ironically, both were wrong. The Whig settlement of 1689 was inspired by modern liberty, the French Revolution by republican liberty. Of note here is the manner in which these men interpreted the two revolutions, not the veracity of their interpretations.

Moreover, Fox did not advocate for popular sovereignty during this debate. He openly upheld the principles of mixed government, with

three mutually independent branches coexisting. In the debate on
11 May 1791, Fox maintained

as a principle never to be departed from, that every part of the British dominions
ought to possess a government, in the constitution of which monarchy, aristocracy, and democracy were mutually blended and united; nor could any government be a fit one for British subjects to live under, which did not contain its due
weight of aristocracy, because that he considered to be the proper poise of the
constitution, the balance that equalized and meliorated the powers of the two
other extreme branches, and gave stability and firmness to the whole.[37]

While he accepted the monarchic principle, he wanted to limit its operation in the colonies as much as possible. The American Revolution
had taken place, he believed, not because too much room had been
made for the democratic principle but because "[the rebels] did not
think themselves sufficiently free."[38] Similarly, he accepted that the aristocratic principle should be represented in the colonial institutions. But
because there was no aristocracy, Fox proposed that legislative councillors be elected so that they remain genuinely independent of the governor and the assembly. Fox's suggestion did not flow from republican
principles, since he advocated for a political system governed by the traditional principles of mixed government. In this type of government, the
Commons represents only one-third of the legislative branch. In addition, councillors' primary legitimacy would derive from property ownership; electivity would be merely a device for choosing, from among the
richest members of society, those who would sit on the aristocratic body.
Fox pointed out that the British aristocracy too derived its legitimacy
from property.

What is instructive for our purposes is to note that the Canadian question was not discussed in a vacuum. In adopting the colonial constitution, the British politicians inevitably had to confront the lessons of the
American and French Revolutions. Of course, that does not mean that
the principles underlying these revolutions were in any way reflected in
the Constitutional Act. On the contrary, the debate around the Canadian
constitution tells us that the act in fact served to constitutionalize modern liberty – the form of liberty that had underlain the British constitution for a century – in the colonies.

The act was given royal sanction by George III in June 1791 and took
effect on 26 December. The mixed government it created is predicated
on a balance among the legislative institutions representing the monarchy (the governor), the aristocracy (the legislative council), and the democracy (the representative assembly). The system relies on cooperation

rather than competition among these bodies. While the division between the assembly and the government (strictly under the governor's control) was unorthodox with respect to British practice, the constitution is true to the general principles of mixed government dear to eighteenth-century constitutionalists and jurists.[39]

The constitution is based on neither popular sovereignty (as in the United States) nor national sovereignty (as in France) but the supremacy of the imperial parliament. The colonies had legislatures, not parliaments of their own. Parliamentary sovereignty (albeit that of an imperial parliament) is a characteristic feature of modern liberty. Furthermore, Canadian subjects' political participation was limited by two factors. First, it consisted only of the power to elect members to the assemblies, and these constituted only one-third of the legislature. Second, there was no mechanism, written or conventional – other than refusal to pass the budget – for subjecting the executive to the will of the assembly. This was understandable: the intent of the act was to give the representative institutions the power to oversee the government but not to govern. In short, executive power was the seat of real authority in the colony.

Remarking on the similarity between the English and Canadian constitutions, Lieutenant-Governor John Graves Simcoe stated on 15 October 1792 before the first session of the Upper Canadian Assembly that "this province is singularly blessed, not with a mutilated Constitution, but with a Constitution which has stood the test of experience, and is the very image and transcript of that of Great Britain, by which she has long established and secured to her subjects as much freedom and happiness as it is possible to be enjoyed under the subordination necessary to civilized Society."[40] Earlier, during the Commons debate on the Canadian constitution on 13 May 1791, Simcoe had praised the British constitution. But while the two constitutions were similar in terms of their principles and institutions, there was an important difference between them: the Canadian constitution was a colonial constitution. It was the work of British politicians, and its purpose was to preserve the bonds between colony and empire. If Simcoe made no mention of this reality, Pitt was well aware of it. It was incumbent on the colonial legislature, he said, to obey the principles of the British constitution "as near as circumstances would admit." He continued, "[the constitution] should be extended to all our dependencies, as far as the local situation of the colony, and the nature and circumstances of the case would admit."[41] Burke, too, knew that the colonial constitution could not be an exact replica of the British constitution; "it was evidently the intention of His Majesty's declaration," he stated, "that the laws adopted in Canada should be as nearly as possible similar to those of England.

Indeed, it was usual in every colony to form the Government as nearly upon the model of the mother country, as consistent with the difference of local circumstances."[42]

Thus, while the Constitutional Act was the incarnation of modern liberty in the colonial setting, it could not be a wholesale transfer of the British constitution due to the realities of that setting. The head of state was not a sovereign monarch but the king's representative, accountable for his administration to the Colonial Office. The governor's decisions were in no way beholden to the opinion of his executive councillors, who were *ipso facto* not responsible for those decisions. The legislature was composed of two houses but was in many respects dissimilar to Parliament. In the absence of a colonial aristocracy, an appointed legislative council stood in for the House of Lords. (London planned to create an aristocracy but never followed through.[43]) Unlike the latter, however, its legitimacy emanated from the constitution alone. Conversely, the democratic principle was much more powerful in the colonies than in the mother country, with suffrage extended to a larger proportion of the population. The assemblies took on a more popular cast than the Commons, with its members derived from the scions of rich and noble families. In practice, the colonial constitution functioned precisely opposite to the way the imperial government had hoped. It fostered competition rather than cooperation between the assembly and the councils.

THE CONSTITUTIONAL ACT: AN ANTIDOTE TO THE REVOLUTIONARY THREAT

The passage of the Constitutional Act was certainly influenced by the American and French Revolutions. However, the text of the constitution itself does not embody revolutionary ideals; indeed, it was drafted as an antidote to republicanism. The government believed that by granting an elected assembly it could satisfy both the republicans and the moderns. But what vision of liberty and the state did this act imply? Historians of this period have paid little attention to this question. They have generally depicted the new assemblies simply as the successful outcome of a striving for liberty on the colonists' part. Yet the answer is crucial to an understanding of how the authorities conceived of the individual, his rights and duties, his place in society, and his relations with the government; that is, whether the assembly was seen as taking its place within a republican state or a modern (constitutional) one.

The situation was particularly ambiguous in the context of the British constitution. Two people might claim to admire this constitution without sharing the same understanding of its underlying principles, much less a similar or even compatible political agenda. Blackstone and De Lolme had shown that the English constitution is an avatar of modern liberty because it is founded on absolute rights, mixed government, and parliamentary sovereignty. Yet the English constitution to which the British Radical Price aspired was a republican constitution, based on popular sovereignty and the elective principle.

Thanks to this ambiguity surrounding British parliamentarianism, the Constitutional Act was initially satisfactory to all the colonists, who had yet to become divided over different visions of liberty. The partisans of mixed government could justifiably believe they had obtained a constitution similar to Great Britain's. For example, Samuel Neilson, an adept of modern liberty, published two articles in praise of British constitutional principles in the *Quebec Gazette*. The first, by an author signing as "Solon" (in reference to the Athenian lawmaker), appeared in serial form on 23 February and on 1, 8, and 15 March 1792 and commented on each article of the Constitutional Act. (According to John Hare, the author concealed behind the pseudonym was Jonathan Sewell, who would serve as chief justice of Lower Canada from 1808 to 1838.[44]) The second, by an anonymous author, appeared on 29 March and 5 April. Despite its title, "Esquisse de la Structure et de l'Excellence de la Constitution, accordée à la Province du Bas-Canada par l'Acte du Parlement passé en 1791," it was primarily a defence of the British constitution and the English social order. The analysis was consistent with Blackstone's, although the presentation recalled that of Burke. In these two articles, Neilson offered his readers an interpretation of the Constitutional Act as issuing from the British constitution, the true guarantor of liberty in the colony.

But the partisans of republican liberty, too, could and did claim the constitution as their own, provided they took the phrase "representative assembly" to mean "legitimate legislative power." This was Fleury Mesplet's interpretation. As a faithful advocate of republican liberty, he had always favoured the creation of an assembly in the province, and now there was one. He thus signaled his approval of the Constitutional Act by reprinting part of Solon's article in the *Gazette de Montréal*. The truth was, though, that the republicans had little choice but to accept the constitution. To do otherwise would have been to reject representative government.

Solon's analysis was divided into three parts: a general description of the Constitutional Act, an article-by-article analysis, and a presentation of the political rights he saw as having been granted to Canadians. Mesplet reprinted only the second and third parts. Solon's analysis clearly partook of the principles of modern liberty. The idea of popular sovereignty was nowhere to be found. He repeatedly thanked the British Parliament for a constitution "founded on the principles of the British constitution," thus implicitly recognizing British parliamentary sovereignty over the colony. Moreover, he sang the praises of mixed government, arguing vehemently for an appointed legislative council even as he praised the elected assembly. He even supported the clause creating hereditary titles in the colony. The legislative council, he said, was essential to the new constitution since it served "as a counterweight between the Governor and the people's representatives."[45] In support of this typically modern position – republican ideology has no room for a governing body independent of the people's will – Solon quoted Montesquieu, Blackstone, and De Lolme.[46]

Mesplet must not have realized that the analysis he published was not republican in nature. Had he realized it, he would undoubtedly have published a companion analysis according more closely with his views, as seems to have been his editorial policy. Nevertheless, it is not hard to see how the third part of Solon's article could mislead a reader – or an editor – as to the author's view of the constitution. Solon began the third part:

We shall define the rights which citizens enjoy under this form of Government, & we shall explain the duties they owe to the British Government; such that by instructing our countrymen in the true meaning of the liberty they enjoy at present, we can also inculcate in their minds the respectful & submissive obedience due the system of Magistrates, which was instituted to protect this liberty & deter licence.[47]

He explained that with the creation of the assembly, citizens had acquired four important rights. The first was the right to participate in the legislative process. The second was the right to petition the assembly for redress of injustice and abuse. The third was the power of censure, or the right of citizens to complain of provincial laws privately and publicly, verbally and in writing. This implied a fourth right, which was to lobby one's assemblyman or to vote him out at the next election. A quick perusal of this presentation reveals that all the rights in question have to do with political participation, and one might conclude on this basis that the liberty granted by this constitution was republican in nature. Solon concluded, "Such are the transcendent powers with which the people have been entrusted, which give rise to the precious rights and important privileges enjoyed by free peoples; among these privileges are freedom of the PRESS & trial by jury, which are essential to the protection of subjects' life, liberty and property."[48]

But there is more than a little ambiguity in this presentation of the rights granted to Canadians under the Constitutional Act. While Solon's "rights which citizens will enjoy under this form of Government" were all political rights, serving in turn as a guarantee of civil rights such as freedom of the press and trial by jury, a closer look shows that Solon's presentation was in fact consistent with modern liberty. For one thing, a "system of magistrates" would not be instituted to protect liberty in a republic, where liberty is essentially tantamount to political participation. For another, the reference to "subjects' life, liberty and property" indicates that these were the fundamental rights that the constitution was designed to protect. This was the goal pursued through the granting of new political rights, which would in turn guarantee freedom of the press and trial by jury.

Therefore, the creation of a representative assembly by the British government in 1791 elicited differing views in the colony as to the nature of the constitution and the legitimacy of the state; nevertheless, all colonists were ultimately satisfied with the outcome. Only Mézière put forward a true republican critique of the Constitutional Act, writing to his parents in May 1793 that it "was granted by a foreign parliament, a corrupt parliament that is reaching the moment of its disintegration for having impelled England into shameful league with the crowned heads of Europe against the Rights of man."[49]

The imposition of a constitution modeled on Britain's forced the Canadians to study the constitutionalists (Locke, Blackstone, De Lolme) in order to learn the parliamentary system and discover how they would have to articulate their demands within a constitutional framework.[50] The Canadian elites proceeded to immerse themselves in British constitutional theory and, in so doing, were drawn into the world of modern liberty.

THE DISAPPEARANCE OF REPUBLICAN IDEAS IN LOWER CANADA (1793–1797)

Within a year, the Canadian elites were evincing satisfaction with their new constitution, and no one was in greater haste to sing its praises than the assemblymen themselves. During the first session of the Lower Canadian House of Assembly, the members adopted an address in response to the inaugural speech of the civil administrator, Alured Clarke, reading in part, "truly sensible of the paternal sollicitude of our most gracious Sovereign, in watching over the happiness of his people, and of the justice and benevolence of the Parliament of Great Britain."

They expressed their gratitude for the granting of "a new and liberal Constitution for their colonial government." They added,

We cannot express the emotions which arose in our breasts, on that ever memorable day, when we entered on the enjoyment of a Constitution assimilated to that form of Government which has carried the glory of our Mother Country to the highest elevation.

It is a very high satisfaction to us, to have an opportunity of joining in praise and admiration of the system of the government of Great Britain, which gives to it, so decided a superiority and advantage over other nations.[51]

Doubts about the legitimacy of the new state proceeded to disappear from the discourse of the colonial elites. The Constitutional Act and the assemblies it created had effectively served as an antidote to revolution and to republican ideals in Lower Canada. Official debates now turned towards practical matters, such as the composition of the Assembly and the qualifications of candidates for election.[52] The first session was spent on the choice of a speaker and the question of official language.

This turn away from republicanism was reinforced by the radicalization of the French Revolution in 1792, with the massacres taking place that September and the execution of the king in January 1793. Revolution was losing its lustre – and the promotion of republican ideals in the colony vanished outright with France's declaration of war against Great Britain the next month. The government became less tolerant of a dissident press, not to speak of subversive activities.[53] By the summer, it was cracking down on putatively seditious speech and acts of treason, and would soon take more pro-active measures with the publication of a pamphlet in support of the Militia Act. It used this opportunity to hammer home its own definition of liberty: "that after having obeyed the Law and the Government of his country, each is free to do as he pleases, provided that he harms no one."[54] In any case, the leading advocates of republican liberty were soon gone from the Canadian scene: Mézière left the colony in May 1793 while Mesplet died in January 1794. From then on, although a potentially revolutionary movement persisted among the masses, without leadership it went nowhere.[55]

The situation was the same in Upper Canada, where the constitution's legitimacy was not challenged at this time. The Constitutional Act gave the loyalists what they had been demanding since their arrival in the Province of Quebec: an autonomous province. In the first session of their assembly, the Upper Canadian subjects decided to re-enter the domain of British common law (in place of French civil law). In so doing, they imported not only a legal framework but also a whole manner of conceiving of the social order based on private property, certain individual rights, and equality before the law (as opposed to de facto equality).

In any event, even if the Upper Canadians had wanted to dissent from the new constitution, there was no real means of doing so. The colony's first newspaper, the *Upper Canada Gazette*, was founded in 1793 as a government mouthpiece. Not until 1807 did Joseph Willcocks found an opposition newspaper. For the first fifteen years of Upper Canada's existence, whatever controversy there was among the elites largely revolved around the degree of desirable social hierarchy. While Simcoe wanted to re-create British society and its official church in the Americas, considering any amount of American influence over colonial life to be dangerous and unacceptable, the local elites were receptive to American influence.[56] The important point is that the colonial state was now firmly established, rooted in the principles of modern liberty, and would encounter no significant dissent until the first decade of the new century.

3

The Birth of Reform Movements
in the Canadas, 1805–1828

FOLLOWING THE PASSAGE of the Constitutional Act in 1791, the two Canadas developed in accordance with the ideals of modern liberty. No one seriously questioned them – unsurprisingly, given that war had been declared on the empire. Until 1805, the legitimacy of political power and the colonial state went basically uncontested; there was no reform movement to speak of. Lower Canadians set about learning the rules of the parliamentary system while Upper Canadians accustomed themselves to the new constitutional order. As for the assemblies, they were quite docile with respect to the executive branch. Not until the first decades of the new century were some timid demands for political reform heard. These demands, though arising simultaneous with the revolutionary changes taking place in Latin America (1808–26), retained their own special character. Canadian reformers still thought of themselves as distinct from this Atlantic movement. They remained British constitutionalists, not republicans.

In Lower Canada, the first organized reform movement emerged in 1805 with the formation of a group in the Assembly. From then on, the authorities had a veritable opposition to contend with. But while calling for some refinements to government institutions, this group did not fundamentally challenge or question the state or British constitutional principles. It was organized around the tenets of modern liberty until the 1820s.

In Upper Canada, the first stirrings of reform coalesced at the same time when Robert Thorpe and his followers developed a set of political demands. This group would evolve along a rather different time scale from the Lower Canadian reform movement. It only began to have any influence on colonial politics around 1828, long after a few lone individuals' abortive attempts to found a movement (in 1806–07 and 1818). In the absence of a bona fide reform movement, individual reformers developed their critiques of colonial policy, and the demands ensuing from them, in isolation. In the decade from 1817 to 1828, reformist discourse in Upper Canada bifurcated into modern and republican variants.

THE REFORM MOVEMENT
IN LOWER CANADA (1805–1828)

Lower Canadian policy in this period was shaped by an opposition between reformers and advocates of the status quo. There were three operative power dynamics: between these two groups, between the colonial legislative and executive branches, and between Lower Canada and the empire. No one involved, however, questioned mixed government, modern liberty, or the sovereignty of Parliament.

The Lower Canadian reform movement coalesced in 1805 under the impetus of assemblyman Pierre-Stanislas Bédard. It began in response to a political crisis around the issue of taxation. Parliament was proposing to levy a tax to fund the construction of two prisons – but no one wanted to pay it. Merchants wanted it to apply to real estate, while farmers thought it should apply to commerce. In the course of this conflict, the merchants, who were mostly anglophone and had the support of the legislative and executive councils, founded the *Quebec Mercury* newspaper (1805). Bédard responded by founding and editing *Le Canadien* the following year. This newspaper became the house organ of the colony's first reform movement.[1]

*The Lower Canadian Reformers
and Ministerial Responsibility (1805–1810)*

Louis-Georges Harvey contends that the movement in question adopted a republican discourse from the outset.[2] But while certain articles in *Le Canadien* were republican in tone, Bédard's reform movement largely did not take issue with modern liberty as the basis for state legitimacy and agreed to operate within its bounds. Accepting of parliamentary sovereignty, it merely sought to change how certain parliamentary institutions operated. Bédard limned his position with quotes from Locke and Blackstone (3 June 1809), then spelled it out in a later editorial (11 November). When in 1810 the House and the Legislative Council squared off on the question of judges' ineligibility to sit in the Assembly and petitions favourable to the Council's position began circulating in the colony, Bédard wrote,

When two branches of the legislature are of different opinions on a constitutional point, is it decent, is it honest for anyone, excepting that power which is Superior to both of them, to interfere in their dispute? Who is entitled to judge between two branches of the legislature of this province, other than the Sovereign Power which created it? How could one dare arrogate to himself a power residing solely with the supreme power of the British Empire? These are the effects of that unfortunate Yankeeism which weakens all the ideas of the British Constitution, and obscures from view all but the influence of the populace as a principle of government.[3]

As can be seen, Bédard straightforwardly acknowledged the sovereignty of Parliament. Indeed, he defended it against American democratic principles, for which he expressed open contempt.

Furthermore, the early Lower Canadian reformers were advocates of mixed government. They agreed that legislative power should be held by a legislature composed of three mutually independent entities, each representing one of the traditional orders of society: monarchy, aristocracy, and democracy.[4] The governor represented the king and acted for the monarchy, the Legislative Council was regarded as "the aristocratic branch of the Constitution,"[5] and the Assembly represented the "people."[6] Bédard stressed the importance of the three branches' preserving their independence, since each represented a particular interest within society:

I maintain that above all else they [the assemblymen] must be independent of the Government and the Legislative Council, and that they must have none but the same interests as the public at large. The King, and for him the Government his Representative in this Province, charged with the enforcement of the laws and the proper employment of public monies, naturally seek to have as much power and raise as much in taxes as possible. The Legislative Council, composed of the wealthiest merchants and property owners, sees to the conservation of their immense landholdings and has an interest in increasing revenues, and in having taxes levied per capita rather than on land holdings and luxury items. The House of Assembly, which represents the people or the least wealthy class, must see to it that taxes are paid less on land holdings than on luxury items, much less per capita.[7]

It is interesting to note that the "people" represented by the Assembly, which only accounted for one-third of the legislative branch, was materially different from the republican fiction of the "people." And the legislature itself was not sovereign, for sovereignty rested with the British Parliament. Like all partisans of modern liberty, the Lower Canadian reformers believed that the responsibility to govern – under the watchful eye of the Assembly – rested with the king: "If the King has Prerogatives so as to give him the means with which to govern us, the people also has the right see to it that his Ministers' bad counsel does not cause him to lose his Government."[8]

Finally, the reformers believed that the colonial government had the role of protecting property owners. According to *Le Canadien*, "The more property you own, the greater the number of people who covet what is yours, who are willing to harm you, and, consequently, the more you need the protection of the law and the Government."[9] Modern liberty, with its ethic of accumulation, characteristically accorded great importance to property, recalling Adam Smith for whom "civil government, so far as it is instituted for the security of property, is in reality instituted for the defence of the rich against the poor, or of those who have some property against those who have none at all."[10] Their position also foreshadowed that of John A. Macdonald, who argued at the Quebec Conference of 1864, "The rights of the minority must be protected and the rich are always fewer in number than the poor."[11] The reformers desired political reform, no doubt, but not the overthrow of the political or social order.

They were very much conversant with the works of the great constitutionalists and made copious reference to them to justify their demands, believing that this would stand them in better stead with the authorities.[12] Works by Blackstone – dubbed the "catechism of the Constitution"[13] – De Lolme, and Locke were universally considered authoritative on constitutional matters, for the reformers as much as anyone else.[14] Not a single republican author was quoted or mentioned in *Le Canadien* in the years 1806 to 1810. The closest the paper came was a biography of Charles James Fox, the great Whig leader, on the occasion of his death.[15]

In short, Bédard's protest movement posed no challenge to the colonial constitution, the composition of the legislative branch, or the royal prerogative. It sat comfortably within the confines of the modern liberty on which the colonial state was founded. All the reformers wanted was to alter the workings of the colonial institutions so as to ensure consistency between the policies of the executive and legislative branches.

Having accepted all these constitutional premises, the reformers were left only three avenues through which to channel their demands. One was to call for control over all public spending. Article 4 of the Bill of Rights entitled Parliament to tax its subjects and use the proceeds at its discretion,[16] but Parliament had transferred its taxation power over the colonies to the colonial legislatures with the Declaratory Act of 1778. Theoretically, control over these revenues would have given the assemblies a lever with which to dissuade the executive branch from making unilateral decisions. However, the colony not being self-sufficient at that point, the reformers did not advocate for this reform. A second possibility was to call for the

implementation of a process allowing for the impeachment of public servants guilty of misappropriation, similar to the practice existing in the
mother country.[17] Bédard did not opt for either of these rather straightforward demands. Instead, he chose a third, more complex one: the creation of a provincial cabinet (referred to then as a ministry).[18] Given the
state of constitutional theory at the time, this was a bold and radical in-
novation, all the more fascinating in that Bédard's arguments are totally
original. No one else, not even in the mother country, had come up with
anything similar.

The English Cabinet did not owe its existence to a long period of theoretical discussion but to gradual, empirical evolution. In theory, the king
is the exclusive holder of executive power and as such has two major responsibilities: overseeing the execution of acts of Parliament, and using
a special power known as the royal prerogative, consisting of "those
rights and capacities which the king enjoys alone, in contradistinction to
others, and not to those which he enjoys in common with any of his subjects."[19] The king, for example, was solely responsible for administering
foreign policy, commanding the armed forces, meting out justice, granting honours, and overseeing the Church of England.[20] He was not always
under the strict control of the legislative power, but neither did he enjoy
full-fledged autonomy.

To justify the use of the royal prerogative, and to defend the greatness of the state of which the king was the representative as well as to
secure the loyalty of the subjects, the English constitution had made it
a cardinal principle that "the king can do no wrong." Indeed, he was
even incapable of "*thinking* wrong: he can never mean to do an improper thing: in him is no folly or weakness."[21] The person of the monarch was constitutionally inviolable and sacrosanct. He stood above the
law, beyond the jurisdiction of any court. But since such immunity
threatened the balance of power between different branches of government – putting liberty itself in jeopardy – a mechanism was needed for
subjecting the king to a degree of parliamentary control without thereby undermining his authority; in a word, to keep him from becoming a
despot. That mechanism was ministerial responsibility. Each executive
act had to be approved on behalf of the monarch by a cabinet minister,
or by the whole cabinet. Accountability for the act rested with the minister who approved it.

Ministerial responsibility receives no more than passing mention in
Blackstone and De Lolme, who simply state that the English constitution
entitles Parliament to punish the king's councillors, commonly known as
ministers, for their misdeeds:

For, as the king cannot misuse his power, without the advice of evil counsellors and the assistance of wicked ministers, these men may be examined and punished. The constitution has therefore provided, by means of indictments, and parliamentary impeachments, that no man shall dare to assist the crown in contradiction to the laws of the land. But it is at the same time a maxim in those laws, that the king himself can do no wrong.[22]

These constitutional theorists do not, however, explain the mechanism by which ministers are chosen in the first place. In theory, the king is completely free to choose his ministers (or his prime minister), since only the executive's policies – not its appointments – are subordinate to the will of Parliament (the House of Commons in particular). However, Parliament has a lever over the king – it can cut off his income, prosecute and remove his officials, and dismiss his ministers. The king does better to avert confrontation with Parliament by choosing councillors whom he knows to be acceptable to the Commons. Thus arose the tradition whereby the leader of the party that either holds a majority of seats or (in the case of minority government) secures the confidence of a majority of sitting MPs becomes prime minister. The king's autonomy and power were contingent upon the balance of power among the parties in the Commons as well as the principles of the MPs. When a parliamentary group secures a majority, the king has to choose his ministers from this group, even if he despises it. This in fact happened in 1765–66 and again in 1782, when King George III had to give power to the Marquis of Rockingham's Whigs, whom he detested. As to the monarch's influence over the ministers, that depends on the ministers in question. If they encroach upon the prerogative, the king has no choice but to wait for a change in the parliamentary balance of power. This happened in 1783 with the coalition government led by Charles James Fox and Lord North. Conversely, if the ministers act so as to preserve the prerogative, the king's influence is enhanced accordingly. This was the case under the governments of William Pitt the Younger (1783–1801, 1804–06).

In short, even though the king was the sole holder of executive power, he had to exercise that power through the intermediary of ministers, who were accountable to Parliament for executive decisions they made. This arrangement meant that ministers did not play a merely advisory role: they had to take responsibility for executive acts. However, they always acted in the name of the king, the sole recognized executive authority.

Despite the resemblance between the colonial and British constitutions, the relationship between the legislative and executive branches in the Canadian colonies could not be the same as the relationship between

Parliament and the king. Here too the king was the official holder of executive power, but it was the colonial governor who served as the de facto executive. The governor, however, enjoyed no immunity. He was just a Colonial Office official accountable for his acts to the Secretary of State for the colonies, cabinet, and Parliament – not to mention that the colonial legislative branch was not sovereign but merely a creature of the imperial Parliament.

The Constitutional Act of 1791 created an executive council for each of the Canadas. While these councils occupied a similar position as the cabinet in the British constitution, their powers were not as extensive. They were entrusted with specific responsibilities but were not accountable to the colonial legislatures for executive acts. There was no constitutional reason why they should be, since the governor, unlike the king "who can do no wrong," took full responsibility for his decisions. He could be prosecuted and punished by the British government and Parliament. Thus, in theory, the colonial constitution was simpler than the British constitution since the sovereign power could hold the executive branch directly responsible for its decisions. There was no need for an arbitrary body, the cabinet, to assume the king's responsibility.

In practice, however, the workings of the colonial constitution were more complex than those of its British counterpart. Since colonial governors were directly accountable to the cabinet and Parliament, they could not also be accountable to the provincial assemblies: one cannot serve two masters, as the adage goes. For this reason, the constitution established a total separation between the colonial legislative and executive branches. While this separation was consistent with Montesquieu's conception of modern liberty, it was not consistent with British practice. In the mother country, the legislative and executive branches were linked through the mechanism of cabinet. Therefore, the colonial assemblies played a much less important political role in the colonies than did the House of Commons in Great Britain. The assemblies had no power to oversee and censure the colonial executive branch, as that power rested with the British authorities. That meant they could not play one of the assembly's essential roles in a mixed government: protecting subjects' liberty by overseeing the government. One should not thereby conclude that the colonial constitution was despotic or a threat to liberty. It was the imperial Parliament that protected Canadian subjects' liberty from unreasonable executive acts.

In Lower Canada, this separation between the governor and the Assembly did not initially cause problems. The polarization between the merchants and councillors (anglophone) on one side and the assemblymen (francophone) on the other during the taxation debate of 1805–07 did, however, afford an occasion for Bédard to demand that the relationship between the executive branch and the Assembly be clarified. The reform he called for consisted of a provincial cabinet that would give the Assembly the possibility of overseeing the executive branch. The demand was consistent with the British constitution, but it entailed a major change in the workings of the colonial constitution and, more fundamentally, in the distribution of powers within the empire.

Bédard launched the debate over executive responsibility on 24 January 1807, the first time he advocated for the creation of a Lower Canadian cabinet. He persisted in this demand until his arrest and the closing of his newspaper in March 1810. He always formulated it within the British constitutional framework and based it on the idea that the Canadian constitution must operate in identical fashion to the British constitution (regardless of the fact that Lower Canada was a colony and not a nation).

The point of his demand was not to challenge the sacrosanct status of the king; indeed, Bédard felt the same status should be granted to the king's representative, the governor: "it is true (as could not be denied) that the person of the King's Representative must be sacred and inviolable here, as is the person of the King himself in England." However, "to say that it is the King's Representative who is in charge of everything here is to take away from colonial subjects the right to review public acts of the Government. What purpose, in that case, does their role in Legislation serve, if we deprive them of the means of discovering abuses that could be remedied through this legislature."[23] A correspondent of Bédard's who signed "A.B." made the same point. The idea that ministerial responsibility should not exist in the colony was absurd – in the absence of councillors, the governor alone, acting as the king's representative, was responsible for every executive act. And if so, then the monarchic principle was undermined and shorn of its sacrosanctness:

It is even a maxim of our ministry that there is no ministry here and that it is the Governor who directs everything. This maxim, which has the result of making the King's Representative responsible for all of the ministers' advice, is as unjust as it is unconstitutional, in that it exposes the King's Representative to the loss of the people's trust as a result of his ministers' mistakes.[24]

The reasoning of Bédard and A.B. is based on a constitutionally false premise: that the governor, having taken on the duties of monarchic status, should enjoy its benefits. As they would have it, the governor cannot be held responsible for his administration because he is covered by the monarchic principle; he can do no wrong. Therefore, executive responsibility must fall on the shoulders of his councillors. If it does not, then the colonial constitution is vitiated because the legislative branch has no lever of control over the executive branch, no way to censure executive acts. But if the governor is not responsible and no one else is either – that is, there is no cabinet – then the executive branch can do whatever it pleases, and the result is despotism. What Bédard and A.B. deliberately omitted was that the governor, hence the colonial executive branch, was de facto responsible to the British authorities. The Assembly might lack the power to censure the government, but that did not mean executive responsibility did not exist. To justify the need for a provincial cabinet, its proponents thus had to resort to a selective analysis of how Lower Canada operated as a colony.

Bédard's and A.B.'s analysis fit the bill, and they consequently demanded a fundamental change to the colonial constitution, one in which the executive branch would be accountable to the local legislative branch and not to the imperial authorities. In support of this demand, A.B. emphasized that the governor is surrounded by people (including executive councillors) who do not enjoy the confidence of the House. Their presence

has the effect of sowing continual dissension between the King's representative and the House of Assembly. What the ministerial party could not win in the House by means of debate on the prerogative, or in the newspapers, it will try to win from the King's representative ... and the result is dissension between the King's Representative and the House of Assembly over utter trivialities.[25]

In other words, the governor's decisions, flanked as he was by this ministerial party, were bound to be influenced by it. It was wrong for his councillors to have influence over the executive branch without being responsible for their opinions, especially if the governor himself (as they saw it) could not be held responsible for his decisions. A.B. mentioned that in Lower Canada, this state of affairs had exacerbated the divide between the English and French, with each group controlling separate institutions.

What the reformers were demanding was, in effect, the power to warn the governor away from bad councillors and to punish them as necessary. For Bédard, the solution was to be found in British practice, where

the Cabinet must necessarily have the majority in the House of Commons. As soon as it loses the influence which this majority affords, or as soon as its system no longer appears good, it is replaced. It·may also happen, that when the King wishes to know which of the two systems, the cabinet's or the opposition's, the nation should adopt, he dissolves Parliament. The nation then exercises its judgment by electing those whose system and conduct it approves, and by rejecting those whose system and conduct it likewise disapproves.[26]

While this demand by the reformers was perfectly in keeping with the British constitution and the institutional principles of modern liberty, it was not consistent with the colonial status of Lower Canada.

Unfortunately for Bédard and his associates, Governor James Craig took strong exception to this campaign. On 10 March 1810, with the publication in *Le Canadien* of a poem asking, "When will you dare to turn out / Good people, this rascal / Whom the government wishes to pay / Out of our taille?"[27] Craig found a pretext to take aim at the reformists. Bédard disavowed the poem in the 14 March edition, stating that he deplored its publication and condemning what appeared to be a libel against the governor, but the damage had been done. The governor had the reform leaders imprisoned and their paper shut down. By the time they were released, strict loyalty had become the order of the day: during the War of 1812, the French Canadians as a group fell in step with Craig's replacement, Sir George Prevost.

Significant constitutional debate did not resume until 1814, when a new critique of the Executive Council was published in a memorial denouncing the composition of the Council. Its anonymous authors remonstrated against the selection of councillors from the minority party in the Assembly, such that the executive branch and the Assembly were perpetually at loggerheads.[28] In making this critique, they were denouncing both the political opinions of the subjects called to sit on the Council and their ethnic origin: they were all British.[29] According to the authors, the existence of such an institution was deleterious to the colony in several respects. The councillors, who harboured animosity towards the French Canadians, were giving the governor and the British authorities wrong information. Consequently, the government found itself constantly at odds with the people, the governor and the Assembly being unable to agree on suitable policy. Not to mention that whenever the French Canadians demanded reforms, doubts were expressed as to their loyalty.[30]

But unlike Bédard, the authors of the document did not demand the creation of a cabinet composed of members drawn more or less exclusively from the majority party in the Assembly. They acknowledged that "It is fair for the Governors to be familiar with the two parties." In order for the governor to get to know the French Canadians and take account of their demands without the intermediary of English councillors, the authors proposed that the governor appoint to his executive council "the principal members of the majority in the House of Assembly." The

Council would then become "a place where the two parties can reach agreement and decide together on their plans and projects, and many needless conflicts arising only from the fact that the projects were devised separately, and from the fact that the self-love of those who devised them became committed to supporting them, would be obviated."[31] Thus, the authors did not demand the creation of a provincial cabinet, since their vision of the Executive Council was as an essentially advisory institution on the model of the British Privy Council.[32]

The idea of a Lower Canadian cabinet then disappeared almost entirely from the public scene, with a few exceptions. Pierre Bédard's nephew Laurent relaunched *Le Canadien* on 14 June 1817 and directed it until the end of 1819.[33] Like the older man, he was concerned by the question of freedom of the press. In the summer of 1818, he reprinted De Lolme's writings on the subject, which his uncle had first published in 1808.[34] Laurent Bédard, too, regularly appealed to the authority of Blackstone and De Lolme. Ultimately, on 25 July 1818, he revisited the idea of ministerial responsibility. This discussion, otherwise of little significance, arose from a minor dispute over the responsibility of the civil secretary in regard to acts of government during the Prevost administration.

According to Laurent Bédard, the idea that the governor should take sole responsibility for the acts of his administration made no sense at all. To demonstrate the danger of this idea, he stated that it was "the practice, which always prevailed in France during the Revolution, that the Ministers were in no way accountable for acts of the Government ... All the faults of the administration fell on the leaders of the revolution. Whence the rapidity of the revolutions. Whence the instability of a Government in which the Ministers are accountable for nothing." Justified or not, this statement was highly useful in casting doubt on the status quo in the colony. Following this logic, Bédard stated that "the civil secretary is most responsible for acts of the Administration." He concluded by referring to the principles of the British constitution: "The prerogative has its rules and its maxims. It is entrusted to the head of state, in order to be employed according to the opinion of his Ministers for his greater good." Bédard did not pursue this line of thinking again until February 1819, at which point he added nothing new to the debate but merely reprinted two articles from 1807: the ones by A.B. and Pierre Bédard.[35]

The question of ministerial responsibility resurfaced only once in the 1820s, in an editorial titled "Catéchisme à l'usage du Bas-Canada" that was published by Flavien Vallerand, the new editor of *Le Canadien*, on 22 March 1820. The argument in this case was particularly muddled. Vallerand acknowledged that responsibility for the colonies rested with the minister in London. His comments on colonial ministerial responsibility were limited to the following: "The Executive Council is, more or less, to the Governor as the Ministers are to the King: one should conclude from this that a member of the Executive Council should not be a member of the Legislative Council." This conclusion is perplexing since the King chose his ministers from both houses of Parliament, so there was no reason why the king's executive councillors could not also be legislative councillors. Nevertheless, with this comment, the topic disappeared from reformist discourse for over a decade.

Subsequently, only Étienne Parent devoted much ink to the relationship between the executive and legislative powers, advocating for a form of ministerial responsibility in the 1830s. Parent resumed publication of *Le Canadien* on 7 May 1831 after a six-year hiatus. Though he supported the Patriotes until 1835, he never shared their republican ideals. Like Bédard, Parent endorsed British constitutional principles, and this is why he came to consider a degree of local ministerial responsibility as a possible solution to the problems of Lower Canada.

Parent was well versed in British constitutional matters. He knew that "the king's ministers and counsellors are accountable, at the price of their portfolios, their fortunes, and indeed their lives, for the acts of government." But he could not refrain from noting that the situation was very different in the colony: "Here the ministers and counsellors of the king's representative give any advice whatever, do whatever they wish, appear everywhere to do evil, and when the time comes to account for their advice, they take on an intangible form, they disappear, they become nothing."[36] His criticism of the colonial executive councillors was not intended as a criticism of the royal prerogative as such:

The colony has never claimed that its powers should go beyond the point where they would be incompatible with the maintenance of the King's sovereignty. The colonists have always been and are still willing to leave to the king all the prerogatives and powers which constitute royal sovereignty under the English constitution; but, at the same time, they want the people to enjoy the rights and privileges guaranteed by this same constitution.[37]

Thus, Parent's request for the introduction of ministerial responsibility in the colony was intended as a way of controlling the executive branch within the framework of the British constitution.

Parent's demand diverged from that of Bédard and the authors of the 1814 memorial in that it proposed to make the executive councillors responsible for various departments (ministries). According to Parent, it was necessary in Lower Canada to have a "corps of men on whom it would be incumbent, each in a certain department, to submit measures to the

Houses which are designed to meet the needs of the country ... a Council or provincial ministry composed, as is the case everywhere, of men of influence in the two Houses."[38]

In November 1835, Governor Gosford assured the Canadians that London had no intention of changing the "social arrangements" – an allusion to the Quebec Act – in the colony. Parent was thus more confident than ever of the authorities' good will. Indeed, he wondered whether the reform of the Executive Council might not be sufficient by itself to replace all the other demands made by the Patriotes, especially if the Executive Council could name legislative councillors.[39] Be that as it may, Parent never had enough influence over the Patriotes to secure the acceptance of this reform proposal. Accused of moderatism because he rejected violence in 1836–37, Parent remained on the margins of the Parti patriote until the uprising.[40] The question of ministerial responsibility would only regain importance after the rebellions.

The Lower Canadian Reform Movement (1810–1828)

As we have seen, the idea of a colonial cabinet largely disappeared from the reformists' discourse after 1810. It was not a demand with which they could easily prevail. Though integral to British constitutional practice, the mechanism of cabinet was difficult to explain and articulate, for its theoretical underpinnings had never been made explicit in Britain. The abandonment of this demand did not, however, signify that the reformers had given up. Two other demands were possible within the framework of modern liberty and British institutions. The first concerned Assembly control over subsidies; the second, the impeachment of public servants. In the years from 1810 to 1828, the reformers repeatedly brought up these two mechanisms as means of giving the Assembly some control over the executive branch.

On the second of these, the reformers argued that it was inconceivable to grant certain people immunity from prosecution for misconduct: that would put them above the law. Judges in particular came into the Assembly's line of sight. In 1814, proceedings were begun with a view to impeaching judges Jonathan Sewell and James Monk. In 1817, Louis Charles Foucher was the object of a similar attempt. Even Pierre Bédard, who had become a judge, did not elude the wrath of the elected representatives: similar proceedings were brought against him in 1819. The problem the Assembly faced was that the colonial constitution contained no mechanism allowing for removal of public servants. The Assembly could pass resolutions, but nobody was officially empowered to actually remove a public official. The judges kept their positions.

In 1818, the Prince Regent (the future George IV) announced that he wished to entrust this power to the Legislative Council. The decision does not appear to have been put into practice since reform member François Blanchet was still calling for the implementation of a court of impeachment during a debate in the Assembly on 28 February 1819. He wrote that the establishment of such a court was necessary because "the courts are the only rampart against crime. It cannot therefore be but extremely alarming for this Colony, to see that there is in fact a class beyond the reach of the law."[41] On 31 January 1821, the members resumed debate on a bill to make the Legislative Council the court of impeachment, but the discussion did not bear any fruit.[42]

In 1822, the Assembly asked for sanctions against a legislative councillor, John Richardson, for remarks made at a 25 January Council session to the effect that the Assembly, by virtue of its actions, was comparable to the rebels under Charles I and to the Committee of Public Safety during the Reign of Terror in France. The Assembly asked the Council to punish Richardson even if he could not be removed. It also requested that the governor "remove and dismiss the said *John Richardson* from all Offices and Places of Honour, Trust or Profit which he may hold during pleasure, under His Majesty's Government in this Province."[43] Here again, these proceedings were to no avail: the authorities left Richardson alone.[44]

After failing in their efforts to institute a degree of ministerial responsibility and to create a court of impeachment, with the British government refusing to cooperate, the reformers turned to their last resort, the only mechanism under the British constitution that could allow the Assembly to limit the Crown prerogative: they demanded that the Assembly be given control of all colonial revenues. This demand took centre stage in 1818 when the Prince Regent required the governor, Sir John Coape Sherbrooke, to ask the legislature to bear all costs relating to the civil government of the province.[45] There was nothing radical about this request; the Assembly itself had made the same proposal in 1810.[46] Nothing had come of that proposal, as the War of 1812 intervened, but the prince's demand in 1818 marked the beginning of a long struggle culminating in the rebellions.

In 1819, Laurent Bédard insisted that the Assembly's control of all colonial revenues was the necessary corollary to the royal prerogative within the framework of British mixed government:

Fears that the members of the House will encroach on the Crown prerogative do not seem to us better founded. The crown's power to appoint all officials, and to confer titles of nobility and honour, puts the King above all his subjects, and is what constitutes the English monarchy; and the right, which the people possesses, to raise and grant monies through its Representatives, is what forms the limited monarchy. For, if the crown possessed this power, it would be absolute, and the people would have no guarantee of their liberty.[47]

Flavien Vallerand, Bédard's successor as publisher of *Le Canadien*, stated likewise that "the sacred right, which the English people possess, to raise and allot monies through their Representatives, is a right to which the inhabitants of the country can never be too attached."[48] This right was essential to liberty, since its disappearance would lead to a form of despotism: "Deprive the English of control of their public monies and these proud heirs of freedom, so jealous of their Constitution, would fall in an instant under despotic rule."[49] The assemblyman François Blanchet, owner of *Le Canadien*, reiterated that the structure of the British parliamentary system itself justified the Assembly's demands:

His Majesty's Government, in granting the Inhabitants of Canada a representative Government, took as a model the English Constitution, in so far as circumstances would permit. The Canadians, in receiving the benefits of this Constitution, received with it an experience consecrated by centuries of practice. The powers of the different branches of the Legislature were then defined ... Since the revolution of 1688, it has been a basic law of the Realm, that the Commons holds the exclusive privilege to raise money, to appropriate it, and to attach any such conditions to such appropriation as it pleases. By virtue of this common right, the Assemblies of all the Colonies enjoy this same privilege.[50]

The reformers were quick to insist that they had nothing against the constitution. On the contrary, they maintained that "it would be dangerous to touch a single stone of an edifice as venerable as the English Constitution."[51] All they wanted was for it to be put fully into effect in the colony.

Nevertheless, relations between the Assembly and the executive branch went downhill with the arrival of Lord Dalhousie as governor in 1820. Dalhousie demanded not only that the Assembly pay the expenses of the civil government (which the Assembly was willing to do) but also that it adopt standing appropriations.[52] The Assembly's decision was predictable. Being unable to hold cabinet ministers responsible for their decisions or to impeach public servants, its only means of putting limits on the royal prerogative was to exercise tight control over the budget. Dalhousie, invoking the British constitution, reiterated his request on 11 December 1821 when he asked for a civil list (an appropriation for the operation of the executive and judicial branches) for the lifetime of the king.[53] The Assembly responded directly to the king on 21 January, declaring that it was unable to acquiesce to the demand, much as it might have liked to. It based its refusal on arguments that rejected the governor's analogy between the British and colonial constitutions and highlighted the many differences between them. Here one sees a clear difference from the first generation of reformers, who had made no distinction between the two constitutions.

The Assembly maintained that provincial revenues were unstable and on an overall decline. Under the circumstances, it would be risky to agree to such a long-term allocation for the costs of civil government. It added that the Crown retained control over certain sources of revenue, whereas the Assembly was demanding control over all provincial revenues. In addition the colony's revenues were contingent on imperial laws over which the colonists had no power. Not only would the passage of a civil list for the life of the king impose recurring expenses on the province whose relative weight in the total budget would continue to grow, it would deprive the Assembly of control over revenues. The Assembly further explained that although the civil list was a very small budget item in Great Britain, it would account for nearly the entirety of the colony's spending. By adopting a multi-year civil list, the Assembly would lose all power over the province's fate.

The Assembly further noted that the colonial political system was not identical to the British system:

The division of the Legislative, Executive and Judicial Powers, the independence of the Judges in the functions of their Office, as also the responsibility of the Officers of Government, essential attributes of the Constitution are well marked in *Great Britain;* but do not exist in this Province, where powers and functions which mutually exclude each other are united in the same persons.

In this context, it maintained that the use of colonial revenue "can only in fact be superintended by the Colonial Legislature, and more especially the Assembly, as it is in the other British Colonies; any other mode of control might prove impracticable and illusory." The Assembly thus refused to pass the civil list, maintaining that such an appropriation

would involve an abandonment by the Assembly of one of the most ancient Privileges, and of the Rights most constantly exercised by the Colonial Assemblies. The Assembly would thereby be deprived of that weight in the Legislature which they ought to have, as also would the People whom they represent. They would also thereby divest themselves of the only practicable means of superintending the application of the Public Revenue; Rights and Privileges alike necessary and beneficial to His Majesty's Government and to the security of his Subjects in this Province.[54]

Notwithstanding these objections, the Assembly reiterated its willingness to pay the civil government's expenses on an annual basis.

The crisis came to a head in 1823 when the Legislative Council refused to pass the Assembly's budget. The tension lessened briefly the following year when, in the absence of Lord Dalhousie, Sir Francis Burton came to the colony to serve as lieutenant-governor (a position he'd held in absentia since 1808). But the crisis resumed with even greater intensity in 1827. That year, the spring electoral campaign revolved around this issue. John Neilson, a Lower Canadian representative who testified before the select committee of the House of Commons in 1828 on the Canadian question, made control of subsidies by the Assembly the primary demand of Lower Canadian reformers.[55]

From Reformism to Republicanism (1822–1828)

Prior to 1828, the reformers rarely wavered in their allegiance to the British Empire, nearly always situating their demands within the constitutional framework. They likewise adhered to the tenets of modern liberty, in which participation in the legislative process is only one among a number of rights.[56] They never questioned the balance of power inherent in mixed government; nor did they dispute the legitimacy of the Legislative Council, and they acknowledged the relative autonomy of the executive branch, even though they sought a more effective check on its power. Pierre Bédard and Louis-Joseph Papineau, the speaker of the Assembly, even opined (in 1809 and 1820, respectively) that the Conquest of New France had proved positive in that it had given French Canadians free institutions.[57]

But things began to change after 1820. Reformist discourse progressively took on a republican character. This trend arose in the context of concerns about corruption in the legislative branch. An article in *Le Canadien* of 4 March 1820 argued that an elector must not sell his vote to the highest bidder. While the importance of voter independence is discussed by Blackstone, it is more characteristic of the discourse of republican liberty. On 15 March, the same paper published an article on Andrew Marvell, a colleague of John Milton under the Commonwealth in the 1650s. Marvell was presented as a "martyr of patriotism" for staunchly preserving his independence from the executive branch after the Restoration. Finally, on 14 July 1824, *Le Canadien* published an article on the need for assemblymen to preserve their independence from the administration.

The first direct criticism of the British constitution appeared in the colony in October 1821 under the title "Origine et vices de la Constitution britannique." The anonymous author began by impugning the greatness and superiority of the constitution. He wrote, "in vain would one look for a Lycurgus or a Solon among the English; their vaunted constitution had no other source than the interest of the royal power itself. It is in reality but an incoherent amalgam of different acts successively obtained from their monarchs." Emphasizing the importance of representation in the political system, the author stated that "if on the one hand the people must obey the laws, [these laws] must on the other emanate from their own will." He then upbraided Montesquieu for having admired the English system of mixed government:

Our predecessors were so little acquainted with the essence of the representative mode, that the immortal Montesquieu prostrated himself, as it were, with admiration before the British constitution … More enlightened in our day in regard to the people's rights, we shall praise, with Montesquieu, that which deserves to be praised; but we would be ashamed to profess blind admiration for the defects which dishonour the English Constitution.[58]

After this rather direct introduction, the author criticized the House of Commons, whose members were for sale or obtained their seats in rotten boroughs, as well as the House of Lords, not all of whose members were deserving of the honour.[59] Finally, he criticized the Crown, stressing that the United States had succeeded in entrusting an elected representative with executive power.[60] It should be added here that the Lower Canadian perception of the United States, which started out essentially negative, grew increasingly positive after 1815.[61]

The reformers' references also became more diversified in the 1820s. The time was gone when Blackstone and De Lolme would suffice to justify their demands. True, *Le Canadien* still mainly appealed to partisans of modern liberty – Voltaire, Montesquieu, Blackstone, Charles James Fox, Benjamin Constant, Germaine de Staël[62] – but it now also referred to republican authors such as Jean-Jacques Rousseau. Even though the Rousseau passages quoted did not generally concern politics, their provenance indicates that the reformers were now conversant with the republican principles developed in the corresponding works. *Le Canadien* published several excerpts from *Encyclopédie* articles (including the *Discourse on Political Economy*, which presaged the argument in the *Social Contract*), the fifth book of *Émile* (containing a summary of the *Social Contract*), and *Julie, or the New Heloise.*[63]

Another trend after 1818 that offered a glimpse of the reform movement's edging towards republican liberty was its insistence on control of subsidies. De Lolme, who had recognized the importance and effectiveness of this limit on the royal prerogative, nonetheless believed that its wholesale application could be potentially dangerous to the stability of the constitutional order: "there might be the danger, that, if the parliament should ever exert their privilege to its full extent, the prince, reduced to despair, might resort to fatal extremities; or that the constitution, which subsists only by virtue of its equilibrium, might in the end be subverted."[64] One cannot help but observe that De Lolme's analysis proved prescient in the Lower Canadian case. The dispute over subsidies exasperated the reformers. With London's refusal to countenance ministerial responsibility or impeachment of public servants, the only way to make their demands heard was to withhold subsidies, at times leaving the government and the judiciary in difficult economic straits. In the end they were led to reject constitutionalism altogether and to adopt republicanism.

The dispute over subsidies was a prelude to another serious dispute beginning in June 1822, when a bill was tabled in the House of Commons to unite the two Canadas. This measure seriously shook the Canadians' confidence in the British government. According to Philip Buckner, the goal of the authorities in proposing the union was to consolidate their position in British North America, resolve the sharing of customs revenues between the two Canadas, and gradually assimilate the French Canadians. According to Helen Taft Manning, the anglophone elite of Lower Canada saw it as a way of circumventing French Canadian domination of the Assembly.[65] News of the bill was initially disbelieved when it reached the colony; *Le Canadien* even took it for a hoax.[66] When the text of the bill arrived, *Le Canadien* declared it unjust because it changed "the political constitution of the country, without providing to those concerned by this measure, as regards the preservation of the liberty of their persons and the security of their property, [an opportunity] to have their demands heard."[67] Petitions were circulating by the autumn.[68] A large meeting was held on the Champ de Mars in Montreal on 7 October. The Legislative Assembly formally adopted an address to the King in early 1823, as did the Legislative Council. Papineau and Neilson were sent to the United Kingdom to fight the bill. But the Upper Canadians were equally opposed. John Beverly Robinson, the attorney general of Upper Canada, and John Strachan, the soul of the Upper Canadian elite, officially expressed their point of view in London between 1822 and 1824.[69] Rather than have the question debated, the government dropped the bill without bringing it to a vote after the member James Mackintosh objected to voting on the union without the Canadians having been consulted.

At this point, the reformers were still working within the English constitutional system. Papineau, the speaker of the Assembly and the leader of the reformers, explained in a letter to Louis Guy that fall that his group opposed the union for two reasons. First, the aim of the bill was to destroy French laws and customs as well as Catholic institutions. Papineau went as far as to call for the support of the clergy to improve the chances of defeating the union. In other words, he was defending the Quebec Act. Second, he contended that the parliamentary institutions created by the Constitutional Act of 1791 had been obtained thanks to the efforts of the greatest statesmen England had ever known: William Pitt, Lord Grenville, and perhaps even Edmund Burke, who had spoken in favour of the act in the House of Commons. It was wrong, said Papineau, for the French Canadians to be deprived of their constitution and their rights. In tactical terms, he had grasped the importance of not being perceived to be driven by "racial" considerations. He was at pains to specify that all the constituted powers of the colony objected to the union. And to prove that the struggle did not pit two ethnic groups against each other, Papineau proposed to send a "good Englishman" of the Calvinist faith as the spokesman for the movement – here he was alluding to John Neilson. This choice was all the more symbolic in that Neilson was Scottish and Presbyterian.[70] In short, Papineau had not yet abandoned the constitutional framework. His position resembled that of the Assembly, which adopted an address framed within the bounds of modern liberty.

In this address to the king, the Assembly explained that the Canadians were "sincerely attached to the Form of Government under which [they have] the good fortune to live" and that they trusted in the justness of the British government. Going further, the Assembly expressed its satisfaction with the Constitutional Act, which, "modeled on the Constitution of the Mother Country, by some of the greatest and wisest of its Statesmen, establishes Powers sufficient to reform Abuses, repair Wrongs, appease Discontent, and provide for the general Good of the Province." While such a statement may seem surprising coming from an Assembly that had failed in all its attempts to "reform Abuses, repair Wrongs, [and] appease Discontent," it confirmed that the reformers were not yet calling for a change in the constitutional framework.

The Assembly was more than just satisfied with the structure of power in the colony: it appreciated the division between the two Canadas. It stated in this regard that

The Separation of this Province from Upper Canada was, on the part of the Imperial Parliament, an Act of Justice and Benevolence towards the Inhabitants of both Provinces, giving all of them the means to keep intact the Rights and Privileges which were guaranteed to them by Honour of the Government.

While national rights (along with other rights) are accommodated by this sentence, the framework allowing for their maintenance is characteristic of modern liberty since it was imposed by Parliament. Parliamentary sovereignty is neither challenged nor questioned. In any event, the Assembly had yet to conceptualize the republican "people" since it went on to state that the policy adopted in 1791 had "Secured forever more to the Government of Your Majesty the unshakable Confidence, Affection, and Loyalty of all the Classes of Your Majesty's Subjects in this Colony." The use of the phrase "all classes of subjects" implies that the population of Lower Canada had multifarious interests. The Assembly concluded by stating that

Not only do the Reasons giving rise to the Adoption of this Statute still exist in all their force, but they have even acquired a degree of additional force as a result of the favorable Experience which the Inhabitants of this Province have had of them, and because they rightly regard them as the permanent foundation of their Laws, their Institutions, and their most dearly held Rights.[71]

While the Canadian reformers defended the integrity of their province within the bounds of modern liberty, they were beginning to push at those bounds and to question British intentions. What is more, Papineau's visit to London in 1823 had an unintended effect. While officially successful, his visit left a bitter aftertaste. He who so admired British society and the constitution was greatly chagrined by the inequalities he observed. This seems to have been the source of his disenchantment with the British constitution and, by the end of the decade, his stated preference for the American model.[72]

The Lower Canadian reformers' shift from constitutionalism to republicanism was more readily accomplished after 1822 in that they had long been affirming that the Assembly represented the "people." Such an argument can take on a republican cast when the "people" in question ceases to correspond to the democratic component of mixed government to become instead the republican fiction. This ambiguity around the concept of the people was key to the progressive transition between modern liberty and republican liberty among the Lower Canadian reformers. The transition was facilitated by the fact that the speaker of the Assembly was also the majority leader. In the British parliamentary system, the speaker of the House of Commons plays the role of arbiter between the party in power and the opposition parties, while the majority leader is the prime minister. By this division of labour, the British system acknowledges the plurality of interests represented in the House, an essential element of democracy within the framework of mixed government. Things worked differently in the colonies. Since the majority leader was also the speaker, he did not speak for the majority but for the whole body. Thus, he could, as time went on, claim to be speaking on behalf of the people. The combination of the duties of speaker and majority leader in a single person made it possible to structure the conflict not as one between colonial and British interests but as one between the people (who spoke through the voice of the Assembly) and the other colonial institutions (Legislative Council and governor) that were infringing its rights.

The shift from the modern to the republican conception of liberty took place progressively. An early sign of it appeared in 1826 when the Parti canadien became the Parti patriote. The reformers' new banner evoked the one in which the rebels of the Thirteen Colonies had draped themselves. In early 1827, with the colonial electoral campaign in full swing, the daily *La Minerve*, published by Ludger Duvernay, published articles that were clearly republican in tone, touching on issues such as corruption and virtue. But it was the next year that things really changed. The governor's persistent refusal to make any concessions to the reformers, as well as the torpid pace of reform afterward, led certain reformers to prosecute their struggle with recourse to republican liberty.

Modern liberty, by this time, had nothing to offer them: it formed the very sinew of the state they were struggling against and put the acts of the sovereign power beyond appeal. To serve the reformers' aims, any alternative ideology would have to accommodate a different source of legitimate authority in the colony. Republicanism served this purpose. As the eighteenth-century revolutionary movements had shown, republican principles were subversive: they allowed one to appeal successfully to the people as the source of all legitimate authority, and in so doing to challenge the established order. Thus, the shift to republican discourse in the Canadas made perfect sense in that it served the interests of those who adopted it.

The transition was facilitated by the fact that republican discourse – no less than constitutional discourse – had accommodated mixed government in the eighteenth century. This resemblance between the two ideologies allowed Lower Canadian reformers to glide almost imperceptibly towards republicanism. In this they could follow the example of the majority of British Radicals who had articulated a coherent republican discourse without ever abandoning the constitutional framework.[73] No matter that republican mixed government is a completely different creature from its constitutional cousin, with sovereignty in the hands of the people rather than a tripartite parliament. The reformers had only to stand the British constitution on its head for it to take on a republican form (see Figure 3.1).

Mixed constitutional government, as it existed in the colony, dictated that legislative power rest with the legislature, which represented the sum of the interests of the monarchy (the king), the aristocracy (the upper house), and the democracy (the assembly). In this system, the assembly represents the people, construed as the portion of the population belonging to neither the aristocracy nor the monarchy. The assembly constitutes one-third of the legislative branch, alongside the upper house and the monarch. This form of government works if all three legislative partners collaborate. The members of the Lower Canadian Assembly could demand a greater share of power by asserting their rights and privileges as a party to the legislative system. In doing so, they remained within the framework of modern liberty, and this is what they did until 1828. However, faced with London's refusal to countenance reform of any kind, the members had to invoke some other justification for their demands. That justification would have to establish the primacy of the Assembly over the imperial parliament, the governor, and the other two branches of the colonial legislature, or else they could not reasonably persist in their demands. Republicanism and its elective principle fit the bill. The Assembly was the sole institution elected by the inhabitants of the province; ergo, it and it alone spoke on behalf of the people. Of course, for this justification to be valid, the word *people* had to be redefined to refer to the republican fiction, and it duly was.

The Patriotes would not reject the empire and the monarchy until the end of the 1830s, yet their adoption of the republican ideal changed the nature of their movement. They ceased to be reformers demanding changes to the workings of the colonial institutions – and became revolutionaries. After 1828, calls for reform were no longer heard. The reformers now advocated for a reinterpretation, and ultimately a total remaking of the constitution. They demanded neither more nor less than the reconfiguration of political and social dynamics in the colony: a Lower Canadian republic.

This fundamental ideological transformation took place so gradually that no one noticed until the 1830s. It was only when the Patriotes' discourse had become clearly republican that those reformers who still

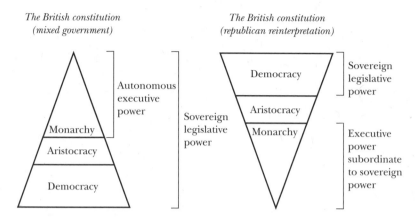

Figure 3.1
Two interpretations of the British constitution

subscribed to the principles of modern liberty realized what had happened. Acting on this realization, John Neilson and Étienne Parent, two important architects of the Lower Canadian reform movement, quit the party and were politically marginalized (at least initially) as a result. The republicans came to consider their former allies' moderate stance as a betrayal. Neilson, who had taken part in all the battles of the 1820s alongside the reformers and who had twice (in 1823 and 1828) represented them in London, broke with the party definitively in 1834 during the debate over the Ninety-Two Resolutions. In the ensuing months he helped organize the Constitutional Association of Quebec and became its president the following year. This association was one of the pillars of the defence of modern liberty and the constitution until 1837.[74] As to Parent, he took his distance from the Patriotes around 1835–36. Note that these two defections occurred in Quebec City, a region that did not join the 1837 uprising. The moderates, it seems, may have retained some authority locally. It remains that by the time of the Rebellions, their influence over the Patriotes was essentially nil.

THE UPPER CANADIAN REFORMERS (1805–1828)

The situation in Upper Canada for the period of 1805 to 1828 hardly bears comparison with that of Lower Canada. The province was much smaller and less developed. Its main issues of concern had to do with immigration, land distribution, and American influence rather than the division of powers that so preoccupied the Lower Canadians. No bona fide political reform movement appeared until 1828. While there were two reform-related episodes, they were primarily the work of isolated individuals. In one case (1805–07), Judge Robert Thorpe found himself at the head of a small group of malcontents; in the other (1818), Robert Gourlay organized a petition campaign. Both these attempts failed and their instigators left the colony.

Robert Thorpe's Early Reform Attempt (1806–1807)

The first stirrings of reform appeared in the colony around 1805.[75] As in the neighbouring province, these efforts stemmed from an ethnic conflict – to wit, a small number of Irish subjects complaining of favouritism by the executive branch towards an equally small number of Scottish merchants.[76] What appeared as an ethnic dispute on the face of it was reinforced by personal considerations. A small group of malcontents had gathered around executive councillor Peter Russell, either out of family ties (in the case of Joseph Willcocks, William Willcocks, and William Warren Baldwin) or friendship (in the case of Thorpe).[77] Russell had administered the colony from 1796 to 1799 and hoped to succeed Peter Hunter as lieutenant-governor on the latter's death in 1805. He did not get the job; Francis Gore did, after a short interregnum in which Alexander Grant administered the colony (1805–06). Russell's failure to secure the appointment was the catalyst for his partisans to become active on the colonial political scene (though he himself did not join them).[78]

Thorpe's involvement with the reformers was also stoked by professional disappointment. Arriving in Upper Canada the preceding year as a puisne judge, he had his sights set on becoming chief justice, a position he had held in Prince Edward Island (1801–04). In attempting to secure this position, Thorpe played a double game. Even as he joined Russell's circle, he carried on a correspondence with the British authorities in an attempt to set himself up as an authority on Upper Canadian affairs and the man who, given his contacts with the malcontents, had the best chance of restoring harmony to the colony;[79] he wrote that if appointed chief justice, he could achieve this "in twelve months or less."[80] When he learned he had been passed over for chief justice in favour of the provincial attorney general,[81] Thorpe cast his lot with the reformers while still hoping to be appointed to the executive and legislative councils.[82] Faced with London's inaction and at the instigation of a group led by William Willcocks, Thorpe agreed to run in a by-election for a seat left vacant after reformist assemblyman William Weekes was killed in a duel. He was elected in December 1806 and became the leader of the reformers.

Despite how their adversaries depicted them, the Thorpe group (with the possible exception of Joseph Willcocks) were not republicans.[83] They never gave the slightest indication of intending to overthrow the established order. On the contrary, England was for them the very paragon of a free country.[84] Moreover, Canada's political system was the envy of the Americans. It would become, Thorpe said, "the asylum to which in the first tumult thousands will fly with their property and in the first convulsion between the Northern and the Southern States, it will be the post to rally round the Royal Standard, and be the means of reuniting a great portion of America again to Gt. Britain."[85] Thorpe made no bones about his admiration of the British constitution and the tenets of modern liberty. His 1806 campaign slogan was "The King, the People, the Law, Thorpe and the Constitution."

For Thorpe, law was a central element of liberty; he stated in October 1805,

A young country particularly calls for care and attention; the bad habits of infancy are the miseries of age; but nurtured by your energy and zeal, we will advance to maturity, laden with the blessings of Constitution and Commerce … As we love liberty, we must uphold the law, for liberty consists in freedom from restraint, except such as established law imposes for the good of the Community; therefore when the restraints of the law are overthrown, anarchy reigns, until the people in this lassitude of contention, succumb to tyranny, feeling the worst of Governments better than none.[86]

This definition of liberty as preserved by law recalls that of Montesquieu. Thorpe also refers to the importance of commerce, a central feature of modern liberty, contrary to the ethic of virtue and the agriculturism inherent in republican liberty.

Thorpe's complaint, in reality, stemmed not from any disagreement with the form of the constitution but from anger and jealousy directed at certain individuals. As he explained to Edward Cooke, Under-Secretary of State for War and the Colonies,

The British Parliament gave the Colony the British Constitution yet the Executive never would suffer the public money to be accounted for before the House of Assembly and for the pitiful patronage of one thousand a year, the people were deprived of the very object they came to enjoy. The Province adopted the English Law, but the people found that power influenced the decisions of the Courts and defeated the verdict of the juries. In short, the liberality of the Crown, the wisdom of Parliament and the system agreed on by the greatest politicians England ever produced as the only mode by which the province could be retained was all despised and the converse pursued. The few were aggrandized and enriched; the many were to be oppressed and impoverished ... The shadow of the British Constitution was given to the many and the substance retained for the few.[87]

From the outset, and in contrast to what occurred in Lower Canada, the Upper Canadian reformers made Assembly control over subsidies their principal demand.[88] The matter at issue was relatively straightforward. In the years 1803 to 1805, with no opposition from the Assembly, the executive branch had drawn on provincial coffers to pay some of the costs of the provincial administration and justice system.[89] But on 1 March 1806, the Assembly demanded that the money spent be reimbursed. They stated that "the first and most constitutional privilege of the Commons has been violated."[90] The governor prorogued the session. Thorpe and his collaborators set themselves up as the advocates for the Assembly's right to control public money.[91] Thorpe's adherence to this principle and his hatred for the lieutenant-governor and his circle were so intense that, when the Assembly retroactively approved the subsidies on 7 March 1807, he was one of only two members to vote against the measure.[92]

This first Upper Canadian reform effort, although contemporaneous with the Lower Canadian movement, was not comparable to it. First, the reformers were a minority in the Upper Canadian Assembly; indeed, Thorpe at times found himself the sole member voting for or against a resolution.[93] Second, unlike Bédard, Thorpe was not sincerely attached to the colony. From the time he learned that he would not be appointed chief justice, he continually requested a transfer to another colony: Cape of Good Hope or any other destination characterized by "a good climate."[94] Finally, while the Lower Canadian reformers were connected with the legislative branch (the Assembly), their Upper Canadian counterparts held positions linked to the judiciary (Thorpe) and the executive branch. Charles Wyatt was surveyor general, William Jarvis provincial secretary, Joseph Willcocks sheriff of the Home District. To defeat these reformers and defuse their movement, all Gore had to do was fire them – which he did in the spring of 1807. Gore also suspended Thorpe from the court of King's bench and ultimately secured his recall by the British government.

This initial attempt to organize a reform movement in Upper Canada produced meagre results indeed. It left behind a newspaper founded by Joseph Willcocks, the *Upper Canada Guardian* (1807–10), and a work by John Mills Jackson, *A View of the Political Situation of the Province of Upper*

Canada (1809), whose thrust was to denounce the colonial administration and defend Judge Thorpe. Willcocks, much more radical than Thorpe, continued to defend his ideals in the Assembly until 1812, attracting a few other members into his camp.

Robert Gourlay and the Emergence of a Republican Critique

In Upper Canada, as in the next-door province, the War of 1812 had the immediate effect of quieting dissent. Loyalty, not reform, was the order of the day. Although the war ended with a victory for the status quo, it left a legacy of some distrust of the Americans, both those who lived in the neighbouring republic and those who had moved to the colony before 1812. From 1814 until 1826, the British government continually infringed the rights of its subjects of American origin (apart from the Loyalists). The Upper Canadian identity that developed was increasingly consonant with the concept of loyalty, which the elite considered synonymous with Toryism or conservatism.[95] The importance given to loyalism and its conservative colouration hindered the emergence of a true reform movement in Upper Canada.

Against this backdrop, a single attempt to organize an opposition movement – hardly more successful than the first – took place in the 1810s. It was the work of Robert Gourlay, a Scottish settler whose wife had inherited land in the colony. Upon arrival in 1817, Gourlay sought to become a land agent working to encourage immigration. To this end, he attempted to purchase a large tract of land. He also busied himself with the compilation of statistics concerning the province and its agriculture. His land application denied, in February 1818 Gourlay set about challenging the colonial government and the ban on land sales to Americans. He proposed to set up a commission of inquiry into the state of the province and launched a petition to the Prince Regent that led to a convention held at York (now Toronto) that July.[96] Gourlay's brash style and facility at making enemies drove away his allies, Thomas Clark and William Dickson in particular. In November, Isaac Swayze, the member for Niagara, denounced him as having violated an 1804 statute titled An Act for the Better Securing of this Province against All Seditious Attempts or Designs to Disturb the Tranquillity thereof, for failing to take an oath of allegiance after an absence of several months from the colony. Gourlay was found guilty on 10 November. His refusal to leave Upper Canada (he considered the expulsion illegal) led to his arrest by the authorities on 4 January 1819. He was deported on 21 August.[97]

Back in Britain, Gourlay tried to restore his tarnished reputation and obtain justice. He petitioned the English Parliament. He attempted to obtain the support of Sir James Mackintosh, the MP who had responded to Burke's reflections on the French Revolution with a radical work titled *Vindiciæ Gallicæ*. Gourlay also requested the help of Lord Holland, political heir to the great Whig leader Charles James Fox.[98] Alongside the data in his *Statistical Account of Upper Canada* (1822), he recounted his adventure in the colony in an attempt to mend his reputation.[99]

Gourlay's discourse drew inspiration from republican liberty throughout his early career, including his time in Upper Canada. He was quite comfortable with his reputation as a radical: "I have been called a reformer, a radical, and a radical reformer; and, provided my notions of reform are rightly understood, have no objection to any one of these appellations."[100] Gourlay's ideas were formed during the Napoleonic wars when the Radical movement was dominated by John Cartwright, William Cobbett, Henry Hunt, and Sir Francis Burnett. Like his fellow Radicals, Gourlay adapted his discourse to the necessities of the moment. In Great Britain in the 1810s, he sympathized with the hardship of the poor and the workers. In this he followed the Radicals' drift towards workers' issues, which led them to Chartism in the 1830s.[101] He became versed in the methods used by the Radicals in that era, especially mass meetings and petitions – thus his participation in the famous meeting at Spa Fields on 2 December 1816, which degenerated into a riot. The situation greatly worried the British authorities, and they reacted by suspending habeas corpus and enacting various repressive laws.

Gourlay's discourse in Upper Canada did not step out of this mould. His analysis of the colony's problems and his suggested solutions were consistent with the overarching themes of English Radicalism: political corruption, taxation and inadequate representation, virtue as a prerequisite to liberty, the evils of commerce, the dangers of wealth accumulation, parliamentary reform. In the preindustrial context of Upper Canada, he adopted the traditional radical rhetoric favourable to smallholders and directed his remarks at "the Resident Land-Owners of Upper Canada." His first address in October 1817, however, did not deal with Upper Canadian problems. Not that none were on his horizon; rather, he believed they would soon be rectified. Since his land application was pending a response from the York authorities, he opted for prudence. He began by stating that "my present Address, therefore, waves all regard to political arrangements: it has in view, simply to open a correspondence between you and your fellow-subjects at home."[102] He kept his promise. He explained that his sole objective was to publicize Upper Canada in the mother country with a view to encouraging investment and immigration. It was in no way, he said, a matter questioning colonial ties; on the contrary, he wrote, "a society of a superior kind may be nursed up in Canada by an enlarged and liberal connexion with the mother country ... [Such a] connexion ... appears to me to promise the happiest results to the cause of civilization."[103] Going further, he argued for the superiority of British civilization over American civilization: "Many of you, Gentlemen, have been bred up at home, and well know how superior, in many respects, are the arrangements and habits of society there, to what they are on this side of the Atlantic."[104] He maintained nonetheless that the destiny of Upper Canada would remain out of reach if only the poorest settled there.

Gourlay's early optimism gave way to bitterness at the beginning of 1818 when his land application was rejected. His second address "to the Resident Land-Owners of Upper Canada" in February betrayed this disillusionment. In a more acerbic, indeed radical tone, he attacked the executive branch and its partisans in the colony. He was now drawing directly upon the principles of republican liberty. He called for the "people" to mobilize and put pressure on the authorities to obtain the political reforms he saw as essential to the development of the colony:

This country, I am convinced, cannot be saved from ruin by temporizing measures, nor by the efforts and reasoning of any individual. If it is to be saved, reason and fact must speedily be urged before the throne of our Sovereign, by the united voice of a loyal and determined people: if it is to be saved, your Parliament now assembled must be held up to its duty by the strength and spirit of its constituents: a new leaf must be turned over in public conduct; and the people of Upper Canada must assume a character, without which all Parliaments naturally dwindle into contempt, and become the mere tools, if not the sport, of the executive power.[105]

The people did not, he believed, have a genuine voice in a mixed legislature: it was an entity unto itself, not a composite of the interests represented in the two houses. The reference in the above quote to voter influence over elected officials is a key tenet of republican representation. Fear of the executive branch as the source of parliamentary corruption is a direct legacy of the Commonwealthmen. And extraparliamentary agitation, including petition campaigns, was the main tool of the English radicals in the 1810s.[106]

If Gourlay worried about the Upper Canadian situation, he remained confident in the virtue of the province's inhabitants, which gave him hope that a good government would soon be in place: "It is my opinion, that in all countries the goodness of government keeps pace with the virtuous spirit of the people; and in no country has this spirit less to contend with than here."[107] The will of the virtuous people must be sovereign: "Our constitution, which has been refining for ages, and the spirit of which is purity, has often been lauded, for its effects are irresistibly impressive, but it has been seldom understood. It is that beautiful contrivance *by which the people, when perfectly virtuous, shall become all-powerful;* but which reins back their freedom in proportion to their vice and imbecility."[108]

Gourlay also averred that "the grand purpose of government is the protection of our persons and property."[109] While the word "property" used here might suggest an adherence to modern liberty on Gourlay's part, his writings elsewhere show this was not the case. As early as 1809, Gourlay had denounced wealth accumulation as a threat to civic virtue, a corrupting force.[110] He hoped for a world in which "enlightened men would not only think of themselves as individuals, and play only at the *game of getting.*"[111] His rejection of the ethic of accumulation went hand in hand with a contempt for commercialism:

Trust me, sophistry has stolen from the genius and industry of the people its reward ... It has succeeded to a wish in imposing the false doctrine of commercial strength, because great merchants could purchase boroughs – because great merchants reaped the profit, and had always plenty to spare to maintain this system of delusion. Can commerce add one acre to the island? ... No. But this island is not only the residence of its own merchants; it is the rendezvous of worn-out governors, of petty tyrants, and of gorged wealth from all corners of the earth. Commerce is necessary to supply these with luxuries; conquest and rule are necessary to supply their sons with objects of ambition and opportunities to spoil.[112]

Gourlay hoped that "upon the ruins of the altars of Mammon" the British people could establish "a temple for virtue and a sure hold for freedom."[113] In an 1815 essay titled "To the Labouring Poor of Wily Parish," he made no bones about his fear of wealth: "Riches will always bestow power and foster tyranny."[114] This stance can also be found in his *General Introduction to Statistical Account of Upper Canada*, where he quotes Mackintosh's *Vindiciæ Gallicæ* on the perils of wealth concentration in the hands of the few: "Property alone can stimulate labour ... But though it is necessary, yet, in its excess, it is the great malady of civil society. *The accumulation of that power, which is confirmed by wealth in the hands of the few, is the perpetual source of oppression and neglect to the mass of mankind.*"[115] Gourlay's unceasing contempt for wealth, the clearly republican character of his 1818 addresses, and the audience to whom he directed them indicate that his defence of property concerned the small property holdings on which citizens' independence is predicated, not the unbridled accumulation of wealth.

For Gourlay, it was essential to restore the operation of the fundamental principles of the British constitution in Upper Canada. He thus acknowledged the sacrosanctness of the king; still, he did not concede any autonomy to him. Like all the Radicals, he regarded the king as nothing more than the "grand Executor" of the constitution. Thus, he maintained that "in courtesy and fiction everything belongs to him: in fact, little or nothing."[116]

In April 1818, Gourlay published a third address to the landowners of Upper Canada whose content was just as radical and republican as the previous one. It was clear that he no longer had any confidence in the Upper Canadian institutions. Nothing good was to be expected from an Assembly so servile to the governor. That servility, he believed, was due to the presence of too many corrupt individuals in the Assembly, with the result that representation itself had been corrupted.[117] His attack, that is, was not on individuals but on the political system as a whole: "It is not the men, it is the *system* which blasts every hope of good; and, till the system is overturned, it is vain to expect anything of value from *change* of Representatives or Governors."[118] He explained that "the people of every nation may at any time put down, either domestic tyranny or abuse, – they may, at any time, lay a simple foundation for public prosperity."[119] This statement goes beyond the right of resistance to tyranny to adumbrate the basis for popular sovereignty. Gourlay indeed recalled a previous statement of his to the effect that the English constitution was "that beautiful contrivance by which the people, when perfectly virtuous, shall become all-powerful."[120] Like all the Radicals, he insisted that his only goal was to rescue the social contract from abuses of the constitution: "The constitution of this province is in danger, and all the blessings of social compact are running to waste. For three years the laws have been thwarted, and set aside by the executive power; for three sessions have your Legislators sat in Assembly, and given sanction to the monstrous – the hideous, abuse."[121]

In keeping with his commitment to extraparliamentary protest, Gourlay called on the landowners and indeed all the subjects of Upper Canada to rally around a petition campaign. He explained in his third address how people could assemble and organize to petition in each district. The citizens of each district could raise funds and elect representatives who would then gather at a provincial convention where they would adopt a petition to the Prince Regent. The Upper Canadians, he argued, should keep in mind the ultimate goal of the movement, which was governmental reform: "on such an occasion, and under such circumstances as the present, every party, and every personal prejudice, should be put down, every eye should be resolutely bent on the one thing needful – a radical change of system in the Government of Upper Canada."[122] He opined that the colonists "have only to put trust in the success of their own virtuous endeavours" in order for the change to take place. Finally, he asserted that the petition "will shew that, though the rights of Parliament may be trifled with, those of the people of Upper Canada are not so easily to be set at defiance."[123]

Neither the petition nor the convention – held at York in July 1818 – had the desired influence. Gourlay's deportation put an end to this second attempt at organizing an Upper Canadian reform movement after just a few short months. Its importance in historical context, however, outstrips its concrete achievements. While Gourlay never came close to putting the state in jeopardy, he did succeed in introducing English Radical ideas to the Upper Canadian scene. These ideas, when coupled with the extraparliamentary protest he urged, were revolutionary in import. Had they succeeded, they would have entailed a fundamental transformation of the political system created by the Constitutional Act in 1791.

Reformers Divided: Reform in Upper Canada during the 1820s

Reform became a more popular idea among Upper Canadians in the ensuing decade but did not, as in Lower Canada, result in a unified reform bloc.[124] The reformers here were divided intellectually and organizationally into constitutional-leaning individuals such as William Warren Baldwin and his son Robert, and republican-leaning individuals such as William Lyon Mackenzie. As in the neighbouring province, however, the republicans gradually displaced the moderns without conflict – almost as a matter of course.

William Warren Baldwin was the highest profile modern reformer of the 1820s. A high-born Irishman, he had immigrated with his father to Upper Canada in 1799. He settled in York in 1802 and became connected with the councillor Peter Russell and with the Willcocks family. Having earned a medical degree in 1797 from the University of Edinburg, he changed careers in 1803 and became a lawyer. Starting in 1806, he held various positions in the Upper Canadian public service. That year he met Robert Thorpe and other reformers but escaped the purges dealt the reformers by Lieutenant-Governor Gore. Baldwin was elected to the House of Assembly in 1820 and quickly distinguished himself as a defender of the British constitution and the social order. An admirer of Blackstone, said to have been his inspiration for becoming a lawyer, Baldwin drew upon the Irish experience of the late eighteenth century to promote a form of colonial sovereignty.

Baldwin was defeated in the 1824 elections but re-elected in 1828,[125] and it was in the latter year that he first came forward with a demand for responsible government. That summer, a reform committee that he chaired petitioned London for several reforms, including

that a Legislative Act be made in the Provincial Parliament, to facilitate the mode in which the present constitutional responsibility of the advisers of the local Government may be carried practically into effect; not only by the removal of these advisers from office, when they lose the confidence of the people, but also by impeachment for heavier offences chargeable against them.[126]

The petitioners called for the introduction of two mechanisms to give the Assembly some control over the executive power: executive council responsibility for administrative acts, and the power of the Assembly to impeach and remove officers guilty of crimes. This dual demand, albeit inspired by British practice, was inconsistent with the constitution because of the way it was formulated. Executive council responsibility in particular violated two constitutional principles. First, while the responsibility of the British Cabinet was well established in practice, it had never been officially legislated in the home country, so there was no precedent for this type of legislation; moreover, the Upper Canadian constitution, being subordinate to the will of Parliament, could only be amended by that body. Second, the petitioners were demanding two very different reforms but had not grasped or explained the subtle differences between them. Executive council responsibility concerned the workings of the executive branch while impeachment concerned the personal responsibility of officers of the Crown.

In a letter to the British prime minister, the Duke of Wellington, on 3 January 1829, Baldwin clarified his position on ministerial responsibility. He explained what he meant by the idea of making executive councillors responsible:

The principle alluded to is this, the presence of a Provincial Ministry / if I may be allowed to use the term / responsible to the Provincial Parliament, and removable from Office by his Majesty's representative at his pleasure and especially when they lose the confidence of the people as expressed by the voice of their representatives in the Assembly; and that all acts of the King's representative should have the character of local responsibility, by the signature of some member of this Ministry.[127]

The petition was briefly studied in the House of Lords on 14 May and summarily rejected. It was not officially tabled in Parliament because it was deemed to contain a personal attack on the British M P William Huskisson, in violation of parliamentary rules. Furthermore, Lord Goderich and the

Duke of Wellington rejected the idea of granting the Assembly the power of impeachment.[128] Wellington rejected the principle of ministerial responsibility in the colonies on the grounds of their geographical location. He stressed that the colonists could always complain of the lieutenant-governor's decisions to the British government. Thus ended the first attempt to obtain a form of ministerial responsibility in Upper Canada. Baldwin and his son Robert both lost their seats in the electoral debacle of 1830. From that time on, William Lyon Mackenzie, a partisan of republican liberty who survived the debacle, gained in stature until he became the acknowledged leader of the reformers, without ever holding an official position among them. The moderates' hour of glory would not arrive until after the rebellions had passed.

A Scottish immigrant to Upper Canada in 1820, Mackenzie founded a reform newspaper, the *Colonial Advocate and Journal of Agriculture, Manufacture & Commerce*, four years later. The paper began in Queenston (now Niagara-on-the-Lake) but moved to York in November 1824. It was not a financial success. Despite a print run of eight hundred, it could manage only 330 subscribers. Things were so dire that after 18 April 1825 the paper only appeared irregularly, and not at all between 16 June and 8 December 1825. In April 1826, Mackenzie, who strove to become the king's printer, declared he would no longer discuss politics. Yet he continued to reprint reformist essays on various questions and regularly attacked the York political elite. On 8 June 1826, he recounted the sad tale of a duel of 1817 in which John Ridout had lost his life to Samuel Jarvis. In retaliation, a group of young York Tories – Jarvis, Charles and Raymond Baby, John Lyons (the governor's private secretary), and Henry Sherwood – vandalized the paper's offices and destroyed MacKenzie's presses. He sued and won. The attack had boomeranged against the complicit political elite, since the victory in court saved the newspaper from bankruptcy.

Elected for the first time in 1828, Mackenzie was one of the most active reform members in the next two years. He helped form several committees on matters as varied as the Bank of Upper Canada, agriculture, commerce, the post, and patronage.[129] While he never championed a single cause after the fashion of Robert Gourlay, Barnabas and Marshall Spring Bidwell, and Egerton Ryerson, it is false to assert, as Aileen Dunham has, that Mackenzie did not have "a decided policy" between 1824 and 1837.[130] He was in fact the Upper Canadian who best articulated the discourse of republican liberty in the province.

His embrace of these principles had begun as early as 18 May 1824 when he clearly stated them in an essay that occupied most of the first edition of the *Colonial Advocate*. He began by taking distance from the

English Radicals, with whom any perceived association would not be beneficial to him. By the same token he dissociated himself from Robert Gourlay: "We have never been disloyal subjects nor radical reformers: we have neither joined Spa-fields mobs, nor benefitted by the harangues of Hunt, Cobbett and Watson. – We are not disappointed land speculators; and as we were not in Canada when Mr. Gourlay's Convention took place, we are, of course, no Gourlayites."[131]

But Mackenzie never really managed to distance himself from the radicals. Claim as he might that he was not a Gourlayite, he could not resist quoting the man at length in his address and stating, "we consider Mr. Gourlay to be really a very honest man, and a sincere well wisher of the country."[132] References to the Gourlay episode in Upper Canada, to Gourlay's fate in Britain, and to his reform activities were omnipresent in the paper during its first four years.[133] Mackenzie also attempted to take distance from the Americans, but here too he could not refrain from admiring them: "We would never wish to see British America an appendage of the American presidency; yet would we wish to see British America thrive and prosper full as well as does that Presidency."[134] The *Colonial Advocate* never missed an opportunity to highlight the divide between what it regarded as American progress and Canadian stagnation.

On the level of principles, Mackenzie proudly stated, "we have made our election: it is to have only one patron, and that patron is the People; – the people of the British Colonies."[135] Even though he did not define the term in more detail, the context for his address indicates that Mackenzie was alluding to the republican fiction of the people. He believed that the people must keep clear of corruption. He distrusted the accumulation of wealth that went along with commercialism. Like all the republicans, he was an enemy of luxury and conspicuous consumption; he valued the simple, frugal life. What is more, he lamented that money in Upper Canada was concentrated in the hands of a few people. Conversely, he expressed his approval of the United States, where the distribution of wealth was more equal, "where it is, thanks to their free institutions and home manufactures, in every body's hands and in plenty."[136] Mackenzie also advocated for an agriculture-based economy. While he knew full well that agriculture could not prosper without the support of manufacturing and commerce, he complained that, in the colony, these two activities were in the hands of British capitalists, who corrupted the population with their economic power: "luxury is encouraged and the simplicity of our manners lost."[137] He thus became an advocate for local manufacturing and colonial commerce.

According to Mackenzie, not only did the commercial system and the concentration of wealth destroy the colonists' economic independence, it also caused them to be indebted, and hence to lose their moral and political independence. That meant their representatives were exposed to corruption as well. Candidates for the Assembly were too tied, or became too tied after their election, to the executive power of the province. Corruption prevented elected officials from working on their constituents' behalf, from being "the constitutional representatives of the whole body of the people of the Province [and from] speak[ing] the sentiments and act[ing] according to the wishes of that body."[138] Mackenzie enjoined his compatriots to get rid of corrupt representatives: "Stir yourselves, like men, and strike at the roots of corruption, in the persons of our late corrupt representatives."[139] Mackenzie's appeal to the independent farmers of the colony – insofar as they still were independent – was consistent with the spirit of republican liberty: "On you alone, Farmers, does Canada rely. You are the sole depositories of civil and religious liberty."[140]

Mackenzie was not, in that early year of 1824, ready to go on the attack against the British constitution. Like most of the English Radicals, he attempted to situate Upper Canadian radical thought within the constitutional framework. He emphatically denied wishing to bring down the constitution or the government, taking note of "the ever memorable and never to be sufficiently praised blessings of the British constitution and government."[141] And in case his loyalty was in doubt, he was, although "sincerely attached to freedom," of the opinion that it was "not incompatible with a limited monarchy ... We like American liberty well, but greatly prefer British liberty. British subjects, born in Britain, we have sworn allegiance to a constitutional monarchy and we will die before we will violate that oath."[142]

Mackenzie's limited substantive aim was to point out the shortcomings of the colonial constitution, with its selfish executive power, servile legislative council, subordination to the Crown, and established church. Only in 1829, after his visit to the United States, did the constitution itself become the target of his attacks.

MODERN LIBERTY VERSUS
REPUBLICAN LIBERTY IN THE COLONIES

As we have seen, the basis of the colonial state was not seriously called into question until around 1828. In Lower Canada, the reformers were still thinking along the lines of modern liberty, while in Upper Canada, the reformers' influence was still quite limited. The situation changed rapidly after 1828. From then on, all was turmoil in the colonies. In Lower Canada, the clash between the Assembly and the governor took on the appearances of all-out war. The election of 1827 confirmed the reformers' hold on the Assembly, and Louis-Joseph Papineau was re-elected speaker. Dalhousie rejected this choice and prorogued the legislature, using this opportunity to purge the militia as well. The reformers' patience was being sorely tested, and tensions ran high in the colony.[143]

In Upper Canada, the situation was hardly better. By that same year, three issues – clergy reserves, American property rights, and patronage – had become particularly contentious. More circumstantial recriminations added to the tension. The reformers were outraged that the loyalty of a radical assemblyman, John Matthews, had been called into question and his pension temporarily suspended for proposing to sing the American hymns "Yankee Doodle" and "Hail Columbia" at a theatre show. They also rallied around William Forsyth over his run-in with the army concerning his right to own land on the Niagara Peninsula. Finally, the dismissal of reform-minded judge John Walpole Willis, whose story recalled Thorpe's in that he had hoped to become chief justice of the colony, angered the reformers.[144]

On top of all this, a third attempt to organize a broad reform movement in the colony soon materialized.[145] In 1828, Upper Canadian reformers of all stripes, modern and republican, joined forces. Their union enabled them to win control of the Assembly in that year's elections. Unfortunately, the new assembly lacked leadership, and while several committees were struck, very few reforms came to pass. In fairness to the reformers, they had no experience as either a movement or a parliamentary majority. They barely had time to get their bearings when elections were called unexpectedly on the death of King George IV. The reformers, with their meagre track record to that point, were defeated. This event marked the start of the radicals' ascendancy over the moderates.

The British government was more than conscious of the problems afflicting the colonies: it was buried under petitions from the Canadas, the most popular being the one presented by John Neilson, Denis-Benjamin Viger, and Augustin Cuvillier on behalf of eighty-seven thousand Lower Canadians. Casting about for a response, the government struck a select committee of the House of Commons to study the grievances.[146] The committee report, tabled 22 July 1828, was largely favourable to the reformers' demands. The colonial assemblies, it said, should control all provincial revenues. The administration should be reformed. Jesuit property in Lower Canada should be given over to education. The legislative councils should be made more independent. The clergy reserves, which hampered the development of the colony, should be liquidated and the proceeds divided up among all Protestant denominations. And there were numerous other recommendations.[147]

Nevertheless, the committee perceived the problems as solvable within the constitutional framework and did not envisage any major modification of the existing structures.

The report also roundly criticized Governor Dalhousie for his conduct during the ongoing, years-long conflict with the Lower Canadian House of Assembly. The British Cabinet seized the opportunity to replace him and the lieutenant-governor of Upper Canada, Sir Peregrine Maitland, both staunch enemies of the reformers, with James Kempt and John Colborne, respectively. Despite its wish to be done with the colonial problems, the British government had very little time to devote to them. It was caught up with much more pressing problems at home, including the repeal of the Test Act (1828), the emancipation of the Catholics (1829), the demise of the Tory government and the historic Whig victory (1830), the adoption of the Reform Bill (1832), the abolition of slavery (1833), and the reforms of the Poor Laws (1834). The government's resulting inertia was the straw that broke the camel's back. The reformers concluded that minor reforms would no longer do: what had to be changed was the colonial political structure itself.

All the overlapping conflicts in play – between the reformers and the conservatives, between the assemblies and the councils, between the agrarian interest and the commercial interest, and between the colony and the empire – ultimately came down to a clash of principles: republican liberty versus modern liberty. The reformers rejected modern liberty and mixed government as defined by the Constitution of 1791. They adopted republican liberty and began to press for a republican makeover of colonial government. By the end of the 1820s, the political crisis had degenerated into an ideological crisis, and by the middle of the next decade, republicanism was clearly a threat to the British colonial institutions. However, the reformers-turned-republicans did not initially grasp that their demands were now even more unacceptable to the British authorities.

4

"We, the people": Republican Liberty
in the Canadas, 1828–1838

THE YEAR 1828 marked the start of the ten years of greatest turmoil in Canadian history. Never had the colonies witnessed such intense agitation, such a fundamental challenge to the state. At this time, a number of crises – political, colonial, economic, social, ethnic, structural, and conjunctural – all came together. Yet the period had begun under rather favourable auspices, with the British authorities recalling Dalhousie and Maitland, a gesture appreciated by reformers in both provinces. Nevertheless, the opposition between the reformist assemblies and the governors, assisted by their councils, would intensify throughout the 1830s.

In Lower Canada, relations eased between the Assembly and the governor and councils during the administration of the more conciliatory James Kempt (1828–30). But the next year the conflict resumed. The minister responsible for the colonies, Lord Goderich, arranged for Parliament to pass a law transferring control of nearly all colonial revenues to the assemblies, without requiring the prior adoption of a permanent civil list or one that would endure for the life of the king. With this legislation, the minister hoped to satisfy the Patriotes and put an end to the subsidy crisis going on since 1818. He hoped the assemblies would appreciate this openness and would enact a civil list voluntarily, thus rendering the executive and judicial branches independent of the legislature. While the Upper Canadian Assembly quickly obliged, its Lower Canadian counterpart refused. The Patriotes knew that a long-term civil list would minimize their political influence, since the subsidy vote was their only lever over government. The result was that instead of resolving the subsidy problem, the British government's new approach made the situation considerably more complicated. Now, when the Patriotes refused to adopt the budget – which they continued to do – the colonial government no longer had sufficient funds to operate.

The subsidy crisis was soon exacerbated by an institutional crisis. In 1831, the Assembly began to question the value and legitimacy of the Legislative Council. Around 1833, the Patriotes began demanding that it be made elective, and this became a central demand of the Ninety-Two Resolutions adopted in February 1834. These resolutions summarized the complaints and demands of the Patriotes; they were, in effect, the charter of Lower Canadian republicanism. The British government struggled to react, finally opting to send a commission of inquiry to Lower Canada in 1835. It was headed by Lord Gosford, who thereby replaced Matthew Aylmer as governor. The new governor's instructions specified that London was prepared to be conciliatory but did not intend to reform the colonial institutions in accordance with the Patriotes' demands. Gosford, keeping this information to himself, negotiated skillfully and gradually won the French Canadians' trust. But his efforts were demolished when Sir Francis Bond Head, the lieutenant-governor of Upper Canada, published London's instructions to Gosford in January 1836, revealing that they contained no promise of reform. The governor's credibility collapsed and the colony plunged into a crisis from which it would only emerge through rebellion. London's refusal to countenance a republican reform of the colony's institutions was confirmed by Parliament's adoption of ten resolutions, known as the Russell Resolutions, in March 1837. News of the resolutions reached the Lower Canadians several weeks later. Adding insult to injury, Parliament announced that it would allow the governor to appropriate the colony's revenues, without the legislature's approval if necessary. The Patriotes reacted by holding public assemblies between May and October 1837, and the tension mounted rapidly.

In Upper Canada, the reformers won the elections of 1828 and controlled the Assembly for the first time. Their victory, however, was short-lived: their inability to adopt concrete measures precipitated their electoral defeat in 1830. The Tories retook the Assembly, with just a few isolated reformers remaining. One of them, William Lyon Mackenzie, became the preeminent figure of the Upper Canadian radical movement thanks to his efforts on the Assembly committee of inquiry into the matter of representation in 1831 and his repeated expulsion from the House in 1831–32. The next winter, Mackenzie went to London to present his grievances. In the 1834 elections, the radicals regained control of the Assembly. In early 1835, Mackenzie struck a new committee on the colony's grievances in reaction to statements made by Lord Stanley who, as chair of a Commons committee on Canadian affairs in 1834, had claimed that all was well in Upper Canada. The Assembly was quick to reiterate its demands. The committee's *Seventh Report on Grievances*, tabled in April 1835, became the charter of Upper Canadian radicalism. The arrival of Bond Head as the new lieutenant-governor in early 1836 restored a measure of calm and raised hopes for change; indeed, his initial stance was one of openness and conciliation. He even included three reformers, among them Robert Baldwin, on the Executive Council. But, as we have seen, he had no intention of altering the structure of the colonial government. He continued to administer the province without consulting his council. Disillusioned, the executive councillors asked him to commit to regular consultation; he refused, and the councillors resigned in March 1836. Assemblyman Peter Perry formed a committee to study the matter. In its report of 14 April 1836, the committee sided with the resigning councillors. The lieutenant-governor dissolved the legislature and called elections, and the radicals lost control of the Assembly. Robert Baldwin left for the British Isles, and with his departure the reformers who leaned towards modern liberty were definitively marginalized. As in Lower Canada, the radicals now dominated the reform movement.

One important reason for the widening chasm between the Patriotes and the radicals on the one hand and the constitutionalists and the British authorities on the other has to do with the former's conversion to republicanism. This was an understandable result of over twenty years of fruitless struggle. The reformers had always articulated their demands within the framework of constitutionalism and had never (with the exception of Robert Gourlay) challenged the legitimacy of the colonial state, yet they had achieved nothing since 1805. Stronger arguments were needed, and republicanism provided them. By arguing that power was legitimate only if it emanated from the people, the Patriotes and the radicals equipped themselves to challenge the sovereignty of Parliament and the legislative councils.

This ideological shift positioned the Patriotes and the radicals within the republican movement of protest that had shaken the ancien régime in Europe and America to its foundations. The new, increasingly well-articulated rhetoric, particularly resembling that used by the American revolutionaries,[1] pulled the colonies into the axis of the Atlantic revolutions – of which the Canadian rebellions thus, in many respects, constitute the final chapter.

The adoption of republicanism in the colonies was double-edged: it gave the Patriotes and the radicals a solid justification for their demands, but by the same token it posed a threat to colonial power and the sovereignty of Parliament. Republican ideas clashed frontally with the vision of the local constitutionalists and the British authorities. On one side were those who conceived of power relations in republican terms; on the other, those who still interpreted the colonial constitution as an avatar of modern liberty and British constitutionalism.

LOWER CANADIAN PATRIOTES
AND UPPER CANADIAN RADICALS

While the ideologies in play in the two colonies were the same, the republican opposition was not equally strong. In Lower Canada, the Patriotes controlled the Assembly throughout the 1830s. It was the most important and effective tribune they had. In addition, they could count on the support of certain newspapers, particularly *La Minerve* and *The Vindicator.* Yet their unity was never total, but varied according to circumstances, even within the Assembly. They were led by Louis-Joseph Papineau, a lawyer and seigneur who became speaker of the Assembly in 1815. Around him was a hard core of members: Louis Bourdages, Édouard-Étienne Rodier, Louis-Hippolyte La Fontaine, Augustin-Norbert Morin (who also founded *La Minerve* in 1826), Daniel Tracey and Edmund O'Callaghan (successive publishers of *The Vindicator*), and Robert Nelson. Joining them were Patriotes from other walks of life, such as the businessman Édouard-Raymond Fabre, who owned a bookstore where the Montreal Patriotes met and also owned *The Vindicator* starting in 1832; Ludger Duvernay, owner and publisher of *La Minerve* as of 1827; Dr Wolfred Nelson, and the Swiss-born Amury Girod. In 1828, the movement was largely centred around Montreal.

In Upper Canada, the radical movement was much less influential and organized. Mackenzie, its leader, though he never officially led the reformers in the Assembly, was the most important radical politician and polemicist. As an assemblyman (1828–32, 1834–36), he published the province's principal radical newspaper, the *Colonial Advocate* (1824–34), and its successor *The Constitution* (1834–37). Among his allies were Marshall Spring Bidwell (speaker of the Assembly, 1828–30 and 1834–36), John Rolph, and Charles Duncombe.

The colonial advocates of republican liberty most certainly did not share a single discourse, nor a single vision of an ideal republic; on the contrary, there were always significant differences of opinion between them. In ideological terms, it was possible to share the same principles and values yet still conceptualize republican institutions in different ways. Though it later became standard, for instance, to describe monarchy and republic as polar opposites, there was no necessary opposition between them. Executive power could rest with a monarch, elected or hereditary, who had no power over the legislative branch; he would be nothing more than the highest-ranking public official in government. In rhetorical terms, the colonial republicans differed in the vehemence of their discourse. In general, until 1836, they made every effort to stay within the law; far from crying revolution, they professed their loyalty to

anyone who would listen. Yet their underlying message was unequivo-
cally revolutionary; expressions of loyalty could not completely obscure
this fact. And even though the colonial republican leaders articulated a
rather coherent discourse, local allies of the movement, such as those
taking the floor at the Lower Canadian public assemblies of 1837, frequently departed from it. There were two possible reasons for this diver-
gence. First, the language of republicanism lent itself to misuse and
misinterpretation; while its approach to corruption, virtue, and faction
were quite specific, its call to liberty was not. Second, while the provin-
cial-level elites developed their discourse within the framework of the
British constitution,[2] as had Price, Mackintosh, and the English Radicals
before them,[3] the local elites were less skillful at inserting republican
discourse into the British framework. They often borrowed language
from the rhetoric of modern liberty even as they sought to express un-
abashedly republican concepts.

In Lower Canada a significant source of contention among republicans concerned the proposed abolition of the seigneurial system. This
issue surfaced around 1837 when the rural population and the local
elites sought to use the crisis as an opportunity to demand social and
economic reforms. They did not want the revolution to be limited to the
political sphere: they wanted it to transform social and economic institutions as well. They would not be satisfied with a mere transfer of sovereignty from Parliament to Lower Canada, as had happened in France in
June 1789 when sovereignty passed from the king to the nation. Rather,
they demanded an end to privilege, as the French National Assembly
had proclaimed on 4 August 1789.[4] Their demand was perfectly consonant with the ideal of equality found in republican liberty, but it did not
garner the support of all the Patriotes; Papineau, for one, opposed it.
The whole question turned on the definition of equality. Like all republicans, Papineau believed in equality. However, republican equality primarily concerns itself with the economic and political independence
of citizens; it has little to say about the despoilment of private property.
For Papineau, the seigneurial system was not an obstacle to the economic independence of Lower Canadians, since the colony's farmers were in
some sense owners of their own land, and ownership implied independence. He stated in 1836 that "the ministers sought to put the aristocratic principle into full effect in the Canadas, whose social constitution
is essentially democratic, where everyone comes into the world, lives and
dies a democrat; because everyone is a land-owner; since no one owns
but a small parcel of land."[5] The fact that censitaires had to pay seigneurial rights did not ipso facto deprive them of their economic independence; ergo, their political independence was intact. The seigneurs could

not corrupt them or buy their votes. Papineau therefore maintained that the seigneurial regime did not violate citizens' equality, so there was no reason to abolish it.

There was also an important ethnic difference between the republicans of the two provinces. The Lower Canadian Patriotes were more numerous, more influential, and better organized than the Upper Canadian radicals, and their electoral base was solider, but in addition it was composed of a large majority of French Canadians. The ethnic divide between French and British became gradually more marked and was highly visible by the eve of the rebellions. But the ethnic question was not, it must be emphasized, fundamental to the Patriotes' discourse, which strove to be as inclusive and welcoming as possible. Anglophones, including Daniel Tracey, Edmund O'Callaghan, and the Nelson brothers figured among the most prominent of the Patriotes, who also published a Montreal English-language newspaper called *The Vindicator*. Even the Lower Canadian declaration of independence of February 1838 was the work of an anglophone, Robert Nelson. There is a further fact casting doubt on the idea that the battle lines in Lower Canada formed between ethnic groups. Allan Greer has remarked that older-stock inhabitants of both provinces – who were French-speaking in Lower Canada and either of British or American origin in Upper Canada – tended to rally around the reform movement while new British arrivals preferentially sided with the government. Seen from this angle, the ethnic divide in Lower Canada appears more as a quirk of history than as a fundamental, irremediable difference between the two colonial experiences.[6]

Another distinction to be made between the two colonies concerns the question of loyalty. Of course, accusations of disloyalty were made against both the Patriotes and the radicals throughout the 1830s – and were vehemently denied until the eve of the rebellions. However, the charge had much more impact in Upper Canada, where the colonists' identity had been built on the idea of loyalty to the empire since 1812. While charges of disloyalty merely glanced off the Patriote party, which dominated the Assembly throughout the decade, they considerably eroded electoral support for the Upper Canadian radical movement whenever the issue was debated. In particular, the calls for loyalty issued by Lieutenant-Governor Bond Head during the 1836 election, as well as by Governor Charles Metcalfe in 1843, facilitated the Tory victories.

The republican colonial elites did, however, all share some common ideals and values, a single way of understanding society and its fundamental rules. The Patriotes and radicals all strove to establish a republic. They always acted in the name of the people and fought for republican liberty. In a word, the republican movements in both provinces were drinking from the same intellectual spring.

PATRIOTES, RADICALS, AND THE ATLANTIC WORLD

The Patriotes and radicals of the 1830s linked their political agenda to that of the Atlantic republican movements. They drew inspiration from, or invoked the authority of, other theorists of republican liberty. These references elucidate both the intellectual genealogy of their demands and the outcome they desired. More fundamentally, they gave respectability, credibility, authority, and in fact legitimacy to those demands. And this was precisely the point of the references: to declare a kinship with the broader Atlantic revolutionary movement.

There were references, among others, to Thomas Paine, Richard Price, and Thomas Jefferson.[7] Charles James Fox, too, was often invoked by republicans on both sides of the Atlantic. Even though he was never a republican, the great Whig politician (who spent most of his career in the opposition) sometimes used the rhetoric of republican liberty to score points against the governments of William Pitt and Henry Addington. For example, he defended the French Revolution and the "rights of man" by likening them to the Glorious Revolution. He also defended popular sovereignty and even drank a toast to it in 1798. While his definition of the people corresponded to the modern conception and not the republican fiction, colonial adherents of both ideologies could claim him as their own because of the absence of published writings clarifying his thoughts on the matter.[8] Fox's co-optation by the republican colonists gave them a degree of respectability and shielded them from charges of sedition. Robert Gourlay referred to Fox in his *Statistical Account of Upper Canada* (1822); likewise, Papineau described Fox as "the man most dedicated to the advancement of human happiness." The text of the Ninety-Two Resolutions deplored that this visionary's advice had been disregarded when the Canadas were created.[9]

The more the tension mounted, the more the colonial republicans stepped up their references to republican intellectuals who had never collaborated with the British government. In the summer of 1837, Mackenzie even reprinted *Common Sense*, Thomas Paine's 1776 pamphlet advocating for the independence of the Thirteen Colonies.[10] As well, appeals to American republicans became louder: Benjamin Franklin, George Washington, and Thomas Jefferson were invoked to highlight the revolutionary potential of the colonial crisis. Mackenzie's *Sketches of Canada and the United States* (1833) used a quote from Jefferson as an epigraph and quoted Franklin in the body of the text.[11] The Patriotes too appealed to the fathers of the American republic. In 1835, in Assembly debate over the appointment of an agent in Great Britain to replace Denis-Benjamin Viger (1831–34), Papineau warned the mother country that if Canada were subjected to Parliament as the American colonies had been before the war of independence, Britain would find itself facing Jeffersons and Washingtons in Canada.[12]

When the proponents of republican liberty became exasperated, they drew upon outright revolutionary sources. Papineau, during a debate in 1833 on electivity and the colonial institutions, hailed the seventeenth-century reign of Cromwell, founder of the Commonwealth: "It will be recalled how Jamaica was torn away from Spain under the administration of Cromwell, who brought the glory of England to its highest point, and who made sure it was respected by all Europe; to a point which has never been surpassed and rarely equaled since."[13] The allusion was not at all innocent. The proud Mackenzie, in an 1836 article, invoked the heroes of Scottish independence as well as such enemies of the English monarchy as William Wallace, the Earl of Argyll, and William Russell.[14]

Not only did the republicans appeal to the example of the British radicals and American revolutionaries of yore but they also sought the support of Radicals in Parliament. The Upper Canadians developed a special relationship with Joseph Hume, who had fought for Catholic emancipation, repeal of the Test Act, and parliamentary reform.[15] In a letter to Mackenzie of 29 March 1834, Hume supported the colonists' demands, drawing parallels with the United States and France and, in general, saying what Mackenzie could not: that the colonies should be independent.[16] He took the opportunity to support the Patriotes as well. Mackenzie used this letter to justify his political struggle:

As to Mr. Hume's reference to the example of America in 1776, it does indeed furnish an excellent and salutary lesson to the statesman – and with regard to his prediction that freedom from life legislators, military domination, land-jobbing, established priesthoods and irresponsible government must be the result of the continued misconduct of the authorities here and their abettors in the Colonial Office, I do sincerely believe it is the truth.[17]

Meanwhile, the Patriotes were building ties with John Arthur Roebuck, the member for Bath, who became the Assembly's agent in the House of Commons in 1835.[18] Roebuck conveyed their demands without altering the language thereof. He predicted that if the desired reforms were not granted, "our dominion will cease within a very few months after the people shall have become convinced that the government of this country has definitively determined not to grant them."[19]

All these references and examples tended to track the political evolution of the colonies. At first they were situated within the British framework, and later within the Atlantic framework. While they did not initially constitute an explicit threat to the established order, their continual repetition carried a potentially revolutionary message. The tenser the situation became, the more the references took on the character of direct and explicit threats, albeit always couched in language that allowed their authors to elude charges of sedition.

The radicalization of the republicans was also evident in their references to the American example. They exalted American republicanism and its institutions, depicting the United States as a quasi-mythic republic, an ideal model to be followed. Papineau, during a debate on electivity, forthrightly stated, "of all these forms of government, the one whose system has, without parallel, produced the most happy results, has been the pure or very slightly modified republicanism of the confederated states of New England."[20] The Ninety-Two Resolutions (particularly resolutions 41 to 45 and 50) also invoked the American example. On the eve of the rebellions, Papineau described the US Constitution as "the most perfect governmental structure which genius and virtue have yet raised up for the happiness of men in society."[21] The situation was essentially the same in Upper Canada, especially given that many of its subjects had come from the neighbouring republic. Mackenzie told his readers that *Sketches of Canada and the United States* would discuss "the success of the experiment of self-government, attempted for the last half-century by a majority of its inhabitants."[22] He made good on this promise, lavishing praise on the institutions of Illinois, Vermont, and New York.[23] And he proved the superiority of the US Constitution over the Upper Canadian one by stating, "I have never yet met an American who would prefer another system of government to his own."[24] The invocation of the American Revolution was, from the first, intended as a veiled threat against the colonial institutions. Indirect and tacit it may have been, but it was no less subversive for that. The republicans were well aware of the implications and the inevitable outcome of their political struggle – a republic in British North America: "It is certain that before much time has passed, all America must be republican."[25] On the eve of the rebellions, the threat was even more direct.

Thus, colonial republicans drew inspiration from the Atlantic world, first from Great Britain and later from the United States to a preponderant degree. But the fact that they finally appealed to the American example more often than to British writings does not necessarily lead to the conclusion of their "Americanness." Their choice of references was a rhetorical strategy more than an instance of geographical determinism. They could go further, they felt, by identifying with a victorious example rather than with a tradition of opposition. In doing so, they naturally migrated towards the republican model of the United States and away from the modern framework of Great Britain. This shift had a clear practical advantage as well: as professed republicans, the Patriotes believed they could rely on American support in the event of conflict with Britain. Nevertheless, republican liberty was not the exclusive property of the United States or the Americas – Europe of course had its republicans as well. Finally, the American model was a useful one because it encapsulated the rejection of imperialism. The brute fact that ultimately became clear to the colonists was that republican liberty would not be possible within the empire. They could continue to plead their loyalty, but their choice of references made increasingly clear that they had lost all hope of reform. And if this realization pointed to revolution, the American example showed that it could succeed in North America.

LIBERTY AND EQUALITY: PATRIOTES, RADICALS, AND REPUBLICAN RHETORIC

If the colonial republicans could readily invoke the names, speeches, institutions, and lives of the proponents of republican liberty to justify their political quest, it was because they shared the same vision of society. Their discourse indicated that for them, a free man was a politically involved one.[26] They did not reject civil liberties as such (though they spoke little about them), but considered the most essential of these to be the right to collective self-government. The point here is that the Patriotes and radicals cannot be mistaken for liberals. Political freedom, defined in republican terms as political participation and popular sovereignty, was their primary interest. Civil liberties, the chief concern of liberals, were of secondary importance. The Canadians' goal was not to protect themselves from tyranny but to control the state. In this sense they were ideologically closer to nationalism than to liberalism.

The discourse of 1830s republicans in the two Canadas was characterized by a quintessential feature of republican argumentation: that liberty and equality go hand in hand. Liberty, they believed, could only exist within an egalitarian society. Equality – not just equality before the law but genuine socioeconomic equality – was the pivotal principle around which society should be structured. Not that the republicans advocated the leveling of all fortunes; they did, however, believe that excessive disparities between the richest and the poorest would preclude the possibility of a republic. It was only natural that Papineau and Mackenzie should be disturbed by the inequalities they observed when visiting the United Kingdom (in 1823 and in 1832–33, respectively),[27] and would formulate a discourse pitting the two continents against each other, a discourse that regarded the American experience as having done more for the cause of equality than the British one. In general, this opposition was paired with invidious comparisons between monarchy / aristocracy and democracy, but always with a clear focus on the importance of equality.[28]

The best way, the republicans believed, to ensure that equality would exist in a preindustrial republic was to base it on independent smallholders, who were seen as the foundation of the perfect society. According to Amury Girod, a Swiss immigrant to Lower Canada who rallied to the Patriotes' cause early on and was a "general" at the Battle of Saint-Eustache (1837), "property is one of the primary causes of all good and evil in society. If it is equally distributed, knowledge and power will be also ... Liberty will, sooner or later, be the certain result."[29] Similarly, Marshall Spring Bidwell held that "an equal division of property in a country was most favorable to its morality and happiness." Bidwell was "sure the country would be more free, more moral, more happy, if there was a pretty equal diffusion of property, than if it were principally accumulated in the hands of a few," and he "wished there might be none very wealthy, and none very poor."[30] Mackenzie, for his part, quoted Raynal: "People of America! ... Be afraid of too unequal a distribution of riches, which shows a small number of citizens in wealth, and a great number in misery, – whence arises the insolence of the one and the disgrace of the other."[31] For the majority of republicans, equality was already a social fact in the Canadas. It was a matter of changing the political institutions to make them conform to the social reality and ensuring that laws were designed to safeguard equality.

In Upper Canada, for example, the reformers worked throughout the 1820s and 1830s to abolish the principle of primogeniture for people who died intestate.[32] In each year from 1824 to 1834, they attempted to have this law repealed, but the Legislative Council always opposed the attempt. The abolition of primogeniture was a typically republican struggle aimed at preventing people from building their fortunes through inheritance (de facto inequality). According to Bidwell, the implications of primogeniture for Upper Canadian society were grave: "The effect of the law of primogeniture is to create a landed aristocracy, or in other words, to throw the land of the Province into the hands of a few persons, and to leave the great body of the people, without any permanent interest in the country."[33] The republicans' struggle had political resonance as well, since political participation was based on property rights. Hume, Roebuck, and Papineau supported the Upper Canadian radicals on this issue.[34] Mackenzie advocated for repeal by referring to the US example: "the British Colonists (now the United States), in all cases where the law of primogeniture, half-blood, and entail prevailed, hastened to abolish these unnatural laws the moment they were freed from the restraints which the machinery of colonial government had imposed upon their wishes and judgement."[35]

In Lower Canada, primogeniture was not discussed in the same terms. In his testimony before a committee of the House of Commons on 10 June 1828, Viger explained that primogeniture did not apply because the Quebec Act had recognized French civil law, in which this principle did not exist: each heir was entitled to an equal share, regardless of the testator's intent. Confusion arose only in townships where the application of French civil law was contested. For Judge Samuel Gale, who testified before the same committee on 8 and 13 May 1828, English law should apply in these townships, and with it the right of primogeniture. Neilson (24 May) and Viger (10 June) contended that Canadians had always understood that French civil law extended to these regions, despite the allodial title under which they were held.[36] In practice, the Patriotes implicitly opposed primogeniture when they called for the repeal of the Canada Tenures Act of 1826 and the Canada Trade Act of 1833, whereby English law was introduced into allodial lands.[37]

Just as central to this egalitarian current was the fight against the banks. Banking concentration in the colonies made a nonsense of the principle of equality and allowed corruption to spread. Just as Thomas Jefferson had opposed Alexander Hamilton on this question in the 1790s, the colonial republicans fought against the banks, which they saw as undermining equality and attacking the foundations of society. Papineau stated,

Of all the engines now in operation to injure the interests of the Country, the most powerful is the bad direction which has been given to the operations of the Bank. The most efficacious and the most immediate means which the Canadians have to protect themselves against the fury of their enemies, is to attack them in their dearest parts – their pockets – in their strongest entrenchments, the Banks ...

The unequal distribution of wealth that results when banks favor the monopolies of one political coterie, is another social evil which they inflict.[38]

This opposition led to the founding of the Banque du Peuple in 1835.[39] On this question, Mackenzie was in step with the others: "I have not room to enumerate the several monopolies under which Lower Canada suffers, but they are many and grievous, and have, doubtless, tried the temper of the Legislative Assemblies. One of them, the Bank of Montreal, operates very unfavourably to public liberty; its managers are chiefly merchants, connected with houses here and in the United States."[40] Mackenzie's position resulted from the fact that the Upper Canadians were themselves fighting their banks, and he delivered a disquisition against them.[41] All the colonial republicans, in fact, believed that "labour is the true source of wealth,"[42] and in the preindustrial era, working generally meant working the land. Generalized ownership of small plots of land would provide a solid social basis for the republic.

The principles of equality before the law and social equality were coupled with another principle, that of "moral" equality. It was incumbent upon citizens, small landowners, to be virtuous, which meant essentially three things to the republicans. First, a virtuous citizen was economically and socially independent, hence immunized against corruption. Second, this independence implied a commitment to simplicity and frugality. Charles Duncombe stated in his report on education in Upper Canada "that frugality and economy in a money-making country like ours, are virtues that ought to be taught the youth of the land, by the examples of their preceptors as well as their precepts."[43] Even more so, the republicans sang the praises of daily life and poverty. Mackenzie gave this advice to his fellow citizens:

Be diligent – persevere – neither eat, drink, nor wear anything that is not of the produce of your own farm – if you can avoid doing so – until your lands are paid for, and a freehold title recorded and in your pocket. Rather miss a good bargain than grasp at too much with the risk of getting in debt. If your clothes be plain and clean, never care although they be coarse. You will be valued by your conduct, and not by your clothes. As to food, your own mutton and beef, and pork and veal, and butter and cheese, and potatoes and corn, and poultry, &c. raised at home, will render you as independent as King William IV.[44]

Living the simple life, then, was what guaranteed citizens their equality, their independence, and their incorruptibility. The frugality of daily life would necessarily have implications for politics, for the republicans wished to live in a simple state that did not cost too much to administer.[45]

Finally, republican virtue implied that citizens must put the general interest before their own private interest – in a word, they must be patriotic. Colonial discourse was imbued with this republican virtue. In 1836, Papineau wrote that he could not but "applaud virtue in all its guises."[46] In the assembly of Saint-Constant in 1837, he approved "the virtuous majority of our house of assembly."[47] He reminded his children as well that patriotism was the highest-minded sentiment one could possess: "there is no sentiment more honest, no duty more pressing, than love of country."[48] In Upper Canada, Duncombe complained, in his report on education of 1836, that "the lessons of the nursery, the general course of domestic training, the policy of common schools, and the rewards and honors of the colleges, all tender to beget and foster a criminal selfishness."[49] In order to curtail this selfishness threatening the general interest, he proposed to reform the educational system so as "to provide for the education of youth in direct reference to the wants of the world." This approach was essential since an individual "cannot be educated wrong for *any* of the purposes of life, who is judiciously educated in reference to the public good."[50] The republicans believed that thus educated in patriotism, citizens would have the capacity to fight tyranny. As Mackenzie summed it up, "However perfect the constitution of any government may be, it will speedily resolve itself into an engine of tyranny and oppression unless there is intelligence, patriotism and manly virtue enough in the great body of the people to check the corruption engendered in man by the possession of power." Unfortunately, in Upper Canada, "the prevalence of individual interests, over the general welfare [was] the fatal defect of th[e] government."[51] It was the absence of patriotism that had perverted the constitution.

In the colonies, as elsewhere in the Atlantic world, the republicans held that virtue is threatened by corruption, which can take various forms. One of these forms was dependence on government. The republicans believed that their adversaries opposed the republican agenda because they were not independent. This was a recurring accusation against the legislative councillors: "It was acknowledged by all that there was no independence in the Legislative Council, where independence should be, if it is to be found anywhere."[52] This being the case, the councillors did not deserve the title of citizen. Another form of political corruption manifested itself in the form of an Assembly of members who also worked for the government. Since they received a salary from the executive branch, they could not be trusted to vote independently.[53]

Thirdly, corruption could mean a preference for money and enrichment over simplicity and frugality. In this sense, the call for a boycott of English products in 1837 was not only practical but symbolic: "Gold is the god they worship, let us kill their god," wrote Papineau.[54] Mackenzie went as far as to paint money as the great threat to liberty: "Had it not been for the paper money lords the people of the Canadas would at this day have been free and independent."[55] Thus, corruption in this sense meant putting one's personal interest before the public interest – the antithesis of patriotism.

More specifically, corruption could be synonymous with the electoral irregularities that Mackenzie continually denounced throughout the period.[56] It could at times be associated with deception (*duperie*), the term used by the assembly of Saint-Marc (May 1837) in its first resolution. The participants accused the Gosford Commission of having been sent to "deceive and corrupt the nation's representatives and betray the people's good faith."[57] It could also manifest itself in the form of government mismanagement. Finally, it could signify institutional parasitism and sinecures.[58] All these forms of corruption were denounced by the republicans during the 1830s.

THE REPUBLICAN FICTION OF THE PEOPLE

In the Canadian colonies, the republicans made direct appeals to popular sovereignty. According to Mackenzie, "an enlightened people are the only safe depository of the ultimate powers of society."[59] His colleague Papineau also discussed this form of sovereignty,[60] as did the local elites. In a letter to his wife, Papineau mentioned that Dr René-Joseph Kimber of Trois-Rivières had held a housewarming party decorated, among other things, with a banner bearing the inscription, "Long live the sovereign people, freedom, and equality."[61] At the banquet for St John the Baptist's Day in 1835, assemblyman Édouard-Étienne Rodier celebrated "The People, the legitimate source of all political power."[62] As the tension mounted, popular sovereignty was loudly proclaimed: "The people is made to dominate and not to be dominated; its voice must be listened to; its will consulted, its laws observed and its orders obeyed."[63]

Popular Sovereignty and Legislative Power

The will of the sovereign people could be expressed in two ways: either in a written constitution, as in the United States, or through the legitimate voice of legislative power. This power, which Jean-Jacques Rousseau called the Sovereign, was fundamental to republican discourse. Citizens were considered free to the extent that they participated in it. Since the size of states made it impossible for all citizens to participate directly, republicans invoked the principle of representation.[64] For Thomas Paine, a republic was a state in which the legislative body is elected in accordance with the principle of representation. Liberty, for a citizen of an eighteenth- or nineteenth-century republic, primarily meant participation in the *legislative process* through one's *elected representatives*. A republic thus constituted would be based on the general will or popular sovereignty, as expressed in the laws enacted. Although legislative power rested de facto with the elected representatives, the "people" (in whose name they spoke) was not the sum of the republic's inhabitants, nor was it the sum of the representatives themselves. It was the legal fiction that legitimized power relations.

Political struggles in the colonies revolved around the legitimacy and importance of the legislature throughout the 1830s. For the Patriotes and radicals, the colonial government ought to be structured around elected assemblies, which expressed the people's will. This conception of republican liberty served the interests of those putting it forward, of course, since they could and often did control the assemblies but could not hope to control the other parts of the legislature. It was an argument that, if accepted, would entitle the republican colonists to have their demands granted by London.[65]

With the Patriotes holding a majority of seats in the Assembly of Lower Canada, the equation of the Assembly with the people was easy to make. They could plausibly claim to speak for the people they represented. Papineau stated in the Assembly that he alone was "competent to represent the [people's] sentiments" and that the members "represent the people."[66] The Assembly itself claimed to speak "in the name of the people we represent ... as the representative of the people."[67] Similarly, the first resolution of the assembly of Malbaie, held 25 June 1837, stated that the House of Assembly constituted "the sole constitutional conduit for the wishes and desires of the Canadian people."[68]

The Upper Canadian radicals did not control the Assembly; they had to be more cautious. To put too much emphasis on this body as the interpreter of the people's will would confer legitimacy on the constitutionalists, who controlled the Assembly from 1830 to 1834 and again from 1836 until the end of the colony in 1841. Even so, Mackenzie did occasionally refer to the Assembly as being the people's representative.[69]

The political weakness of the Upper Canadian radicals helps to clarify our understanding of how, for the republicans, the fiction of the people was thought to be embodied in the legislative branch. In this case, it was paradoxical for the radicals to claim to speak for the people and liken their adversaries to a faction when they themselves were a minority in the Assembly. To justify this stance, they claimed that the imbalance had been caused by faulty electoral mechanisms. In a speech to the Assembly on 22 January 1831, Mackenzie complained of the corruption of certain members who had taken on various executive duties, and also of the unfair allocation of seats.[70] Deploring that the Assembly did not have the power to censure a bad government, he called for an inquiry into the state of representation in the colony, and a committee to study the issue – chaired by Mackenzie – was formed.

The committee's report, tabled on 16 March 1831, reached a conclusion as devastating as it was predictable: "the imperfect state of the representation in the House of Assembly is and has been the cause of much evil to the Community."[71] The report continued, "an imperfect state of the representation places too great power generally in the hands of one class of the Community." Since a minority had managed to dominate the representative body, the people, who should have been able to impose their will, were reduced to petitioning to have their voices heard.[72] The report further concluded that the existing system of representation was inequitable when judged according to either population or property values. Finally, it denounced corruption on the Legislative Council, made up of persons intimately linked to the executive power, and also in the Assembly. If bills to initiate an inquiry into the banking system and to abolish primogeniture had not passed the Assembly, it was because the members did not actually represent the people's will.[73] Given all these problems, the committee opined that "it becomes so much the more essential on the part of the people that the representation in their House should be as perfect as possible."[74]

For the republicans, then good representation was essential for the proper expression of the people's will. Good representation necessitated an assembly elected by independent small landowners and candidates not derived from the colonial elite.[75] As to the members, it was incumbent upon them to represent their electors.[76] According to the Upper Canadian radicals, the Assembly would truly represent the people when virtuous electors made their wishes known through a fair and legitimate electoral system – and this entailed control by the republicans. It was they and only they, so it was claimed, who could defend the public interest against private interests.

Popular Sovereignty and the Legislative Council

While all republicans agreed that sovereignty rested with the people, they were not of one mind on the specific institutions that would allow for the public interest to prevail. For many years they agreed that popular sovereignty should be framed within a system of mixed government in which monarchic and aristocratic elements would be allowed to guide the decisions of the sovereign democratic power. In Lower Canada, the rhetoric of mixed government allowed for a seamless passage between the constitutionalism of the 1820s' reformers and the republicanism of the 1830s' Patriotes. Once the conversion to republicanism had taken place, the Patriotes abandoned the rhetoric of mixed government, leaving it entirely to the constitutionalists. From then on, the Patriotes and the radicals rejected any aristocratic presence – and, *a fortiori*, any collaboration between aristocracy and democracy in the colonies – as illegitimate. They demanded that the aristocratic role be wiped from the constitution. In this contention, the Canadians hewed closer to the French republicans than to the American rebels, who never abandoned the rhetoric of mixed government.[77]

This rhetorical shift was laden with consequences in the colonies, where legislative power was vested jointly in the governor (the monarchic principle), the legislative councils (the aristocratic principle), and the assemblies (the democratic principle). Throughout the 1830s, the republicans contested the legitimacy of the legislative councils. Republican liberty resided wholly in a sovereign assembly representing all citizens; ergo, to entrust an appointed council with veto power was nonsensical – indeed offensive.

To protect the people's will from that veto, the republicans proposed that the legislative council be either abolished or made elective. Initially, Papineau reasoned that it was redundant and called for its abolition: "Two legislative bodies in a colony are a [needless] complication of the workings of government, if they represent the same interests."[78] Not to mention that an elective council might compete with the Assembly. Here again, Papineau's thinking approached that of the French republicans, who had opted in 1789 for unicameralism over American bicameralism. In 1832, however, he and the other republicans rallied to the idea of an elected council, seeing this measure as a way to wrest control of it away from the "enemies of the people." The application of the elective principle would, Papineau maintained, transform these factious and corrupt individuals into "apostles of the rights of man."[79] This demand became the chief rallying cry of the Patriotes. Thirty-four of the Ninety-Two Resolutions (numbers 9 to 40, 51, and 54) dealt with the Legislative Council, its utility, and its composition. The members of the Council were accused of forming a faction and promoting their private interests (19, 39), being enemies of the people (18), acting as an aristocracy (21), and failing (along with those who appointed them) to keep the broader interests of the province at heart (10, 23, 32). Under such circumstances, only the application of the elective principle to the Council could resolve the colony's problems (11 to 14, 17, 27, 28, 36, 40).

For the republicans of Upper Canada as well, the election of the Council appeared essential; unlike the Patriotes, however, they did not dedicate all their efforts to this demand. In the "Seventh Report on Grievances," the committee chaired by Mackenzie wrote, "the legislative council neglect and despise the wishes of the country on many important matters which a council elected by the freeholders would not."[80] The committee concluded that "elective institutions are the only safeguards to prevent the Canadas from forming disadvantageous comparisons between the condition of the colonists and the adjoining country."[81] To bolster its arguments for electivity, the committee appealed to the authority of sympathetic British politicians:

The opinions of Mr. Fox, Mr. Stanley, Earl Grey, Lord Erskine, Mr. Ellice, Mr. Hume, Sir James Mackintosh, Mr. O'Connell, Mr. Washburton, and many other eminent British Statesmen, have been expressed in favor of elective institutions as the most suitable for the Canadas; and it appears to Your Committee that Mr. Stanley correctly describes the Legislative Council as being "at the root of all the evils complained of in both Provinces."[82]

In 1837, Mackenzie accused the British government and the Legislative Council of having detracted from the public good, adducing several examples of essential bills that were never passed by the Council.[83] On this basis, he argued that reform was urgent.

Legislative Supremacy

The legislative branch being central to the republican political system, the Patriotes and radicals took little interest in the executive branch. Generally speaking, they believed that, once deprived of its revenues and isolated through reform of the Legislative Council, it would have no choice but to submit to the will of the people and enforce the laws enacted by the Assembly.

But the Patriotes and radicals did at times address the putative relationship between the legislative and executive branches. While they ruled out mixed government at an early stage of their campaign, they continued for the most part to believe in the separation of powers, a constitutional standard across many societies.[84] In capsule, the legislative branch would set rules for life in society; the executive branch would enforce them, and the judiciary would judge those who disobeyed the rules. The executive and judicial branches would not be independent, but rather subordinate to the legislative branch.

This idea of the legislature as the seat of power and freedom explains why neither the Patriotes nor the radicals advocated a constitutional mechanism to harmonize the relationship between the legislative and executive powers. In Lower Canada, the Patriotes' demands always targeted the Legislative Council. They never, for instance, called for "responsible government," in which the governor would choose executive councillors from among assemblymen who had the people's confidence.[85] The executive, they reasoned, had no role to play in representing the people's will; its only job was to put that will into effect. Following this logic, the Assembly censured Patriote-aligned member Dominique Mondelet and his brother Charles-Elzéar in November 1832 when Dominique accepted an appointment to the Executive Council. With a different conception of the role of the executive, this appointment might have been perceived as something positive, a voice for the Patriotes on the Council. Instead, it was perceived as a betrayal.[86]

Moreover, the demand for responsible government is nowhere among the Ninety-Two Resolutions. Consequently, the issue was barely touched upon by the Commons committee that studied the colonial situation in 1834 based on the recommendations of the committee of 1828 and the resolutions brought to London by the Lower Canadian assemblyman Augustin-Norbert Morin. During his testimony before the committee, the matter of the executive branch was only superficially addressed. To the question, "Would not having two chambers springing directly from the people make the Executive in fact dependent upon the people?" he replied, "it would make the Executive responsible to the country, and we consider most distinctly that this must be the case."[87] Thus, what the Patriotes wanted was to put the executive power under guardianship. They did not call for a strong executive power that would enjoy some independence, even if subjected to legislative oversight, as the reformers in the camp of modern liberty preferred. No resolution to this effect was adopted by the public assemblies held in the province during the spring and summer of 1837.[88]

While the situation in Lower Canada was straightforward, with the Patriotes' discourse eclipsing all non-republican reform proposals, the situation in Upper Canada was more complex because reformers who formulated demands consistent with the constitution were not totally marginalized until the spring of 1836. The Upper Canadian reform movement did not speak with a single voice. Mackenzie-styled republicans coexisted with Baldwinist reformers, although the latter became more discreet and lost influence after 1830. It was clear nonetheless that the Upper Canadian radicals were not calling for executive responsibility in the form of trusted executive councillors; indeed, this option was barely discussed before 1836. Their appeals for a responsible executive were characteristic of the discourse of republican liberty, for this demand never appeared alone; it was always complementary to others, and secondary to legislative reform. In 1830, Mackenzie summarized his demands in five points: give the Assembly total control of provincial revenues (with a few exceptions); guarantee judicial independence; reform the Legislative Council; instate responsible government; and protect the equality of all religious denominations.[89] He reiterated this reform agenda in his *Almanack* of 1834.[90]

In its "Seventh Report on Grievances," the equivalent of the Patriotes' Ninety-Two Resolutions, Mackenzie's committee began by making several observations about the Legislative Council, then turned to a consideration of the legislative-executive relationship. The committee noted that the British practice of ministerial responsibility did not exist in the colony. It went on to present the three main positions on the ideal executive-legislative relationship for the province. The first was the status quo, favoured by John Strachan and his followers. The second was to create a provincial ministry (cabinet) that would have to earn the confidence of the Assembly – probably a reference to Baldwin's position. According to the report, Mackenzie had allegedly stated in a letter to Lord Goderich that "with some modifications [this position] might be productive of a greater share of good government and public prosperity than is at present enjoyed by the people."[91] The third position was to make the Executive Council elective, since if the British government were to retain control over patronage appointments in Upper Canada, any provincial cabinet would be rendered ineffective. The committee gave this third option the closest scrutiny, in conjunction with its recommendation of an elected legislative council; indeed, the application of the elective principle was central to the report. The idea of responsible government was not advocated.

As the rebellion approached, Mackenzie's position was clear. In August 1837 he declared, "we, therefore, the Reformers of the City of Toronto, sympathizing with our fellow citizens here and throughout the North American Colonies, desire to obtain cheap, honest, and responsible government, the want of which has been the source of all their past grievances, as its continuance would lead them to their utter ruin and desolation."[92] The three characteristics mentioned – cheap, honest, responsible – were typically found conjoined in republican discourse. In November 1837, Mackenzie outlined a constitution in which the chief executive would not be responsible but elected (article 58).[93] In his proclamation as president of the "provisional government" of Upper Canada, he continued to demand that the governor and the principal government officials be elected within the framework of a legislature based on republican principles. He stated that he wanted "a Legislature, composed of a Senate and Assembly chosen by the people, an Executive, to be composed of a governor and other officers elected by the public voice."[94] In short, the Upper Canadian republicans were not partisans of the cabinet system of responsible government.

For the Patriotes and the radicals, the elective principle was not necessarily meant to apply only to the principal executive officers. Since liberty equaled the right to govern oneself, citizens had to be allowed to choose their servants. Certain lower-level officials, then, should also be elected. In Lower Canada, the republicans attempted to apply the elective principle to the fabriques and to railway inspectors. In Upper Canada, the radicals had the judiciary in their sights; judges had once been elected in Great Britain, so there was no reason why they should not be elected in North America.[95] This proposal was heard from Mackenzie as early as January 1828. Subsequently, the radicals tried to revoke from sheriffs the power to compile jury lists; the executive-appointed sheriffs were viewed as servile, corrupt employees.[96] In 1836, the Assembly passed a bill that made local elected officials responsible for drawing up a jury list from among all the men between twenty-one and sixty years of age in their township. In these attempts to implement electivity in a number of different institutions, the republicans were seeking to defend the cause of liberty – the right of citizens to political participation in the broad sense.

THE SOVEREIGN PEOPLE AND COLONIAL INDEPENDENCE

Let there be no doubt: to assert the ideal of popular sovereignty in the British colonial context was an act of subversion. Sovereignty could not belong to the people and to Parliament at the same time, for in the republican conception a sovereign people is necessarily independent from other peoples. It cannot be subordinated to an empire. To accept submission would be to lose its sovereignty – and a people that is not sovereign ceases to exist. For this reason, the republican discourse of popular sovereignty not only threatened the colonial government: it called the entire structure of the British Empire into question. Papineau and Mackenzie were referring to this issue when they stated that "no nation wishes to obey another for the very simple reason that no nation is capable of commanding another."[97] More generally, the republicans extended their concept of equality and liberty to states. As the English Radical Richard Price said at the time of the American Revolution: "This equality or independence of men is one of their essential rights. It is the same with that equality or independence which now actually takes place among the different states or kingdoms of the world with respect to one another."[98]

The republicans argued that the Canadians were the ones best placed to look after their own interests, while the British government had other issues to address in administering its empire: "We of Canada are less anxious to encourage, by specious misrepresentations, a vast influx of settlers from Europe, ignorant of the situation of the country, and therefore too apt to be careless of its true interests, than we are to obtain the blessings of self-government and freedom for those who now constitute the settled population."[99] Furthermore, the British administrators allegedly understood nothing of colonial affairs. Most of the Colonial Office secretaries had never even visited the colonies and were not kept abreast of colonial affairs by their representatives and officials.[100] While Lord Gosford's arrival in 1835 blunted this critique to a degree, the publication of his instructions in January 1836 reinforced the Patriotes' belief that Britain's inadequate understanding of the colonies was permanent. Given this, it was pointless to strive for agreement on the colonists' demands.

Initially too weak to demand independence outright, the colonists limited their demands to reform of the empire.[101] This strategy could only work if Britain did not feel threatened, and so His Majesty's subjects made a point of expressing their loyalty. In public, the colonists did not take issue with the empire itself, only with its political institutions.[102] In private, they were less polite. Papineau wrote to his wife, "I do not think it possible to be happy and well treated under the colonial regime. Even with the greatest desire to be fair, how can a governor be fair at all times when he is surrounded by so many scoundrels?"[103]

Taking as an axiom that two peoples should not be made to belong to the same empire by force, the republicans attempted to reform the British Empire in order to make it compatible with popular sovereignty. They proposed to reverse the roles so that it would no longer be the mother country profiting from the colonies but vice versa: "Our reasons for being attached to the mother country reside first and foremost in the powerful protection it offers us against attacks from without. In the advantageous outlet it offers for our products through reciprocally useful trade. It is to this end that it must multiply its colonial possessions."[104] However, the threat was never far away: "that is what Ireland and British America demand – and this is what they will be strong enough to take within a very few years, if others are unjust enough to withhold it from them."[105]

Despite their expressions of loyalty, the republicans clearly regarded the empire as an aberration. Sovereign peoples could unite in a confederation with others but their submission to an empire was inconceivable. A close analysis of colonial political discourse suggests that the republicans did not believe in the imperial system: it could not and must not survive. With the American and Irish examples in mind and with appeals to the authority of the celebrated historian Catharine Macaulay, Mackenzie noted that it is impossible to place two legislatures under the same executive.[106] Ultimately, the republicans believed that it was up to Canadians to decide on their allegiance to the empire.[107] London, of course, thought differently, and would conclusively enforce that allegiance in 1837–38.

As of 1836, with Lord Gosford's mission going awry, anger was palpable in the colony. By the following year, any lingering doubts that Great Britain had definitively broken the social contract with the colonies were gone. The eighth Russell resolution, allowing the governor to appropriate colonial monies without the Assembly's consent, was a declaration of war against the Lower Canadian people. From here on, the republicans would feel justified in rebelling.[108] Accession to independence was the only avenue left: "We have not evoked the prospect of independence from the British Crown, but we are mindful that the destiny of the continental colonies is to separate from the parent state when the unconstitutional action of a legislative power residing in a faraway country has become unbearable."[109]

On 15 November 1837, Mackenzie published a draft constitution in which he attempted to make the Upper Canadian "people" the source of state legitimacy. It began with this characteristic expression: "We, the people of the State of Upper Canada." The entire document is built on the notion of a sovereign people, whose legitimacy is enshrined in the preamble and reiterated in the final article: "All powers not delegated by this Constitution remain with the people." This draft is true to republican ideals. It is based on legal and social equality (5–7, 16). It makes the elected legislative branch the seat of all power, and gives it control over all revenues (55). The constitution establishes a separation of powers between the legislative and executive branches (43, 47, 48), abolishes sinecures (54), and subordinates military to civilian power (10). It lets the governor pardon convicted criminals but does not allow him to intervene in cases of impeachment by the legislative branch (61). The legislative branch thus dominates the executive and judicial branches. The elective principle applies to various political institutions, including the militia (11), the assembly and the senate (22), the governor (58), justices of the peace and commissioners of the courts of request (66), and sheriffs, coroners, clerks, and registrars (74). The draft constitution guarantees the conventional rights of Upper Canadians: right of assembly (12), freedom of the press (13), trial by jury (14), and protection of property (15, 20). Finally, the agrarian ideal is implicitly encapsulated in this constitution, since the state is not permitted to create commercial or banking companies.[110]

In Lower Canada, Robert Nelson issued a declaration of independence (as opposed to a draft constitution) on 28 February 1838, appealing to the sovereignty of the people and declaring the establishment of the Republic of Lower Canada (Article 2). Nelson's Article 15 provides for the holding of a convention to draft a constitution. The tone is reminiscent of republican rhetoric, with the principle of equality given central importance (e.g., equality of First Nations people [3], abolition of seigneurial tenure [5–6]). Conventional rights, including freedom of the press (11) and trial by jury (12), are guaranteed. The declaration is notable for Nelson's relative lack of elitism with respect to leaders such as Papineau. For example, it extends the franchise to all men ages twenty-one and over for election of convention members.[111] In general, it presents a democratizing thrust – one possible direction for republicanism in the nineteenth century.

PEOPLE AND FACTION: REPUBLICAN EXCLUSION

For the republicans, there were two conditions for the enjoyment of liberty: being a member of the people *and* participating in the legislative process. A non-participating member of the people is not free in the republican sense, which does not mean that he cannot enjoy certain rights granted by the Sovereign. A denizen of a republic – for example, a visiting foreigner or a person expelled because of his actions – could even, conceivably, be a member of neither the people nor the Sovereign. This person would still be governed by the laws of the republic. In a word, a republic would be governed by rules of inclusion and exclusion.

As to exclusion from the Sovereign, certain individuals, although members of the people, might not be allowed to participate in the legislative process because they are not entitled to vote. The French constitution of 1791 called them "passive citizens." Men deemed incapable of being free, generally due to poverty, were put in this group. Lest there be any doubt, elitism was a characteristic of eighteenth-century republicanism as much as of modernism: its institutions were not democratic in today's sense but in fact closed to the masses. Rousseau, for instance, was partial to an elected aristocratic system,[112] while Gabriel Bonnot de Mably circumscribed the class of electors in a highly reductive way. In *Phocion's Conversations* and *Droits et devoirs du citoyen*, he maintained that artisans and the poor should not be allowed to vote.[113] The English Radicals espoused an equally truncated democracy. The nineteenth-century idea of universal suffrage was utterly foreign to them; they supported census suffrage.[114] They also knew that democracy can be just as tyrannical as monarchy.[115] It is relevant to observe that of all the eighteenth-century republicans, Robespierre, with his early opposition to census suffrage, was the least elitist.[116]

In the colonies, suffrage was generously granted in 1791 to all householders owning land or paying sufficient rent in Quebec City, Trois-Rivières, Montreal, and William-Henry (now Sorel).[117] In practice, because preindustrial Canadian society was primarily based on working the land and most families were landowners, suffrage was quite widely enjoyed.[118] The republicans, it is worth mentioning, never paid much serious attention to city dwellers. For them, the perfect republic was based on agriculture, and so the peasants were their main concern. When the Patriotes turned their attention to electoral reform, the positions they adopted were imbued with eighteenth-century elitism. While they did not seek to alter voting eligibility for the Assembly, they wanted to make the elected legislative council a more elitist chamber. In a petition to the king of 20 March 1833, the Assembly of Lower Canada declared, concerning reform of the Council,

There only remains, may it please your most gracious Majesty, the principle of election to rest upon, as being capable in practice of presenting an analogy with the second branch of the legislature of the United Kingdom. We entertain no doubt of the result of the adoption of this principle, if the election depended upon a numerous body of electors composed of the best ingredients and the best interests of the colony; and if the choice were confined to persons possessed of a certain easy degree of fortune, without, however, raising that qualification so high that such choice could only be made, in any case, but out of a small number of elegible [sic] persons.[119]

Two of the Ninety-Two Resolutions mention the possibility of requiring higher qualifications for the Council than for the Assembly as well as imposing more stringent eligibility criteria.[120] In short, the Patriotes adopted an elitist attitude just like all the other republicans. Because of the relative equality among Canadians, the consequences of such elitism would have been milder than elsewhere (e.g., France).

Women formed a second population group deemed incapable of political participation. The Constitutional Act of 1791 had granted suffrage to landowners, some of whom were female. While women were traditionally disenfranchised in Britain, nothing – neither law nor tradition – prohibited female landowners in the colonies from voting, and some women availed themselves of their right after 1791.[121] It was only seriously challenged once, in 1834 – when the Patriotes attempted to abolish it.[122] This stance seems surprising: What argument could be put forward in support of it? How could men who were demanding the franchise – let alone the Patriotes, with their rhetoric of freedom based on political participation – turn around and deprive women of it?

Nothing in republican theory made women's exclusion from the Sovereign (legislative power) mandatory, even though republican discourse was inflected by gender-related considerations from the sixteenth century onward.[123] A number of women participated in defining and promoting the ideals of republican liberty in the eighteenth century. Catharine Macaulay, in *The History of England* (1763–83), situated republican principles within a historical framework and, in *Letters on Education* (1790), argued for women's emancipation. Mary Wollstonecraft was the first, before Mackintosh and Paine, to respond to Edmund Burke with her *Vindication of the Rights of Men* (1790). In 1792, she published *Vindication of the Rights of Woman* in response to Rousseau's remarks on women. She denounced the inferiority of girls' education as well as the subordination of women in society. In France, the first person to argue for women's political rights was a man, Antoine Nicolas de Condorcet, who made this argument in three texts: *Lettres d'un bourgeois de New Haven* (1787), *Essai sur la constitution et les fonctions des assemblées provinciales* (1788), and *Essai sur l'admission des femmes aux droits de la cité* (1790). The following year, Olympe de Gouges published her *Déclaration des droits de la femme et de la citoyenne* (1791). The Girondist Marie-Jeanne Roland hosted a salon during the Revolution while Pauline Léon and Claire Lacombe founded a revolutionary women's club in Paris in the spring of 1793, succeeding where Théroigne de Méricourt had failed several months earlier. In the United States, two Revolution-era documents argued for women's rights: *The Sentiments of an American Woman* and *The Sentiments of a Lady in New Jersey* (both 1780).[124] Thus, it was perfectly possible to conceive of a republic in which women were full-fledged participants in legislative power. If the eighteenth-century revolutionaries and the nineteenth-century Canadian republicans did not, it was because they did not want to.

In practice, the Atlantic revolutions did not do much to expand women's rights.[125] In the United States, women did not acquire equality with men; rather, the Revolution harped on the ideal of domesticity and maternity.[126] In France, a few laws favourable to women were enacted during the Revolution, putting limitations on a husband's rights over his wife and children (1790) and making divorce legal (1792). But French women did not win suffrage, and the few laws that benefited women were soon repealed by Napoleon and Louis XVIII.[127] Before setting women's exclusion down to republican ideology, though, it should be noted that Great Britain underwent a similar evolution at the same period.[128] The truth is that the will to exclude women transcended ideology: it was rooted in mindsets, in the ambient political culture, in inherited legal frameworks, and in societal norms. One might imagine that the thinkers of the day made an effort to propound a cohesive ideological justification for the fact of women's exclusion, but the truth is that there was a general lack of debate on the question, in Lower Canada as elsewhere, as if debate were needless. Republicans differed from others on the woman question only in the justification given for exclusion, which had simply to do with certain prejudices that none of them was willing to challenge.[129]

According to Nathalie Picard, women's suffrage as an issue was ignored by the Patriotes until after 1827. In 1831, they passed two laws officially excluding women from politics. The first, An Act to Secure to and Confer

upon Certain Inhabitants of this Province, the Civil and Political Rights
of Natural-born British Subjects (I William IV c.53), granted certain
rights to men only (sections 1 and 2). The second, An Act to Incorporate
the City of Montreal (I William IV c.54), specifies that an elector must
be male (section 2). The exclusion of women embodied in these bills
does not appear to have given rise to vigourous debate – there was
little need, since these laws merely legalized what most considered nor-
mal.[130] The situation was not much different in March 1834 when
the Assembly passed a law banning women from voting. Debate was
limited to a few comments heard during debate over electoral reform
in general.

The debate leading to the passage of this act was structured in such a
way that it was women's suffrage, and not the desire of the members
(whether Patriotes or constitutionalists) to revoke it, that appeared
anomalous. It was largely contained within a brief exchange between
Augustin Cuvillier (a reformer-turned-constitutionalist) and Papineau.
No one rose to defend women's suffrage or to challenge their exclusion,
since all sides were of one mind on the matter. The question that should
concern us is why.

In Lower Canadian discourse, situated at the crossroads of French and
British thought, two arguments could have been used to justify women's
exclusion. The first came from the Commonwealthmen, who had considered elector independence to be an essential component of freedom.
To be free, individuals had to be equal and virtuous – that is, independent of undue influence on their electoral choices, capable of putting
the public good ahead of their private interests, and satisfied with a simple life. But women could not be virtuous in this sense. They were not
economically independent since a married woman did not generally
own property. In British law, everything belonged to the couple, and the
couple was under the husband's authority.[131] Being economically dependent, she could not be politically free. Following this logic, unmarried
female property owners should have been able to vote in Great Britain
– but they did not. Tradition weighed heavier than the law. It is interesting that the Commonwealthmen, who sought to reconfigure the legitimacy of the state and promote political participation, never gave much
thought to women's suffrage, but so it was.[132] As to the few radical texts
promoting women's emancipation, they managed little influence over
the movement. The Commonwealthmen's silence meant that their ideal
of equality and virtue was of little use to the Patriotes' in their effort to
revoke women's suffrage.

Instead, Papineau turned to French republican rhetoric. Rousseau was
probably the most influential republican thinker on this question. In his

novel *Julie, or, The New Heloise* (1757) and in his *Émile* (1759), he expounded on women's physical and moral inferiority and on their subjection to the tyranny of the passions. As he wrote in *Social Contract* (1762), "the impulsion of mere appetite is slavery."[133] Not only were women corrupt for this reason; they threatened men's freedom because of their power to corrupt. Since women could not be politically virtuous, they could not participate in politics. Yet the republicans went to some lengths to define a different meaning of virtue that applied to women. The future of the republic demanded it, for women were responsible for the education of children,[134] and hence for the transmission of patriotic values. The republicans explained that thanks to a sound education, women could learn to control their impulses and become chaste and modest. This education would make them virtuous in this specific sense. Feminine virtue, thus acquired, would allow women to play their role as patriotic mothers – their only true role in the republic.[135] In short, republican virtue was gender-based: men were virtuous if economically and politically independent, women if they evinced modesty in their moral and social behaviour.

It seems clear that this dual signification of virtue made its way into Lower Canadian values, and it was indeed around the concept of feminine modesty that Papineau structured his arguments on 27 January 1834. During the debate over a proposed reform of electoral law, Papineau criticized certain sources of electoral corruption that he regarded as standing in the way of liberty. He began by denouncing the intervention of legislative councillors in the electoral process; this, he said, was an affront to the people's liberty. He then objected to the fact that returning officers were appointed by the governor. Finally, he devoted a sentence or two to women's suffrage as a problem to be resolved:

As to the custom of giving women the vote, it is appropriate to eliminate it. It is ridiculous, it is odious to watch wives being dragged onto the hustings by their husbands, daughters by their fathers, often even against their will. The public interest, decency, and the modesty of the sex demand that these scandals not be repeated. A simple motion in the House, excluding these persons from the right to vote, would avert much unseemly behaviour.[136]

The construction of the argument adheres to republican principles and prejudices. By including women's suffrage on his list of concerns right after legislative and executive corruption, Papineau implies that it too is a source of corruption. He appeals to modesty as a characteristic of women. To demonstrate that virtuous women should not wish to get involved in politics and that Lower Canadian women are virtuous, he

contends that those who voted did so against their will, goaded into it by
the men. Papineau's comment to the effect that a mere motion by the
Assembly could prevent women from voting is indicative of his conception of the social contract. In republican theory, this contract cannot be
modified without the unanimous consent of the parties. Ergo, for
Papineau, women had never been parties to the contract: it was between
men only. Women's suffrage, inasmuch as it existed in the colony, had
been an aberration from the start. The debate was over no sooner than
it had begun: the Assembly passed the bill abolishing women's suffrage
without further debate.

The Patriotes did make an appeal to women in 1837, but they did so
within a republican framework in which women's contribution is encouraged outside the formal political sphere. Papineau, speaking to women
at the assembly of Saint-Scholastique on 1 June 1837, did not impugn
women's place in Lower Canadian society:

I call upon the women of Canada, I adjure them to follow a shining example
given, in a time like this, by the patriotic women of America, and to help me,
to help us all destroy this revenue from which our oppressors forge chains for us
and for our children, and to discourage, by every means in their power, the consumption of these items which pay duties.[137]

Unquestionably, for the republicans, women's participation had to
take place within the domestic setting.[138] It is unfortunate that the debates on women's exclusion were not longer, since they would have
taught us much about how exclusion from the Sovereign functioned in
republican thought.

But as regrettable as it was, and as much as certain citizens and groups
might complain about it, exclusion from the Sovereign had much less
serious implications than exclusion from the people. Anyone who opposed the people's will set himself apart from it, forming a faction. The
concept of faction offers insight into this principle of exclusion.

Historians have generally invoked nationalism – termed ethnic by
some authors, civic by others – to explain the principle of exclusion articulated by the Patriotes. In his *Economic and Social History of Quebec,
1760–1850*, Fernand Ouellet contended that the Patriotes were nationalists who hid a retrograde, conservative, ethnic ideology under a democratic liberal discourse.[139] In this he echoed the conclusions of Lord
Durham.[140] More recent historiography has presented the Patriotes' ideology as an outgrowth of civic nationalism (liberal according to Yvan
Lamonde and Marcel Bellavance, republican according to Louis-Georges
Harvey).[141] These attempts to place the Patriotes' discourse within a

nationalist framework can primarily be set down to a search for the roots of contemporary Québécois nationalism. But the Patriotes' discourse was not, strictly speaking, nationalist: it was republican pure and simple.[142] It was structured around a sovereign people and its institutions, not around a nation. While the thought structures of republicanism and nationalism resemble each other, there are important differences. As Maurizio Viroli explains in his work on patriotism, "The crucial distinction [between republicanism and nationalism] lies in the priority or the emphasis: for the patriots, the primary value is the republic and the free way of life that the republic permits; for the nationalists, the primary values are the spiritual and cultural unity of the people."[143] Continuing along these lines, he writes, "Whereas the enemies of republican patriotism are tyranny, despotism, oppression, and corruption, the enemies of nationalism are cultural contamination, racial impurity, and social, political, and intellectual disunion."[144] By this definition, the Patriotes of the 1830s were manifestly working within the republican tradition.

Generally speaking, the Atlantic republicans did not appeal to a people defined in terms of culture or ethnicity. It is true that Rousseau clearly articulated the national cultural characteristics of Corsica and Poland in his draft constitutions, while the French Revolution included a Francization campaign. But one must not confuse the accessory with the essential, the accidental with the inevitable. The appeal to ethnicity or culture was never a fundamental part of republican thought prior to the revolutionary era. Jeremy Bentham and Thomas Paine, both Englishmen, were made citizens of the French Republic. Belonging to the republican people was a matter of political allegiance, submission to the body politic, not ethnic origin.[145]

As for the Patriotes, they never articulated an ethnic or racist discourse: it was always culturally inclusive, calling for the collaboration of all reformers regardless of ethnic background. As Papineau said in May 1837, "whoever comes to share our fate, as an equal, is a friend who will be welcome, no matter what his place of birth may be."[146] The public assemblies held in Lower Canada in the summer of 1837 passed highly inclusive resolutions. The most enlightening comes from the assembly of Saint-Scholastique (1 June 1837), whose sixth resolution forthrightly states,

We heartily call for union among the inhabitants of this Province from all beliefs and all languages, and origins, that for the common defence, for the honor and preservation of the Country each must make the sacrifice of his prejudices, and we must all extend our hands to obtain a wise and protective government, which, in restoring harmony, shall at the same time cause agriculture, commerce, and national industry to flourish. And we reassure our fellow subjects of British origin of our fraternity and our trust, they who have, above the wheedling and the antipathies of power, joined us in our demands. That we have never entertained and, to the contrary, have always reproved the unfortunate national divisions which our common enemies have maliciously tried and still try to foment among us, and we must loudly proclaim that the fact alleged in the reports relayed to the government of His Majesty that the struggle here was between inhabitants of British origin and those of French Canadian origin, is a malicious assertion belied by the well-known character of the French Canadian inhabitants; and that as for us, whatever be the fate of the Country, we shall work without fear and without reproach as in the past, to guarantee the whole people, without any distinction, the same rights, equal justice, and shared liberty.[147]

Thus, the Patriotes refused to make background, language, or religious beliefs into criteria for exclusion from the people. Robert Nelson's declaration of independence, moreover, indicates that the Republic of Lower Canada would be bilingual (article 18).

The Patriotes did, of course, perceive the animosity between the French Canadians and subjects of other backgrounds. When they referred to it, however, it was to contend that the responsibility for this animosity lay with the Legislative Council: "it is the Council itself which, after having been remodeled, revealed the baseness of its predilections and its antipathies, declared itself the organ and the passive instrument of a faction, dedicated itself to fomenting and protecting national distinctions."[148]

In the 1830s, this approach was the only one that made sense. From a political standpoint, there was no need for the Patriotes to appeal to cultural characteristics: if the people succeeded in gaining control of all legislative power, the nationality of the majority would no longer be threatened. In strategic terms, the advantage of this approach was to attract British subjects favourable to their reform agenda. The Patriotes generally attempted to cultivate good relations with the English-speaking community, using the Assembly and the newspaper *The Vindicator* for this purpose. The fifty-fifth of the Ninety-Two Resolutions specifies in this regard that "the wishes and interests of the majority of [the anglophones] are common to them and to their fellow-subjects of French origin, and speaking the French language; that the one class love the country of their birth, the other that of their adoption; that the greater portion of the latter have acknowledged the generally beneficial tendency of the laws and institutions of the country."[149] This policy of openness did not, however, produce the intended results. As Allan Greer notes, tensions mounted between English and French speakers during the 1830s. Some factors explaining the rise of ethnic tensions were the arrival of large numbers of immigrants, which upset the linguistic balance of the province; the epidemics to which immigration gave rise; the difference between the needs of long-established subjects (francophones) and new arrivals (anglophones); and the refusal of British immigrants to break ties with the mother country.[150] The fact that the anglophone constitutionalists simultaneously articulated a principle of exclusion against the French Canadians exacerbated these ethnic divisions. Be that as it may, the Patriotes did not find such division desirable, nor did they encourage it.

In fact, the Patriotes attempted to present the political struggles of the two Canadas as one and the same. The Patriote-led Assembly pointed out that

there are on this portion of the American Continent, more than a million of His Majesty's Subjects, composing the Colonies of *Upper* and *Lower Canada*, who, speaking different languages, and having a great diversity of origin, laws, creeds and manners, characteristics peculiar to them respectively, and which they have severally the right to preserve as inhabitants of a separate and distinct Province, have yet come to the conclusion that the institutions common to the two countries ought to be essentially modified, and that it has become urgently necessary to reform the abuses which have, up to this day, prevailed in the administration of the Government. We rejoice that we have, in our just claims, the support of our brethren of *Upper Canada*. This support will demonstrate to Your Honorable House and to our fellow subjects in all parts of the Empire, that we have been sincere in our declarations, that the circumstances and wants of the two Canadian Provinces do indeed require a responsible and popular government, and that we have been actuated by no narrow views of party or of origin in demanding for many years, from the authorities of the Mother Country, that such a Government may be granted us.[151]

Conversely, this stance enabled the radicals of Upper Canada to link their demands to those of the Patriotes. On 27 November 1828, Mackenzie wrote to John Neilson, who had not yet broken with the other reformers, to tell him that a union between the reformist forces in the two Canadas could be profitable.[152] In 1837, Mackenzie thanked the French Canadians for their contribution to the cause of liberty and asked his fellow citizens "to make common cause with their fellow citizens of Lower Canada, whose successful coercion would doubtless be in time visited upon us, and the redress of whose grievances would be the best guarantee for the redress of our own."[153] National distinctions would only disappear once the provincial institutions had been reformed according to republican designs. The people would then be masters of their own fate and cultural distinctions would no longer provoke animosity.

While the Patriotes did not put too much emphasis on the ethnic question, they did at times allude to it. For example, while the third of the Ninety-Two Resolutions states that British subjects are welcome in Lower Canada, subsequent resolutions (51, 75–6) denounce them as having monopolized government positions and of having interests different from those of the majority. Nevertheless, the Patriotes' discourse was more culturally inclusive than that of their adversaries.

All things considered, the republicans did articulate a principle of exclusion, but one that was justified on the basis of political rather than ethnic considerations. For them, belonging to the people was a matter of accepting the idea of the people and the logic of republicanism. To make common cause with the people was to be a member of it. Conversely, to be an enemy of the people – that is, to be a political enemy of the Patriotes and the radicals – was to exclude oneself from the people. The worst charge one could make against a group of individuals was to accuse them of factiousness – the core characteristic of an enemy of the people.

The American Revolution had certainly been much less bloody than the French, but it too had excluded enemies of the people on the basis of this principle. The difference in the outcome had to do with the nature of the enemy. For the Americans it was a foreign power: Great Britain. In signing the peace of 1783, the enemy admitted defeat and the threat of reconquest disappeared. The loyalists, who could not remain in the republic because they had thrown in their lot with the enemy, as well as anyone else who did not want to stay for some reason, simply left the United States. In France, the enemy was domestic: the aristocracy. In his 1789 work, the Abbé Sieyès affirmed that the privileged did not belong to the nation because they sought to defend "not the general interest, but the private one."[154] That being the case, these aristocrats were internal enemies of the people and had to be destroyed.[155] Two methods were possible. The revolutionaries first attempted to subordinate the privileged by force, as with the passage of the Civil Constitution of the Clergy in 1790. In this the French republicans merely followed Rousseau's dictum: "whoever refuses to obey the general will shall be constrained to do so by the entire body: which means nothing other than that he shall be forced to be free."[156] However, as the situation evolved, the revolutionaries met with resistance from the elites. Exile might have been a solution, as it was in America, but since the émigrés were fomenting a counterrevolution on the border in the hope of regaining power and crushing the people, exile was no guarantee of security. The guillotine became the solution to the problem of the excluded. Because the aristocrats and the privileged – the king chief among them – posed a threat to the people, they had to be eliminated. The Terror was merely the expression of the republican principle of exclusion in its most intransigent form.[157] It is the best representation of what J.L. Talmon called totalitarian democracy.[158]

While the situation in Lower Canada, as in Upper Canada, never reached such dramatic levels, the colonial republicans wielded the rhetoric of factionalism with great skill, presenting the bureaucrats and merchants controlling the councils as the enemy of the people. For Papineau, the executive power "must also know that a faction and a fraction are the same thing, and that the commercial cabal, which claims to rule everything here, is not the strength of this country ... The wishes of the mass of the population must be obeyed."[159] The Assembly of Lower Canada sent the king a petition that described the Legislative Council in unequivocal terms: "this Body, *far from being attached to the Country, and making part of it,* represent[s] only favoritism, monopolies, and privileges."[160] In Upper Canada, Mackenzie adopted and publicized the phrase "Family Compact" in his *Sketches of Canada and the United States.*[161] By pointing out the improper ties binding members of the ruling class (and hence their reciprocal dependency), he attacked the whole political organization of the province. Not only were the members of the elite corrupt (non-independent) but they formed a particular body within Upper Canada that was parasitic on the body politic.[162]

When the rebellions came, the rhetoric of factionalism was ever present. According to the drafters of the "Address of the Confederation of the Six Counties to the People of Canada" (24 October 1837), the existing officials "have joined together in a faction driven only by private interest to oppose all the reforms, to defend all the iniquities of a government that is the enemy of the rights and freedoms of this colony."[163] The people was threatened and had to defend itself.

5

The Primacy of Rights:
Modern Liberty in the Canadas,
1828–1838

IN THE 1830s, Upper and Lower Canadian republicans presented themselves as the champions of liberty. They claimed to be defending the people against the tyranny of the colonial oligarchy, and they demanded fundamental constitutional reform. Their demands fit clearly within the overall thrust of Atlantic republicanism. Squaring off against this revolutionary protest movement was a powerful group of adversaries determined to defend the colonial constitution. This conflict has long been presented as one between conservatives and reformers, defenders of order and aspirants to liberty. The scheme is not incorrect per se, but it does give the impression that order and liberty are antithetical concepts – and nothing could be less certain. The republicans may have held the ideal of liberty aloft, but this did not equate in their minds to anarchy. Their ideal state was just as well-ordered as a monarchy or any other state. The republic they envisioned was predicated on a specific type of political organization, well-defined power relations, a particular social hierarchy, and a principle of exclusion. Moreover, the republicans were not the only ones in the Atlantic world to espouse liberty: so, with equal vehemence but without sharing the republican ideal, did Montesquieu, Voltaire, Blackstone, and De Lolme, to name only a few. And so did the partisans of the colonial constitution, whose conception of liberty found its underpinnings in the Constitutional Act of 1791.

Modern liberty, like republican liberty, engendered a spectrum of ideologies in the Atlantic world, and in the Canadas specifically. Its partisans were divided into reformers, who wanted to adapt the structures of the British parliamentary system, and constitutionalists, who were content with the status quo or with only minor adjustments to political or social organization. While a few 1830's reformers (Étienne Parent, the Baldwins) continued to situate their demands within the constitutional framework, the polarization of political forces in both Upper and Lower Canada meant that they would be progressively marginalized, leaving a starker opposition between republicans and constitutionalists. To the latter, the constitution guaranteed all the liberty the colonists needed. It was republicanism – the "tyranny of the majority" in their eyes – that threatened their liberty.

Historians have long depicted the (self-described) "constitutionalists" as conservatives – which they were, if the word is taken to mean specifically that they wanted to preserve the constitutional framework intact (and they were joined in this, as the conflict heated up, by reformers such as John Neilson). But not all the constitutionalists were ideological conservatives. They did not all subscribe to an organic, hierarchical society resulting from a pact between the living and the dead, a society rooted in tradition.[1] Nor were all of the reformers liberals: some, such as Denis-Benjamin Viger, were ideologically conservative.[2] What is more, new portrayals of the constitutionalists as liberals have begun to enter the historical literature. This may be going too far in another direction: while several of them acknowledged the existence of inviolable individual rights, beginning with property rights, and a number of their speeches sat comfortably within the Whig tradition, the liberal concept of the individual is largely absent from their discourse.

Prior to 1828, in the absence of any serious challenge to the Constitutional Act of 1791, the defence of the state and the social order was a sporadic affair, the work of individual constitutionalists reacting to circumstances or to reformers' demands. In 1810, when tensions were mounting between Great Britain and the United States, John Strachan, the renowned teacher and Anglican minister at Cornwall (who became an archdeacon and then the bishop of Toronto), published *A Discourse on the Character of King George the Third*. This pamphlet strove to educate Canadians about the nature of the constitution in the hope that this would encourage them to defend the colony against the American menace. Strachan thought of himself as a friend of liberty but rejected the United States and France as appropriate models to follow.[3] Liberty in Britain, he argued, was "placed on a much firmer basis than that of the American States."[4] The Canadians ought to consider themselves lucky to have a constitution modeled on that of the mother country, one

founded upon the most equitable, rational and excellent principles: a constitution of free and equal laws, secured on the one hand against the arbitrary will of the sovereign, and the licentiousness of the people on the other; a constitution which has become the fruitful source of heroes, the nourisher of liberty, the promoter of learning, art and commerce: a constitution which protects and secures the life and liberty of every individual, and whose pure administration has been experienced for fifty years through a king who delights in being the guardian of freemen and the father of his people.[5]

Strachan's discourse falls firmly within the precincts of British constitutionalism and modern liberty. For him, the constitution guarantees equality before the law, but nothing more. Legal equality is the necessary and sufficient condition for individual liberty, and the state is responsible for protecting it. Liberty is in turn bound up with two other rights: property and security, and the three form a more or less inseparable whole:

Does any person doubt whether the British be the freest nation on earth, let him tell me where property and its rights are so well protected. This is the life and soul of liberty. What shall oppression seize when property is secure? Even a tyrant will not be wicked for nothing; but the motives and objects are removed, and the seed of oppression destroyed, when property is safe. By this, life and liberty are rendered sacred.[6]

Strachan goes on to present liberty as deriving from experience, not theory. The emphasis on prescription (experience) recalls the writings of Edmund Burke:

Nothing is more absurd than to suppose a nation free, because it possesses a written constitution which is little regarded in practice. Before a people can be called free, their freedom must have been tried. It must have given permanent proofs of its health. It must have braved the most terrible storms – weathered the attacks of tyranny on the one hand, and of faction on the other. And what is more, this freedom must have become the foundation of the public manners – it must have stamped itself on the people who enjoy it. And such is the freedom of the British nation; it has undergone all these trials, and it has been triumphant.[7]

Strachan minimizes the value of the constitutional innovations introduced after the American Revolution, appealing to the authority of Locke, De Lolme, Blackstone, and Montesquieu:

The framers of their constitution have been called wise, but this production does not prove it. Let any person read Locke's treatises on government, De Lolme on the British constitution, Blackstone, Montesquieu, with a few other authors who wrote before the minds of men were agitated with successive revolutions, and compare them with the slimsy [sic] productions which have deluged the world since the American revolution, and they will be forced to confess, that in this subject, we seem to go back.[8]

In practice, he favoured the maintenance of the social hierarchy and the bonds between church and state.

Subsequently, in 1822–23, certain constitutionalists seized on the debate over Britain's proposed union between Upper and Lower Canada as an opportunity to put forward a defence of the constitution. On this question, they were not all in agreement. Certain Lower Canadians, particularly those living in the Eastern Townships and Montreal, favoured a union that would liberate them from minority status with respect to the French Canadians.[9] The union was opposed, however, by a majority of the legislative councillors of Lower Canada. For them, the Constitution of 1791 had "eminently promoted the welfare and prosperity of this Province ... secured the peace and happiness of all classes of His Majesty's Subjects, and ... strengthened the bond of union with the Mother Country."[10] In Upper Canada, the constitutionalists (notably Strachan, who had become an executive councillor in 1815 and a legislative councillor in 1820, and John Beverley Robinson, attorney general of Upper Canada) were equally opposed to the projected union. Strachan wrote to Robinson that a united legislature would be "a Babel, half roaring French, half English."[11] Robinson, in a long letter to Lord Bathurst, explained that the union would be deleterious since it would put Protestantism and English-speaking subjects in the minority with respect to a group of Catholic French Canadians who would unite to fight their assimilation. Nor would it guarantee the instatement of English civil law throughout the new colony. Robinson believed that the only desirable union would bring together all of British North America.[12] This proposal was supported by Jonathan Sewell, chief justice of Lower Canada.[13]

These few writings aside, it was not until the 1830s that a robust defence of the constitution and of modern liberty would be heard in the colonies. With the emergence of an articulate republican discourse, the constitutionalists found themselves obliged to make explicit their vision of power and social relations.

CONSTITUTIONALISM IN THE TWO CANADAS

The constitutionalist forces in the two colonies exhibited significant differences. In Lower Canada, they were largely anglophone, with a few French Canadian allies (Augustin Cuvillier, Pierre de Rocheblave, Dominique Mondelet, and Charles Clément Sabrevois de Bleury, for example). They dominated the Legislative and Executive Councils but not the House of Assembly, which was held by reformers from 1806 to 1828 and by republicans from then on. The conflict between republicans and constitutionalists took on an institutional cast, with the Papineau-led

Assembly on one side and the governor and the councils (whose members included Jonathan Sewell, Peter McGill, George Moffatt, and John Molson) on the other.

The Lower Canadian constitutionalist forces also mobilized outside the Assembly. Under the impetus of John Neilson, who broke with the Patriotes for good in 1834, the Quebec City constitutionalists founded the Constitutional Association of Quebec in December of that year. This was a reaction to the re-election of the Parti patriote on a platform based on the Ninety-Two Resolutions. The Montreal constitutionalists followed suit in January 1835, founding the Constitutional Association of Montreal. These two groups had the support of newspapers such as the *Quebec Gazette*, the *Montreal Gazette*, and the *Montreal Herald*. The Lower Canadian constitutionalists formed a number of other associations and held public assemblies in the years 1834 to 1837.[14]

The defence of the constitution also involved the publication of books and pamphlets. The most interesting Lower Canadian author was certainly Adam Thom, a Scottish immigrant who came to Montreal in 1832. From January to December 1833 he edited the *Settler, or British, Irish and Canadian Gazette*, in which he promoted the anglicization of the colony. He then taught at the Montreal Academical Institution before becoming, in 1835, editor of the *Montreal Herald*. At the end of that year, he published the *Anti-Gallic Letters*, a response to the inaugural speech of Governor Gosford and one of the best defences of the Canadian Constitution. As the title of the work suggests, this defence was contained within an all-out attack on the domination of the Patriotes and the survival of French in Lower Canada. Thom was important enough for Lord Durham to name him, in August 1838, assistant commissioner on the commission on municipal administration. He left Lower Canada in 1839 for the Red River Colony, where he was put in charge of codifying that colony's laws.[15]

In Upper Canada, the constitutionalists were much more powerful than the republicans, commanding the allegiance of more or less the entire colonial elite. Partisans of modern liberty dominated the two councils throughout the period, and the Assembly as well (with a hiatus from 1834 to 1836). Extraparliamentary organizations were much less important here as vehicles for their participation in politics, for high-profile constitutionalists generally held official positions. John Beverley Robinson, leader of the Family Compact, was attorney general from 1819 to 1829 and chief justice from 1829 to 1862. John Strachan was an executive councillor from 1815 to 1836 and a legislative councillor from 1820 to 1841. Robert Baldwin Sullivan, after supporting his reformer cousin Robert Baldwin for a time, switched allegiance and was appointed to the

Executive Council in 1836, becoming a legislative councillor in 1839.[16] To these names one could add Christopher Hagerman, solicitor general and member of the House of Assembly for Kingston, and Allan MacNab, member for Hamilton and Speaker of the Assembly from 1837 to 1841.

The Upper Canadian constitutionalists published their own pamphlets denouncing republican ideas. The most interesting, *The Affairs of the Canadas in a Series of Letters* (1837), was the work of Egerton Ryerson, a Methodist minister and editor of the *Christian Guardian* for most of the 1830s. Ryerson began his public career in 1826 when he published a defence of the Methodists' loyalty in William Lyon Mackenzie's *Colonial Advocate*. He maintained ties to the reformers until 1833, when he went to Great Britain to negotiate a merger between the Upper Canadian Methodists and the British Wesleyans. The trip gave him some distance from colonial politics, and he became convinced that the colonial reformers wanted to destroy the Constitution and sever ties with Britain. In 1836, writing as "A Canadian," he published letters in the *Times of London* denouncing the colonial republicans and accusing radical British MPs Joseph Hume and John Arthur Roebuck of having goaded them down the road to sedition. The letters resemble Thom's writings in both tone and argumentation. On his return, Ryerson broke with the reformers and took a public stance in favour of the Constitution,[17] publishing his letters in pamphlet form. He did maintain his opposition to the clergy reserves, however.

To sum up, the constitutionalists were not equally strong in the two colonies. They controlled the political institutions of Upper Canada to a greater degree than those of Lower Canada and were less involved in extraparliamentary activities. There was also an important difference in the tone of the emerging constitutionalist discourse. In Lower Canada, the constitutionalists were on the defensive between 1828 and 1834. In the latter year, the situation turned critical with the adoption of the Ninety-Two Resolutions, which posed a direct threat to the Constitution and, as they saw it, to liberty itself. The outraged constitutionalists mobilized aggressively against this threat, giving notice that they would use force if necessary. In Upper Canada, the threat waned after 1830 with the reformers' electoral defeat. They then sat in the opposition until 1834, and while their electoral victory that year worried the authorities, their crushing defeat two years later gave reassurance as to the loyalty of the colony's inhabitants. To a large extent, it was not until after the rebellions that the Upper Canadian constitutionalists articulated a bona fide defence of the Constitution.

In short, while a similar ideological opposition between republicans and constitutionalists was enacted in both colonies, the enactment was much starker in Lower Canada. Still, it may be said that all the constitutionalists, regardless of circumstances obtaining, position held, tone adopted, and media used, generally espoused the same constitutional principles and the same conception of liberty.

LIBERTY, PROPERTY, AND SECURITY: CONSTITUTIONALIST RHETORIC IN THE CANADAS

For the moderns, liberty amounted to the enjoyment of certain basic rights. According to Blackstone, these rights "may be reduced to three principal or primary articles; the right of personal security, the right of personal liberty, and the right of private property."[18] If these rights were not spelled out in the Constitution of 1791, it is because there was no reason for it: they formed the very core of the British Constitution. The colonial constitutionalists were fully versed in these rights. The Constitutional Association of Quebec explained that "the enjoyment of equal rights with our fellow subjects, and that permanent peace, security and freedom for our persons, opinions, property and industry … are the common rights of British Subjects."[19] For them, the guaranteed enjoyment of these rights was the essence of liberty. Throughout the 1830s they argued passionately for these rights and took issue with anyone perceived as threatening them.

Personal liberty was certainly the most ambiguous of these rights, for it was never given any formal definition in the colonies. Nevertheless, all those assembled under the banner of modern liberty concurred that personal liberty exists where all members of society obey reasonable laws that do not violate anyone's personal autonomy.

In practice, this definition had a number of ramifications. One was religious tolerance. Subjects were free to subscribe to the faith of their choice. This freedom had been acquired in England in 1689 with the passage of the Toleration Act and had been passed along to the inhabitants of the colonies.[20] As Strachan put it, "All parties retain the right of worshiping God as their consciences direct, and of educating their children as they please."[21] In the mother country, however, such tolerance was not synonymous with true religious freedom for more than a century thereafter. Until 1828, when it was repealed, the Test Act deprived Nonconformists of certain civil and political rights; likewise, the British and Irish Catholics were not emancipated until 1829. Religious freedom in fact came earlier to the colonies than to Britain: Nonconformists and Catholics were allowed to profess their faith without penalty after 1774.

Still, colonial religious cohabitation was not without strife. In 1820s' Upper Canada, a problem arose with an attempt by the British authorities and the local constitutionalist elites to make the Anglican Church the established church of the colony and to grant it those tracts of land that had been reserved by the Constitutional Act for the support of all the Protestant clergy. The Anglicans argued that this had been the clear intent of the London authorities. Such an interpretation was inevitably and vehemently contested by the other Protestant denominations and by the Catholic Church, with political support from a number of reformers and radicals. Emboldened by the absence of clear-cut legal discrimination, these denominations demanded their share of the clergy reserves, pointing out that Anglicans, while forming the largest denomination in Upper Canada (until the 1840s), only accounted for a fraction of the population.[22] Their economic demand was incommensurate with their demographic weight.

There was, it should be noted, no necessary contradiction between the existence of an official church and the principle of religious tolerance, as Britain's example proved. According to Strachan, even the great Whig reformer Charles James Fox had declared himself "the friend of a religious Establishment, *because* I am the friend of toleration without restriction."[23] That was because the argument for an official church and the privileges pertaining to it was made on social and often essentially political rather than religious grounds. For eighteenth- and early nineteenth-century advocates of modern liberty, the role of religion was one of education and social control, and the benefits of this role should not be denied the colonists.[24] Strachan wrote, "by the Law of England the Church is an integral part of the State, and being well aware of the advantage, which the people at large derive from this union was solicitous to extend to the Canadas the blessings of a Constitution, assimilated as much as possible to that of the Mother Country." Specifically concerning the preservation of social order, Strachan cited a report of the Executive Council of Upper Canada that specified, "It is of great importance that the Constitution in Church and State should be so interwoven with the whole social system in Upper Canada, as to engage men's interests as well as their feelings in its support, and make it in popular and daily estimation, no less essential to the *security of property* than to the preservation of religion, and maintenance of good order."[25] Thus, the constitutionalists insisted on a distinction between denomination and institution that allowed them to square their attempt to award the clergy reserves to an official church with their belief in modern liberty. Special church status could coexist with freedom of conscience. Their position simply pointed to a highly inegalitarian view of legitimate political and social relations in society.

Freedom of expression was another important form of liberty for the moderns – but it did not imply that anyone could say anything. Subjects should be allowed to express themselves freely, but always with respect for their peers. Freedom of expression would not, for example, provide a shield to hide behind while wrongly accusing another. One person's freedom stopped where another's began. And what allowed each person to distinguish the limits of his own freedom was his capacity for reason. Thus, a person misusing this freedom could be held to account. As Blackstone explained,

the liberty of the press is indeed essential to the nature of the free state; but this consists in laying down no previous restraints on publications, and not in freedom from censure for criminal matter when published. Every freeman has an undoubted right to lay what sentiments he pleases before the public, to forfeit this is to destroy the freedom of the press; but if he publishes what is improper, mischievous or illegal, he must take the consequences of his own temerity.[26]

While there was no official pre-publication censorship in the British world, persons believing themselves to have been defamed could sue and have the perpetrator imprisoned. Such a posteriori censorship encouraged self-censorship and proved highly practical for colonial officials seeking to silence their detractors. Governor Craig closed down *Le Canadien* in March 1810 for a poem deemed offensive, and several journalists were imprisoned for libel during the 1820s and 1830s. In Lower Canada, Ludger Duvernay, editor of the Patriote paper *La Minerve*, was imprisoned in 1828, 1832, and 1836, and his colleague Daniel Tracey, editor of *The Vindicator*, was imprisoned in 1832. The journalist Étienne Parent was imprisoned for four months in early 1839 for an article published in *Le Canadien* (in his case the charge was sedition). In Upper Canada, the journalist Francis Collins was imprisoned (1828–29) for referring to the "native malignancy" of John Beverley Robinson in an article published in the *Canadian Freeman* (16 October 1828).[27] And Mackenzie was expelled from the Legislative Assembly in 1831–32 for his writings in the *Colonial Advocate*. Lawsuits filed by the constitutionalists against the reformers during the 1830s indicate the nature and limits of the version of freedom of expression to which the constitutionalists subscribed.

To these civil liberties, the constitutionalists added political freedom, or the right of subjects to participate in politics by electing assemblymen. Note that voting was not synonymous with modern liberty in the minds of its partisans: it was a condition for and a component of liberty. The constitutionalists never wavered from their support for representative institutions, though they always situated them within the framework of mixed government.

The constitutionalists' version of liberty also entailed the existence of an impartial judiciary, though this aspect was little discussed.[28] The principles underlying the colonial justice system corresponded to those of the mother country, featuring various mechanisms designed to preserve subjects' liberty and protect them from arbitrariness. One was the rule of law, a fundamental characteristic of the British Constitution that obliged judges to adhere to the Constitution in their decisions. Another was judicial independence.[29] While the executive power appointed judges, it had no right to interfere with their work. And a third was trial by jury, "the boast and the glory of BRITISH subjects all over the world," "the palladium of BRITISH liberty ... the sacred bulwark of their liberties."[30] This mechanism guaranteed individuals the right to be judged by their peers.

Equality, too, was integral to modern liberty – Locke referred to it as a natural right – but in a more restrictive sense than in republican liberty. The constitutionalists were only interested in equality before the law, never de facto equality. On the contrary, the constitutionalist elites in the two Canadas generally held a hierarchical vision of society. Some defended the preexisting social order based on rank or social status while others argued for a meritocracy based on financial success.[31] The constitutionalists of Lower Canada, who considered themselves unjustly treated, used every available forum – petitions to the king, resolutions and other documents by the constitutional associations of Montreal and Quebec City, political speeches, polemical writings – to demand equal rights for all during the 1830s.[32] The constitutionalists of Upper Canada, who largely controlled the political system, believed that such equality already existed in the colony.

Finally, the partisans of modern liberty considered two other rights to be inviolable: property and security.[33] Protection of property, as the fruit of a person's honest labour (at least in theory), was elevated to a distinct right early on. If the constitutionalists rejected republicanism it was to some extent because they feared that the republicans would not treat property with the same respect. Thom quoted John Adams on this subject:

Suppose a nation, rich and poor, high and low, ten millions in number, all assembled together; not more than one or two millions will have lands, houses, or any personal property; ... Would Mr. Needham be responsible that, if all were to be decided by a vote of the majority, the eight or nine millions who have no property, would not think of usurping over the rights of the one or two millions who have? Property is surely a right of mankind as really as liberty. Perhaps, at first, prejudice, habit, shame or fear, principle or religion, would restrain the poor from attacking the rich, and the idle from usurping on the industrious ...

The moment the idea is admitted into society, that property is not as sacred as the laws of God, and that there is not a force of law and public justice to protect it, anarchy and tyranny commence.[34]

   This vision of things was not very different from that of Adam Smith, for whom property was the most basic of rights. For the constitutionalists, then, the republicans threatened the colonies not only with political tyranny, in which individual rights would no longer be inviolable, but also with violation of property rights.[35]

   Property was doubly important for the constitutionalists. An inalienable right, it was also, for many of them, the basis of their philosophy of life. Against the republicans' ethic of virtue and frugality, the constitutionalists – or at any rate the wealthiest and most conservative among them – pitted an ethic of accumulation. Property accumulation was the very source of happiness, the thing that made it possible. The pursuit of happiness was a sacred and inviolable right: ergo, so was the right to protection of property. The constitutionalists who adopted this view held in contempt those whom they perceived as not sharing it. The opprobrium heaped on the French Canadians during the 1830s stemmed in part from their willingness to live a simple life:

The Canadian habitants have not that "*auri sacra fames,*" the parent of so much good, as well as of so much evil. They are content to live in no better houses, wear no better clothes, travel over no better roads, and to be no greater men than their fathers; and they are content likewise to raise their oats, and their potatoes, among grass and thistles ... They are people of few wants.[36]

   The constitutionalists, for their part, agreed that accumulation of property (whether real or personal) was virtuous, but not necessarily on the kind of society that this implied. Lower Canadian merchants favoured a society based on trade while other Lower Canadians and certain Upper Canadians (e.g., Robinson and Sullivan) still harboured a societal vision based on large estates and landholdings. Both groups' perspective remained preindustrial and highly inegalitarian.

   This ethic of accumulation went hand in hand with a firm commitment to trade and commerce. For the adherents of modern liberty, commerce was a guarantee of order and liberty. As Adam Smith had put it, "Commerce and manufactures gradually introduced order and good government, and with them the liberty and security of individuals, among the inhabitants of the country, who had before lived almost in a continual state of war with their neighbours, and of servile dependency upon their superiors."[37] The constitutionalists were strong proponents of large trade-facilitating public works projects such as canals, which they regarded as synonymous with progress. They opined that the French Canadians' lackadaisical attitude towards infrastructure investment stood in the way of commerce, progress, and ultimately happiness. The Lower Canadian Assembly's refusal to develop the colony's infrastructure during the 1830s was indeed problematic, and continually decried by these observers, since it was no use investing in Upper Canadian infrastructure without a corresponding effort down river.

Another charge leveled at the Lower Canada House of Assembly was that of stealing Upper Canadian property.[38] Customs duties charged on products imported into the colonies were paid in Lower Canada. The government there was supposed to remit a portion of these revenues to its neighbour, but revenue sharing between the colonies was a perpetually contentious issue. Upper Canada complained that it was not receiving its fair share and accused Lower Canada of hindering its development. Constitutionalists in both colonies contended that the French Canadians, with their simple way of life, were certainly not the consumers of these products – and that meant the Upper Canadians were being deprived of their rightful revenues.

Another complaint came from Lower Canadian constitutionalists who claimed that the Patriote-led Assembly was using taxation as a means to oppress the English Canadians:

These means, derived in great part from the petitioners, are now avowedly employed for the purpose of subjugating the persons, property, and freedom of the petitioners to the mere will and pleasure of a power derived from a majority of one distinct portion of the population only, proclaiming its "French origin" by solemn resolves of its Representatives, and manifestly held together by feelings and prejudices averse to other origins, and acted upon by ambitious and self-interested individuals.[39]

Given this perceived oppression, it was only natural that the Lower Canadian constitutionalists would want to deprive those they perceived as oppressors of the means of harming them, and so they supported the Upper Canadian demands.

Security was the third basic right of British subjects – so basic that it was at times conflated with liberty itself. Montesquieu wrote, "The political liberty of the subject is a tranquillity of mind arising from the opinion each person has of his safety."[40] More specifically, the British subject's right to security "consists in a person's legal and uninterrupted enjoyment of his life, his limbs, his body, his health, and his reputation."[41] In the nineteenth century, the right to security was closely associated with the right to property and to liberty. These three rights were nearly inseparable since liberty, to which every individual in a society is entitled, "is natural liberty shorn of that part which made individuals independent and created community of property, in order to live under laws which procured to them security and property."[42]

The colonial constitutionalists too considered security to be inseparable from liberty and property. Their objection to the Patriotes' demands and actions in Lower Canada was motivated by the fear that if the Assembly became the centre of colonial power, then "security for [their] liberties, lives and properties" would evaporate.[43] In Upper Canada, Tory MP Henry Sherwood expressed the views of many constitutionalists when he wrote in the report of the Assembly's committee on the state of the provinces in 1838 that the Constitution of 1791 contained "all the elements necessary for the most perfect security and enjoyment of Civil and Religious Liberty."[44]

The constitutionalists' conception of liberty can thus be summarized as enjoyment of individual autonomy with respect to other individuals and the state. It was a radically different conception from the republicans' and it implied a correspondingly different approach to the organization of power in a modern state.

PARLIAMENTARY SOVEREIGNTY WITHIN MIXED GOVERNMENT

For the constitutionalists, liberty was most definitely *not* predicated on public participation in politics and did not imply the supremacy of the legislative branch. Liberty did not reside in the state as a matter of principle; the state was merely the mechanism that had been devised for the protection of liberty. On this view, the republican conception of liberty was tantamount to tyranny.

The constitutionalists insisted on observance of the principles of modern liberty undergirding the British constitution, "the noblest system of Government that has ever been consecrated to freedom." This constitution was free because it was "adverse at once to despotism on the one hand, and to popular licentiousness on the other."[45] They likewise insisted on adherence to the Constitutional Act of 1791, which they saw as having engendered "the best system of Government that ever existed on earth, and from which they derive all the personal security, the worldly prosperity, and religious happiness which they enjoy." This system was presented as "the Colonial Charter of the rights and liberties of BRITISH subjects in this part of the dominions of the Empire."[46] The constitution offered all manner of guarantees of the freedom of British North American subjects. Robinson, for his part, believed that no oppression was possible or even conceivable under this system: "under the British Government, and in this age to dread the civil or religious prosecution of a whole people is to fear an imaginary danger."[47]

As a consequence of this position, the constitutionalists opposed republican principles mightily. Popular sovereignty, the idea that power in society and the state emanated from a monolithic fiction known as the "people," was an aberration. This fiction, they objected, could be invoked falsely to justify all manner of abuses. Furthermore, power would in practice rest with a single body, the assembly, where an elected majority could falsely be claimed to represent the will of the whole "people."[48] The majority could then proceed to oppress a minority who disapproved of its decisions, to depict that minority as an enemy of the people rather than a group with its own particular needs. The minority would be at the mercy of the majority. Finally, a sovereign "people" might assert its will to be law, only to express that will in an unreasonable manner. For the constitutionalists this was a considerable defect, since their conception of liberty was based on reason.

Thus, the constitutionalists repaid the republicans' hatred of their ideology in kind. The republican ideology had to be combated, since if allowed to triumph it would be wielded according to the whims of a majority interest group and to the detriment of individual rights. The constitutionalists were convinced that they would wind up slaves in the colony if their adversaries won: "the uncontrolled domination of the majority would deprive the minority of any and every guarantee for property, liberty or life."[49] As a result, they remonstrated bitterly against Lord Gosford's concessions to the Patriotes. Thom argued that the governor had, in his inaugural speech of October 1835, essentially ratified the majority's right to tyrannize the minority: "Your lordship ... has most liberally established the democratic principle, that the majority is everything and the minority nothing; that 'the great body of the people' is omnipotent and the small body of the people is powerless."[50]

There was an element of paradox in the constitutionalists' conception of the relationship between the individual and the state. On the one hand, their conception of liberty as synonymous with individual autonomy caused them to fear the state. On the other, they knew that liberty could not exist without it, that individual freedoms, property, and security could never be guaranteed. They resolved this dilemma by envisioning structural limitations on the capacity of the state to violate individual rights.

In this conception, sovereign power rested not with the "people," an immanent fiction, but with Parliament, a representative institution operating within a framework of mixed government. Structurally more complex than the republican vision, this conception consisted not of an indivisible,

142   *The Idea of Liberty in Canada*

monolithic "people" but of an aggregate of different societal interests. The will of Parliament transpired as an aggregate of the wills of the monarchy, the aristocracy, and the democracy, which last was further subdivided into distinct interests. Parliamentary sovereignty implied an understanding that these varying interests all deserved respect and should be allowed to square off legitimately within society and the state.

But despite what the constitutionalists thought, their political system too was predicated on an intellectual fiction. The "monarchy," the "aristocracy," and the "democracy" did not really exist in the colonies. There was a king, of course, but only on paper; in practice, the chief executive or governor of each colony was just a functionary of the Colonial Office. Nor was there anything resembling an aristocracy – the legislative councils were composed of individuals who, if they had lived in the mother country, would have sat in the House of Commons. As for democracy, it was not so much about representation of individual citizens of the colony as about representation of the interests they constituted.

In this context, the constitutionalists argued that something should be done to keep the majority of rural French-speaking Lower Canadians, as represented by the Parti patriote, from holding a majority in the Assembly, since they represented just one societal interest among several. The other interests in society, including the interests of merchants, did not have their fair share of representation. The Constitutional Association of Quebec condemned this state of affairs in 1835:

In prosecution of the views of the party to which those evils are mainly ascribable, that portion of the population of the province which has been by them designated as "of British or Foreign origin," has virtually been, and now is, deprived of the privilege of being heard in the Representative Branch of Government, in support of their interests and views. The portion of the population thus proscribed, amounts to about one hundred and fifty thousand souls, or one fourth of the whole, and comprises nearly all the Merchants, the principal Members of the Learned Professions, a large body of skilful and wealthy Artizans and Mechanics, and a great number of respectable and industrious Agriculturalists, possesses extensive real estate, and holds by far the greatest portion of the capital employed in the pursuits of trade and industry, all which interests are liable to be burdened, and in fact have been injuriously affected, in consequence of the proceedings of the said party and of the majority of the same origin by whom they have been supported in the Assembly of the Province.[51]

To provide for better representation of these interests, the moderns thought it necessary to gerrymander the electoral map, a practice they saw as perfectly consistent with the Constitution:

The British Constitution, on the contrary, besides checking popular impulses by two hereditary branches of the legislature, prevents, by the nicest adjustment of dissimilar constituencies, the majority of the people from returning the majority of representatives. In Lower Canada, in particular, the uncontrolled domination of the majority would be fatal to the welfare of the proscribed and calumniated minority.[52]

In the British Constitution, the separation between monarchy, aristocracy, and democracy was complemented by the separation between the executive, legislative, and judicial powers:

It is, my lord, a fundamental maxim of the British constitution, that the legislature, the executive and the judiciary should be so far independent of each other, as that not one of the three should either control the others or be controlled by them. Such, in fact, must be the fundamental maxim of the constitution of every free state. For the concentration of all the powers of the state in the hands of an individual or of a party is the very essence of despotism.[53]

In theory, executive power rested with the king, legislative power with Parliament, and judicial power with the courts. But again this separation of powers was more theoretical than real in the British – hence the colonial – constitution. All three branches of government involved collaboration among the different orders of society. The king, for example, played a role in the legislative process through the institution of royal assent. A bill could no more become law without royal assent than without a majority vote in the House of Commons (or its colonial equivalent, the assembly) or the House of Lords (the legislative council). Conversely, while the primary role of M P s and lords was legislative, they were not uncommonly asked to advise the king on executive matters. As to the judiciary, it should be remembered that the king, as "the fountain of justice,"[54] had the power to appoint judges. Judges, for their part, played a direct role in the legislative process: In Lower Canada, they were allowed to sit in the Legislative Assembly until 1811,[55] while they sat on the Executive and Legislative Councils until 1831 (they were barred thereafter, although the chief justice did retain his seat as speaker of the Legislative Council). Finally, judges could be consulted by the colonial executive, a fact to which Robinson took no exception:

As Chief Justice I am, like my brother Judges liable to be called on for reports, and opinions and advice in those cases in which recourse should be had in England to the Judges, and in no others – I have no concern in the executive affairs of the Colony, and no claim or wish to be consulted in any of them, except where they have so direct a bearing upon the general administration of justice, as to make such a reference proper.[56]

If the constitutionalists defended the separation of social orders (monarchy, aristocracy, democracy) and powers (executive, legislative, judicial), they rejected "the absurdly republican doctrine of a *complete* separation of 'the principal bodies of government.'"[57] More than tradition, it was the British Constitution that condoned this direct relationship among the powers.[58] To demonstrate the rightness of this reasoning, Thom appealed to the authority "of one of the most distinguished jurists of the [United States]" whom he presented implicitly, without stating it, as a republican. According to this jurist, an admirer of Montesquieu, the only way for power to check power involved a "partial participation of each in the powers of the other; and by introducing into every operation of the government in all its branches, a system of checks and balances, on which the safety of free institutions has ever been found essentially to depend." If Thom withheld the name of the quote's author, it was because Judge Joseph Story was a jurist whose writings in fact sat comfortably within the ethos of modern rather than republican liberty.[59]

The relationship between the executive and legislative powers was, in sum, much more complex for the constitutionalists than for the republicans. In the republican framework, executive power emanated from legislative power and could be closely supervised by it. In the parliamentary framework, executive power did not emanate from legislative power and was not subordinate to it: it was an autonomous power with prerogatives of its own. In order to ensure the smooth running of the parliamentary system, a mechanism was needed to keep the executive and legislative powers from being at loggerheads. The British had created such a mechanism: the Cabinet.

While the British model had been replicated to a considerable degree in the colonies, the constitutionalists opposed the creation of provincial cabinets. These would be redundant, they argued, since the British cabinet, if not the colonial assemblies, had the power to hold the colonial executive powers accountable for their acts vis-à-vis the House of Commons (the king, as noted, was above personal responsibility). The governor (or lieutenant-governor) was accountable to the British government, which was in turn accountable to Parliament. For the constitutionalists, this chain of accountability constituted a sufficient check on executive power.

Indeed, they contended that this model had served the colonists well. For Robinson in particular, the British government had proved a better friend of liberty than the assemblies. Had the executive councillors constituted a cabinet in the past, he argued, good laws opposed by the assemblies would never have been passed, since to advocate them would have been to lose the confidence of the legislature. He gave the example of the abolition of slavery: it would not have happened, he said, in colonies where the assemblies opposed abolition.[60]

The constitutionalists did, however, think that certain high-ranking officials should sit in the assembly to speak on behalf of the government. Their presence would allow the government to explain its policies to the members and the legislative councillors. The result would be better communication between the executive and legislative powers. This arrangement would have the further benefit of stimulating colonial development, since it would allow the government to argue for its investments and propose specific measures for adoption. Conversely, the opportunity for legislators to hold paid executive duties would encourage them to moderate their positions:

The man who at a public meeting or in his place in the assembly puts forth extravagant claims for his constituents, or for the Province upon the Legislature the Government or the mother country in the full knowledge that he ought not to succeed and without the desire to do so may for the time be popular, but when he is placed in high office under the Government he is under the necessity of acting instead of talking. He has to a certain extent to be moderate prudent and just.[61]

The constitutionalists believed that the job of member of Parliament would attract more qualified individuals if the members had access to such executive positions. One could not, after all, expect people to run for the assembly if the fact of winning a seat disqualified them from promotion within government.[62] In this respect, the constitutionalists' position was diametrically opposed to that of the republicans. James Mackintosh had made the reverse argument in 1791: "the exclusion [of Cabinet ministers from Parliament] is equivalent to that of all men of superior talent from the Cabinet: for no man of genius will accept an office which banishes him from the supreme assembly, which is the natural sphere of his power."[63]

The constitutionalists thus defended the colonial constitution, under which the governor was accountable to the king and the Imperial Parliament for his executive decisions. If the colonial assemblies disapproved of those decisions, they could withhold their support, petition the king or Parliament, or seek the removal of officers having committed wrongful acts. Consistent with the modern concept of liberty, the constitutionalists believed that the executive branch should be autonomous, with the legislative branch acting in response to the governor's decisions.

Clearly, then, modern liberty took a different institutional form in the colonies than in the mother country. Nevertheless, the constitutionalists contended that the colonial constitution obeyed the overarching principles of mixed government. They defended it fiercely, believing that it alone could protect liberty, security, and property. The maintenance of a balance of executive and legislative power in relation to the monarchy, the aristocracy, and the democracy was essential, since it placed checks on potential abuses of state power. Barring a highly improbable conspiracy among the three orders of society and the two branches of government, such a thing could never take place.

For all these reasons, the constitutionalists likewise defended the legitimacy of the colonial institutions throughout the 1830s. That legitimacy, they said, did not depend on whether the institutions were appointed or elected, but on their mutual independence. Appointment was just as legitimate as election, for appointees represented different interests from elected officials. Conversely, an institution became illegitimate as soon as it attempted to upset the balance of power in its favour.

Constitutionalists in both Canadas defended the rights and powers of the assembly as well as the elective principle fundamental to its legitimacy. They held that the right of representation, "the best legacy of our fathers,"[64] was central to the British system. In a context in which political participation was itself a form of individual liberty, as well as the basic condition for liberty in general – since it prevented power from becoming concentrated – the constitutionalists acknowledged that the Constitutional Act of 1791 allowed for participation in a manner that did not violate but rather protected individual liberties: "We govern, and are governed by, ourselves. We have free institutions of our own, sufficient to secure to us every just right and privilege to which a BRITISH subject is entitled."[65] And even though they had not always controlled the Assembly in Lower Canada, the constitutionalists there could not conceive of living without it:

We will not, of course, submit to any other system of Government than a Constitutional one – that is a Government modelled upon that of the Mother Country ... We will not, you may be sure, submit to be again governed by a Governor and Legislative Council, however well appointed and enlightened they might be. It would be a system of government and legislation altogether adverse to our rights and liberties, as BRITISH subjects ... It is a species of oligarchical tyranny, as contrary to the principles of BRITISH freedom, as to the elective and democratical system which the Assembly is desirous of establishing amongst us ... We are entitled to the full and free exercise of a Constitutional Government.[66]

This said, the Lower Canadian constitutionalists denied being swayed "by idle apprehensions of a Government of the people and for the people." They demanded "a Government of 'the people,' truly represented, and not a French faction; the Government of an educated and independent race, attached to the principles of civil and religious liberty, and not that of an uninformed population, striving for domination, and seeking to perpetuate in America, the institution of feudal Europe."[67] They would oppose any attempt by the French Canadians to invoke the elective principle as a pretext for upsetting the balance of power in favour of the Assembly and thereby imposing their will on others: "We are no enemies to the elective principle in the abstract. Under proper restrictions it is the basis of our Constitution. But we are enemies to its indiscriminate application – we are enemies to an application which must of necessity subjugate an English minority to a French majority."[68] This is a clear statement of the difference between the republican concept of the people posited by the Patriotes (a monolithic fiction) and the modern concept of the people posited by the constitutionalists (a composite of different interests).

In the colonies – according to the constitutionalists – aspirations to democracy (people's power) were threatening the balance of power. In Lower Canada, this threat was especially great, for the Assembly was dominated by the Patriotes throughout the period – and they were alleged to be perverting institutions, abusing privileges, and threatening the constitutional order: "the efforts of the Assembly have been obviously directed, for several years past, to the attainment of power and influence, at the expense of the Crown, and in direct violation of the constitutional rights and privileges of the Legislative Councils."[69]

On this view the republicans' actions and demands, including those seeking to ensure the Assembly's ascendancy over the other branches of government, were illegitimate. First, the republicans asserted that the Assembly was not just one institution among others but the paramount institution, the only one predicated on the elective principle. The constitutionalists disagreed, arguing that the republicans were simply abusing the legitimacy of the colonial assemblies.

Second, the republicans' demands did not accommodate the different interests present in the colony. The Lower Canadian constitutionalists accused the Patriotes of having gerrymandered ridings to favour agrarian interests and their own party: "The majority in the House of Assembly is not a deliberative majority, acting for the good of the whole, and representing the great interests of the country, but a French majority, acting on national distinctions, (a line drawn by themselves,) and opposing all English interests."[70] The constitutionalists, it should be noted, were not concerned about gerrymandering in the abstract; rather, they inveighed against its use as a means of elevating the Patriotes' interests above their own. As the "progressive," commercial, British interests of the colony, they believed they should have a bigger voice in the Assembly.

Third, the constitutionalists accused the French Canadians and the Patriotes of perverting the Constitution. The French Canadians as a group were not independent but in thrall to demagogues (the Parti patriote): "The only duty of the free and independent electors was to register the decree of the demagogues."[71] Thom noted, for example, that candidates for the Assembly were not chosen by the voters but by the party.[72] Ironically, the constitutionalists generally refused to acknowledge that the Patriotes represented the views of the French Canadians until the outbreak of the rebellion.[73] This expedient allowed them to minimize the importance of the Assembly within the framework of the Constitutional Act. Yet after 1838 the constitutionalists deliberately conflated Patriotes and French Canadians with the goal of discrediting and more easily subordinating the whole French population.

In Upper Canada, the legislative councillors accused the Assembly of failing to respect the powers and privileges of the other political institutions. The Assembly, it was asserted, was prone to combating the power of the Legislative Council by illegitimately withholding support from important measures or by substituting its own bills at the last minute.[74]

The constitutionalists position was that both the assemblies and the legislative councils were legitimate and irreproachable as institutions within the framework of mixed government. The councils' independence from the other bodies was assured through lifetime appointments of their members without the possibility of recall. This put them beyond executive control.[75] In addition, the executive and legislative councils were alleged to be "substantially independent" (especially by the end of the 1830s). Thom, writing about Lower Canada, stated,

[the] Legislative Council of *thirty-six* members contains *two* Executive Councillors; an Executive Council of *eight* members contains *two* Legislative Councillors ... Of *thirty-six* members, only *ten* hold official situations. Since 1829 have been appointed *twenty-one* legislative councillors, unpolluted by the name of a single officer of the government. So unvarying a course of liberal policy has ... rendered the legislative council substantially independent.[76]

Ryerson, arguing similarly, cited a dispatch of 5 March 1834 from Governor Aylmer to Lord Stanley in which Aylmer stated that only seven of the eighteen councillors appointed since 1828 had ever held government positions (e.g., the chief justice and the bishop of Quebec City).

Ryerson thought it would be hard to imagine a more independent legislative council than Lower Canada's.[77] The Legislative Council of Upper Canada likewise rejected the charge of excessive overlap between the two colonial councils:

Much industry has been used to inculcate the persuasion that the Legislative Council is a body composed of persons solely connected with the Government by official station, and therefore unlikely to exercise an unbiased and independent judgment ... It is perfectly well known, and the public are daily witnesses of the fact, that the most important and critical measures before the Council, as well as the more ordinary business, have been for years past constantly discussed and disposed of in an assembly of gentlemen, among whom perhaps there was not one, and seldom more than two or three who held any public office of emolument, while the great majority of those usually present are in fact as independent of the Crown as they are independent from their circumstances and station in society.[78]

Not only were the legislative councillors independent, said the constitutionalists, but they acquitted themselves well in practice. They acted with diligence and sobriety. Unlike the republican assemblies, they abided by the Constitution and worked to preserve the balance of power.[79] They also took on the role of representing interest groups absent from the assemblies or whose rights had been violated by the republicans. In Lower Canada, the constitutionalists thought that the Legislative Council had proven particularly useful in the face of the Patriotes' illegitimate agitation. Since the opposition Assembly members had often been powerless to assert minority interests, the Legislative Council had stepped into the breach, rejecting bills it perceived as constituting an abuse of power. In this way, it provided virtual representation for anglophone commercial interests: "the English inhabitants of Lower Canada are as powerless in the house of assembly, as if they were disfranchised; and that, but for their virtual representation in the legislative council, they would be the legitimate slaves of the unbroken and unbending majority."[80] Meanwhile, the Legislative Council of Upper Canada assured the king that its conduct was beyond reproach: "Your Majesty should possess the satisfactory assurance that a Constitution, which in principle is well adapted to secure liberties and advance the prosperity of this Colony, has not in practice been abused by the Legislative Council."[81] It was on this view the legislative councillors who effectively preserved the constitutional equilibrium.

The legislative councils being independent,[82] they were ipso facto legitimate. The republicans claimed that only electivity would secure the councils such legitimacy; the constitutionalists countered that such a reform would destroy it. Elected councillors would represent the same interests as the Assembly, thereby losing their independence from it. The colony would become "a republican democracy,"[83] its constitution deformed, and liberty would be at an end. In Lower Canada, the Council was presented as the last rampart against the oppression of anglophones. The *Montreal Gazette* asserted that if the Legislative Council became an elected body, the British subjects of Lower Canada would become "the helots of democratic principles and elective institutions."[84]

In Upper Canada, the constitutionalists defended not only Legislative Council independence but also the royal prerogative (executive power), which, they contended, kept the Assembly from becoming tyrannical when captured by the republicans. Robinson approved a posteriori Francis Bond Head's decree of 1836 dissolving the Assembly. This decision, he said, had allowed for the election of a majority of loyal members, whose presence had then made it possible for the government to react firmly against Mackenzie's uprising.[85] In a similar vein, he objected to granting the Assembly the powers of either prorogation or dissolution, as was envisaged for the proposed Canadian union in June 1839. The delegation of this power would, he said, impinge on the royal prerogative, which "is part of the law and constitution of Parliament, as ancient and as well defined as any other. It is no usurpation of the Sovereign; and the people of Canada are not impatient under it."[86]

For the constitutionalists, in short, mixed government (including an independent, appointed legislative council) had to be safeguarded, for its disappearance would upset the balance among monarchy, aristocracy, and democracy – and concentration of power was the prelude to tyranny. Liberty would die on the vine. Contrariwise, if the sources of supreme power in the colony – the Imperial Parliament, the colonial constitution, and the institutions emanating from it – were given due respect, liberty would blossom.

MODERN LIBERTY AND COLONIAL STATUS

While the principles of modern liberty were identical in Great Britain and the Canadian colonies, the implications of parliamentary sovereignty in the context of mixed government differed. The mother country was governed by a local parliament, but the colonies were subjected to a faraway authority: the Imperial Parliament. No constitutionalist during the 1830s ever questioned this arrangement, and several accepted and defended it. The *Montreal Gazette*'s editor wrote,

It ought always to be borne in mind, that Colonies, whether conquered, or planted by settlers from the Mother Country, form no part of that country, but distinct

and dependent dominions, subject to the control of the Imperial Government and Parliament, and incapable of assuming any law, privilege or authority, except as these may be conferred upon them by the Parent State ... Let it be remembered that the Colonies have no right to go a single step beyond the authority conferred upon them by the parent state ... that they are, and of right ought to be, subordinate to, and dependent upon, the Imperial Crown and Parliament of Great Britain.[87]

This subordination of the colonies to the Imperial Parliament was not a limitation on liberty because the mother country and the colonies were "the same nation and people having but one interest, and knowing but one general object and design ... Let us, by every means in our power, cultivate the most friendly intercourse with our Colonies, and foster their growth in prosperity and wealth, in connexion with the interests of the Mother Country."[88] The constitutionalists had no trouble accepting the imperial framework because they saw themselves as subjects of the empire, not as second-class subjects. Moreover, this allegiance was voluntary: "there is no man who will not admit, that the question of remaining a dependency of the British Crown rests entirely with ourselves."[89]

And political participation was only one liberty among others. There was no necessary antithesis between enjoyment of liberty and subordination to an Imperial Parliament in which they had no voice, since subjects of the empire enjoyed the same rights wherever they lived: "it is, therefore, absolutely necessary that BRITISH subjects in the Colonies – no matter how far removed from the Mother Country – should know and feel that they belong to the same national family – *that their rights, liberties, and immunities are the same* – and that the prosperity of both solely depends upon the closeness and intimacy of their intercourse."[90] Empire and liberty were perfectly compatible – one defined the framework of the state, the other the nature of power relations between individuals and the state.

Finally, the empire was not merely compatible with liberty: it was the best guarantee of it. The Constitutional Association of Quebec argued that

among the advantages to be derived from this connexion, there is none which they more highly prize, than that *settled Government, Constitutional freedom and security of person and property,* which the experience of ages has proved preeminently to distinguish the British Constitution of Government, firmly supported as it has been, by the intelligence and wisdom of a public spirited and patriotic People.[91]

Likewise, the Solicitor General of Upper Canada, Christopher Hager-man, maintained that Parliament protected the liberty of subjects throughout the empire:

Every part and parcel of the British Constitution that was necessary for the practical purposes of good government in this Province had been extended to it. The British Constitution, consisting of King, Lords, and Commons, each branch possessing its peculiar rights, powers and prerogatives, and the laws and institutions of the Empire, were not confined to Great Britain and Ireland, – their influence reached throughout all the widely extended dominions of the British Empire, and shed their protecting power and blessings to the remotest portion of the realms and possessions of our Sovereign and the people of Upper Canada are as much protected by that Constitution as if they lived in an English County.[92]

The colonists' liberty was all the better protected in that political power was divided not only among the monarchic, aristocratic, and democratic powers, as defined in the Constitution of 1791, but also between the provincial legislature and the Imperial Parliament. The constitutionalists argued that the possibility of collusion among the six constituent powers of Parliament and the legislature in an attempt to oppress the Canadian population was very remote. Furthermore, the Imperial Parliament could arbitrate conflicts between these entities and maintain balance among them. This was essential in Lower Canada, where the Patriotes threatened to upset that balance.

The second major difference between the mother country and the colonies was that the colonies had a written constitution, taken in practice to be the embodiment of Parliament's will. A colonial law or power derived legitimacy not from being enacted by a local legislature but from its conformity to the Constitution.

Since Parliament – a representative institution providing for the expression and cooperation of different interests in society – was sovereign and because liberty consisted in the enjoyment of certain rights, the partisans of modern liberty could, unlike the republicans, countenance their inclusion in an empire. The particular makeup of the state was of no importance in itself; what mattered was that the state – whatever its form, size, or power – guaranteed protection of liberty, property, and security.

MODERN LIBERTY AND EXCLUSION

Modern liberty, like republican liberty, operated on the basis of certain principles of exclusion. To begin with, modern liberty was based on reason, so persons considered to lack reason – children, women, the incapacitated, and others – could not enjoy the same rights as other individuals. Second, the constitutionalists organized their institutions in such a way that they would protect liberty, property, and security. In this institutional context, the democratic representative assembly served as a check on the aristocratic and monarchic pretensions of the other institutions. But for the assembly to play its role, both the voters and the members had to have a material interest in the defence of these basic rights. The best way to achieve this was to disqualify from voting and holding office those persons who did not have such an interest. Owning property thus became a second prerequisite for political participation. Since most men in the colonies owned property, this exclusionary criterion was of limited relevance. But a third criterion – allegiance to the British culture, language, religion, customs, civil laws, and social institutions – was a highly relevant and oft-articulated principle of exclusion during the 1830s.

The early partisans of modern liberty, particularly Locke in his *Second Treatise of Civil Government* (1690), developed a rhetoric of what they termed "natural rights." As co-opted by the eighteenth-century republicans – notably Thomas Paine in his *Rights of Man* (1791) – this rhetoric came to be associated with the movement towards revolution, which, coupled with the rise of British nationalism,[93] in turn instigated a change in the rhetoric of modern liberty in the last third of the eighteenth century. By 1765, Blackstone was referring not to natural rights but to "absolute rights," while De Lolme preferred the term "birth-rights," but they amounted to the same thing:

Private liberty, according to the division of the English lawyers, consists, first, of the right of *property*, that is, of the right of enjoying exclusively the gifts of fortune, and all the various fruits of one's industry; secondly, of the right of *personal security;* thirdly, of the *locomotive faculty*, taking the word liberty in its more confined sense.

Each of these rights, say again the English lawyers, is inherent in the person of every Englishman; they are to him as an inheritance, and he cannot be deprived of them, but by virtue of a sentence passed according to the laws of the land. And, indeed, as this right of inheritance is expressed in English by one word (*birth-right*), the same as that which expresses the king's title to the crown, it has, in times of oppression, been often opposed to him as a right, doubtless of less extent, but of a sanction equal to that of his own.[94]

That liberty, property, and security were now being described as absolute rights or birth rights rather than natural rights did not change much in the British Empire, at least for the British. The republicans too, particularly the American rebels, spoke of both natural rights and, at times, birth rights. What distinguishes the modern and republican discourses on this point is what lies behind these terms – namely, the values they were thought to embody.

The Canadian constitutionalists preferred the rhetoric of birth rights to that of natural or inalienable rights.[95] These rights were as sacred as natural rights, but "birth-rights" suggested the possibility of denying certain rights on a hereditary basis – a possibility exploited by the constitutionalists.[96] To wit, in order to enjoy the inalienable rights guaranteed by English law, a person had to belong to the British nation.

In Upper Canada, subjects of American origin were, from 1814 to 1826, victims of exclusion at the behest of the London authorities. Following the War of 1812, Henry Bathurst, the Secretary of State for War and the Colonies, ordered a halt to the acquisition of land by subjects born in the United States until they had resided in the colony for seven years, this on the grounds that they were a threat to the state.[97] Loss of property rights meant loss of political rights, and thus these subjects saw their liberty curtailed. Though this policy was abolished in 1827, animosity between British and American colonists persisted until the rebellions. Moreover, the political struggle of the 1830s was at times interpreted by contemporary observers as a clash between British colonists (partisans of colonial institutions and modern liberty) and American colonists (partisans of republican institutions and liberty):

In this country unfortunately the settlement of American citizens has been too much permitted and encouraged. And thus in the bosom of this community there exists a treacherous foe[.] The vicinity of the arena for the discussion of extreme political fantasies infects this population, many of the natural born Subjects of the Crown are carried away by the plausibility of republican doctrines, and by the gratification to self conceit, which would be the consequence of every man being not merely a speculative but a practical statesman.[98]

This interpretation was reinforced by the fact that certain republican leaders (Marshall Spring Bidwell and Charles Duncombe, for example) were themselves American immigrants or direct descendants thereof.

Nevertheless, the Lower Canadian Patriote rebellion of 1837 forced the Upper Canadian constitutionalists to reinterpret the political crisis. They despised American republican institutions as much as ever, yet the rebellions had changed the game. Mackenzie's insurrection had been readily put down with the help of militia and volunteers. The looming threat had been contained, the loyalty of Upper Canadians convincingly demonstrated. Furthermore, the American government's official neutrality on the conflict had made it difficult to perceive the American colonists as a fifth column. It was the Patriote rebellion that surprised and frightened the Upper Canadian constitutionalists, who concluded that the French Canadians and their aspirations to independence posed the greatest threat to the empire. If these aspirations were to come to fruition, Upper Canada would be cut off geographically from the mother country.

The newly perceived French Canadian threat threw into perspective the differences between American and British Upper Canadians. All of a sudden, the ethnic kinship between the two groups was rediscovered. Were they not all originally from the mother country? Were they not all brothers?

Springing from a common origin, having a common language, and actuated by the same enterprising spirit, their relations in peace are so intimately blended, that if war should ever come it must be attended with unusual calamities. I believe that at least the present generation are not likely to see the time when the government of the United States, or the people of most intelligence and property in that country, will desire to see their peace with England interrupted.[99]

The unity of the two peoples, more so than institutions and values, was now the primary concern of Upper Canadians. They quickly recast the conflict in ethnic terms as one between the Anglo-American people and the "[French] Canadian nation," as James Craig had called it in 1810. There was nothing original about this interpretation, of course, for the Lower Canadian constitutionalists had been harping on it for years. The January 1836 address of the Constitutional Association of Montreal to the inhabitants of British America stated that "the same ardour for improvement ... distinguishes their race throughout the North American continent."[100] The principle of exclusion adopted by the Lower Canadian constitutionalists had now found favour across the colonial border.

To justify the exclusion of the French Canadians, the constitutionalists resorted to a three-step argument. First, they presented the people of British North America as forming a whole that was in turn a fraction of the imperial citizenry. The British people of North America spoke English and were loyal to the empire. They stood for liberty, security, property, and the British institutions. Ethnicity and loyalty went hand in hand. Robinson wrote,

[Upper Canadians] are living in the enjoyment of the English law, both civil and criminal, administered in the same manner as in England. The English language is universally spoken; and recent events have shown that there is among the people generally a sound feeling of attachment to their constitution and government, a strong sense of duty to their Sovereign, and a determination to resist any danger that seems to threaten their connection with the British Crown.[101]

Second, they imagined an Anglo-American "race" characterized by its entrepreneurial spirit and industriousness – a race to which the French Canadians did not belong. The United States, after all, had known equally great success, albeit in spite of the Americans' political choices:[102] its development was due, rather, to the the their membership in the English race and to the solidarity that existed between Britain and America.[103] (Robinson asserted that the major infrastructure projects in the United States had been financed by the British and built by the Irish.) In this way, ethnicity ("race") replaced political values – that is, different conceptions of liberty – as an inclusionary criterion in Upper Canada. But by the same token it became an exclusionary criterion: the French Canadians were suddenly the real menace.

As mentioned, this approach had appeared earlier in Lower Canada, especially among Montreal constitutionalists. The problem was said to be caused by the fact that "the majority of the inhabitants are alien in their origin, habits, laws, language, and institutions from those of the nation at large; and that no attempt has before been made to render them uniform with those of the Parent State."[104] According to the Constitutional Association of Montreal, the struggle in Lower Canada was "between feudalism and rational liberty – domination and equal rights – French-Canadian *nationalite* and the spirit of universal liberty."[105] The institutional avatars of this ethnic conflict were to be found in the House of Assembly and the Legislative Council. The constitutionalists argued that the French Canadians wanted to impose their domination and accede to independence – and in this they were right. Where they erred was in asserting that independence would necessarily be based "on principles of national distinctions."[106]

The constitutionalists were simply incapable of making a distinction between ethnic nationalism and republicanism. They believed that all the reformers were alike in basing their proposed reforms on ethnically exclusionary criteria. In support of this view, and in an attempt to prove that the French Canadians were closing ethnic ranks, they confounded a scattered few nationalist texts with the republican discourse of the Patriotes. Thom and Ryerson, for example, both quoted an incendiary essay published in *La Minerve* on 16 February 1832 that stated,

There exist here two parties entirely opposed in their interests and customs, the Canadiens and the English. The first, born French, have those habits and character, and inherited from their fathers a hatred for the English who, in turn, seeing in them the sons of France, detest them. These two parties can never come together, and will not always remain at peace; it is a poor amalgam of interests, customs, languages and religion, which sooner or later will lead to a collision. Many believe in the possibility of a revolution but think it far off; I think it will not be long in coming ... The greatest misfortune for the politician, he says, is to obey a foreign power; no humiliation, no torment of the heart can compare to that.[107]

Thom was certainly right to read ethnic exclusion into this quote; the problem is that it was not representative of Patriote thinking (and was disclaimed by the paper's editor four days later). For the constitutionalists, all the reformers could only be thinking along ethnic lines. It was an understandable mistake, one made later even by such historians as Maurice Séguin, who regarded the editorials of the nationalist Étienne Parent as representative of the Patriotes' discourse.[108]

Ethnicizing the political struggle of Lower Canada was doubly expedient to the constitutionalists. On the one hand, they could elide discussion of republicanism by putting the emphasis on nationalism;[109] on the other, they could argue that ethnic affinity explained why Lower Canada was the only truly disloyal colony. An effort was therefore put into depicting the French Canadians as the antithesis of the British North Americans. They were disloyal. Their disloyalty threatened the colonies' ties to the empire. And they placed limits on British immigration to achieve their disloyal ends. In so doing, they unjustly deprived the imperial race of its due since "every British subject inherits a title to a share of the lands [in Lower Canada]."[110] The French Canadians' relative lack of education explained the ease with which their leaders dominated and manipulated them, their overall lack of political sense. In a phrase, they were "[an] ignorant, harmless, idle, and superstitious people."[111]

To the constitutionalists, the French Canadians were contemptibly frugal, preferring subsistence agriculture to commerce. Moreover, they stood for an old feudal structure and outdated laws (the seigneurial system, described as a "barbarous code"[112]) that were seen to be hampering the province's development. Even worse, they obstinately refused to encourage infrastructure development.[113] The perceived ethnic conflict was, in short, bound up with a perceived economic conflict. Both Lower Canada and Upper Canada were allegedly harmed as a result, so much so that the Upper Canadian elite envisaged a scheme to geographically circumvent their laggard neighbours: "The anti-commercial proceedings of the French faction, my lord, have driven the inhabitants of Upper

Canada to contemplate a scheme, which, if successful, must be fatal to the 'commercial classes' of Lower Canada. Our brethren, my lord, have been compelled to think seriously of making New York the sea-port of Upper Canada."[114]

It need hardly be stressed that this image of the French Canadians was neither accurate nor innocent. It was simply a device with which the constitutionalists attempted to marginalize their political adversaries. Not that they admitted to wishing to deprive anyone of his rights or liberty; it was that the French Canadians themselves were incapable of being free: "[French Canadians] are unfit to sustain their own just rights and interests, and are necessarily totally unqualified to be entrusted with the rights and interests of others."[115] The French Canadians were, on this view, inimical to the liberty of others.[116] They neither understood nor subscribed to the concept of the separation of powers in a mixed government. Lacking an elementary grasp of the concept of liberty, they had commandeered the colony's representative institutions for nationalistic purposes.

According to the colonial constitutionalists, language was central to the Lower Canadian conflict: "a social union of two races of different languages ... is impossible."[117] Therefore, the French Canadians had to be assimilated as quickly as possible. Peter McGill, the president of the Constitutional Association of Montreal, declared after the rebellion of 1837 that "the period had arrived when some determinate course of action should be adopted for securing the rights of the British inhabitants of Lower Canada – that this Province should be made a British Province in fact as well as in name."[118] The British nation was the only one entitled to exist in North America.[119] The French Canadians had to be assimilated to the English language, for only this would allow them to cast off their cultural heritage and take on English values and lifeways. The ensuing cultural uniformity would inevitably be beneficial:

Whatever may be the nature and principle of the social institutions of a nation, they must be rendered uniform throughout, otherwise the motley superstructure will soon fall to the ground, and be crumbled into ashes. There is no other method of rendering the bond of union binding upon all parties, or of cementing those ties by which alone a whole people can be actuated by one general and absorbing sentiment.[120]

Linguistic assimilation would have to be accompanied by education. By assimilating and receiving a better education, the French Canadians would come to understand their true interests and acquire a new appreciation for the British institutions that guaranteed their rational liberty.

In this way, the French Canadians' loyalty would be secured: "if it was the object of GREAT BRITAIN to perpetuate her connexion with those Provinces, she must unite them into one people and government, having the same institutions, laws and language, as well as an identity of rights and liberties with the inhabitants of the Parent State in as far as they could be extended to our Colonial possessions."[121] Assimilation would serve the interests of all concerned. Lord Durham had only to bend an ear in 1838 to discover the main conclusion of his report.

6

Citizens, to Arms!
The Rebellions of 1837–1838

AFTER 1828, the political situation in the Canadas degenerated. Historians have traditionally interpreted the crisis of the 1830s as the crystallization of an opposition between conservatives and liberals, between partisans of the status quo and promoters of reform, between retrograde and progressive forces (though which were which depends on the observer). To this political clash, historians of Lower Canada have added an ethnic one: British versus French Canadians.[1] While ethnicity has been given less emphasis in accounts of Upper Canada, the presence of Americans in the rebel camp has not gone unnoticed. Historians such as Donald Creighton have explained the crisis as a confrontation between commercialism and agriculturalism while Fernand Ouellet, Stanley Bréhaut Ryerson, and others have construed it as a social class struggle, with national allegiance an extra factor in Lower Canada.[2] Gérald Bernier and Daniel Salée have minimized the importance of the national question in Lower Canada, emphasizing the transition from a feudal or precapitalist mode of production to a capitalist mode.[3] Richard Larue has presented the Patriote/Tory standoff as an identity crisis based on questions of allegiance and origin, while David Mills has studied the question of loyalty in Upper Canada.[4] Allan Greer has presented the rebellions as a struggle around two different visions of democracy, parliamentary and plebeian.[5]

One thing is certain: the Canadian rebellions were not (as viewed through the lens of ideology) groundbreaking in the Atlantic context. The political program of the Patriotes and the radicals positioned them firmly within the republican tradition. Republicanism came comparatively late to the Canadas with respect to the better-known experiences of the United States, the United Provinces, France, Ireland, and the rest of continental Europe. Nevertheless, a perfectly recognizable variant of this tradition took its place in Canadian history during the era 1828–38.[6]

Likewise, constitutionalism sprang from the Enlightenment concept of liberty developed and first put into practice in Great Britain. The Canadian experience thus more closely resembles the Country / Court conflict of eighteenth-century Britain and America (as described by Pocock) than it does the revolutions of Europe and South America, which for the most part pitted revolutionaries against an arbitrary power. And the Canadians of the time could perceive these parallels. John Strachan implicitly compared the colonial struggle of the 1830s to the opposition between Whigs and Radicals in Britain at the time of the French Revolution: "in the Colonies there are only two classes of Politicians[:] Whigs and Radicals."[7] Need it be recalled that Edmund Burke never considered himself anything but a Whig?

What I posit, then, is that the Canadian crisis of the 1830s and its culmination in the rebellions can in part be explained by ideological considerations. The conflict grew up around two irreconcilable visions of the ideal society and the legitimate state. These visions were in turn rooted in different conceptions of liberty and the natural rights and responsibilities of the individual – vis-à-vis himself, society, and the state. The ultimate outcome was the incapacity of the two sides to agree upon the form that the political institutions of the colonies should take.

There was, to be sure, nothing excessive about the reformers' demands at the outset; these were perfectly compatible with British practice and could have been granted without ado by the imperial government. Republican demands were another matter: absent a revolution, they could not be accommodated. When Papineau, the Nelson brothers, Bidwell, Mackenzie, and the other reformers adopted the republican rhetoric of liberty, they transformed a practical problem – what was the best mechanism for preserving harmony between the legislative and executive branches of government? – into a political problem concerning the legitimacy of the colonial constitution. In so doing, they transformed a solvable problem into an insoluble one.

With the clash of these two visions, institutional reform began to slip out of reach. What was fair and legitimate to one side looked immoral and unjust to the other. It is hard to imagine the two groups seeing eye to eye on anything at all under such circumstances. Tensions mounted and violence became increasingly predictable – especially since the more moderate reformers, the ones like Étienne Parent and Robert Baldwin who accepted the modern framework, found themselves increasingly marginalized on the political scene.

All this said, the clash of ideologies fails to account fully for the extraparliamentary conflict of 1837–38. The two conceptions of liberty, after all, had at times joined forces against a common foe; consider the collaboration between the *anglomanes* and the *américanistes* in the initial months of the French Revolution. And there was no reason why a state based on modern ideals such as the British Empire could not accommodate a republican-styled opposition. In contemporaneous Great Britain, Joseph Hume and John Arthur Roebuck carried on an equally radical (republican) discourse, yet neither was persecuted because they posed no threat to the state. The republicans in the colonies, Lower Canada especially, were much stronger – strong enough to threaten the foundations of the colonial state. It was this threat that made the situation politically explosive.

TOWARDS AN IMPASSE

In Lower Canada, the Patriotes controlled the House of Assembly throughout the decade while the constitutionalists dominated the Legislative Council. Facing each other were two conceptions of liberty, two sets of rules causing a head-on confrontation between institutions that were supposed to collaborate. The whole situation was untenable, and the resulting paralysis was leading towards rebellion.

Decades before, the opposition between these two conceptions of liberty had already become apparent. With the Constitutional Act of 1791, the William Pitt government had attempted to force the different interests present in the colonies to compromise by imposing a mixed government upon them, but this approach had merely institutionalized the existing social antagonisms. Lower Canadian politics evolved in a manner that pitted the elected Assembly, representing the interests of a majority-French farming population, against the appointed Legislative Council, representing a majority-English commercial elite. The economic and social nature of this clash, and its crystallization in the colony's political institutions, could not have been better conceived to hasten the confrontation between the two conceptions of liberty.

By the late 1820s, the identification of political institutions with social groups and conceptions of liberty was almost complete. The Assembly had become a republican institution, the Council an elitist one dedicated to defending the constitutional order. Commissioners Lord Gosford, Charles Grey, and George Gipps, in their 1835–36 inquiry into the political situation in Lower Canada, found these facts to be self-evident.[8]

The political situation in Upper Canada was less problematic, for the radicals did not control any institution (except the House of Assembly from 1834 to 1836).[9] They could and did make noise on the political scene, but they posed no threat to the state. Despite their different levels of strength, however, both groups derived from the same intellectual sources.

Ironically, the reformers adopted republican rhetoric at a time when the British government was becoming more conciliatory.[10] The timing could scarcely have been worse. From 1828 on, and especially with the Whig victory of 1830, the British government genuinely sought to make substantial political reforms in response to the colonial reformers' demands. London's first sign of openness was the formation, in 1828, of a select committee of the Commons on the Canadian question. The committee tabled a report favourable to the colonists' demands on 22 July of that year. Around the same time, the government recalled unpopular governors Maitland (Upper Canada) and Dalhousie (Lower Canada). On 29 September, Sir George Murray, the minister for the colonies, cautioned the new administrator for Lower Canada, James Kempt, that a conciliatory approach was the order of the day. He enjoined him to convey to the province's two councils "the necessity of cultivating a spirit of conciliation towards the House of Assembly and of terminating, if possible, those dissensions with which the province has been too long agitated."[11] This injunction set the tone of imperial policy on Canada for nearly a decade.

Another Commons committee met six years later to determine what had become of the proposed reforms. The committee acknowledged that, while not all the proposals had been taken up, "a most earnest anxiety has existed on the part of the Home government to carry into execution the suggestions of the Select Committee of 1828 ... and Your Committee have observed with much satisfaction, that in several important particulars their endeavours have been completely successful."[12] While the Patriotes' discontent had only increased, Britain still believed it could find common ground. The Tory government of Robert Peel (November 1834–April 1835) planned to send a commission of inquiry headed by Lord Aberdeen,[13] but this initiative was aborted when the Peel government fell.

Lord Melbourne's Whig government, replacing Peel, decided to follow an analogous policy and strike a new commission to inquire into the affairs of Lower Canada. The role of commissioners Gosford, Grey, and Gipps was twofold. Lord Glenelg, secretary of the Colonial Office, asked them on the one hand to report on the implementation of the proposed reforms – he believed, in fact, that "His Majesty [had] spontaneously advanced considerably beyond the limits recommended by [the] authors"[14] – and on the other to propose additional reforms that might serve to resolve the conflict between the government and the Assembly. The commissioners were put on notice: "You proceed to Lower Canada on a mission of conciliation and peace."[15]

In London, from 1828 to 1837, successive administrations drew on the conclusions of the "Report from the Select Committee on the Civil Government of Canada" of 1828 to effect reforms in the hope of resolving the problems poisoning Canadian politics once and for all. The changes made were diverse, and I shall limit the discussion here to reforms concerning political institutions, since this was the core problem that sparked the 1837 uprisings. In response to the colonists' complaint of collusion between the judicial and executive branches, Lord Goderich, the secretary of the Colonial Office in the early 1830s, implemented one of the recommended reforms when he announced (in a dispatch of 8 February 1831 to Matthew Aylmer, governor of Lower Canada) that the government would no longer appoint judges to the Legislative Council. Henceforth only the chief justice would be allowed, since his advice was at times needed.

Next, the government dealt with the control of colonial revenues, one of the oldest bones of contention between the Assembly and the governor of Lower Canada. The 1828 report had proposed to give the assemblies control of these revenues. In 1831, the government finally asked Parliament to pass this reform and the result was the passage, on 22 September, of the Canadian Revenue Control Act.[16] The Crown thereby gave the colonial assemblies control over revenues belonging to it, in the spirit of the Act to Establish a Fund towards further Defraying the Charges of the Administration of Justice and Support of the Civil Government within the Province of Quebec in America of 1774.[17] However, contrary to the proposal of 1828, the government did not require the prior adoption of a civil list – the minister simply trusted the Assembly to provide for the independent operation of the executive and judicial branches. The government in London having made judges independent of the executive branch, it hoped that the Assembly would follow suit and make them independent of the legislature.

Finally, the 1828 report had proposed to make the legislative councils more independent by altering their composition. While the British government never considered abolishing the appointment process, it did attempt to make appointments in a manner that established a distinction between the legislative council and the executive branch. After 1828, the number of legislative councillors holding other positions in government declined substantially in both Canadas.[18] The councillors indeed became more independent from the executive, as Robinson, Ryerson, and Thom boasted they had. In 1834, the governor of Lower Canada, Matthew Aylmer, maintained that all councillors named after 1828 were prosperous enough that none had to depend on the executive.[19] Even the Patriote Augustin-Norbert Morin had to admit, when testifying before the Commons committee on Lower Canada on 12 May 1834, that independence had in fact been achieved.[20] In Upper Canada, according to an analysis by André Garon, only four of the nineteen councillors named after 1829 held another government position.[21] While there was still some overlap, it was much less than before.

The authorities also gave consideration to the French Canadians' complaints of exclusion.[22] The government wanted to correct this injustice and give them a greater share of Council seats. It did not at all share the ethnically exclusionary criteria adopted by the Lower Canadian constitutionalists at that time. The breakdown of appointments to the Legislative Council is particularly enlightening as to the authorities' thinking on this question.

While they had, in 1792, decided to appoint an equal number of English- and French-speaking councillors, the balance between the two linguistic communities had not always been maintained. In particular, Dalhousie's administration (1820–28) had been marked by efforts to exclude French Canadians from power. But this trend was reversed in the next decade. Lord Goderich stated in a dispatch to Aylmer on 7 July 1831 that "if it can be shewn, that the patronage of the Crown has been exercised upon any narrow and exclusive maxims, they cannot be too entirely disavowed and abandoned."[23] In 1835, Lord Glenelg even urged Governor Gosford to engage in some form of affirmative action on the French Canadians' behalf:

Between persons of equal or not very dissimilar pretensions, it may be fit that the choice should be made in such a manner as in some degree to satisfy the claims which the French inhabitants may reasonably urge to be placed in the enjoyment of an equal share of the Royal favour. There are occasions also on which the increased satisfaction of the public at large with an appointment, might amply atone for some inferiority in the qualifications of the persons selected.[24]

This expressed intent to put an end to official French Canadian exclusion (in the hope of ending the political crisis) was in fact put into practice, even up to the eve of the rebellions. In August 1837, Lord Gosford appointed ten members to the Council, including seven French

Canadians (Table 6.1),[25] resulting in parity between the two linguistic groups (Table 6.2). French-language councillors actually formed a deliberating majority on the Council at the end of 1837.

Not only did the government appoint more French speakers, it appointed more reformers. In March 1837, Glenelg directed Gosford to expand "the Legislative Council ... to include a sizable number of members 'holding opinions, in general, with those of the majority, but not concurring in their extreme demands.'"[26]

The British government also tried to appoint more reformers (some but not all French Canadian) to the Executive Council in the 1830s. The earlier administration of Matthew Aylmer had, in October 1830, recommended the appointment of five executive councillors including three reformers: Papineau, Neilson, and Mondelet.[27] The first two of these had refused, a fact for which Aylmer declined responsibility in 1834. He also, in a dispatch to Lord Aberdeen of 18 March 1834, rebutted the charge included in the Ninety-Two Resolutions to the effect that French Canadians were being excluded from government employment. He stated that since October 1830, 80 out of 142 paid positions, 295 out of 580 unpaid positions, and 151 out of 330 "commissions for rulings on small cases" had gone to French Canadians.[28]

All these conciliatory efforts were, however, destined for failure, whether London knew it or not. No reform within the bounds of modern liberty could satisfy the republicans, and the imperial authorities were not going to step outside those bounds. The reformers' adoption of republican discourse had certainly placed their demands on a firmer footing but, by the same token, it had put the prospect of reform out of reach. The British government and the colonial councils would never accede to republican demands: to do so would be to countenance the destruction of their form of government and, with it, the conception of liberty on which it rested.

Neither the Canadian Revenue Control Act of 1831 nor the French Canadian appointments resolved the conflicts. One pernicious problem created by the act was how it led to executive and judicial dependence on the assemblies. London had hoped that the assemblies would respond in equally conciliatory fashion by adopting a long-term civil list, giving the executive and judicial branches the independence necessary to fulfill their constitutionally mandated role of protecting liberty in the colonies. While the Upper Canadian Assembly acceded to this request (which did not prevent the radicals from complaining of the executive's financial independence[29]), the Lower Canadian Assembly continued to oppose it. The Patriotes simply did not regard independent executive and judicial power as a positive thing. Papineau's outrage was unsurprising: "Have

Table 6.1
Appointments to the Legislative Council of Lower Canada, 1828–1837

Period	Number of appointments	Anglophones		Francophones	
1792	14	7	50%	7	50%
1793–1811	19	14	74%	5	26%
1812–1819	22	9	41%	13	59%
1820–1828	7	6	86%	1	14%
1828–1837	33	12	36%	21	64%
Total	95	48	51%	47	49%

Table 6.2
Composition of the Legislative Council of Lower Canada, 1828–1838

Date	Number of councillors	Anglophones		Francophones	
31 December 1827	23	18	78%	5	22%
31 December 1832	36	23	64%	13	36%
31 December 1836	34	21	62%	13	38%
31 December 1837	39	21	54%	18	46%
Councillors active in October 1837*	31 (of 40)	13	42%	18	58%

*"Despatch from the Earl of Gosford to Lord Glenelg," 19 October 1837, BPP-C-C, 9:72.

there ever been any other English colonies where the authorities have stumbled so badly as to demand a civil list for the lifetime of the King[?]"[30] Twelve of the Ninety-Two Resolutions specifically dealt with this issue and the need for the Assembly to control all provincial revenues.[31] Thus, the well-intentioned Canadian Revenue Control Act had the unintended effect of giving the Patriotes a lever over the other branches of government – one they proceeded to use, withholding monies from the other two branches as necessary to apply pressure to their adversaries. It need hardly be added that the resulting dissension within the Lower Canadian polity was not salutary.

Similarly, the British government thought that by making appointments less partisan it would satisfy the reformers and dispel the political crisis. But no appointment would have been enough to satisfy the republicans. What was at stake was not power but its source of legitimacy – either the people or Parliament. The British authorities could not satisfy the republicans because their reasoning was contained within the framework of (British) parliamentary sovereignty, constitutional mixed government, and the separation of powers.[32] Parliament, in this conception, was the source of legitimate power in the colony. The House of Assembly of Lower Canada was just a creature of Parliament, the colonists were mere subjects; their will was not law. But it was precisely these constitutional principles that the republican-dominated Assembly rejected. In the resulting atmosphere of heightened tension, Lord Gosford warned the Assembly that it would be the author of its own misfortune if Parliament was forced to intervene in the Lower Canadian crisis.[33]

There was simply no way for the two camps to reach an accommodation. London's empire was modern through and through, and could not be reconceived as something else. The radicals rejected any reform that took the modern framework for granted, since it gave primacy to the executive. For them, reform worthy of the name would have to demolish the foundations of mixed government and erect a republic in its place. By the time the Whigs came to power in 1830, it was too late to avert the impending conflict.

Not only did the British government fail to appease the republicans, but its attempts to do so displeased colonial constitutionalists for whom any concession was an attack on liberty. They understood that the republicans' demands were incompatible with the British constitution and feared that London would sacrifice mixed government to achieve peace – hence their vehement denunciations of British policy. They too felt that London shared responsibility for the colonial crisis: "The evils which oppress us have been aggravated by the various and temporising policy of successive administrations ... The tendency of their measures has been to compromise the dignity of the Home Government and to confer a sanction upon the pretensions by which our interests are assailed."[34]

Adam Thom was one opponent of conciliation who based his argument on a perceived threat to modern liberty. Any concession to the republicans, he asserted, only accentuated that threat. He took the additional step of equating republicans with French Canadians, and both with foreigners. This group, he argued, was "petted ... at the expense not merely of abstract principles but of the *natural rights* and the covenanted claims of His Majesty's English subjects."[35] Such concessions ineluctably led to the destruction of the English form of government. Gosford's concessions were immoral, implying that the government was acting as if "the 'constitution' ... vests all power, executive, judicial and legislative, in the anti-British hands of 'its natives.'"[36] The ultimate outcome was to consecrate the domination of the republicans over the constitutionalists. It signified "that the French majority shall be everything and the English minority nothing"[37] – in other words, the advent of tyranny. At stake for Thom was the victory of liberty (the basic rights of subjects) over democracy (the will of the majority), and democracy was winning. A final point he made was that any attempt at conciliation would impair trade and the development of the colony. All things considered, a firm stance was the only answer to republican agitation.

But, to repeat, if an extraparliamentary clash was becoming increasingly unavoidable in Lower Canada, it was not largely the fault of imperial intransigence, nor republican bad faith for that matter. It was because the clash between two visions of society and public order paralyzed the colonial state and made conciliation illusory. Under these conditions, Thom was correct to point out that "the concessions, which have been made to the self-constituted Assembly, have not only aggravated the grievances of its constitutional opponents but have rendered impracticable any adequate remedy for those grievances."[38]

CITIZENS, TO ARMS!

As the conflict worsened, the two camps struggled with increasing intensity to split the Gordian knot. Violence became a conceivable solution, a desirable one, and ultimately a probable one – a self-fulfilling prophecy. The two camps both came to consider themselves justified, as perceived victims of tyranny, in calling for a violent response. For the republicans, the colonial elite had turned into an oligarchy (breakdown of the aristocratic principle) who disrespected the sovereign people; for the constitutionalists, the republicans posed a threat to life, liberty, and property since they opposed mixed government.

As the rebellions drew nearer, the republicans made people's rights the ultimate argument for their demands, one that legitimized revolt.[39] At that point, the republicans found it necessary to join forces to defend their rights. Since the British government was betraying the social contract by flouting the popular will, the people were entitled to use force in response.[40]

The republicans began early in the decade to articulate the option of violence. A November 1832 *La Minerve* article proffered thinly veiled threats: "The people shall attempt to obtain redress of their grievances, by the constitutional means they have used, albeit with little success until now; and if these means do not succeed they will see what is to be done next."[41] The following year, Mackenzie warned the British authorities that the challenge they were facing was just as significant as the one the American Revolution had posed to George III and his prime minister

Lord North.[42] The threat inherent in this allusion to that "noble era in the annals of British freedom"[43] – a relatively recent defeat sustained by Great Britain – could hardly be missed. It was a canny allusion, implying the threat of violence without unmistakably brandishing it (as an allusion to the bloody French Revolution would have).

As positions hardened, the threat to the established order edged out into the open. By 1836–37 the appeal to the American example was explicitly aimed at inciting revolt. If Parliament could not accept the colonists' demands, that was a difficulty that was "great, but ... not new ... not insurmountable. This omnipotent parliament was gloriously defeated by the Americans."[44] The republicans' threats were directed not only at the imperial authorities but also at the constitutionalists who sided with them. Papineau warned that "the enemies of the people have more to fear and to suffer from the discontents of the people, than to gain by the corruptions of the Government."[45]

Starting in 1836 in Upper Canada and in May 1837 in Lower Canada, the opposition went extraparliamentary. In Lower Canada, where the future of British North America was at stake, public assemblies followed one another in rapid succession during the spring, summer, and autumn of 1837. The struggle took on a more popular cast. Appeals to economic pressure (boycotts of imported products) and acts of civil disobedience proliferated. Lord Gosford banned these assemblies in July, but it was too late: his authority had evaporated. Papineau ridiculed the governor's proclamation. Since it did not emanate from the people, it could not have the force of law: "These proclamations have no force. It is only when something is prohibited with the sanction of the House of Assembly that the prohibition has the force of law. Proclamations such as the governor's are but scraps of paper."[46]

On the eve of the rebellion, the threats being expressed were as overt as they could be: "After seventy-seven years of English domination, we are led to view our country as being in a state of misery as compared with the flourishing republics which had the wisdom to shake off the yoke of the monarchy."[47] Even more direct was the address of the Assembly of the Six Counties:

The wise and immortal drafters of the AMERICAN DECLARATION OF INDEPEN-DENCE set down in that document the tenets upon which alone the rights of man are based, and called for and propitiously established the institutions and the form of government which alone can guarantee in perpetuity the prosperity and the social accord of the inhabitants of this continent, whose education and customs, tied to the circumstances of their colonization, demand a system of government entirely dependent on the people and directly accountable to it.[48]

And for anyone who had not understood that the time for delay had passed, the first resolution of the Assembly of the Six Counties was a translation of the American Declaration of Independence written by Thomas Jefferson:

That following the example of the sages and Heroes of 1779 [sic], we hold these truths to be self-evident, that all Men are created equal; that they are endowed by their Creator with certain unalienable Rights; that among these are Life, Liberty, and the pursuit of Happiness; that to secure these Rights, Governments are instituted among Men, deriving their just Powers from the Consent of the Governed; that whenever any Form of Government becomes destructive of these Ends, it is the Right of the People to alter or abolish it, and to institute new Government, laying its Foundation on such Principles, and organizing its Powers in such Form, as to them shall seem most likely to effect their Safety and Happiness.[49]

During this same assembly, Wolfred Nelson declared that "the time has come; I advise you to put aside all your tin plates and spoons, in order to melt them down and make bullets out of them."[50] Dr Cyrille-Hector Côté added, "The time for speeches is past – what we must now send our enemies is lead."[51] Not everyone was in such a hurry to take up arms. Papineau did state in May 1837 that "the time of trials has arrived," but his remark did not mean he approved of the rebellion that November – he did not.[52] Nevertheless, by the fall, the Lower Canadian republicans knew they were headed for armed conflict. Their demands could not be fulfilled any other way. While the actual uprising may not have been premeditated (no more than the formation of the French National Assembly in June 1789), it was increasingly foreseeable.

The situation was similar in Upper Canada, although most of the calls to arms issued from Mackenzie alone. In July 1837, he asserted that the colony was on the verge of revolution:

Canadians! It has been said that we are on the verge of a revolution. We are in the midst of one; a bloodless one, I hope, but a revolution to which all those which have been will be counted mere child's play. Calm as society may seem to a superficial spectator, I know that it is moved to its very foundations, and is in universal agitation ... The question today is not between one reigning family and another, between one people and another, between one form of government and another, but a question between privilege and equal rights, between law sanctioned, law fenced in privilege, age consecrated privilege, and a hitherto unheard of power, a new power just started from the darkness in which it has slumbered since creation day, THE POWER OF HONEST INDUSTRY ... The contest is now between the privileged and the unprivileged, and a terrible one it is. The slave snaps his fetters, the peasant feels an unwonted strength nerve in his arm, the *people* rise in stern and awful majesty, and demand in strange tone their ever despised and hitherto denied rights.[53]

In November, he distributed a broadside titled "Independence" that advocated rebellion.[54]

For moral and intellectual justification, the republicans turned to Rousseau's version of the social contract. The clauses of that contract by which colonial political life should be governed were, in capsule, as follows: "To choose one's representatives, to see no portion of their laws [repealed], no new law given, no part of their property taken away, without the consent expressed by their delegates, such were the privileges acquired by our fathers, such are the birthrights, the inalienable rights of their children." Note that the right to political participation was, for the republicans, the most basic natural right. All the others, including property, were contingent rights, predicated on the people's will. As long as the social contract was respected, the people could continue to obey the established authority: "The observance of these rights is the condition of the social pact, which alone binds subjects to the authority. It is entitled to obedience only in so far as it does not stray from these principles." Citizens were relieved of this duty of obedience if the authorities violated the contract; more than that, such a violation created a new duty: "resistance to oppression, the duty of the subject, the duty of the fathers who did not intend for their progeny to be slaves." Papineau explained that once the social contract was broken, only the resort to sufficient force would allow the empire to keep its colonies: "If England treats us as British subjects must be treated, it is entitled to our submission and our recognition: if it does not, it could command obedience. It is strong but it will never be entitled to our recognition, and to our submission for only as long as it remains strong."[55] Allegiance to the empire could only be willing, never coerced:[56] Rousseau would not have put it any differently.

The people, being sovereign, could legitimately rise up against a power that flouted their will as expressed by the legitimate legislative power. The idea of colonial oppression, that the people were unjustly subjected to a foreign power, pervades colonial republican writings of the period. Rebellion was justified because the British government had violated the contract binding the colonies to the empire. The constitutionalists, not the republicans, shouldered the blame: it was they who should be held to account. From 1834 to 1837, this rhetoric of the broken, despised, demolished social contract was omnipresent. Nearly all the public assemblies of 1837 mentioned this betrayal and accused the British government of being the source of the oppression. In June 1837, the Assembly of Sainte-Scholastique adopted a resolution affirming that the Russell Resolutions reflected "the considered approval [by London] of the corrupt, oppressive system whose discontinuation we were falsely led to expect." The Russell Resolutions sought to "gradually and systematically overturn the liberties, rights, institutions, and *the very existence of the People of this Province.*"[57] The people felt threatened and had to act.

Despite these direct threats, the constitutionalists did not believe a republican revolt was possible and in this they singularly underestimated their adversaries. In Lower Canada, even the usually alarmist Thom opined in 1835: "Canadians ... will never rise in arms against the British government."[58] As late as the fall of 1837, the constitutionalists did not apprehend a full-scale insurrection:

As to the general rising against the Government by the mass of the population – still I trust under the influence of their venerable and respected pastors, and holy religion which inculcates loyalty to the Sovereign, and obedience to the laws, I think there are no grounds for alarm, – but under the circumstances and from the causes I have mentioned, there being reason to apprehend partial disturbances.[59]

The constitutionalists showed equal lack of foresight in Upper Canada. Despite Mackenzie's threats, Lieutenant-Governor Francis Bond Head redeployed the province's British troops to Lower Canada, where the situation seemed more unstable.

Like the republicans, the partisans of modern liberty crafted their rhetoric to justify revolt against oppression. For them, however, the power of Parliament was officially "absolute and without control,"[60] and their discourse was more circumspect. But as Locke had explained, there was a limit on Parliament's power and that was the purpose for which it had been created: to guarantee security and property, the public good and adherence to natural law (including the right to life and liberty).[61] Blackstone agreed with Locke in theory but believed that the limit was, in practice, inapplicable.[62] And even so, Parliament could theoretically never behave tyrannically, since the institution was a composite of societal interests that would not plausibly conspire to deprive one group of its liberty.

In the parliamentary context, only the executive could pose a real threat to liberty, since executive power was vested in a single individual. Blackstone explained that executive power was limited by the subjects' right to rise up against a tyrannical prince.[63] Such a revolt would be difficult to justify, but not impossible. Two conditions were necessary. First, a free state had to degenerate into a tyranny. Mixed government turned tyrannical when the executive power violated the law or overstepped its authority, either by infringing individual rights and freedoms, destroying property, or threatening security. Second, the tyrant had to direct violence against the people. In so doing, he would be declaring war, and the people would be justified in resorting to arms.[64]

The colonial constitutionalists were as concerned with the right of revolt as their republican counterparts. However, in their minds it was they who were being victimized. The republican oppressors were foreigners: French Canadians in Lower Canada, Americans or their admirers in Upper Canada. The constitutionalists rejected charges of racism, claiming it was these other groups who were fomenting distinctions based on origin, particularly in Lower Canada: "what, in short, has been the uniform policy of the assembly for many years, but a systematic scheme for 'fostering national animosities and distinctions?'"[65] The French Canadians' attitude was especially reprehensible in that they had no reason to complain. It was thanks to London's generosity that they had been able to preserve their customs, culture, and language:

To the French Canadians the connexion of Canada and Britain is eminently advantageous. It is only by the solemn guarantee of the mother country that their privileges can be long respected or their institutions long preserved, for it is an undeniable fact that their cherished privileges and institutions, whether right or wrong, sound or unsound, would meet little sympathy and little indulgence from a legislature composed as the majority of any federative legislature would be, of colonists of *British* extraction.[66]

Moreover, the French Canadians had, thanks to the conquest, inherited British freedoms. The Constitutional Association of Montreal stated in this regard that French-language subjects were

in the full and complete security of their persons and property, in the free and unrestricted enjoyment of their religious worship, their ancient civil laws, their native and beloved language, and of an equality of rights and privileges in the provincial representative government with their fellow-subjects of British and Irish origin, in possession, moreover, of a numerical popular majority.[67]

According to the constitutionalists, "in no part of the British Empire have the blessings of a mild and just Government been more fully enjoyed than in Lower Canada."[68] Finally, they denied that the French Canadians were victims of systematic discrimination in their own province. Responding to the seventy-fifth of the Ninety-Two Resolutions contending "that Britons hold a majority of provincial offices," Thom argued that the reverse was true: "the Canadians hold a majority of public appointments, political, military and judicial."[69] He reached this conclusion by counting French Canadians who held positions in the seigneurial militia and as justices of the peace. Thom knew full well that the Patriotes would disavow all French Canadians appointed to executive or legislative positions, regardless of their numbers,[70] since their concern was with the legitimacy of the system, not the identity of its office holders. Yet the constitutionalists invoked these numbers to justify their contention that the French Canadians formed "a highly favored people,"[71] and on this basis denied the legitimacy of the republicans' impending revolt.

And since they felt that their liberty was threatened by the Patriotes' demands and actions, the constitutionalists were considering taking up arms themselves. Thom, for example, appealed to the memory of the great reformer Fox, who had claimed to adhere to "the general principle of resistance; the right inherent in freemen to resist arbitrary power, whatever shape it may assume, whether it be exerted by an individual, by a senate or by a king and parliament united. This I proclaim as my opinion; in support of this principle I will live and die."[72]

The spectre of armed resistance invoked by Thom and others in Lower Canada targeted two perceived enemies. Referring to the Patriotes, Thom wrote in the *Montreal Gazette*, "Britons must either arouse in their majesty and put down their oppressors, or quietly submit to the yoke already prepared for them," at the risk of becoming "the perpetual and irredeemable serfs of a despotic, ignorant, anti-commercial and ANTI-BRITISH faction."[73] By 1835 he was envisioning "an English insurrection ... an insurrection not against a British King but against a French Vice-roy."[74] But Thom also urged opposition to those British ministers who were too conciliatory for the constitutionalists' tastes. He explained that "The English inhabitants of this province wage war not with the British people but with the British cabinet, not with his Majesty but with his Majesty's Ministers, not with the law but with its dishonest and 'cheerful' violators."[75] The idea that it was the ministers who had to be combated and not the monarch stemmed from the principle that "the king can do no wrong." In the British context, the king wore the crown; the ministers bore responsibility for executive acts. The threat was alarming enough that commissioners Gosford, Grey, and Gipps mentioned it in their second report to London:

The English portion of the community, and especially the commercial classes, will never, without a struggle, consent to the establishment of what they consider little short of a French republic in Canada: we believe that if the measures they regard in this light were adopted, the presence of a commanding British force might become necessary to prevent a collision between the two parties.[76]

Before the rebellions, then, the Canadian constitutionalists had acknowledged a right to revolt and were discussing the circumstances under which it could be asserted. After the rebellions, they continued to discuss it in language designed to prove that the republican uprising had been illegitimate. The attorney Charles Dewey Day, later deputy judge advocate at the Patriotes' trial, principal pro tempore of McGill University, and member of the commission to codify Lower Canadian civil law (1857–66),[77] made this argument on the grounds that there had never been a threat to "personal liberty, property [and the] rights of conscience of the subject."[78] Even Étienne Parent, the reform-minded journalist who had remained faithful to the modern concept of liberty throughout the decade, admitted that "there did not ensue from the existing order that degree of oppression which can drive a people to despair."[79]

The same discourse was heard in Upper Canada from Chief Justice Robinson. At the opening of the trial of rebels Samuel Lount and Peter Matthews, he reiterated the conditions for legitimate revolt in the eyes of a partisan of modern liberty – namely, where liberty, property, and / or security are in jeopardy. These conditions had not obtained:

Every man who obeys the laws is secure in the protection of life, liberty, and property ... No man could deprive you, by force or fraud, of the smallest portion of the fruit of your labour, but you could appeal to a Jury of your country for redress, with the certainty that you would have the same measure of justice dealt out to you, as if you were the highest and wealthiest persons in the Province ... In short, you were living in the enjoyment of as full security against injury of every kind as any people in the world.[80]

How had these basic protections come about? Robinson argued that "it is no longer in the power of a Prince or Governor to sport with the interests and lives of those over whom he rules, to such a degree as to drive them to the desperate remedy of rebellion."[81] Executive power, in short, was too circumscribed to allow for the kind of tyranny that would justify the rebels' actions. While that statement may seem farfetched today, it was much easier to defend in the preindustrial world. As Allan Greer has noted, the preindustrial state did not have the means "of exercising direct and constant control over 'civil society.'" To a great extent, society governed itself. Order was kept by justices of the peace and militia captains in the formal sphere, and by mobs informally. The modern state, with law enforcement officers deployed more or less systematically across the territory, is a creation of the industrial era.[82]

Robinson hastened to add that if tyranny was no longer possible, "it is especially so in respect to the Empire of Great Britain, where the Government is emphatically a Government of the laws, and where a well-balanced Constitution affords the means of obtaining a remedy, without violence, for every injury, public or private."[83] Instead of taking up arms, the rebels could have asserted their rights before the courts or left the country. Clearly, the distance between the republicans and the constitutionalists was unbridgeable on this point. The republicans' whole stance was predicated on an assertion not that individual rights had been violated, but that the will of the people had been thwarted.

The consistent through line of the constitutionalists' discourse was their emphasis on absolute individual rights. The rebellions could only have merit if those rights were directly threatened. That was the basis on which they justified their own threats of violence. They sought to use "the means which they can most effectually employ to maintain their rights as British subjects under the established Constitution."[84]

FROM RHETORIC TO REALITY: THE OPPONENTS READY FOR WAR

The situation became explosive in the Canadas because the two opposing forces, in addition to their bellicose rhetoric, began readying themselves physically for an eventual clash. Though the proverb says that "if you want peace, prepare for war," it is equally true that those who prepare for war rarely have peace in mind.

In Lower Canada, the power base of the Parti patriote consisted of the small elites who organized the people's assemblies of 1837 and promoted pressure tactics such as boycotts of imported products. That year also saw the formation (officially, if not in actual fact) of committees of correspondence and a call for a convention with the election of certain delegates. In October, a paramilitary organization, the Société des Fils de la liberté, was founded, whereas the rebellion of 1838 itself took place under the auspices of a second paramilitary organization, the Frères chasseurs. This rudimentary organization may well have been insufficient to guarantee the success of the revolution, but its existence shows that the Patriote movement had deeper roots in the population than did the radical movement in Upper Canada. And, given the intellectual and political impasse in which Lower Canada found itself at this time, any attempt to organize the masses was bound to be perceived as a threat.

The constitutionalists organized as well, founding the Constitutional Association of Quebec in 1834 and the Constitutional Association of Montreal the following year. They also established a paramilitary group in December 1834 – the British Rifle Corps – and wrote to Governor Gosford to offer their services. This group's aim was to preserve "the connection which exists between Great Britain and Lower Canada, and to maintain unimpaired the rights and privileges confirmed to them by the Constitution."[85] Gosford declined the offer on 28 December, stating that no one's rights were threatened and that, if they should become threatened, the responsibility for their protection would fall upon the state, not individuals.[86] The British Rifle Corps was dissolved but was replaced in 1837 by a similar outfit, the Doric Club.

Even as the republicans looked forward to a new political order in the colonies, the constitutionalists were preparing to defend their liberty. The executive committee of the Constitutional Association of Quebec called for an inquiry into the means to assure "the security of all the rights and liberties, civil and religious, which the inhabitants of all classes and denominations in this Province now enjoy, of right are entitled to."[87] As to those constitutionalists who took up arms, they did so because their foe was "threatening the destruction of their lives and properties."[88]

The details of these rather limited paramilitary organizing efforts are not pertinent here. What is important is that a conflict originating in formal political institutions now moved into the extraparliamentary arena. In Lower Canada violence had long appeared unavoidable, whereas in Upper Canada the republican agitation had looked as if it could be contained. The situation degenerated in both provinces, however, when the two camps began rhetorically invoking and justifying the use of violence. This discourse by the Lower Canadian republicans and constitutionalists, both asserting the right to take justice into their own hands, condemned the colonial state to death.

By 1837 everyone knew where the conflict was headed. There was no avoiding violence because neither side was willing to renounce its principles. The republicans were not going to re-enter the ambit of modern liberty and accept parliamentary sovereignty when they had been clamouring for popular sovereignty for a decade. Neither were the constitutionalists and the British government going to agree to reorganize the colonial political system around the elective principle. The constitutionalists of Lower Canada, having devoted considerable ink to depictions of the French Canadians as fanatics, were bound to be horrified at the idea of the Legislative Council's falling under their control; nor was London going to entrust the republicans with the future of its empire. Violence became the preferred means of settling the conflict, and with the adoption of the Russell Resolutions in March 1837, the powder keg was lit.

THE LIMITS OF CONCILIATION:
FROM THE RUSSELL RESOLUTIONS TO THE REBELLIONS

In March 1837, Lord Russell tabled ten resolutions in the House of Commons in response to the republicans' demands. The principles underlying these resolutions (which were never officially passed into law) accorded with the positions of the committee of 1828 and the imperial government. In the fourth resolution, the government made explicit its refusal to countenance the electivity of the Legislative Council. It knew that to do otherwise would spell victory for the Parti patriote in both houses of the legislature and hence the end of mixed government. The government did, however, specify that "it is expedient that measures be adopted for securing to that branch of the Legislature a greater degree of public confidence."[89] In April 1837, Lord Glenelg reminded the governor that "it is our intention to advise his Majesty to make an addition to the Legislative Council, by a careful selection of men of property, character and influence in the Province, of liberal views, and entitled to the respect and confidence of the public, but not committed to the extreme opinions."[90] London's refusal was nonetheless guaranteed to ire the republicans who, as we have seen, had no room for the aristocratic principle, nor for allegiance to empire, in their philosophy.

The fifth resolution rejected ministerial responsibility. In practice, this meant that neither the reformist interpretation of this concept (a harmonization of executive-legislative relations, such as through the creation of a provincial cabinet) nor the republican interpretation (subordination of the executive to the Assembly) would enjoy the government's favour. Still, it recognized the expediency of "improv[ing] the composition of the Executive Council in Lower Canada."[91] In a dispatch dated 14 July 1837, Glenelg instructed Gosford to renew the Executive Council as per the recommendations of the third commissioners' report of 1835–36.[92] Predictably, the fifth resolution was decried by the Patriotes, for whom all appointments by London were illegitimate. Indeed, the seventh and eighth resolutions of the Assembly of the Six Counties (October 1837) denounced all of Gosford's appointments.[93]

But the most objectionable resolution in the Patriotes' eyes was the eighth. It gave notice of impending British legislation to allow Gosford to defray the arrears on the administration of justice and civil government, something the Assembly had been refusing to do since 1834. The resolution, directly inspired by the report of Gosford, Grey, and Gipps, was designed to overcome the Assembly's obstruction on this issue. It was not a law per se but a threat of legislative action and thus a reaffirmation of Parliament's sovereignty. The government hoped to frighten the Patriotes into passing the subsidies themselves, so that coercion would no longer be necessary. This conciliatory side of London's stance – it claimed to be willing to make certain changes to the Constitution in return – was evinced with utter clarity in Lord Glenelg's instructions to Lord Gosford that the Assembly should be convened for a voluntary vote on subsidies:

You will further express to the House of Assembly the anxious hope that you may not be compelled to exercise the extreme power with which the Parliament has declared its intention of investing you, in order to discharge the arrears due for public services in the colony, for the payment of which the faith of the Crown has been repeatedly pledged. You will inform them, that the chief object with which they are called together at present is that before the Bill founded on the Resolutions shall reach Lower Canada, they may have an opportunity of rendering that part of it which rests on the 8th Resolution unnecessary and inoperative, by a grant of the supplies requisite for the purposes for which it is intended to provide. You will further express to them the earnest desire of his Majesty's Government to co-operate with them in the removal of every obstacle to the beneficial working of the existing constitution, and in the correction of every defect which time and experience have developed in the laws and institutions of the Province, or in the administration of its government.[94]

Such statements may well have been made in good faith, yet the aim of the eighth resolution was clearly to undermine the power of the Lower Canadian House of Assembly. The Patriotes realized they were about to lose their only lever over the constitutionalists. To a republican, the eighth resolution was completely illegitimate, a frustration of the people's will. And so once again in August 1837, the Patriotes refused to grant the subsidies.

If London thought it could escape the impasse by showing its teeth without having to bite, it was wrong. Not only did the Russell Resolutions fail to secure a subsidy vote, they stirred up a wave of unrest that took menacing form in the public assemblies of 1837. At the end of August, a peaceful solution to the conflict was almost inconceivable: no longer was there any compromise that would satisfy both camps. Violence appeared as the only way for the Patriotes and radicals to assert their rights. Armed conflict would determine the conception of liberty that would characterize the Canadas for the foreseeable future.

In late November, the Patriotes finally took up arms in Saint-Denis and Saint-Charles. While they won the first battle, they lost the second, as well as another that took place in Saint-Eustache a few weeks later. The Upper Canadian radicals followed suit. In many respects, the Upper Canadian rebellion was merely an echo of the one taking place across the provincial border. In December, Mackenzie struck while the British troops stationed in his province were away fighting the Patriotes. Without the Lower Canadian rebellion, Mackenzie's associates would probably never have opted for violence, since they would have been greatly outgunned. But the difference between the two insurrections was qualitative, not merely quantitative. While the Lower Canadian uprising resembled a revolution,[95] a genuine attempt to remake the state with appeals to the masses for support, the Upper Canadian uprising was more like an attempted coup by a small number of partisans.

History records that both revolts were put down in blood by the British army, fighting alongside the Upper Canadian militia and volunteers in both provinces. The declaration of independence proclaimed by Robert Nelson in February 1838, the second Lower Canadian uprising in the autumn of that year, and the Upper Canadian raids of 1838–39 led to further military and legal repression.[96]

MODERN LIBERTY VICTORIOUS

While the crisis in Upper Canada could be resolved within the constitutional framework, since the conflict there was purely extraparliamentary, the crisis in Lower Canada had more serious implications. The rebels were charged with treason and their leaders were imprisoned or exiled, while their newspapers – *La Minerve, The Vindicator*, and *The Constitution* – were shut down. With them, a whole vision of society disappeared, along with a corresponding definition of liberty. Put another way, the first victim of the Lower Canadian revolt was republican liberty itself. In its place, modern liberty triumphed in the Canadas.

Though it may seem paradoxical, the second victim was in fact the Constitution of 1791 – the embodiment of modern liberty in the Canadas. The rebels, after all, held a third of the legislature and were not likely to be voted out. Instead, mixed government would have to be sacrificed. On 10 February 1838, London suspended the Lower Canadian constitution, to the great joy of the constitutionalists for whom the rebels had abdicated by resorting to force: "the Assembly of Lower Canada, as established and composed under the existing laws, is altogether incompetent to the performance of the important duties assigned to it by the Constitution ... has virtually abdicated its high office, and has thus rendered it of paramount and immediate necessity to provide a remedy for the evil." This interpretation recalls the manner in which the Glorious Revolution of 1688 had been interpreted before it.[97] A few days later, Lord Gosford resigned and was replaced by Sir John Colborne, commander of the British troops in North America. Executive power returned to the colonial administrator, while legislative power was entrusted to a special council answerable to the administrator.[98]

As questionable as these measures might appear from the standpoint of modern liberty, they were actually not inconsistent with it. The moderns (e.g., Locke and Montesquieu[99]) generally accepted the idea that rights, freedoms, and parliamentary rules could be suspended in order to protect liberty from a conspiracy. London used an analogous argument to justify its policy, as the Home Secretary, Lord Russell, explained:

As much as the suspension of constitutional government in Lower Canada is to be regretted, it will not be without a very considerable compensation, if, during the interval, arrangements should be maturely and wisely made for securing to the people at large the benefit of those social institutions from which, in former times, the thoughts of the local legislature were diverted, by the controversies which then agitated the provincial society.[100]

The special council did not violate the tenets of modern liberty since it allowed the government to continue to manage, temporarily and legally, a province whose assembly had attacked the constitution. The reform-minded Lord Durham, a friend of Russell's and the new governor of British North America appointed in March 1838 (he arrived in the colony in May), likewise considered the suspension of the constitution as regrettable as it was necessary.[101]

In the colony, the *Montreal Gazette* argued that the state of anarchy reigning in the province had dictated a firm-handed – indeed authoritarian – solution: "We have already expressed our opinion with respect to the necessity of the Autocracy under which we at present live in this Province, considering the anarchy and confusion in which we have been involved by the treasonable projects of the House of Assembly, supported by an ignorant and prejudiced constituency … We know, that anarchy is always the precursor of despotism."[102] Even Parent (the only reformer who could still speak freely in 1838, for he was not a Patriote and had argued against the rebellions), reassured by Durham's appointment, accepted the provisional government:

Long before this day, we predicted that the agitators were leading this country into despotism, for despotism was always the inevitable consequence of anarchy and licence, but we had not foreseen that this despotism would manifest itself in such a benign form and with such encouraging expectations … To accept good-heartedly the provisional state of affairs presented to us, and in the same sentiments in which it is offered to us, is the best means of seeing it promptly give place to the free government we are promised.[103]

The British government's decision would even be approved of at a much later date by John Stuart Mill, who wrote in 1861,

I am far from condemning, in cases of extreme exigency, the assumption of absolute power in the form of a temporary dictatorship ... But its acceptance, even for a time strictly limited, can only be excused, if, like Solon and Pittacus, the dictator employs the whole power he assumes in removing the obstacles which debar the nation from enjoyment of freedom.[104]

Implicit in this comment, apparently, are the lessons derived from the Canadian experience. Mill was well aware of the rebellions since he had commented on them in the *London and Westminster Review* in 1838. Although initially favourable to the rebels' cause and opposed to the suspension of the constitution, he ultimately, in August 1838, sided with Durham and by the end of the year had become his staunch defender, a position from which he never wavered thereafter; indeed, he still held it when writing his autobiography.[105] In short, this great liberal did not, in 1861, decry the suspension of the constitution or the sending of a "dictator" to the colonies, but legitimized this policy a posteriori, since it had allowed for the renewal of imperial policy and the introduction of the principle of "internal self-government" into the colonies.

And if the temporary suspension of the constitution and the existence of the special council were not in and of themselves inconsistent with the logic of modern liberty, neither was the form taken by the special council. The fact that the council did not allow for broad political participation did not constitute a fundamental problem since modern liberty is primarily a matter of private rights – liberty, property, and security – and the council's role was very much to guarantee them. In addition, the council was not, strictly speaking, despotic. It was not the embodiment of arbitrariness or tyranny, nor was it beholden to the will of a particular institution or person; rather, it was the temporary embodiment of parliamentary sovereignty, the rule of law, and the separation of powers. Therefore, no abuse of power was possible, as Robinson explained:

It is certainly not a representative form of constitution, though if it were to be maintained for some years, it would be easy and perhaps advisable to make the special council in part elective. But it is very far from being a despotic Government. It is a written constitution conferred by Parliament, in which the limits of executive and legislative authority are defined, and the laws are as supreme as in any other country; and it is surely a strange description of despotism in which nothing can be done contrary to law, and in which the law, so far from depending on the will of the executive, can only be changed with the concurrence of a council of twenty members, taken from the worthiest, most respectable, and most intelligent inhabitants of the province.[106]

The council set about making decisions within a clear framework of modern liberty, putting an emphasis on the security of persons and the state. It issued orders creating the urban and rural police (1838–40), establishing special courts to try the rebels, regulating taverns (1840), and setting up courts and prisons in certain districts (1841). On the specific issue of property and its protection, it issued orders relating to bankruptcy (1839), the commutation to freehold of the seigneurial rights held by the Montreal Seminary (1840), the dredging of Lake St Pierre (1838), the construction of the Chambly Canal (1840), and the establishment of registry offices (1841).[107]

But the special council's reign could only be considered legitimate if it was temporary. Britain immediately set about rethinking its Canadian policy, always of course within the framework of constitutionalism and modern liberty. It sought to restore balance among the powers in the colonies – an essential element of any constitution based on modern liberty – without re-creating the problems of the 1830s. In the three years following the rebellions, Lord Durham, Lord Russell, and Charles Poulett Thomson each devoted effort to this task. Though the future of British North America remained uncertain, there was no longer any doubt that it would be based on the modern concept of liberty.

Conclusion:
Liberty As the Foundation
of the Canadian State

THE YEAR 1837 could have been for Canada what 1776 and 1789 were for the United States and France. It was the year when republicans in the two Canadas tried to overthrow the government. They sought to establish a new, republican ideal of power and social relations in which all citizens are equal and politically independent. Both these characteristics would be rooted in the economic independence afforded by small landholding. In such a society, the incorruptible, virtuous, patriotic citizens would be duty bound to put the public interest above their private interests. From an institutional standpoint, they would be free as long as they had a voice in the primary branch of the state: the legislative branch, expressing the will of the sovereign people.

True, the Canadian uprisings came much later than the American, European, and South American revolutions, but they were not different at the level of ideology. Had they succeeded, we would now think of them as the "Canadian revolutions." But they did not succeed: simply put, the republicans lost the war. With their victory in the late 1830s, the pro-British forces put a final end to the cycle of the Atlantic revolutions. The republican ideology did not completely and definitively disappear from the Canadian scene (it was articulated in the 1840s by a few French Canadian reformers, and by the Red Party and certain Clear Grits after that), but its partisans would never again be influential enough to pose a threat to the state.

The victory of the constitutionalist forces in 1837–38 consecrated the defeat of republicanism and republican liberty in Canada. It was not fated to be the ideology that would form the sinew of the Canadian political system. But does this mean that liberty itself was irrelevant to the nineteenth-century development of the Canadian state? No. The defenders of the Canadian constitution, whether or not they favoured reform, stood without a doubt for a political and social order based on liberty as they envisioned it. Different as it was from the ideals of the Atlantic revolutionaries, modern liberty was just as much a product of the Enlightenment, and formed the basis for the Constitutional Act of 1791.

This conception of liberty rested on three fundamental principles. The first was the centrality of civil liberties, including habeas corpus, freedom of conscience, freedom of association, and freedom of the press. While the scope of these rights was limited as compared with the present day, they were nonetheless recognized as inviolable. The second and perhaps most important principle was the right to private property, which was generally coupled with an ethic of accumulation. Personal enrichment was not considered a vice, a threat to the social order or the state, but rather as evidence of the constructive use of liberty. The third principle was the security of persons and property. In terms of colonial political organization, this concept of liberty entailed the sovereignty of the British Parliament and found form in colonial institutions structured around the principles of mixed government.

The failure of the 1837–38 insurrections thus marked the victory of modern liberty in the Canadas. In due course, modern liberty as the foundation of the state became an unquestioned postulate of Canadian politics. The vast majority of politicians and intellectuals rallied around it and around the institutional arrangements ensuing from it.[1] In the wake of the Durham report of 1839, debate in the colonies focused on the question of union and, more fundamentally, that of executive responsibility. Colonial reformers in the early 1840s took up where Pierre-Stanislas Bédard had left off in the first decade of the century, wiping away thirty years of unproductive conflict.

The development of Canada is thus to be situated within the constitutionalist tradition of Locke, Montesquieu, and Burke, not within the republican tradition of Rousseau.[2] It is the former tradition, underpinned by modern liberty, that constitutes the organizing principle of Canada's intellectual and political history. It fostered the emergence of a liberal order founded on the principles of liberty, equal rights, and property,[3] and it is this order that forms the basis for the modern Canadian state.

Notes

1 The historians Frank Underhill and Donald Creighton and the literary critic Northrop Frye have argued that Canada remained on the margins of the Enlightenment. On this subject, see Underhill, *In Search of Canadian Liberalism*, 12; Creighton, *The Road to Confederation*, 142–3; Frye, *Divisions on a Ground*, 48, 77. The American sociologist Seymour Martin Lipset contrasted the revolutionary identity of the Americans with the counterrevolutionary identity of the Canadians: see Lipset, *North American Cultures*, 2–10, 13–14; Lipset, *Revolution and Counterrevolution*, 31–63; Lipset, *Continental Divide*, 1–56, 59–60.

2 For a general interpretation of the period considering both the liberal and loyalist principles of the colonists, see Jerry Bannister, "Canada as Counter-Revolution: The Loyalist Order Framework in Canadian History," in *Liberalism and Hegemony*, ed. Constant and Ducharme, 99–146.

3 David Armitage, "Three Concepts of Atlantic History," in *The British Atlantic World*, ed. Armitage and Braddick, 11–27.

4 For example, Canada (under both the French and British regimes) is mentioned only a few times in Bernard Bailyn's 2005 book, *Atlantic History*. It is given scarcely more attention in Armitage and Braddick, eds., *The British Atlantic World*. The loyalists are mentioned in passing by Alison Games in her chapter, "Migration," 48; the acquisition of new territories to the north of the Thirteen Colonies and the Seven Years' War are succinctly covered by Elizabeth Mancke in her chapter "Empire and State," 192–4; Eliga Gould, in his chapter "Revolution and Counter-Revolution," 211, notes that the Constitutional Act of 1791 was conceived as a reaction to the American Revolution and republicanism. The loyalists are given better coverage in Keith Mason, "The American Loyalist Diaspora and the

Reconfiguration of the British Atlantic World," in *Empire and Nation,* ed.
Gould and Onuf, 239–59. There are a few exceptions; see, for example,
Mancke, "Early Modern Imperial Governance"; Mancke, *The Fault Lines*;
Faragher, *A Great and Noble Scheme*; Banks, *Chasing Empire.*

5 Wallot, "Révolution et réformisme"; Wallot, "Frontière ou fragment";
Gilles Paquet and Jean-Pierre Wallot, "Nouvelle France / Québec / Canada:
A World of Limited Identities," in *Colonial Identity,* ed. Canny and Pagden,
95–114; Stewart, *The Origins*; Denys Delâge, "The Fur Trade of New
France," in *The Atlantic World,* ed. Benjamin, Hall, and Rutherford,
139–44; Allan Greer, "French Colonization of New France," in *The Atlantic
World,* ed. Benjamin, Hall, and Rutherford, 191–5; Ajzenstat and Smith,
eds., *Canada's Origins*; Kelly, *La petite loterie*; Choquette, *Frenchmen into
Peasants*; Pritchard, *In Search of Empire*; Harvey, *Le Printemps*; Christie, ed.
Transatlantic Subjects.

6 "Americanness" (*américanité*) is an approach that focuses on the similarities between Quebec and the other nations of the Americas. It argues that
these similarities originate in the fact of the province's being geographically situated in North America. See, for instance, Bouchard, *Quelques
arpents d'Amérique.*

7 It was literary theorists who developed the thesis of Quebec's
Americanness. For literary studies, see Rousseau, *L'image.* Yvan Lamonde
was the first historian to take an interest in this thesis; see Lamonde,
"American Cultural Influence in Quebec: A One Way Mirror," in *Problems
and Opportunities,* ed. Hero, Jr., and Daneau, 106–26. Lamonde revisited
this argument in *Ni avec eux ni sans eux* and in "L'ambivalence historique
du Québec à l'égard de sa continentalité: Circonstances, raisons et signification," in *Québécois et Americains,* ed. Lamonde and Bouchard, 61–84.
For the new societies thesis, see Bouchard, *The Making of the Nations.* For
the nationalities framework, see Bellavance, *Le Québec.*

8 For the continental perspective, see Smith, *Canada: An American Nation?*
For the imperial perspective, see Manning, *The Revolt*; Burroughs, *The
Canadian Crisis*; Buckner, *The Transition;* Lawson, *The Imperial Challenge.*

9 On the subject of French, American, and British influences over Quebec
history, see Lamonde, *The Social History,* 3–46; Lamonde, *Allégeances.*

10 Michael Braddick, "Réflexions sur l'État en Angleterre (XVIe–XVIIe siècle)," *Histoire, Économie et Société* 24 (2005):42, cited in Dessureault,
"La Crise," 173.

11 Reinhart Koselleck, "*Begriffsgeschichte* and Social History," in *Futures Past,* 86.

12 Historians who have studied the nature and influence of certain concepts
over Canada's development have mainly focused on the concepts of loyalty (Mills, *The Idea of Loyalty*) and equality (Larue, "La Crainte").

13 I use the words *liberty* and *freedom* as synonyms. In doing so I follow scholars such as Berlin, "Two Concepts of Liberty," 121; Hayek, *The Constitution*

of Liberty, 421n1; and Foner, *The Story of American Freedom*. Most encyclopedias of political thought still do likewise; see, for instance, Miller, ed., *The Blackwell Encyclopaedia*, 163–6, 291; Sheldon, *Encyclopedia of Political Thought*, 113, 187–8; Hammond, *Political Theory*, 134, 190. Some scholars have nonetheless discussed the difference between the meanings of these two words; see, for instance, Fischer, *Liberty and Freedom*, 1–15; Pitkin, "Are Freedom and Liberty Twins?"

14 For a definition of republican liberty, see Skinner, "The Republican Ideal of Political Liberty."

15 For the origins of the expression and a definition of "modern liberty," see Constant, "The Liberty of the Ancients"; Hexter, "The Birth of Modern Freedom"; J.H. Hexter and R.W. Davies, "Series Foreword," in *Parliament and Liberty*, ed. Hexter, vi–ix. On the birth of the modern self (individual) in the seventeenth century, see Taylor, *Sources of the Self*. For a discussion of the difference between a possessive (modern) conception of individualism and a more transcendent (republican) conception, see Coleman, "The Value of Dispossession."

16 On this question, see Kaiser, "This Strange Offspring."

17 Greer, *The Patriots and the People*, 3–19; Greer, "1837–38: Rebellion Reconsidered," 7.

18 On this issue, see Ducharme, "Closing the Last Chapter."

19 For a general history of the implementation of the new institutions by the state in United Canada, see Careless, *The Union of the Canadas*, and also Greer and Radforth, eds., *Colonial Leviathan*. On the repression that followed the rebellions and made it possible for this new order to be put in place, see Greenwood and Wright, eds., *Canadian State Trials*, vol. 2. On the codification process, see Young, *The Politics of Codification*. For the development of the school system, see Corrigan and Curtis, "Education"; Curtis, *True Government*; Curtis, *Ruling by Schooling Quebec*. For the development of the municipal system, see Michèle Dagenais, "The Municipal Territory: A Product of the Liberal Order?" in *Liberalism and Hegemony*, ed. Constant and Ducharme, 201–20. On responsible government, see Stewart, *The Origins*. On the development of the bureaucracy, see Piva, "Getting Hired"; Piva, "Debts"; Curtis, "The Canada 'Blue Books'"; Hodgetts, *Pioneer Public Service*. On the management of poverty, disease, and delinquency, see Fecteau, *La liberté du pauvre*. For statistics, see Zeller, *Inventing Canada*; Curtis, *The Politics of Population*.

20 McKay, "The Liberal Order Framework"; Fecteau, *La liberté du pauvre*.

21 On the Whig (or liberal) intellectual foundations of the Canadian state before 1840, see Peerce, "The Anglo-Saxon Conservative Tradition"; Peerce, "The Myth"; Cook, "John Beverly Robinson," 79; Ajzenstat, "Modern Mixed Government"; Ajzenstat, *The Political Thought*; Ajzenstat, "Durham and Robinson"; McCulloch, "The Death of Whiggery."

22 In *Revolution and Rebellion,* J.C.D. Clark argues as well that liberalism did not appear in England before the 1820s. In this regard, he writes, "To attempt to write the history of liberalism before the 1820s is thus, in point of method, akin to attempting to write the history of the eighteenth-century motor car" (103).

23 For example, in his *The Politics of Liberty,* Lee Ward presents the history of the eighteenth-century Anglo-American world as a competition among three very different versions of Whiggism. The first, more conservative version was structured by James Tyrrell and based on the sovereignty of Parliament. Ward depicts the other two versions as radical. According to his argument, John Locke articulated a more liberal version, and it became the one taken up by Thomas Jefferson, while Algernon Sidney laid the groundwork for a more republican version that found favour with Thomas Paine. On the relationship between Whiggism and liberalism, see Burrow, *Whigs and Liberals,* 1–20.

24 The word *democracy* is construed here as the political ideology of today based on popular sovereignty, universal suffrage, and political participation by the masses, not in the sense of "deliberative democracy" as employed by Jeffrey L. McNairn in his *Capacity to Judge.* On the relationship between republicanism and communism, see Talmon, *The Origins of Totalitarian Democracy.* On the relationship between republicanism and socialism, see Nemo, *Histoire des idées,* 779–1005, which incorporates ancient republicanism along with the variety espoused by Jean-Jacques Rousseau and the Jacobins into his history of the evolution of socialism from Greece to Marx and Lenin. See also Bevir, "Republicanism."

25 Clark, *The Movements;* Kenneth D. McRae, "The Structure of Canadian History," in *New Societies,* ed. Hartz, 219–74; Ryerson, *Unequal Union.*

26 See Létourneau, "L'Avenir du Canada"; Létourneau, *A History for the Future,* 3–29, 100–50; Létourneau, "Pour un autre récit de l'aventure historique québécoise," in *Les idées en mouvement,* ed. Bélanger, Coupal, and Ducharme, 53–73. While Létourneau is the historian who has done the most work on creating a new analytical framework for Quebec that goes beyond the national framework, he is not the only one to have found this a fertile approach; see, for example, Bélanger, "Les historiens révisionnistes"; Bélanger, Coupal, and Ducharme, Introduction to *Les idées en mouvement,* 10–11; Dagenais, "S'interroger."

27 See Lamonde, *The Social History,* 65–237; Harvey, *Le Printemps.*

28 On this subject, see Baechler, *Qu'est-ce qu'une idéologie?,* 65–105.

29 On this subject see, for example, Wallot, "Religion."

30 On the clergy reserves, see Wilson, *The Clergy Reserves.*

CHAPTER ONE

1 Palmer and Godechot, "Le problème," 219–39; Palmer, *The Age of the Democratic Revolution*; Godechot, *France and the Atlantic Revolution*, 27–121; Godechot, "Revolutionary Contagion." On recent French historiography concerning the late eighteenth-century revolutions, see Lemarchand, "À propos des révoltes." It should be noted that the thesis of Palmer and Godechot has had a cool reception, with several Marxist and French historians finding that this interpretation was the product of an excessively ideological approach in the context of the Cold War. Eric Hobsbawm, for example, has maintained that "the French Revolution ... remains *the* revolution of its time, and not merely one, though the most prominent, of its kind" (*The Age of Revolution*, 52). For Hobsbawm, only the Industrial Revolution appears to have been of equal importance, since both revolutions enabled the bourgeoisie to establish its hegemony. On this issue, see Palmer, "American Historians," 883–4; Bailyn, *Atlantic History*, 24–30.

2 On the American influence on several European countries, see, for example, Library of Congress, *Impact of the American Revolution*; Newman, ed., *Europe's American Revolution*; Schulte Nordholt, *The Dutch Republic*; Dickinson, ed., *Britain and the American Revolution*; Conway, *The British Isles*; Morley, *Irish Opinion*.

3 For a general approach to the English, North American, and European revolutions, see, for example, Bourdin and Chappey, eds., *Révoltes et révolutions*; Jourdan, *La Révolution, une exception française*; Solé, *Les Révolutions de la fin du XVIIIe siècle*; Malia, *History's Locomotives*, part 2. For the ties binding the American, British, and French republicans in the late eighteenth century, see Andrews, *The Rediscovery of America*. For a comparison of the French and American revolutions, see Arendt, *On Revolution*; Higonnet, *Sister Republics*; Dunn, *Sister Revolutions*. For a study of the eighteenth- and nineteenth-century revolutions from a national standpoint, see Morrison and Zook, eds., *Revolutionary Currents*. For the Anglo-American world, see Bailyn, *Ideological Origins*; Wood, *Creation of the American Republic*; Pocock, *The Machiavellian Moment*, 333–552. For the troubles in Geneva during the 1760s and between 1789 and 1794, see Linda Kirk, "Genevan Republicanism," in *Republicanism*, ed. Wootton, 290–300; Golay, *Quand le peuple devint roi*. For the patriots' revolt in the United Provinces, see Geyl, *La révolution batave*, 5–116; Schama, *Patriots and Liberators*. This latter work is set within the Atlantic framework but covers this history from a national standpoint. See also Pocock, "The Dutch Republican Tradition," in *The Dutch Republic*, ed. Jacob and Mijnhardt. For the Austrian Netherlands revolt, see Polasky, *Revolution in Brussels*. On France, see Baker, *Inventing the French Revolution*. On the attempted Irish Revolution of 1798, see Swords, *The Green Cockade*; Gough and Dickson, eds., *Ireland and the French*

Revolution; Smyth, *Revolution, Counter-Revolution, and Union*; Small, *Political Thought in Ireland*; Bartlett, Dickson, Keogh, and Whelan, eds., *1798: A Bicentenary Perspective.*

4 For the Saint-Domingue/Haitian revolution, see Geggus, ed., *The Impact of the Haitian Revolution*; Geggus, *Haitian Revolutionary Studies*; Gaspar, Geggus, and Hine, eds., *A Turbulent Time*; Dubois, *Avengers of the New World*; Dubois, *Colony of Citizens*; Blackburn, "Haiti, Slavery, and the Age of the Democratic Revolution." For Latin America, see, for example, Uribe-Uran, ed., *State and Society*; Rodriguez O., ed., *Mexico in the Age of Democratic Revolutions*; Rodriguez O., *The Independence of Spanish America*; Adelman, *Sovereignty and Revolution.* While the Portuguese and Brazilian experience was distinct from the Spanish imperial one, its history has nonetheless been integrated recently into this Atlantic framework; see Paquette, *Imperial Portugal.* For a history of the Atlantic revolutions that includes the South American revolutions, see Klooster, *Revolutions in the Atlantic World.* For a more American than Atlantic perspective, see Langley, *The Americas in the Age of Revolution.* For a rejection of the Atlantic framework as a way of understanding the Latin American revolutions, see Lynch, *Simón Bolívar.*

5 Palmer, *The Age of the Democratic Revolution*, 1: 3–24.

6 Palmer, "Notes."

7 The United States was seen at that time as the product of liberalism; see, for example, Rossiter, *Seedtime*; Hartz, *The Liberal Tradition.*

8 Fink, *The Classical Republicans*; Robbins, *The Eighteenth-Century Commonwealthman.*

9 John Dunn was the first to question the influence of John Locke in Great Britain in the first half of the eighteenth century (*The Political Thought*, 7–8). This analysis was taken up by several historians, e.g., John Pocock, "The Myth of John Locke and the Obsession with Liberalism," in *John Locke*, ed. Pocock and Ashcraft, 3–24.

10 Certain historians have disputed this chronology and have found this discourse in England before 1650; see Peltonen, *Classical Humanism.*

11 Bailyn, *Ideological Origins*; Pocock, *Politics, Language and Time*; Pocock, *The Machiavellian Moment*; Pocock, *Virtue, Commerce and History*; Skinner, *Liberty before Liberalism*; Wood, *The Creation of the American Republic.*

12 See also the following collections: Wootton, ed., *Republicanism and Commercial Society*; Gelderen and Skinner, eds., *Republicanism.*

13 For England, see, for example, Dickinson, *Liberty and Property*; Norbrook, *Writing the English Republic*; Scott, *Commonwealth Principles.* It was also applied to eighteenth-century Ireland in Small, *Political Thought in Ireland.* A number of US historians have borrowed the framework of Pocock, Bailyn, and Wood; e.g., Banning, *The Jeffersonian Persuasion*; McCoy, *The Elusive Republic*; Ross, "The Liberal Tradition Revisited and the Republican Tradition Addressed," in *New Directions*, ed. Higham and Conkin, 116–31;

Hutson, "Country, Court and Constitution"; Elkins and McKitrick, *The Age of Federalism*. For a presentation of the American historiography on the debate concerning the nature of the Revolution – specifically, whether it was liberal or republican – see Shalhope, "Toward a Republican Synthesis"; Shalhope, "Republicanism"; Rodgers, "Republicanism." For the French case, Pocock's framework has mainly been taken up by English-speaking authors; see, for example, Wright, *A Classical Republican*; Baker, *Inventing the French Revolution*, especially chapters 1, 4, and 6; Baker, "Transformations," 32–53; Kylmäkoski, *The Virtue of the Citizen*; Jainchill, "The Constitution"; Monnier, "Républicanisme et révolution française"; Saint-Victor, *Les racines*. While Carol Blum's *Rousseau and the Republic of Virtue* is not aligned with this historiographic current and analyzes the concept of virtue from several angles, a number of its chapters (6, 8–14) echo the concerns of other Atlantic historians. For a discussion of French republicanism in general, see Nicolet, *L'idée républicaine*, 1–186. On Rousseau's influence on the French Revolution, see Barny, *Prélude idéologique*; Furet and Ozouf, eds., *Le siècle*; Van Kley, ed., *The French Idea*. This framework has also been applied to the sixteenth- and seventeenth-century history of the United Provinces: Gelderen, *Political Thought*; Nicolaas C.F. van Sas, "The Patriot Revolution: New Perspectives," in *The Dutch Republic in the Eighteenth Century*, ed. Jacob and Mijnhardt, 91–119; J.G.A. Pocock, "The Dutch Republican Tradition," in *The Dutch Republic in the Eighteenth Century*, ed. Jacob and Mijnhardt, 188–93. Some historians have treated Dutch republicanism as belonging to a separate current from Atlantic republicanism; see, for example, Herbert H. Rowen, "The Dutch Republic and the Idea of Freedom," in *Republicanism and Commercial Society*, ed. Wootton, 331–6; Albertone, "Democratic Republicanism."

14 D.A. Brading is one of the few authors to have used Pocock's framework to study revolution in South America: *Classical Republicanism*, 8–16.

15 See, for example, Wallot, "Révolution et réformisme"; Wallot, "Frontière ou fragment." See also Jean-Pierre Boyer, "Le Québec à l'heure des révolutions atlantiques."

16 On the American Revolution, see Trudel, *Louis XVI*; Lanctôt, *Canada and the American Revolution*; Lawson, *The Imperial Challenges*; Monette, *Rendez-vous manqué*. On the American Revolution's influence on the rebellions, see Harvey, "Importing the Revolution." On the repercussions of the French Revolution for Canada, see Galarneau, *La France devant l'opinion*; Boulle and Lebrun, eds., *Le Canada et la Révolution française*; Grenon, ed., *L'Image de la Révolution française*; Simard, ed., *La Révolution française*. For the Loyalists, see Condon, *The Envy*; Brown and Senior, *Victorious in Defeat*; Moore, *The Loyalists*; Walter Stewart, *True Blue*; MacKinnon, *This Unfriendly Soil*; Errington, *The Lion*. On the construction of a Loyalist myth, see Knowles, *Inventing the Loyalists*.

17 Milobar, "The Origins."

18 Gordon T. Stewart, *The Origins of Canadian Politics*; Ajzenstat and Smith,
    "Liberal-Republicanism: The Revisionist Picture of Canada's Founding,"
    in *Canada's Origins*, ed. Ajzenstat and Smith, 1–18. See also Ajzenstat, *The
    Once and Future Canadian Democracy*; Ajzenstat, *The Canadian Founding*.

19 Harvey, "Importing the Revolution"; Harvey, "Le mouvement patriote
    comme projet de rupture (1805–1837)," in *Québécois et Américains*, ed.
    Bouchard and Lamonde, 89–112; Harvey, "The First Distinct Society:
    French Canada, America and the Constitution of 1791," in *Canada's
    Origins*, ed. Ajzenstat and Smith, 79–108.

20 Greer, *The Patriots and the People.*

21 Kelly used an analogous analytical approach in *Les fins du Canada*.
    However, this time, he reconceptualized Pocock's theory in nineteenth-
    century terms by constructing an analytical framework in which the vi-
    sions of Alexander Hamilton (heir to the Court ideology) and Thomas
    Jefferson (heir to the Country ideology) squared off. Kelly went on to
    explain that the foundations of Canadian political customs rest on a
    Hamiltonian understanding of politics, contrary to the Jeffersonian
    approach adopted in the nineteenth-century United States.

22 Bailyn, *Ideological Origins*. Kramnick criticized the sidelining of Locke by
    historians of the Atlantic world in "Republican Revisionism Revisited." He
    reintegrated Locke into eighteenth-century history in *Republicanism and
    Bourgeois Radicalism*. Appleby criticized the opposition between Lockean
    liberalism and republicanism in *Liberalism and Republicanism*. Banning,
    "Jeffersonian Ideology Revisited," saw the need to specify that the eigh-
    teenth-century versions of republicanism and liberalism were not at odds.
    In *The Sacred Fire of Liberty*, he presented James Madison as both a liberal
    and a republican. Wood sided with Banning in "Ideology and the Origins
    of Liberal America," 634.

23 Sullivan, *Machiavelli*; Rahe, ed., *Machiavelli's Liberal Republican Legacy.*

24 Pangle, *The Spirit of Modern Republicanism*; Rahe, *Republics Ancient and
    Modern*; Yarbrough, *American Virtues*. Even M.N.S. Sellers acknowledged
    in 1998 that American republicanism, though its roots might lie in antiq-
    uity, was not ipso facto incompatible with liberalism. On the roots of
    American republicanism in antiquity, see *American Republicanism*. On the
    fact that this form of republicanism was compatible with liberalism, see
    also Sellers, *The Sacred Fire.*

25 Hulliung, *Citizens and Citoyens*; Ward, *The Politics of Liberty*, 325–425. Eric
    Foner, *The Story of Freedom*, saw no need to draw a distinction between
    liberalism and republicanism. It is notable that certain other historians
    continue to consider liberalism the ideology that underpins the entire
    Anglo-American experience; see, for example, Lerner, *The Thinking
    Revolutionary*; Webking, *The American Revolution.*

26 On this issue, see Braud, *Sociologie politique*, 94–199.

27 Fecteau, "Lendemains de défaite," 28.

28 See, on this subject, Thompson, *The Making of the English Working Class.*

29 On the continuity of English politics from 1660 to 1832, see Clark, *English Society.*

30 For example, Paul Hoffmann, *Théories et modèles*, presents different models concerning different facets of liberty (the medical concept, the question of free will, different political models, moral liberty). David Miller, ed., *Liberty*, presents three distinct concepts of liberty: republican, liberal, and idealist.

31 On medieval liberty, see David Harris Sacks, "Parliament, Liberty, and the Commonweal," in *Parliament and Liberty*, ed. Hexter, 93–4; Harding, "Political Liberty"; Bayley, "The Idea of Liberty"; Carlyle, *Political Liberty*, 1–22. More generally, see Davis, ed., *The Origins of Modern Freedom.*

32 Reid, *The Concept of Liberty.* For a teleological definition of Western liberty treated as having a more or less unique definition, including civil and political rights, see Grayling, *Toward the Light.*

33 Hobbes, *The Leviathan*, 2 (21:262–68).

34 De Lolme, *Constitution*, 2, 5–9 (169–91); Rousseau, "Considerations on the Government of Poland," 171–4; Staël, *Des circonstances actuelles*, 109–12, 243; Montesquieu, *Spirit*, bks. 2–8, 8–125.

35 Benjamin Constant, "The Liberty of the Ancients."

36 Ibid., 317.

37 Ibid., 311.

38 Ibid., 310–11.

39 Ibid., 316.

40 Berlin, Two *Concepts of Liberty.*

41 On the philosophical debate over negative and positive liberty, see Ryan, ed., *The Idea of Freedom*; Skinner, "The Idea of Negative Liberty: Philosophical and Historical Perspectives," in *Philosophy in History*, ed. Rorty, Schneewind, and Skinner, 193–221; Taylor, "What's Wrong with Negative Liberty," in *Philosophy and the Human Sciences*, 213; Pettit, *Republicanism.*

42 For the opposition between the *anglomanes* and the *américanistes*, see Appleby, "The American Model for the French Revolutionary," in *Liberalism and Republicanism*, 232–52. Frances Acomb, *Anglophobia in France*, 30–42, prefers to speak of the opposition between Anglophile and Anglophobe liberals (i.e., republicans and Physiocrats). On Anglomania in France, see also Grieder, *Anglomania in France*, 7–31; Egret, *La Révolution des notables.* While Gordon Wood believes that the opposition between Republicans (Jeffersonians) and Federalists (Hamiltonians) ended with the Constitution of 1787, the victory of federalism, and the disappearance of classical republicanism *(The Creation of the American Republic,*

606–18), others believe that this opposition persisted throughout the 1790s and even later; see Pocock, *The Machiavellian Moment*, 526–45; Banning, *The Jeffersonian Persuasion*; Banning, *Conceived in Liberty*; Elkins and McKitrick, *The Age of Federalism*; Buel Jr, *Securing the Revolution*; Cunningham, *Jefferson vs. Hamilton*.

43 Locke's case is peculiar. In his *Second Treatise on Civil Government*, he defended both natural rights and political participation. This ambiguity made it possible for post-1750 partisans of both republican liberty and modern liberty to appeal to his authority. However, Locke may be considered the founder of modern liberty, since his arguments revolved around the inalienable natural rights of individuals rather than popular participation and popular sovereignty. Moreover, Locke's writings devote little or no attention to the question of sovereignty. As Jean Terrel writes, "Locke developed his theory of natural law and the contract without reference to sovereignty" (*Les théories du pacte*, 234). And popular sovereignty is the fundamental feature of republican state organization.

44 Before the mid-1770s, the Physiocrats shared the principles of modern liberty in that they sought to further economic development without unnecessary restraints, but this freedom did not entail the need for subjects' political participation. Generally speaking, the Physiocrats kept their distance from popular sovereignty before the middle of the decade. However, with Turgot's dismissal from his position as controller-general in 1776 and with the success of the American Revolution, Turgot, Du Pont de Nemours, Condorcet, and other Physiocrats came to adopt the republican concept of liberty; see Acomb, *Anglophobia in France*, 42–50, 89–123.

45 This concept of equality formed the basis for the "Conspiracy of the Equals" of 1796 in France. This conspiracy sought to overthrow the Directoire, to reinstate the Constitution of 1793, and to abolish private property. With the Industrial Revolution, this idea of equality gave birth to socialism.

46 Priestley, "An Essay on the First Principles of Government," in *Political Writings*, 25.

47 Jean-Jacques Rousseau, "Plan for a Constitution," 148. As well, Rousseau wanted to slow down the circulation of money, not suppress it altogether ("Considerations on the Government of Poland," 213).

48 Jaucourt, "Natural Equality," 170. On the representativeness of this definition, see Delaporte, "Idée d'égalité, thème et mythe," 118. For a good discussion of the issue, see Chisick, "The Ambivalence of the Idea of Equality."

49 In Locke, the natural rights of individuals are defined as the right to life, liberty, equality, property, and security. A century later, Blackstone explained that "the first and primary end of human laws is to maintain and regulate these absolute rights of individuals." He reduced the number of

natural rights to three, which he summarized as security, liberty, and property (*Commentaries*, 1, 1 [1:120]). In the first article of the *Federalist Papers*, Alexander Hamilton wrote that he wished to analyze the new constitution with a view to discerning in it, among other things, "the additional security which its adoption will afford to the preservation of that species of government, to liberty, and to property" (36).

50 Smith, *Inquiry*, 1, 10 (2:55). See also Locke, "Second Treatise of Government," 5, 45, in *Political Writings*, 283; Blackstone, *Commentaries*, 1, 1 (1:134).

51 Blackstone, *Commentaries*, 1, 1 (1:125); Smith, *Inquiry*, 5, 1 (2:321).

52 Montesquieu, S*pirit*, 11 (6:151). Phrase copied by Jaucourt, "Liberté politique," 2:212, and rephrased by De Lolme, *Constitution*, 1 (12:123).

53 Montesquieu, S*pirit*, 12 (2:183). See also Russell, *An Essay on the History of the English Government*, 116.

54 Rousseau, "Considerations on the Government of Poland," 210. Rousseau suggested that the Polish "learn to know a different happiness than that of fortune" (ibid., 176).

55 Priestley, "An Essay on the First Principles of Government," in *Political Writings*, 31.

56 Robespierre, "On Subsistence," in *Virtue and Terror*, 56.

57 The word *sovereignty* is also used to mean political independence, while a third usage concerns the division of powers between levels of government in a federation. For this last usage as applied to the United States, see Kammen, *Sovereignty and Liberty*. On sovereignty in general, see Mairet, *Le principe de souveraineté*; Hoffman, *Sovereignty*; Philpott, *Revolutions in Sovereignty*; Cazzanigo and Zarka, eds., *Penser la souveraineté*.

58 On popular sovereignty, see David, *La souveraineté du peuple*.

59 Rousseau, *The Social Contract*, 50.

60 For example, Robespierre stated in a speech given at the Assemblée nationale in October 1789 that "governments of any sort are established by the people for the people" (*Oeuvres*, 20). On popular sovereignty and the idea of the general will, see Thomas Paine, *The Rights of Man*, 103, 114; Price, "Observation on the Nature of Civil Liberty," in *Political Writings*, 23–4, 28–9.

61 It is difficult to define the exact nature of the republican people, since it is essentially the reification of an idea. It is more than an abstraction or concept. Nor is it a representation. It cannot "allow one to see an absence" (*donner à voir une absence*) since the people represents nothing: it is. Conversely, it cannot merely be the "exhibition of a presence" since it is itself always absent. In politics, the MPs represent the people, who "exhibit its presence." (On representation, see Chartier, "Le monde comme représentation," in *Au bord de la falaise*, 67–86, 79 for the quotes). Dorland and Charland speak of a metaphysical reality when they consider the source

of state legitimacy (*Law, Rhetoric and Irony in the Formation of Canadian Civil Culture*, 146–7). In this regard, we can state that the people is the metaphysical principle that gives meaning to republicanism. However, I prefer to use the word *fiction* (in its legal sense) rather than *metaphysical principle* (in its ontological sense). In law, a fiction is an "artifice of legal technique … consisting of 'making as if,' supposing a counterfactual with a view to producing an effect in law" (Cornu, *Vocabulaire juridique*, 382). The people is a fiction that serves to legitimize the republican state.

62 Morgan, *The Rise of Popular Sovereignty*, 13.

63 Rousseau, *The Social Contract*, 2 (3:60).

64 Price, "Additional Observation on the Nature and Value of Civil Liberty, and the War with America," in *Political Writings*, 78–9.

65 Rousseau, "Considerations on the Government of Poland," 190. There exists an exception to this principle of representation. Since the members elected in the Estates-General of 1789 did not receive a mandate to draft a new constitution for France, they could not justify the creation of the national assembly with resort to the republican conception of representation. Instead, they appealed to the concept of representation inherent in modern liberty.

66 Bailyn, *Ideological Origins*, 169–75.

67 The French text of the Séance de la flagellation is reproduced in Flammermont and Tourneux, publishers, *Remontrances du Parlement de Paris au XVIIIe siècle*, 2: 554–60, 557 for the quote.

68 Rousseau, *The Social Contract*, 2 (6:67). This definition is more pertinent than that of Laurence Cornu, who contends that republicanism can only exist in a kingless republic (*Une autre république*).

69 See, for example, Harrington, "Oceana," in *The Commonwealth of Oceana*, 25. On mixed government and the seventeenth-century English republicans, see Fink, *The Classical Republicans*; Richard, *The Founders*, chapter 5. On mixed government in the work of Rousseau, see Rousseau, *The Social Contract*, 3, 4–8, 90–104; Cranston, "Jean-Jacques Rousseau." On mixed government and the American rebels, see Wood, *The Creation of the American Republic*, 197–255. On the identification of mixed government with republicanism, see also Smith, *The Republican Option*, 38.

70 On the French case, see Ran Halévi, "La république monarchique," in *Le siècle*, ed. Furet and Ozouf, 166–96; Furet and Halevi, *La monarchie républicaine*.

71 Montesquieu, *Spirit*, 11 (4:150).

72 Locke, "Second Treatise on Civil Government," 6, 57, in *Political Writings*, 289; cited in Blackstone, *Commentaries*, 1, 1 (1:122).

73 In the American case, Hamilton argued for the role of the Supreme Court as the guardian of the Constitution against all possible abuses of power (*Federalist Papers*, no. 78, 466–71).

74 Burke, "Speech at the Conclusion of the Poll, 3 November 1774," in *The Writings*, 3:68–9. See also Burke, *Reflections*, 297, 304; De Lolme, *Constitution*, 1 (4:53).

75 Price, "Additional Observation on the Nature and Value of Civil Liberty, and the War with America," 1, in *Political Writings*, 77.

76 Paine, *The Rights of Man*, 33.

77 For the Physiocrats, see La Rivière, "L'ordre naturel et essentiel des sociétés politiques," in Daire, ed., *Physiocrates*, 463; De Lolme, *Constitution*, 1 (9:79); Gay, *The Party of Humanity*, 91; Hazard, *European Thought*, 332–4.

78 De Djin, "Aristocratic Liberalism."

79 Constant, "The Liberty of the Ancients," 324, 323, 326, 327.

80 It was the place given to liberty within the framework of nineteenth-century Anglo-American liberalism and conservatism that differentiated the two ideologies. The liberals made this liberty the core of their ideology while the conservatives subordinated it to prescription and respect for the social order.

81 Moreover, the parliamentarians themselves never acknowledged having carried out a revolution in 1688. According to the official version, it was James II who vacated the throne, forcing Parliament to invite William and Mary to reign over England. See the Bill of Rights (1689).

82 For an analysis of the Glorious Revolution and the liberty at the source of this revolution, see Jones, ed., *Liberty Secured?* In political terms, the fundamental political difference between the settlement of the revolutions of 1688 and 1776 is well elucidated in John M. Murrin, "Great Inversion, or Court versus Country: A Comparison of the Revolution Settlement in England (1688–1721) and America (1776–1816)," in *Three British Revolutions*, ed. Pocock, 368–453.

CHAPTER TWO

1 On the development of printing and the book in British North America, see Fleming and Lamonde, eds., *History of the Book*; Hare and Wallot, "Les entreprises d'imprimerie."

2 Hare, *La pensée socio-politique au Québec*, 19–28; Wallot, "Frontière ou fragment."

3 A good study of how the American Revolution influenced the Province of Quebec remains to be written. For a diplomatic history, see Trudel, *Louis XVI*. For a more factual history, see Lanctôt, *Canada and the American Revolution*.

4 See *Journals of the Continental Congress, 1774–1789*, 1:105–13 (address of 1774); 2:68–70 (address of 1775); 4:85–6 (address of 1776). These addresses are somewhat ambiguous as to the concept of liberty that they embody, as would be expected since they precede the Declaration of Independence. The three letters were written before independence came

to be seen by the Congress as the sole alternative. It is clear from these
letters that the transition from the modern conception of liberty (which
existed in the colonial setting) to the republican conception and independence was not yet fully consummated. Thus, the address of 1774 cited two
passages from Montesquieu. The first affirms that "in a free state, every
man, who is supposed a free agent, *ought to be concerned in his own government:* Therefore, the *legislative* should reside in the whole body of the *people*, or their *representatives.*" This idea is redolent of republican liberty, yet
Montesquieu was an advocate of modern liberty. The Congress then added a typically modern definition of liberty: "The political liberty of the
subject is *a tranquility of mind*, arising from the opinion each person has of
his *safety*." But despite their ambiguity, these addresses advertised a republican conception of liberty since they placed primary emphasis on subjects' right to participate in the legislative process: "the first grand right, is
that of the people having a share in their own government by their representatives chosen by themselves." (107). Next came trial by jury, habeas
corpus, and freedom of the press (107–8).

5 Biographical data on Mesplet is taken from Lagrave, *Fleury Mesplet*.
6 On the *Gazette littéraire de Montréal*, see Nova Doyon, "Valentin Jautard, un
   critique littéraire à la Gazette littéraire de Montréal (1778–1779)," in
   Portrait des arts, ed. Andrès and Bernier, 101–8.
7 On Canadians' appraisal of the revolution between 1789 and 1792, see
   Galarneau, *La France devant l'opinion*, 105–39.
8 For Franklin, see *Gazette de Montréal*, 13 October 1786, 10 November
   1786, 29 December 1786, 3 June 1790, and 30 September 1790; for
   Paine, see 8 September 1791; for de Mably, see 6 October 1786 and
   1 September 1791; for Price, see 17 November 1791; for Priestley, see
   13 October 1791; for Sièyes, see 20 October 1791.
9 For Paine's essay, see 1 and 8 December 1791; for the essays against
   Burke, see *Gazette de Montréal*, 20 January 1790 and 24 February 1790.
10 *Gazette de Montréal*, 26 January 1792.
11 See *Gazette de Montréal*, 1 January 1789. Another article by Sidney ap-
    peared on 22 January 1789. For the works of Sidney, see *Discourses
    Concerning Government*.
12 Genêt's appeal is reproduced in Brunet, "La Révolution française," 158–62.
13 Wade cites the memorial in "Quebec and the French Revolution," 349–51.
14 Wallot, "En guise de conclusion," 433.
15 The campaign for the repeal of the Quebec Act began in November 1774
    when merchants petitioned the king and the two houses of Parliament.
    They regarded the new law as a threat to their property, security, and com-
    merce, most notably because it abolished habeas corpus and trial by jury.
    See Shortt and Doughty, eds., *Documents Relating to the Constitutional
    History, 1759–1791*, 2:589–91.

16 See "Petition of Sir John Johnson and Loyalists," 11 April 1785, and petition by Western loyalists dated 15 April 1787, reproduced in Shortt and
Doughty, eds., *Documents Relating to the Constitutional History, 1759–1791*,
2:773–7, 949–51.

17 The movement received the backing of British merchants trading to
Quebec after 1774. See their memorials of 1774, 1786, and 1788, repro-
duced in Shortt and Doughty, eds., *Documents Relating to the Constitutional
History, 1759–1791*, 1:501–2, 2:796–801, 2:952–3.

18 Pierre Tousignant has shown that the French Canadians were not absent
from the movement for representative institutions, but there was certainly
no unanimity on the question ("La genèse," chapter 6).

19 *Petitions from the Old and the New Subjects.*

20 Du Calvet, *Appel à la justice de l'État*, 143–321.

21 Haldimand qtd. in Cruikshank, "The Genesis of the Canada Act," 179.

22 Knowles, *Inventing the Loyalists*, 18.

23 In addition to the petitions, motions, and memorials mentioned above,
see the letter of 2 November 1785 from Montreal merchants and the
letter of 9 November 1785 from Quebec City merchants, reproduced
in Shortt and Doughty, eds., *Documents Relating to the Constitutional
History, 1759–1791*, 2:801–3, 803–5, as well as "Mémoire et Requête des
Sousignés Marchands et Citoyens des villes de Québec et de Montréal,
tant en leurs Noms qu'aux Noms de leurs Constituants," reproduced
in *Gazette de Montréal*, 18 December 1788. While certain opponents of
a house of assembly based their position on arguments having nothing
to do with liberty, others took up the rhetoric of modern liberty. This
was perfectly logical, since for the moderns, participation in power was
not equivalent to liberty itself; it constituted one liberty among others.
Thus, "A Citizen of Quebec" objected to the granting of an assembly,
arguing that the province's subjects were not living under an oppressive
regime. He added that if an assembly were granted, it would be to the
advantage of those English who had ties to the mother country. Finally,
he contended that Canadians already enjoyed as much freedom as it
was possible to have. On the one hand, the Quebec Act guaranteed
"their religion, liberties and laws"; on the other, "the people of Canada
are in fact well satisfied with the present form of government; their personal liberty is secured to them by an Ordinance ... which gives them
the benefit of the Writ of Habeas Corpus ... Their property is protected
by laws, usages, and customs of Canada, to which, by long experience
of their fitness for their country, they are strongly attached. Their laws
are by no means unfavorable to commerce" (Citizen of Quebec,
Observations, 12, 16).

24 Price, "A Discourse on the Love of Our Country," in *Political Writings*, 190.

25 Galarneau, *La France devant l'opinion*, 335.

26 F. Murray Greenwood has argued that the real threat in the eyes of British
    politicians was to be found in American Republicanism and not the
    French Revolution (*Legacies of Fear*, 61–2).

27 Brun, *La formation*, 12–14. Note that the first two bills predated the French
    Revolution, proving that it was not fear of this revolution that motivated
    the Constitutional Act.

28 Burke's departure was the first major desertion to affect the Whig opposi-
    tion following the French Revolution. There would be others. A large sec-
    tion of the party led by Lord Portland rallied to the government in 1794.

29 *Parliamentary Register*, 29:352–3.

30 Ibid., 388.

31 Ibid., 382.

32 Ibid., 319.

33 Ibid., 337.

34 Ibid., 332.

35 Ibid., 334.

36 Ibid., 392–3. As regards political institutions, "Mr. Fox declared he had
    no difficulty to admit that his principles were so far republican, that he
    wished rather to give the Crown less power and the People more, where it
    should be done with safety, in every government old or new" (ibid., 403).

37 Ibid., 389.

38 Ibid., 403.

39 On the colonial political system, see Buckner, *The Transition*, chapter 2.

40 *Journals of the House of Assembly of Upper Canada* (hereafter *JHAUC*), 1792,
    18.

41 *Parliamentary Register*, 29:380, 393–4.

42 Ibid., 381.

43 Constitutional Act of 1791, 31 Geo. 3 c. 31 (UK), arts. 6-9.

44 Hare, *Aux origines*, 46, 131.

45 Solon, "Pour accompagner la nouvelle constitution," *Gazette de Montréal*,
    15 March 1792 (reprinted from *Quebec Gazette*, 8 March 1792).

46 The first three quotes are from the article titled "Les droits dont jouissent
    les hommes," *Gazette de Montréal*, 22 March 1792 (reprinted from *Quebec
    Gazette*, 15 March 1792.)

47 Solon, "Pour accompagner," *Gazette de Montréal*, 15 March 1792.

48 Solon, "Les droits," *Gazette de Montréal*, 22 March 1792.

49 Mézière, cited in Lagrave, *Fleury Mesplet*, 406.

50 See Wallot, "Révolution et réformisme," 73.

51 *Journals of the House of Assembly of Lower Canada* (hereafter *JHALC*), 1792, 56.

52 A good example of this debate is found in the pamphlet *Dialogue sur
    l'Intéret du Jour, entre plusieurs Candidats et un Électeur libre et indépendans de la
    Cité de Québec*. See the compilation of sources of this nature by Hare, *Aux
    origines*, 150–92.

53 On repression in Lower Canada at this period, see Greenwood, *Legacies of Fear*.

54 Baby, *Un Canadien et sa femme*.

55 On the Canadian elites' attitude towards the French Revolution, see Galarneau, *La France devant l'opinion*. Wallot, while not disagreeing with Galarneau's interpretation, adds to it a popular perspective in "Révolution et réformisme," 362–73. On the influence of the French Revolution on Lower Canada, see also Boulle and Lebrun, eds., *Le Canada et la Révolution française*; Grenon, ed., *L'image de la Révolution française*; Simard, ed., *La Révolution française*.

56 On this issue, see Errington's excellent *The Lion*, 20–54. Not all American influence was republican in nature, since the Federalists and the Whigs shared the modern conception of liberty.

CHAPTER THREE

1 For the debate around the taxation question, see Wallot, "Querelle des prisons dans le Bas-Canada (1805–1807)," in *Un Québec qui bougeait*, 47–105.

2 Harvey, *Le Printemps*, chapters 2–3.

3 *Le Canadien*, 10 March 1810.

4 The English political system was based on this separation of powers, itself derived from antiquity. In France, the separation among the three orders of the Ancien Régime was instead based on the medieval conception of clergy, nobility, and third estate.

5 *Le Canadien*, 21 May 1808.

6 *Le Canadien*, 7 May 1808.

7 Ibid.

8 *Le Canadien*, 16 May 1807.

9 *Le Canadien*, 7 May 1808.

10 Smith, *Inquiry*, 5, 1 (2:321).

11 John A. Macdonald, cited in Brown, ed., *Documents on the Confederation*, 98.

12 For the influence of the British thinkers on Bédard, see also Smith, "*Le Canadien*."

13 *Le Canadien*, 7 May 1808.

14 For Blackstone, see *Le Canadien*, 25 June and 2 July 1808, and 3 June, 24 June, 29 July, and 23 September 1809; for De Lolme, see 25 June, 2 July, 9 July, 16 July, and 23 July 1808; for Locke, see 3 June 1809. The paper also mentions the Bill of Rights (1689) as well as Junius's letters on freedom of the press (1769–72).

15 For the announcement of Fox's death, see *Le Canadien*, 22 November 1806. *Le Canadien* published a biography of Fox on 25 April 1807 and 30 July 1808.

16 De Lolme, *Constitution*, 1 (6:66–7).

17 Blackstone, *Commentaries*, 4, 19 (4:257–9); De Lolme, *Constitution*, 1
    (8:77–8).

18 On this issue, see also Ajzenstat, "Canada's First Constitution," 43–9.

19 Blackstone, *Commentaries*, 1, 7 (1:232).

20 For a description of the powers attached to the royal prerogative, see
    Blackstone, *Commentaries*, 1, 7 (1:245–70); De Lolme, *Constitution*, 1
    (5:61–3).

21 Blackstone, *Commentaries*, 1, 7 *(1:239)*.

22 Ibid., 237. De Lolme and Montesquieu argued similarly; see De Lolme,
    Constitution, 1 (8:76); Montesquieu, *Spirit*, 11 (6:158).

23 Pierre Bédard, *Le Canadien*, 25 June 1808.

24 A.B., *Le Canadien*, 31 January 1807.

25 Ibid.

26 Pierre Bédard, *Le Canadien*, 24 January 1807.

27 *Le Canadien*, 10 March 1810.

28 According to Helen Taft Manning, Fernand Ouellet, and John Finlay, the
    memorial was Bédard's work (Manning, *The Revolt*, 70; Ouellet, *Lower
    Canada*, 88; Finlay, "The State of a Reputation," 72–4). If so, one cannot
    help noting that his request was much more moderate than it had been in
    1807–10. Janet Ajzenstat, however, maintains that François Blanchet and
    J.T. Taschereau were the authors ("Canada's First Constitution," 40–1).

29 "Mémoire au soutien de la requête des habitans du Bas-Canada, à son
    Altesse Royale le Prince Régent, humblement soumis à la considération
    de Milord Bathurst, Ministre d'état pour les colonies," in *Documents of the
    Canadian Constitution, 1759–1915*, 282–3.

30 Ibid., 283–4.

31 Ibid., 285.

32 My interpretation resembles that of Ajzenstat, "Canada's First Constitution,"
    49–51.

33 On the history of the paper and its owners, printers, and editors, see Reid,
    "L'émergence," 13–14.

34 *Le Canadien*, 2, 9, 16, 23 July 1808; 15 August, 5 and 12 September 1818.

35 The two essays initially appeared in *Le Canadien* on 31 January and
    16 May 1807. They were reprinted on 10 and 17 February 1819.

36 *Le Canadien*, 6 August 1831.

37 *Le Canadien*, 29 July 1835.

38 *Le Canadien*, 7 November 1832. On the demand for responsibility, see,
    for example, *Le Canadien*, 25 February 1835, and 12 February, 2 May,
    and 23 May 1836.

39 See *Le Canadien*, 18 and 30 November 1835.

40 For Parent, see Jean-Charles Falardeau, "Parent, Étienne," *Dictionary of
    Canadian Biography* (hereafter *DCB*), 10:579–87.

41 François Blanchet, cited in *Le Canadien*, 3 March 1819.

42 See *Le Canadien*, 7 February 1821. The Executive Council, which also served as the provincial court of appeal, would later be designated as the body responsible for impeachment. This decision would never satisfy the reformers. The issue of the establishment of a bona fide court of impeachment would not properly be resolved before union.

43 *JHALC*, 1821–22, 137.

44 During the 1830s, the impeachment of high-ranking officials became topical again. In 1831, the Assembly instituted proceedings against Attorney General James Stuart, who was dismissed the following year by the minister responsible for the colonies, Lord Goderich. Ironically, it was Stuart who had led the Parti canadien (forerunner of the Parti patriote) in its attempts to secure the impeachment of judges Sewell and Monk in 1814. Be that as it may, the question of impeachment was no longer, after 1818, what drove the Lower Canadian reform movement. In the 1830s, it was the constitutionalists who called for the creation of a court of impeachment so as not to be the "victims," as they put it, of the Patriote-dominated Assembly's anger, especially after the massacre of May 1832 when British troops fired on a crowd of voters in Montreal.

45 *JHALC*, 1818, 8.

46 *JHALC*, 1810, 135–6 (for the address to the king).

47 *Le Canadien*, 21 April 1819.

48 *Le Canadien*, 19 January 1820.

49 *Le Canadien*, 8 October 1823.

50 Blanchet, *Appel*, 2, 20.

51 "D," *Le Canadien*, 8 March 1820.

52 *JHALC*, 1820–21, 44.

53 The request was consistent with British practice; see De Lolme, *Constitution*, 1 (6:68).

54 *JHALC*, 1821–22, 118.

55 Testimony of John Neilson, *British Parliamentary Papers – Colonies – Canada* (hereafter *BPP-C-C*), 1:74–6.

56 For the assemblymen, participation in the legislative process was only one right among others. In an address to the king dated 17 February 1824, the Assembly expressed satisfaction with the benefits that the reign of King George III had allowed Canadians to enjoy, and stated that "none are more highly prized by your Majesty's Subjects in this Province, than the Constitution of Government granted to them by an Act of Parliament ... whereby they are allowed to advise and consent to such Laws as may be found necessary for the peace, welfare and good government of this Province, by means of Representatives freely chosen by themselves" (*JHALC*, 1823–24, 239).

57 Bédard, *Le Canadien*, 4 November 1809; Papineau, "France et Angleterre. Discours électoral, 1 July 1820," in *Un demi-siècle de combats*, 42–5.

58 "Origine et vices de la Constitution britannique," *Le Canadien*,
3 October 1821.

59 "Origine et vices de la Constitution britannique," *Le Canadien*,
24 October 1821.

60 · "Origine et vices de la Constitution britannique," *Le Canadien*,
10 October 1821.

61 On the perception of the American republic in the colony, see Harvey,
"Importing the Revolution," 209–93.

62 For Voltaire, see *Le Canadien*, 16 August 1820; for Montesquieu and
the English constitution, see 13 September 1820; for Blackstone, see
21 November 1821; for Fox, see 22 September 1824; for Constant, see
17 May 1820 (on exile), 31 May 1820 (on political liberty), 7 June 1820
(on punishment of public officers who abet crimes), 14 June 1820 (on
freedom of the press), 26 July 1820 (on personal freedom); for Madame
de Staël and the Revolution, see 8 November 1820.

63 *Le Canadien* does not indicate the source of the works cited, but research into their origin proves highly instructive. Rousseau's text on
women, published 8 March 1820, comes from the *Letter to M. d'Alembert
on the Theatre* (first published as an *Encyclopédie* article in 1757, then separately in 1758), in which he presents certain republican principles; see
Rousseau, *Politics and the Arts*, 87–8, for the quote in *Le Canadien*.
Le Canadien also published a text by Rousseau concerning love of the
fatherland on 12 March 1823, taken from the *Discourse on Political
Economy* (first published in *L'encyclopédie* in 1755, then separately in
1758). The treatment of these principles looks forward to the *Social
Contract*; see *Discourse on Political Economy*, 15–16. On 10 May 1820, *Le
Canadien* published an excerpt from *Julie, or, The New Heloise* (1761) on
women; see *Julie*, 411. It also, on 29 March and 12 April 1820, reproduced several excerpts about women from the fifth book of *Émile*
(1762); see *Émile*, 332, 371 (12 April), 333–4, 353–4 (29 March).
The fifth book contains a summary of the *Social Contract*. On 19 July
1820, *Le Canadien* published an excerpt from the third book of *Émile*
concerning the sunrise; see *Émile*, 131. On 9 August 1820, it published
a short excerpt from the section of the fourth book of *Émile* titled
"The Creed of a Savoyard Priest" (251).

64 De Lolme, *Constitution*, 1 (6:68).

65 Buckner, *The Transition*, 112–21; Manning, *The Revolt*, 151–70. See, for
example, the petition from the inhabitants of the Dunham townships in
Lower Canada favourable to the union (1823), reproduced in "Report
from the Select Committee on the Civil Government of Canada," BPP-C-C,
1:323–6; see also the petition from the inhabitants of the city and county
of Montreal, dated December 1822 and reproduced in *Le Canadien* on
1 January 1823.

66 "When one begins to analyze this new draft constitution, the impossibility of the thing is quickly apparent, and it becomes clear that this is just a story being told to entertain the public" (*Le Canadien*, 19 June 1822).

67 *Le Canadien*, 21 August 1822.

68 See, for example, the petition published in *Le Canadien*, 27 November 1822.

69 Robinson, *A Letter*; John Strachan to Robinson, 1 September 1822, *John Beverley Robinson Letterbook*, cited in Brode, *Sir John Beverley Robinson*, 85; Strachan, *Observations*.

70 Université de Montréal, Baby Collection, u/9417.

71 The petition is found in *JHALC*, 1823, 30.

72 Yvan Lamonde argues that Papineau's final conversion dates from 1827 (Introduction to Papineau, *Lettres à Julie*, 11–12).

73 On this issue, see Epstein, "The Constitutionalist Idiom," in *Radical Expression*, 3–28; Wilson, "A Dissident Legacy: Eighteenth Century Popular Politics and the Glorious Revolution," in *Liberty Secured?*, ed. Jones, 299–334; Pentland, "Patriotism."

74 See Sonia Chassé, Rita Girard-Wallot, and Jean-Pierre Wallot, "Neilson, John," *DCB*, 7:644–9.

75 On this early opposition movement, see S.D. Clark, *The Movements of Political Protest*, 212–33.

76 Anti-Scottish comments by the reformers were frequent; see Thorpe's letters to Edward Cooke and Sir George Shee in Brymner, *Report*, 39, 57. The group of Scottish favourites was sometimes referred to as the "storekeeper aristocracy."

77 On the composition of the group, see Graeme Patterson, "Whiggery," 29.

78 See Graeme Patterson, "Thorpe, Robert," *DCB*, 7:864–5.

79 Thorpe's correspondence with the Colonial Office was published in Brymner, *Report*; he wrote to people as important as the secretary of the Colonial Office and undersecretaries Edward Cooke and Sir George Shee.

80 Thorpe to Edward Cooke, 24 January 1806, in Brymner, *Report*, 39.

81 "Report says Mr. Scott, the Attorney General, is the Chief Justice; from what misrepresentation of him or from what pique against me Ld. Castlereagh has done this I know not, but this you will soon know, that he is perfectly unequal to the situation, that the Governor will be dreadfully perplexed by such an appointment, that the Province will be universally dissatisfied with him, and I think you will soon find out that the Province would have been perfectly satisfied had I been appointed" (Thorpe to Adam Gordon, 14 July 1806, in Brymner, *Report*, 49).

82 Thorpe to Adam Gordon, 14 July 1806, in Brymner, *Report*, 49.

83 According to depositions dated January and February 1807, Joseph Willcocks vaunted the merits of republicanism during an evening at the home of John Mills Jackson: see Brymner, *Report*, 76–80. Andrew James

Young's presentation of Willcocks's demands would seem to prove that they were more radical than those of Robert Thorpe ("American-Upper Canadian Contributions," 28–64). Not to mention that he joined the Americans in the War of 1812.

84 See, for example, Thorpe's response to the Niagara petty jury, a motion filed by William Willcocks with Thorpe and the latter's reply, and a letter from Thorpe to Sir George Shee, in Brymner, *Report*, 55–7, 101.

85 Thorpe to Sir George Shee, 1 December 1806, in Brymner, *Report*, 58.

86 Response to "Address Grand Jury of the Home District to Judge Thorpe," October 1805, in Brymner, *Report*, 65.

87 Thorpe to Edward Cooke, 18 September 1807, in Brymner, *Report*, 111.

88 There is some uncertainty as to whether these reformers ever demanded some form of ministerial responsibility. Such a demand does not appear in the documents published in Brymner, *Report*. However, Graeme Patterson attributes to Robert Thorpe the document titled *Analysis of the U. Canadian Constitution, or a Brief view of the Rights of Persons in U.C., being an adaptation of the 1st. Book of Blackstone Commentaries to the circumstances of the U. Canadians*, which was the subject of an 1829 analysis in the *Upper Canada Herald* and more or less calls for the creation of a provincial minis-try. Unfortunately, the text's authenticity remains difficult to confirm. For our purposes, whether or not it was written by Thorpe is of little conse-quence since it clearly partakes of modern liberty (modeled on the work of Blackstone); see Patterson, "Whiggery"; Patterson, "Thorpe, Robert," *DCB*, 7:865; McRae, "An Upper Canada Letter."

89 The problem is discussed in Alexander Grant to Lord Castlereagh, 14 March 1806, in Brymner, *Report*, 32–3.

90 "Address of the Legislative Assembly of Upper Canada," 1 March 1806, in Brymner, *Report*, 33.

91 See Thorpe to Sir George Shee, 1 December 1806, in Brymner, *Report*, 57; Thorpe to Sir George Shee, 12 March 1807, in Brymner, *Report*, 98; John Mills Jackson to Lord Castlereagh, 5 September 1807, in Brymner, *Report*, 110; "Judge Thorpe to Edward Cooke," 18 September 1807, in Brymner, *Report*, 111.

92 *JHAUC*, 1807, 174–5.

93 Craig, *Upper Canada*, 62.

94 See Thorpe to Sir George Shee, 22 October 1806 and 1 December 1806, in Brymner, *Report*, 50, 59.

95 David Mills, *The Idea of Loyalty*.

96 On Gourlay's petition campaign, see Wilton, *Popular Politics*, 26–7.

97 This biographical summary is taken from S.F. Wise, "Gourlay, Robert Fleming," *DCB*, 9:330–6. On Gourlay, see also Milani, *Robert Gourlay*.

98 For the request for assistance to Mackintosh and Holland, see Gourlay, *General Introduction*, li–lvii.

99 For an analysis of Gourlay's *Statistical Account of Upper Canada*, see Prévost, "Espace public."

100 Gourlay, *General Introduction*, cxxxvi.

101 For an overview of the English radical agenda, 1815–20, see Belchem, *Popular Radicalism*, 37–50. For the link between Thomas Paine and William Cobbett, see Wilson, *Paine and Cobbett*. For an analysis of the Chartist discourse as the heir to the radical discourse of the eighteenth century, see Stedman Jones, "Rethinking Chartism, " in Jones, *Languages of Class*, 90–178.

102 Gourlay, "To the Resident Land-Owners of Upper Canada" (October 1817), in *General Introduction*, clxxxii.

103 Ibid., cxcii–cxciii.

104 Ibid., cxcii.

105 Gourlay, "To the Resident Land-Owners of Upper Canada," (February 1818), reproduced in *Statistical Account*, 2:472.

106 It must, however, be admitted that the principle underlying the petition sits comfortably within the framework of modern liberty, since it implies the autonomy of the executive branch with respect to the legislative branch. The adoption of this measure by the English Radicals shows the practical limits of a republican reinterpretation of the British constitution. It points up the impossible situation in which those nineteenth-century Radicals who did not call for revolution found themselves.

107 Gourlay, "To the Resident Land-Owners of Upper Canada" (February 1818), reproduced in *Statistical Account*, 2:473.

108 Ibid., 480, emphasis added.

109 Ibid., 477.

110 Gourlay, *A Specific Plan*, 82–6.

111 Ibid., 66.

112 Ibid., 79.

113 Ibid., 80.

114 Gourlay, "To the Labouring Poor of Wily Parish," in *General Introduction*, cxxiv.

115 Gourlay, *General Introduction*, clxxv.

116 Gourlay, "To the Resident Landowners of Upper Canada" (February 1818), in *Statistical Account*, 2:480–1.

117 Gourlay, "To the Resident Landowners of Upper Canada" (2 April 1818), in *Statistical Account*, 2:581.

118 Ibid., 2:582.

119 Ibid., 2:583.

120 Ibid.

121 Ibid., 2:582.

122 Ibid., 2:585.

123 Ibid., 2:586–7.

124 Bowsfield, "Upper Canada"; Young, "American-Upper Canadian
     Contributions," 107–32.

125 This biographical summary is taken from Robert Lochiel Fraser,
     "Baldwin, William Warren," *DCB*, 7:35–44.

126 "Petition to the King's Most Excellent Majesty," *JHAUC*, 12th Provincial
     Parliament, 1st session, 15 January–16 April 1835, Appendix, 1:51.

127 William Warren Baldwin to Duke of Wellington, in Doughty and Story, eds.,
     Documents Relating to the Constitutional History of Canada, 1819–1828, 482.

128 See *Hansard's Parliamentary Debates*, 2nd ser., 21:1327–8.

129 This biographical summary is taken from Flint, *William Lyon Mackenzie*,
     9–66.

130 Dunham, *Political Unrest*, 106.

131 *Colonial Advocate*, 18 May 1824, 4.

132 Ibid., 15.

133 Mackenzie mentioned, for example, the convention of 1818 and the
     measures taken against those who participated in it (*Colonial Advocate*,
     27 May 1824 and 26 January 1826); presented a few scenes from
     Gourlay's life (3 June, 8 July, 5 August, and 2 September 1824); pub-
     lished his petitions (10 June and 19 August 1824) as well as some letters
     he addressed to the Canadians (19 August 1824, 8 December 1825, and
     26 January 1826); used his misadventures to demonstrate the flaws in
     the justice system (1 July 1824), and published a poem to Gourlay's
     memory (30 September 1824).

134 *Colonial Advocate*, 18 May 1824, 5.

135 Ibid., 4.

136 Ibid., 2.

137 Ibid., 12.

138 *Colonial Advocate*, 30 December 1824 (excerpt taken from *Edinburgh
     Review*).

139 *Colonial Advocate*, 8 July 1824.

140 *Colonial Advocate*, 18 May 1824, 13.

141 Ibid., 2.

142 Ibid., 5.

143 On the importance of the militia, see Dessureault, "La crise."

144 For an explanation of the crises in this period, see Craig, *Upper Canada*,
     106–23, 165–209. For the more circumstantial crises, see Dunham,
     Political Unrest, 108–16.

145 Clark, *The Movements of Political Protest*, 349–51; Jackson, "The
     Organization," 97.

146 On the formation of this committee in the context of British policy, see
     Burroughs, *The Canadian Crisis*, 28–42.

147 "Report from the Select Committee on the Civil Government of
     Canada," 22 July 1828, *BPP-C-C*, 1:3–13.

CHAPTER FOUR

1 This presentation of the Patriote discourse as partaking of republican ideology is relatively new. Louis-Georges Harvey was the first to adopt this analytical framework in his doctoral thesis for the University of Ottawa in
1990, titled "Importing the Revolution" and published as *Le printemps*.
Allan Greer has analyzed the republican aspects of both the discourse and
local organization of the Patriote movement; see Greer, *The Patriots and the
People*, 120–52, 219–57. This republican interpretation differs from those
of Yvan Lamonde and Marcel Bellavance, for whom the Patriotes articulated a liberal nationalist discourse (Lamonde, *The Social History*, 97–237;
Bellavance, *Le Québec*). It is closer to the older Marxist interpretations that
emphasized the radical and/or democratic aspect of the Patriote discourse
(for two influential Marxist interpretations, see Ryerson, *Unequal Union*,
36–154; Bourque, *Question nationale*). Clearly, these republican, democratic, or liberal interpretations of the Patriote discourse are at odds with that
of Fernand Ouellet, for whom the Patriotes dissimulated their scheme of
establishing an ancien régime society on the banks of the Saint Lawrence
under a liberal democratic discourse (Ouellet, *Economic and Social History*,
440–3; Ouellet, "Les insurrections," 72–3). This last interpretation has
been disputed by both the above mentioned Marxists and by the nationalists, who have defended the Patriotes' nationalist agenda against that of the
Britons (for nationalist interpretations, see Séguin, *L'idée d'indépendance*,
13–34; Lefebvre, *La* Montreal Gazette). For a historiographic overview of
the issue, see Bernard, comp., *Les Rébellions*; Ouellet, "La tradition révolutionnaire au Canada"; Fecteau, "Lendemains de défaite." The ideological
question has been less thoroughly considered for Upper Canada; for a republican interpretation of the radicals' agenda, see Gates, "The Decided
Policy"; Rea, "William Lyon Mackenzie – Jacksonian?"
2 Harvey and Olsen, "French Revolutionary Forms," 390.
3 On the radicals' use of the English constitution, see, for example, James
A. Epstein, "The Constitutionalist Idiom," in *Radical Expression*, 3–28.
4 The assembly of Saint-François, county of Yamaska (held 6 August 1837),
dealt only with the abolition of seigneurial tenure (*Le Canadien*, 18 August
1837). Since it was this small local elite that declared independence in
1838, it sought to abolish privileges.
5 Louis-Joseph Papineau, "La Commision Gosford (Chambre d'Assemblée,
22 février 1836)," in *Un demi-siècle de combats*, 386.
6 Greer, "1837–1838: Rebellion Reconsidered," 9–10.
7 True, the radicals at times co-opted Locke, Montesquieu, and other moderns,
whose writings rather readily lend themselves to republican reinterpretation. The characteristic feature of radical discourse is the repeated reference to the great republican thinkers: Jefferson, Price, Paine, and others.

8 For a good biography of Fox, see Mitchell, *Charles James Fox.*

9 See Gourlay, *Statistical Account*, 2:650; Papineau, "Rejet des Résolutions Goderich (Chambre d'Assemblée, 16 janvier 1832)," in *Un demi-siècle de combats*, 201; the ninth of the Ninety-Two Resolutions, *JHALC*, 1834, 311.

10 *The Constitution*, 19 and 26 July, 2 and 9 August 1837.

11 Mackenzie, *Sketches of Canada*, 9, 27.

12 See Papineau, "Nécessité de nommer un délégué de la Chambre d'Assemblée à Londres (Chambre d'Assemblée, 17 novembre 1835)," in *Un demi-siècle de combats*, 367.

13 Papineau, "Électivité des institutions gouvernementales (Chambre d'Assemblée, 10 janvier 1833)," in *Un demi-siècle de combats*, 215.

14 *The Constitution*, 19 October 1836. William Wallace (1270–1305) was the preeminent Scottish hero. He fought Edward I of England for the independence of Scotland and was executed. Wallace is not pertinent to republican liberty but, within a context of opposition to English imperialism, his name carried great symbolic value. William Russell participated in a republican plot against Charles II in 1683 and died on the scaffold alongside Algernon Sidney. The Earl of Argyll was executed in 1685 for having fomented a Scottish revolt against James II. His goals concerned the rights of Presbyterians rather than political freedom as such. For the conspiracies led by Russell and Argyll, see Robbins, *The Eighteenth-Century Commonwealthman*, 29.

15 For relations with the Upper Canadians, see Buckner, *The Transition*, 28.

16 Hume, *The Celebrated Letter*, 5.

17 *Colonial Advocate*, 12 June 1834.

18 See Buckner, *The Transition*, 28.

19 Roebuck's essay, initially titled "The Canadas and their Grievances," dates from 1835. It is reproduced in augmented form in Roebuck, *Existing Difficulties*, 33 (for the quote).

20 Papineau, "Électivité des institutions gouvernementales (Chambre d'Assemblée, 10 janvier 1833)," in *Un demi-siècle de combats*, 228.

21 Papineau, "Assemblée de Saint-Laurent" (public speech, 15 May 1837), in *Un demi-siècle de combats*, 427.

22 Mackenzie, *Sketches of Canada*, xviii.

23 Ibid., 7 (Illinois), 159–70 (Vermont), 257 (New York).

24 Ibid., 4.

25 Papineau, "Les 92 Résolutions: sur la 1re résolution (Chambre d'Assemblée, 18 février 1834)," in *Un demi-siècle de combats*, 261.

26 The word *man* is used deliberately. Apart from a few republican thinkers such as Antoine Nicolas de Condorcet, Catharine Macaulay, Olympe de Gouges, and Mary Wollstonecraft, women's emancipation was never an issue: liberty was men's affair. See "People and Faction: Republican Exclusion" in this chapter.

27 While Papineau was not a republican in 1823, the class differences he observed in Great Britain indelibly marked him; see his letters to his wife,
5 April to 22 September 1823, *Lettres à Julie*, 72–91, and *Colonial Advocate*,
27 June 1833.

28 See Papineau, "Électivité des institutions gouvernementales (Chambre
d'Assemblée, 10 janvier 1833)," in *Un demi-siècle de combats*, 214;
Mackenzie, Sketches *of Canada*, 15.

29 Girod, *Notes diverses*, 63.

30 Bidwell, *Mr. Bidwell's Speech*, 4.

31 Raynal, cited in Mackenzie, *Sketches of Canada*, 60. The reference is not giv-
en, but it comes from Raynal, *The Revolution*, 161. Mackenzie personally
declared, "Agriculture the most innocent, happy and important of all human pursuits, is your chief employment – your farms are your own – you
have obtained a competence, seek therewith to be content" (*Colonial
Advocate*, 9 September 1830).

32 For an excellent analysis of this issue, see McNairn, *The Capacity to Judge*,
chapter 8.

33 Bidwell, *Substance*, 14.

34 Hume is cited by Mackenzie in *Sketches of Canada*, 305; Roebuck, *Existing
Difficulties*, 29; Papineau, cited in *La Minerve*, 24 January 1833.

35 Mackenzie, *Sketches of Canada*, 305.

36 For the accounts of Gale, Neilson, and Viger, see "Report from the Select
Committee on the Civil Government of Canada," *BPP-C-C*, 1:22–9, 82–5,
145–57.

37 See resolutions 57 to 62 of the Ninety-Two Resolutions; *JHALC*, 1834,
324–6.

38 Louis-Joseph Papineau, *Address*, 14.

39 In 1833, a group of reformist businessmen tried to found the "Banque du
Peuple de la Cité de Montréal." The project failed. A new attempt was
made in 1835, this one successful, and the Banque du Peuple (officially,
Viger, DeWitt and Company until its incorporation in 1843) was born. The
twelve founders, all aligned with the Patriotes, were Louis-Michel Viger,
Jacob DeWitt, John Pickel, Louis Roy Portelance, Thomas Storrow Brown,
Édouard-Raymond Fabre, Pierre Beaubien, John Donegani, Charles S.
Delorme, Peter Dunn, Guillaume Vallée, and François Ricard. On the
Banque du Peuple, see Greenfield, "La Banque du Peuple," 1–9, 13–16.

40 Mackenzie, *Sketches of Canada*, 485.

41 Ibid., 455, 459–60.

42 *The Constitution*, 24 May 1837.

43 Duncombe, *Report*, 59.

44 Mackenzie, *Sketches of Canada*, 350.

45 Papineau stated, "We have need of a simple government, like that of the
United States" ("Rejet des Résolutions Goderich [Chambre d'Assemblée,

16 janvier 1832]," in *Un demi-siècle de combats*, 209). On the same subject, see Mackenzie, *Sketches of Canada*, 47, 56; *The Constitution*, 2 August 1837.

46 Papineau, "A propos du discours de Sir John Colborne à l'ouverture du Parlement provincial du Haut-Canada (Chambre d'Assemblée, 15 février 1836)," in *Un demi-siècle de combats*, 378.

47 See the ninth resolution of the assembly of Saint-Constant, Laprairie (6 August 1837), in *La Minerve*, 14 August 1837.

48 Papineau to Julie, 7 February 1838 (from Albany), *Lettres à Julie*, 363. The Abbé de Mably put it no better: "[the love of one's country] is the very soul of all a patriot's virtues" (*Phocion's Conversations*, 132).

49 Duncombe, *Report*, 22.

50 Ibid., 13.

51 *Colonial Advocate*, 2 June 1831.

52 Papineau, "Rejet des Résolutions Goderich (Chambre d'Assemblée, 16 janvier 1832)," in *Un demi-siècle de combats*, 200.

53 This was one of the major criticisms of Mackenzie's committee on representation in 1831 (*First Report on the State of the Representation*, 7, with list of examples in Appendix E). See Mackenzie, *To the Honorable the Commons*, 3.

54 Papineau, "Assemblée de Saint-Laurent (Discours public, 15 mai 1837)," in *Un demi-siècle de combats*, 435.

55 *The Constitution*, 24 May 1837.

56 See, for example, *Colonial Advocate*, 9 September 1830, "Proclamation by William Lyon Mackenzie, Chairman pro.tem. of the provincial Government of the State of Upper Canada," in Charles Lindsey, *The Life and Times*, 2:367.

57 Assembly of Saint-Marc, held 15 May 1837 (*La Minerve*, 22 May 1837).

58 See Mackenzie, *Sketches of Canada*, 445–6; *Petition of the House of Assembly*, 4; "Seventh Report on Grievances," *JHAUC*, 1835, Appendix, 1:2; Girod, *Notes diverses*, 75–8.

59 *Colonial Advocate*, 9 September 1830. The supreme authority from which power derives is "a free, contented, prosperous and happy people" (Mackenzie, *Sketches of Canada*, 39).

60 See Papineau to Julie, 9 November 1835, *Lettres à Julie*, 309–10.

61 Papineau to Julie, 23 February 1835, *Lettres à Julie*, 297.

62 *La Minerve*, 25 June 1835.

63 "Adresse du Comté de l'Acadie aux électeurs des comtés de Richelieu, Verchères, St. Hyacinthe, Chambly et Rouville" (October 1837), in Bernard, comp., *Assemblées publiques*, 263.

64 Paine, *The Rights of Man*, 100.

65 Papineau, *Address*, 12.

66 Papineau, "Adresse à la Chambre des Communes du Parlement de la Grande-Bretagne (Chambre d'Assemblée, 1 mars 1834)," in *Un demi-siècle de combats*, 306; Papineau, "La Commission Gosford (Chambre d'Assemblée, 22 février 1836)," in *Un demi-siècle de combats*, 414.

67 *Petition of the House of Assembly*, 3.

68 First resolution of the assembly of La Malbaie, Saguenay (25 June 1837), in Bernard, comp., *Assemblées publiques*, 105.

69 For example, Mackenzie stated in 1832, "People of Canada! Your cause is not the cause of one man or of one particular class of men, but of the whole country … An Act of injustice to one man or body of men, is an act of injustice to the community of which he or they are members" (*Colonial Advocate*, 19 January 1832). Elsewhere, he wrote, "The Legislative Assemblies of the colony possess little or no power to redress the wrongs of the people they profess to represent" (Mackenzie, *To the Honorable the Commons*, 2).

70 *Colonial Advocate*, 3 February 1831.

71 *First Report on the State of the Representation*, 4.

72 Ibid.

73 Ibid., 6, 11, 13, 18–20, Appendices B and C (for the disproportionate distribution of seats); 12 (on corruption among councillors); 7, 21–2, Appendix E: list of members receiving a salary from the government (on corruption among members); 16–17, Appendix A (on bills voted down in the Assembly due to imbalanced representation).

74 Ibid., 8.

75 Mackenzie, "On the State of Representation of the People of Upper Canada," reproduced in *Colonial Advocate*, 10 January 1833; Mackenzie, *Sketches of Canada*, 357.

76 See the second resolution of the assembly of Saint-Policarpe (15 October 1837), *La Minerve*, 19 October 1837.

77 On this subject, see Wood, *The Creation*, 197–255.

78 Papineau, "Abolition du Conseil législatif (Chambre d'Assemblée, 11 mars 1831)," in *Un demi-siècle de combats*, 165.

79 Papineau, "Les 92 Résolutions: sur la 1re résolution (Chambre d'Assemblée, 18 février 1834)," in *Un demi-siècle de combats*, 264.

80 "Seventh Report on Grievances," *JHAUC*, 1835, Appendix, 1:11.

81 Ibid., 11.

82 Ibid., 12.

83 Mackenzie, "Declaration," *The Constitution*, 2 August 1837.

84 On the separation of powers and its application in various countries, including Great Britain, France, and the United States, see Vile, *Constitutionalism*.

85 On this issue, see also Greenwood, "Les patriotes," 32.

86 In a very harsh essay, Louis-Hippolyte La Fontaine condemned Dominique Mondelet's acceptance of a seat on the Executive Council as a betrayal: "The month of April, eighteen hundred thirty-two, is the most decisive time in your political career – from then does your apostasy date. In the earliest days of this dire spring, you were still great Democrats; you still professed the principle of popular sovereignty; and of a sudden, by what strange quirk

of fate I do not know, you were seen, in the course of the same month, to avow diametrically opposed principles" (*Les deux girouettes*, 5). La Fontaine was convinced that to hold the position of an officer of government made one unworthy of a seat in the Assembly (11). What transpires from La Fontaine's position is that to be an executive councillor is to be in the pay of the governor; it is not to serve as an intermediary between the executive and legislative branches. A councillor is not and cannot be a minister – he is just the governor's lackey (19–22). Mondelet responded in kind, turning into a sworn enemy of the Patriotes. In *Traité sur la politique coloniale du Bas-Canada*, he advocated better control of the press, which he saw as responsible for many abuses, and opposed making the Legislative Council elective.

87 "Report from the Committee on Lower Canada," 3 July 1834, *BPP-C-C*, 1:126.

88 There was one exception. The assembly of Saint-Marc, held on 15 May 1837, passed a resolution calling for the organization of a delegation to a convention whose agenda would contain "an Executive responsible to the People" (*La Minerve*, 22 May 1837). It should be noted, however, that the phrase "responsible executive" did not, in the Patriotes' parlance, refer to responsible government.

89 *Colonial Advocate*, 9 September 1830.

90 Mackenzie, "A New Almanack," 19, cited in *The Selected Writings*, 205.

91 *JHAUC*, 1835, Appendix, 1:9.

92 Mackenzie, "Declaration," *The Constitution*, 2 August 1837.

93 *The Constitution*, 15 November 1837.

94 Mackenzie, "Proclamation," in Lindsey, *The Life and Times*, 2:364.

95 *Colonial Advocate*, 27 June 1833.

96 On the corruption of sheriffs, see Mackenzie, *To the Honorable the Commons*, 2; Mackenzie to John Neilson (28 December 1835), *The Selected Writings*, 347. The Patriotes, too, denounced the sheriffs; see "Adresse des Fils de la liberté de Montréal aux jeunes gens des colonies de l'Amérique du Nord," 4 October 1837, in Bernard, comp., *Assemblées publiques*, 217. On juries in Lower Canada, see Fyson, "Jurys."

97 Mackenzie, *Sketches of Canada*, 66 (the quote from Papineau is in French in the text). Papineau's exact words were, "Une nation n'en sut jamais gouverner une autre" (One nation can never govern another) (*Address*, 13). It is interesting to note that this sentence was taken up by a number of politicians from different schools of thought. Denis-Benjamin Viger used it in his *Considérations relatives à la dernière révolution de la Belgique* (54). On 16 February 1832, it appeared in an article in *La Minerve* signed "S." This time the emphasis was much more ethnic. The editor of *La Minerve* disowned this article, however.

98 Price, "Additional Observations on the Nature and Value of Civil Liberty, and the War with America," in *Political Writings*, 76–100, 86 for the quote.

99 Mackenzie, *Sketches of Canada*, xx.

100 See *Petition of the House of Assembly*, 19; Mackenzie, "Declaration," *The Constitution*, 2 August 1837.

101 See, for example, Papineau "L'état du pays (Chambre d'Assemblée, 10 mars 1831)" and "Les 92 Résolutions: sur la 1re résolution (Chambre d'Assemblée, 18 février 1834)," in *Un demi-siècle de combats*, 151, 268–9; Mackenzie, *Sketches of Canada*, 461–2.

102 "Notwithstanding the mal-administration of the executive, and the want of confidence felt in the courts of justice, there is yet a powerful feeling of friendship towards England beyond the Atlantic; but the people there, as well as here, wish to be rid of a costly, corrupt, and oppressive system. Ask a Canadian, – Would you desire an established church; the ministers to be paid by the state? He will reply, N O, no; let all denominations be equal. Would you desire the law of primogeniture? – No. The election of your own justices of peace? – Yes. The control over your wild lands and all other revenue? – Yes. Cheap, economical government? – Undoubtedly. The election of your own governors? – Ay. Of your legislative councillors? – Ay. Well then, would you not also wish to be joined to the United Sates? – No, never" (Mackenzie, *Sketches*, 155). Papineau remarked, "We do not want a forced separation, but we are not permitted to discuss the reasons and the causes that could lead to one, though it be assuredly undesirable" (Papineau, "Rejet des Résolutions Goderich [Chambre d'Assemblée, 16 janvier 1832]," in *Un demi-siècle de combats*, 208).

103 Papineau to Julie, 11 February 1829, *Lettres à Julie*, 174.

104 Papineau, "Électivité des institutions gouvernementales (Chambre d'Assemblée, 10 janvier 1833)," in *Un demi-siècle de combats*, 233.

105 Papineau, *Address*, 13. See also the forty-seventh of the Ninety-Two Resolutions in *JHALC*, 1834, 321.

106 "He required no such evidence to convince him of a fact which all history confirmed – namely, that it was morally, politically, and, he might add, physically impossible for two independent legislatures to coexist under one executive" ("Mr. Macaulay's Reply to Mr. O'Connell. – House of Commons, Feb. 1833," cited in Mackenzie, *Sketches of Canada*, 298).

107 See Mackenzie, *Sketches of Canada*, 463, 466; Papineau, "Restitution des biens des Jésuites, (Chambre d'Assemblée, 8 mars 1831)," in *Un demi-siècle de combats*, 145; "Adresse des Fils de la liberté de Montréal aux jeunes gens des colonies de l'Amérique du Nord, 4 October 1837," in Bernard, comp., *Assemblées publiques*, 215; "Grande Assemblée de la Confédération des Six Comtés: Saint-Charles; Procédés du premier jour," *La Minerve*, 30 October 1837.

108 Mackenzie, "Independence," in Lindsey, *The Life and Times*, vol. 2, Appendix F. This idea was echoed at several Lower Canadian public assemblies.

109 Papineau, "Réponse du Comité central et permanent du comté de Montréal à l'adresse de la London Working Men's Association (Adresse publique, septembre 1837)," in *Un demi-siècle de combats*, 491.

110 *The Constitution*, 15 November 1837.

111 The declaration of independence is reproduced in Nelson, *Déclaration d'indépendance*, 25–30.

112 Cranston, "Jean-Jacques Rousseau."

113 Mably, "De la législation," in *Sur la théorie du pouvoir*, 221. See also Coste, *Mably*, 89–90; Guerrier, *L'abbé de Mably*, 184–90.

114 Paine, *The Rights of Man*, 38.

115 Priestley, "An Essay on the First Principles of Government," in *Political Writings*, 28.

116 Robespierre stated in October 1789 that "all citizens, whoever they may be, are entitled to aspire to all degrees of representation ... The constitution establishes that sovereignty resides in the people, in all individual members of the people, and each individual thus has the right to assist in making the laws by which he is bound, and in administering the public weal which is his own. If not, then it is untrue that men are equal as to rights, that every man is a citizen" ("Discours, prononcé à l'Assemblée nationale, October 1789," in *Oeuvres*, 21).

117 31 Geo. 3 c. 31 (UK), art. 20.

118 On the franchise, see Garner, *The Franchise*. For more exhaustive case studies, see De Brou, "Mass Political Behaviour"; Dessureault, "L'élection."

119 *JHALC*, 1832–33, 574.

120 See the twelfth and thirteenth of the Ninety-Two Resolutions in *JHALC*, 1834, 312.

121 The question of women's suffrage is poorly studied; for Upper Canada in particular, no studies on this specific issue have yet appeared. According to Mackenzie's account, women voted in both Upper and Lower Canada during this period (*Sketches of Upper Canada*, 20). The most interesting analysis of gender relations in Upper Canada is Morgan, *Public Men and Virtuous Women*. For Lower Canada, the only in-depth consideration of this topic is Picard, "Les femmes."

122 The Patriotes did not succeed in abolishing women's suffrage because they included this piece of legislation in a broader statute that was rejected by London for other reasons in 1836. The moderns were, it should be stressed, no more open to women's rights than the republicans. Moreover, one of the first measures adopted by the reformers in the United Province of Canada (1849) was the abolition of women's suffrage.

123 See, on this subject, Pitkin, *Fortune*.

124 For Madame Roland, see Dalton, "Marie-Jeanne Roland, Woman Patriot," in *Engendering the Republic*, 55–74. The two American documents are cited in Kerber, *Women of the Republic*, 104.

125 For a general study of this question, see Applewhite and Levy, eds., *Women and Politics*.

126 On women and the American Revolution, see Gundersen, *To Be Useful*; Kerber, *Women of the Republic*; Norton, *Liberty's Daughters*; Cott, *The Bonds of Womanhood*. For a study of the question in the nineteenth century, see Ryan, *Women in Public*.

127 On women and the French Revolution, see McMillan, *France and Women*, chapter 3; Hufton, *Women and the Limits*; Melzer and Rabine, eds., *Rebel Daughters*; Landes, *Women and the Public Sphere*; Blum, *Rousseau*, chapter 11.

128 See in particular Colley, *Britons*; Davidoff and Hall, *Family Fortunes*; Eger et al., eds., *Women*; Mellor, *Mother*.

129 See, for example, Morgan, *Public Men and Virtuous Women*, chapter 2.

130 See Picard, "Les Femmes," 64–7.

131 See Blackstone, *Commentaries*, 1, 15 (1:430–3). Nothing, of course, obliged the republicans to accept this principle of law. They could have proposed to change the situation, but did not do so.

132 My analysis concurs with that of Kerber, *Women of the Republic*, 119.

133 See Rousseau, *Julie*; Rousseau, *Émile*, 5 (321–7); Rousseau, *The Social Contract*, 1 (8:54). This idea was not unique to Rousseau, for de Mably argued similarly; see, for example, the third letter of *Phocion's Conversations*, the third book of *Principes de morale*, and the fourth book of *De la législation*.

134 Rousseau argued that men and women instituted a division of labour when they were still united in a state of nature. Women took care of the home and the children while men went out to hunt ("Discourse on the Origin," 164).

135 On women's role in the private sphere and their role as patriotic mothers, see Rousseau, "Discourse on the Origin," 121–2. The Jacobins, based on the idea of a separation between public and private spheres, banned women from the revolutionary clubs: "When in 1793, the Jacobin Chaumette closed down the women's political clubs, he said, 'the sans-culotte had a right to expect his wife to run the home while he attended public meetings: hers was the care of the family, this was the full extent of her civic duties'" (Siân Reynolds, "Marianne's Citizens? Women, the Republic and Universal Suffrage in France," in Reynolds, ed., *Women, State and Revolution*, 101–22, 113 for the quote).

136 Papineau, cited in *La Minerve*, 3 February 1834. He added later in the debate "that the decency of the sex demanded that she not be dragged into the tumult of elections."

137 Papineau, "Assemblée de Sainte-Scholastique (Discours publique, 1er juin 1837)," in *Un demi-siècle de combats*, 453.

138 On the debate around women's participation in the rebellions, see Greer, "The Queen is a Whore," in *The Patriots and the People*, 189–218; Beverley Boissery and Carla Paterson, "'Women's Work': Women and

Rebellion in Lower Canada, 1837–1839," in Greenwood and Wright, eds., *Canadian State Trials*, 2:353–82. Greer argues that the rebellions were an essentially male affair, to which Boissery and Paterson respond that the absence of evidence of women's involvement in the rebellions is not evidence of their absence. If no women were sued for acts of sedition, it is because the colonial authorities did not wish to acknowledge women's presence in the public sphere. Generally speaking, the question of women's exclusion transcends ideological divisions; it must be addressed within a broader intellectual framework. For a discussion of this issue, see Pateman, *The Problem of Political Obligation*, 60–80, 135–62; Pateman, *The Disorder of Women*, 17–32, 71–117.

139 Ouellet, *Economic and Social History*, chapter 14.

140 Durham, *Report*, 22.

141 Lamonde, *The Social History*, 97–237; Bellavance, *Le Québec (1791–1918)*; Harvey, *Le Printemps*.

142 For a similar interpretation, see Françoise Lejeune, "Patriotisme nord-américain ou nationalisme canadien-français? Les rébellions canadiennes de 1837," in Cottret, ed., *Du patriotisme aux nationalismes*, 169–86.

143 Viroli, *For Love of Country*, 2.

144 Ibid., 1–2.

145 I share Richard Larue's views on this issue, although I would place this allegiance within the framework of republicanism; see Larue, "Allégeance."

146 Papineau, "Assemblée de Saint-Laurent (Discours public, 15 mai 1837)," in *Un demi-siècle de combats*, 431.

147 *La Minerve*, 5 June 1837.

148 Papineau, "Ouverture de la session parlementaire de 1837 (Chambre d'Assemblée, 19 août 1837)," in *Un demi-siècle de combats*, 484.

149 *JHALC*, 1834, 324.

150 See Greer's excellent chapter "Two Nations Warring," in *The Patriots and the People*, 156–68.

151 *JHALC*, 1835–36, 579. Roebuck contends that struggles in the two provinces were one and the same (*Existing Difficulties*, 1, 30).

152 Cited in Mackenzie, *The Selected Writings*, 280–1.

153 Mackenzie, "Declaration," *The Constitution*, 2 August 1837.

154 Emmanuel Joseph Sieyès, *What is the Third Estate?*, 58.

155 The republican discourse at that time was embodied in the person of Robespierre; see *Oeuvres*, "Discours," before the Assemblée nationale, 25 October 1790, 33; Robespierre, "Tableau des opérations de la Convention nationale," 74; Robespierre, "Discours sur la guerre," given to the Jacobins in March 1792, 68, 219; Robespierre, "Discours," before

the Convention, 5 July 1794, 137; Robespierre, "Discours du
8 Thermidor," before the Convention, 26 July 1794, 142, 143, 146.

156 Rousseau, *The Social Contract*, 1 (7:53).

157 On the idea of the internal enemy, see Furet, *Interpreting the French
Revolution*, 28–39, 57–83; Gueniffey, *La Politique de la Terreur*, chapter 7;
Tackett, "Conspiracy Obsession."

158 Talmon, *The Origins*.

159 Papineau, "Les 92 Résolutions: sur la 1re résolution (Chambre d'Assemblée,
18 février 1834)," in *Un demi-siècle de combats*, 255.

160 *JHALC*, 1832–1833, 573, emphasis added.

161 Mackenzie, *Sketches of Canada*, xxiii–xxiv. See also the *Colonial Advocate*,
2 June 1831.

162 On the radicals' struggle against clientelism in Upper Canada, see Noel,
Patrons, Clients, Brokers, 79–111.

163 Papineau, "Adresse de la Confédération des Six Comtés au peuple du
Canada (Adresse publique, 24 octobre 1837)," in *Un demi-siècle de combats*, 497.

CHAPTER FIVE

1 On British conservatism, see Burke, *Reflections*; Disraeli, "Vindication
of the English Constitution," "The Letters of Runnymede," and "The
Spirit of Whiggism," in *Whigs and Whiggism*, 79–172, 173–243, and 245–
68, respectively; Disraeli, *Sybil*. For conservatism in general, see, for example, Kirk, *The Conservative Mind*; Gilmour, *Inside Right*; Scruton, *The
Meaning of Conservatism*.

2 Viger, a stalwart reformer from the start of his career, contributed to
a number of newspapers (the *Montreal Gazette* and *Le Canadien* in particular) during the 1790s and 1800s. In the 1810s and 1820s, he became
an important reformer and a leader of the Parti canadien. In 1828, he
represented Lower Canadian interests before the English Parliament.
In 1829, he was appointed to the Legislative Council but did not sit
for long since he was sent to London in 1831 as the Assembly's agent
in England. He returned in late 1834. Throughout the 1830s, he financed the republican paper *La Minerve* (see Fernand Ouellet and
André Lefort, "Viger, Denis-Benjamin," *DCB*, 9:807–16). Paradoxically,
while Viger remained an important Patriote figure (though his influence
declined throughout the decade), he never shared the movement's
republican ideals. In fact, Viger was a Burkean conservative and had
written admiringly of Burke at the outset of the parliamentary era
(*Considérations sur les effets*, 9–10). His belief in prescription as the basis
of any good constitution – a conservative principle par excellence –
never wavered (*Considérations sur les effets*, 7; *Analyse d'un entretien*, 40;

Considérations relatives à la dernière révolution, 9). Viger went as far as to equate nationality with property (*Considérations relatives à la dernière révolution*, 10). However, his discourse was not nationalist because it was not built around the nation as such but rather around the national order. Viger was a reformer because he feared the threat to this order from the power held by the English within Lower Canadian institutions. He was not a republican and never grappled with the idea of political participation in his writings. He accepted the modern definition of liberty based on individual rights (*Observations de l'hon. D.B. Viger*, 66). Although he acknowledged that social conditions in the colonies were generally egalitarian, he favoured large landholdings and protection of property. On an organizational plane, he did not advocate for popular sovereignty but for a form of mixed constitutional government adapted to the North American context, one in which an independent executive power would be the guarantor of liberty (ibid., 60–1, 19). He did not object to the Legislative Council per se, only to its composition. While not a republican, Viger sided with the Patriotes until the autumn of 1837.

3 Strachan wrote, "I am as friendly to solid liberty as Mr. Jefferson" (*A Discourse*, 59n11).

4 Ibid., 71n14.

5 Ibid., 43. He avers that the Constitution could not be more perfect: "its different parts are so harmoniously combined and incorporated as to produce the greatest possible good; for it not only insures the most extensive civil liberty to every individual, but preserves all the other properties of a good government, dispatch, secrecy, energy, wisdom and union" (iv).

6 Ibid., 20–1.

7 Ibid., 20.

8 Ibid. 55n7.

9 See, for example, the petition of the inhabitants of the Township of Dunham, Lower Canada, dated 1823 and reproduced in "Report from the Select Committee on the Civil Government of Canada," *BPP-C-C*, 1:323–6, and "Petition of the inhabitants of the city and county of Montreal," dated December 1822 and reproduced in *Le Canadien*, 1 January 1823.

10 *Journals of the Legislative Council of Lower Canada* (hereafter *JLCLC*), 1823, 24. Six councillors spoke against the initiative: John Richardson, H.W. Ryland, C.W. Grant, J. Irvine, Roderick Mackenzie, and W.B. Felton.

11 Strachan to Robinson, 1 September 1822, *John Beverley Robinson Letterbook*, cited in Brode, *Sir John Beverley Robinson*, 85. Strachan included his comments and suggested amendments concerning the bill in *Observations*.

12 Robinson, *A Letter*.

13 The idea of uniting not only the Canadas but also British North America was first set out in Sewell and Robinson, *Plan*.

14 Nearly nothing has been written about the Lower Canadian constitution-alists. One exception is Muzzo, "Les mouvements réformistes."

· 15 This biographical summary is taken from Kathryn M. Bindon, "Thom, Adam," *DCB*, 11: 874–7.

16 Brode, *Sir John Beverley Robinson*; Henderson, *John Strachan*; Robert Lochiel Fraser, "Hagerman, Christopher Alexander," *DCB*, 7:365–72; Victor Loring Russell, Robert Lochiel Fraser, and Michael S. Cross, "Sullivan, Robert Baldwin," *DCB*, 8:845–50.

17 R.D. Gidney, "Ryerson, Egerton," *DCB*, 11:783–95.

18 Blackstone, *Commentaries*, 1, 1 (1:125).

19 Constitutional Association of Quebec, "Declaration of the Causes which Led to the Formation of the Constitutional Association of Quebec" (December 1834), in *First Annual Report*, 14. The editor of the *Montreal Gazette* considered these rights and freedoms to be sacred (19 June 1838). When the time came to define them, he spoke of "rational liberty, with se-curity of person and property" (*Montreal Gazette*, 20 February 1838).

20 If the Catholics had to wait longer than the others for tolerance of their faith, it was not essentially because of their belief in transubstantiation but for political reasons (Blackstone, *Commentaries*, 4, 4 [4:52–3]).

21 Strachan, *A Letter*, 101.

22 Fahey, *In His Name*, chapter 2.

23 Charles James Fox cited in Strachan, *A Letter*, 100–1, emphasis added.

24 Smith, *Inquiry*, 5, 1 (3:353–66).

25 Strachan, *A Letter*, 15, 19, emphasis added.

26 Blackstone, *Commentaries*, 4, 2 (4:151). See also De Lolme, *Constitution of England*, 2, (12-13:199–213).

27 Unfortunately, little has been written about freedom of expression in Canada. For a general overview, see Gilles Gallichan, "Political Censorship," in Fleming and Lamonde, eds., *History of the Book*, 320–36; Rutherford, *The Making of the Canadian Media*, 24–8. For the Upper Canadian case in par-ticular, see Romney, "Upper Canada in the 1820s," in Greenwood and Wright, eds., *Canadian State Trials*, 1:505–21.

28 Adam Smith wrote that "upon the impartial administration of justice de-pends the liberty of every individual" (*Inquiry*, 5, 1 [3:325]).

29 Blackstone, *Commentaries*, 1, 7 (1:259). Adam Smith reiterated this idea several times; e.g., "when the judicial is united to the executive power, it is scarce possible that justice should not frequently be sacrificed to what is vulgarly called politics" (*Inquiry*, 5, 1, [2:325]). According to Alexander Hamilton, judicial independence could be considered "in a great mea-sure, as the citadel of the public justice and the public security"; *Federalist Papers*, 466 (see also 467, 470).

30 *Montreal Gazette*, 7 April 1838 and 12 September 1839.

31 On the social order characteristic of the ancien régime in Lower Canada,
    see Greer, *Peasant, Lord, and Merchant*. On social hierarchy in Upper
    Canada, see Noel, *Patrons, Clients, Brokers*, 61–78; Johnson, *Becoming
    Prominent*; Russell, *Attitudes to Social Structure*.

32 See, for example, "Petition of the Undersigned Inhabitants of the City of
    Quebec and its Vicinity" (29 March 1834), in Christie, *A History*, 3:551;
    Constitutional Association of Quebec, "Declaration," in *First Annual
    Report*, 14; Constitutional Association of Montreal, "Report [of the
    General Committee]" (December 1835), in Christie, *A History*, 4:257;
    Thom, *Anti-Gallic Letters*, 35, 71.

33 On the development of the principle of property, see Macpherson,
    Political Theory; on property in the British Empire, see McLaren, Buck,
    and Wright, eds., *Despotic Dominion*.

34 John Adams cited in Thom, *Anti-Gallic Letters*, 109–10. The reference to
    the John Adams essay is not given by Thom. The correct reference is
    Adams, "A Defence of the Constitutions of Government of the United
    States of America," in *The Political Writings of John Adams*, 147–8.

35 See, for example, Constitutional Association of Quebec, "Report [of the
    Executive Committee]" (5 January 1836), in Christie, *A History*, 4:273–4.

36 Robinson, *Canada and the Canada Bill*, 54.

37 Smith, *Inquiry*, 3 (4:181–2). On the good effects of commerce, see also
    Montesquieu, *Spirit*, 20 (1:316).

38 Thom, *Anti-Gallic Letters*, 6–7.

39 Constitutional Association of Quebec, "Report [of the Executive Committee]"
    (5 January 1836), in Christie, *A History*, 4:281.

40 Montesquieu, *Spirit*, 11 (6:151). Phrase copied by Jaucourt, "Liberté poli-
    tique," in *L'encyclopédie*, 2:212, and reformulated by De Lolme, *Constitution*,
    1 (12:123). Montesquieu went on to postulate that "political liberty con-
    sists in security, or, at least, in the opinion that we enjoy security" (*Spirit*, 12
    [2:183]).

41 Blackstone, *Commentaries*, 1, 1 (1:125).

42 Jaucourt, "Liberté civile," in *L'encyclopédie*, 2:211.

43 Constitutional Association of Quebec, "Report [of the Executive Committee],
    (8 March 1836), in Christie, *A History*, 4:298.

44 *Report of a Select Committee of the House of Assembly*, 5.

45 *Montreal Gazette*, 21 October 1837 and 18 October 1838.

46 *Montreal Gazette*, 8 August 1837 and 21 September 1837. In Upper
    Canada, Strachan declared that "by the 31st Geo. 3d, Cap. 31, a regular
    form of Government was established for this loyal and attached popula-
    tion. It confers upon them all the advantages of the British Constitution
    – all the elements of civil liberty to as great an extent as was compatible
    with their enjoyment, or as had ever been possessed by any appendage of
    the Crown" (*A Letter*, 10–11).

47 Robinson, *Canada and the Canada Bill,* 93.

48 Thom, in *Anti-Gallic Letters* (107–8), attacked the idea of popular sovereignty by quoting a long passage from John Adams in which the latter takes issue with Marchamont Needham's idea that popular sovereignty does not threaten individual rights since the people are the best guardian of their own rights. Adams's original text reads: "Marchamont Nedham lays it down as a fundamental principle, and an undeniable rule, 'That the people, that is, such as shall be successively chosen to represent the people, are the best keepers of their own liberties.' ... But who are the people? ... If it is meant by the people, as our author explains himself, a representative assembly, 'such as shall be successively chosen to represent the people,' still they are not the best keepers of the people's liberties, or their own, if you give them all the power, legislative, executive, and judicial; they would invade the liberties of the people, at least the majority of them would invade the liberties of the minority, sooner and oftener than an absolute monarchy ... if one party agrees to oppress another, or the majority the minority, the people still oppress themselves, for one part of them oppress another" (*Defence of the Constitutions,* 3:213–15).

49 Thom (Anti-Bureaucrat), *Remarks,* 132–3.

50 Thom, *Anti-Gallic Letters,* 82. John Bull wrote in an open letter to Gosford that "it is the duty of a man to submit his own inclinations and opinions to the will of the majority. But my Lord, the just power of the majority to determine for the minority, has its bounds ... The rights of each must be respected, because the rights of each are equal. The majority in numbers of the one tribe, does not give it the right to tyrannize over the other" (*Montreal Gazette,* 26 January 1836).

51 Constitutional Association of Quebec, "Declaration," in *First Annual Report,* 9–10.

52 Thom, *Remarks,* 160.

53 Thom, *Anti-Gallic Letters,* 58–9.

54 Blackstone, *Commentaries,* 1, 7 (1:257).

55 In Lower Canada, the issue of judges' eligibility to sit in the Assembly dominated the political scene from 1808 to 1811. The matter was settled with a law disqualifying judges (51 Geo. 3, c. 4).

56 John Beverley Robinson to Arthur, 16 April 1838, *The Arthur Papers,* 1:78.

57 Thom, *Anti-Gallic Letters,* 139, emphasis added.

58 See Blackstone, *Commentaries,* 1, 2 (1:149–50); Bagehot, *The English Constitution,* 9.

59 Cited in Thom, *Anti-Gallic Letters,* 136. Thom did not attribute the quote to its author; it comes from Story, *Commentaries,* para. 540 (1:378).

60 Robinson, *Canada and the Canada Bill,* 67–8.

61 Robert Baldwin Sullivan to Sir George Arthur, 1 June 1838, *The Arthur Papers,* 1:162.

62 "The absolute separation of the three great departments of civil government must have the unfortunate effect of excluding the ablest men of the
country from the most powerful and most dangerous department, the legislature" (Thom, *Remarks*, 33; repeated in *Anti-Gallic Letters*, 138).

63 James Mackintosh, "Vindiciæ Gallicæ," in *The Miscellaneous Works*, 445.

64 Thom, *Remarks*, 165.

65 *Montreal Gazette*, 15 August 1837.

66 *Montreal Gazette*, 19 September 1837.

67 Constitutional Association of Montreal, "Address to the Inhabitants of
British America" (January 1836), in Christie, *A History*, 4:268.

68 W.F. Coffin, speech to the meeting of the Constitutional Association of
Quebec (21 January 1836), *Montreal Gazette*, 28 January 1836.

69 "Address of the Legislative Council of Lower Canada dated 1st April 1833
to the King's Most Excellent Majesty," *JLCLC*, 1835–36, Appendix
EE–166–167.

70 Tristam, *Montreal Gazette*, 23 January 1836.

71 Thom, *Anti-Gallic Letters*, 147.

72 "Can any man, can even any patriot of common understanding, deny that
the Assembly of Lower Canada is, in the strictest sense of the expression,
virtually 'self-elected?' Can any reasonable being doubt, that the liberal
members, as they absurdly and dishonestly style themselves, of the assembly are nominated and appointed by the dominant majority? Who made
the obscure editor of the Vindicator a law-giver? The electors of Yamaska?
No. The mandate of Mr. Papineau 'Elect the bearer'? Yes. Mr. Papineau's
desire to cover the real nature of the contest by the mask of a few English
names, however worthless, induces him to force on his vassals candidates
entirely unknown and thus blindly to prove that the assembly is virtually
'self-elected'" (Thom, *Remarks*, 11).

73 See the sixth resolution of the Rawdon assembly of 29 June 1837 and the
tenth resolution of the Acadie (Napierville) assembly of 24 July 1837, in
Bernard, comp., *Assemblées publiques*, 124, 151.

74 See *Report of a Select Committee of the Legislative Council of Upper Canada*, 33.

75 According to the republicans, the councillors were dependent on the
Crown, since it appointed them. This made no sense to the constitutionalists, since once appointed "they are legislators for life, and can no more
be deprived of the legislative character than any member of the British
House of Lords" (Ryerson [A Canadian], *The Affairs*, 43).

76 Thom, *Remarks*, 22.

77 Ryerson, *The Affairs*, 45.

78 *Report of a Select Committee of the Legislative Council of Upper Canada*, 38–9.

79 "It has never been imputed to them by parliament or by the Government
that they have failed in giving a due support to the rights of the crown on
the one hand, or to the principles of the constitution on the other."
(*Report of a Select Committee of the Legislative Council of Upper Canada*, 141).

80 Thom, *Remarks*, 184. He repeats the remark later: "the English members of the legislative council, who are the virtual representatives of the English population" (*Anti-Gallic Letters*, 5). Ryerson, for his part, stated, "Happy is it for the inhabitants of English, Scotch, Irish, and American origin, who speak the English language, that there is a Legislative Council in Lower Canada; and it is to be hoped that that branch of the Government will be sustained with an integrity and decision, in proportion to its importance. You have wisely concentrated all your forces against the Legislative Council, because you well know that the constitution of that body forms an impregnable fortress for the defence of the Royal prerogative on the one hand, and the protection of the rights and interests of 150,000 British inhabitants on the other" (*The Affairs*, 44–5).

81 "Address to the King," in *Report of a Select Committee of the Legislative Council of Upper Canada*, 44.

82 Robinson wrote on this subject: "As the councils have hitherto been constituted, their members have from the moment of the appointment been, in their character of Legislative Councillors, independent alike of the crown and of the people. They have received no emolument, and the honourable station conferred upon them could never afterwards be taken away." Robinson, *Canada and the Canada Bill*, 140.

83 *Montreal Gazette*, 12 December 1837. On the same theme, see John Bull, *Montreal Gazette*, 20 February 1836; Ryerson, *The Affairs*, 54.

84 *Montreal Gazette*, 30 September 1837.

85 Robinson, *Canada and the Canada Bill*, 155–6.

86 Ibid., 154–5.

87 *Montreal Gazette*, 25 July 1839.

88 *Montreal Gazette*, 28 July 1838.

89 *Report of a Select Committee of the House of Assembly*, 22.

90 *Montreal Gazette*, 1 December 1840, emphasis added.

91 "The Petition of the Undersigned Inhabitants of Lower-Canada," in Constitutional Association of Quebec, *First Annual Report*, 18, emphasis added.

92 Christopher Hagerman, cited in *Important Debate*, 41.

93 On English nationalism, see Newman, *The Rise of English Nationalism*, chapters 4 and 6; Colley, *Britons*, chapter 1.

94 De Lolme, *Constitution*, 1, (9:80–1).

95 The constitutionalists generally used the phrase "birth-right"; see the speech by John Neilson reproduced in the *Montreal Gazette*, 5 August 1837; Robinson, *Address*; Strachan, *A Letter*, 10.

96 It should be noted that the idea of exclusion contained in the phrase "Englishmen's birth-rights" is specific to the English-speaking constitutionalists. The reformers used the term "birth-rights" also, but with an entirely different meaning.

97 See Dunham, *Political Unrest*, 48; Craig, *Upper Canada*, 87–8.

98 Robert Baldwin Sullivan to Arthur, 1 June 1838, *The Arthur Papers*, 1:134.
99 Robinson, *Canada and the Canada Bill*, 48.
100 Constitutional Association of Montreal, "Address to the Inhabitants of British America" (January 1836), in Christie, *A History*, 4:263.
101 Robinson, *Canada and the Canada Bill*, 31. This vision of an Anglo-American people included New Brunswick and Nova Scotia: "In both these colonies the English laws and language exclusively prevail; and everything that is British is valued as it deserves to be. Their inhabitants are a loyal people, contented with their political condition, not impatient of their dependence on England, but glorying in their connection with her" (24).
102 Robert Baldwin Sullivan to Arthur, 1 June 1838, *The Arthur Papers*, 1:135.
103 Robinson wrote, "Undoubtedly, the American people have ever shown, and they daily exhibit a most laudable spirit of enterprise. It has resulted from the characteristics of their race which we share with them." He continued, "Nothing can justly deprive the people of the United States of the credit of being a remarkably energetic, active, and enterprising race; each man in his sphere gives striking proofs of these qualities" (*Canada and the Canada Bill*, 57, 59).
104 *Montreal Gazette*, 18 October 1838. The Upper Canadians adopted this racial explanation; see *Report of a Select Committee of the House of Assembly*, 7; Robert Baldwin Sullivan to Arthur, 1 June 1838, *The Arthur Papers*, 1:176.
105 Constitutional Association of Montreal, "Report [of the General Committee]" (January 1835), in Christie, *A History*, 4:260.
106 *Montreal Gazette*, 16 December 1837. This idea was widely held among constitutionalists in the two Canadas. For example, Ryerson also stated that the Patriotes wanted "nothing less than the establishment of their ancient nationality and ascendancy in the province" (*The Affairs*, 10).
107 "S," *La Minerve*, 16 February 1832, cited in Thom, *Remarks*, 106; Thom, *Anti-Gallic Letters*, 64; Ryerson, *The Affairs*, 22.
108 Séguin, *L'idée d'indépendance*, 17–30.
109 "Any expression of opinion in regard to the superior adaptation to the wants and interests of society of the republican form of Government, or that of a constitutional monarchy, is not required from the Committee. Both forms of government have their advocates; each can be sustained by powerful arguments derived from history and from reason. But the Committee believe that no educated man of unprejudiced mind, will hesitate to denounce *the course pursued by the French Canadian leaders, who, under the specious guise of Reformers, ostensibly desirous of a Government more intimately connected with the will of the people*, as really animated by zeal for the preservation of all those peculiarities which so unenviably distinguish this Province from all other inhabited portions of North America" (Constitutional Association of Montreal, "Report [of the General Committee]" (January 1835), in Christie, *A History*, 4:250, emphasis added).

110 "Petition to the King's Most Excellent Majesty: The Petition of the Undersigned Inhabitants of the City of Quebec and Its Vicinity" (29 March 1834), in Christie, *A History*, 3:551.

111 Ryerson, *The Affairs*, 32.

112 Thom, *Anti-Gallic Letters*, 51.

113 "The French Canadians are not an enterprising people; they care little about commerce, and are not zealous promoters of public improvements; and besides this, it is said, that their laws and customs have an unfavourable tendency and that their ignorance and national prejudices forbid all hope of amendment through the agency of the Legislature" (*Report from the Select Committee*, 68–9). Ryerson made a similar statement (*The Affairs*, 47, note d).

114 Thom, *Anti-Gallic Letters*, 195.

115 Constitutional Association of Montreal, "Report [of the General Committee]" (December 1835), in Christie, *A History*, 4:252.

116 "When a population is unlettered and unenlightened, to entrust them with the unrestricted use of political power would be, in fact, to retard the progress of rational freedom" (Constitutional Association of Montreal, "Report [of the General Committee]" (December 1835), in Christie, *A History*, 4:251–2).

117 Thom, *Anti-Gallic Letters*, 87. Thom continued, "Difference of language must produce difference of feeling. The unity of the former is the only thing that can engender the unity of the latter" (175).

118 "[Meeting of the] Constitutional Association of the City of Montreal" (30 December 1837), in Christie, *A History*, 5:66–7.

119 "… on a continent where none but an Anglo-Saxon nationality can be permanent or permitted" (*Montreal Gazette*, 30 December 1837).

120 *Montreal Gazette*, 17 July 1838.

121 *Montreal Gazette*, 5 November 1839.

CHAPTER SIX

1 See, for example, Maurice Séguin, "Le double soulèvement de 1837," in Bernard, comp., *Les Rébellions*, 173–89.

2 Creighton, "The Economic Background"; Creighton, *The Commercial Empire*, chapter 10; Ouellet, *Lower Canada*, 117–327; Ouellet, *Economic and Social History*, 332–447; Ryerson, *Unequal Union*, 36–154. See also Bernard, comp. *Les Rébellions*, particularly the following papers: W.H. Parker, "Nouveau regard sur les troubles au Bas-Canada dans les années 1830," 162–72; Catherine Vance, "1837: Travail et tradition démocratique," 190–204; Gilles Bourque and Anne Légaré, "Résistance paysanne à l'exploitation petite-bourgeoise et question nationale," 264–83.

3 Bernier and Salée, "Les insurrections"; Bernier and Salée, *The Shaping of Québec Politics.*
4 Larue, "Allégeance"; Mills, *The Idea of Loyalty,* 71–110.
5 Greer, "Historical Roots."
6 Historians have tended to look for the direct influence of the American and French revolutions on Canadian history. If the results of their research have been disappointing, it is because they have tried to force Canadian political evolution into a historical framework that belongs to a different context. It can be useful to look for elements of kinship between Canadian history and the history of another country, but to use the latter as a benchmark is to needlessly constrict one's analysis of Canadian history. What is more, the search for the impact of the revolutions on Canada has generally led these authors to limit their research to the time before 1815, when the "revolutionary era" was ending in Europe (Galarneau, *La France devant l'opinion*; Wallot, "Révolution et réformisme"). Yet the republican justification (whether a priori or a posteriori) for the Atlantic revolutions did not disappear in 1815. This chronological dividing line is at best arbitrary, as a number of historians have realized in recent decades. When Jean-Paul Bernard, Michel Grenon, and Jean-Pierre Wallot studied the putative relationship between the French Revolution and the rebellions of 1837–38, they concluded that the former had a weak influence on the latter (Bernard and Grenon, "La Révolution française et les Rébellions de 1837 et 1838 dans le Bas-Canada," in *La Révolution française,* ed. Simard, 14–38; Wallot, "La Révolution française au Canada, 1789–1838," in *L'image de la Révolution française,* ed. Grenon, 61–104). This conclusion was predictable in view of the Patriotes' and the radicals' tendency to quote American sources. However, before concluding that the American influence over the movement was paramount, one must realize that the Atlantic revolutions, in their American and French phase, were both the daughters of republican liberty. And it was republican principles that the Patriotes and the radicals invoked to justify their demands throughout the years 1828 to 1837 – and even more so during the rebellions.
7 Strachan, "To the Attorney General" (18 April 1834), *The John Strachan Letter Book,* 226. The *St. Catharines Journal,* cited in the *Montreal Gazette,* stated in the same vein, "the contest now going on is between British Reformers, on the one hand, and French revolutionary Jacobins, on the other – rational British freedom under a British Monarch, or abject submission to the domination of a *French* Republic" (*Montreal Gazette,* 19 January 1836).
8 "General Report of the Commissioners for the Investigation of all Grievances Affecting His Majesty's Subjects of *Lower Canada,*" 15 November 1836, *BPP-C-C,* 4:5–6.
9 While the 1836 election was tarnished by irregularities, these "are scarcely enough in themselves … to explain the tory avalanche that buried the

reformers. The tories took over twice as many seats as their opponents" (Colin Read, *The Rebellion*, 9). In fact, Lieutenant-Governor Francis Bond Head's appeal to loyalty served to clarify the issue between allegiance to the Empire (linked to modern liberty) and disloyalty (republican liberty).

10 This section presents a discussion of the thinking of the government in London and of the intellectual framework within which it adopted its policy. For an excellent history of the imperial policy of this time, see Buckner, *The Transition*.

11 "Despatch from the Secretary Sir George Murray, to Lieutenant General Sir James Kempt," 29 September 1828, *BPP-C-C*, 6:219.

12 "Report from the Select Committee on Lower Canada," 3 July 1834, *BPP-C-C*, 1.

13 On Amherst's abortive mission, see Buckner, *The Transition*, 186–9.

14 "Despatch from Lord Glenelg to the Earl of Gosford, The Right Hon. Sir C.E. Grey and Sir G. Gipps, His Majesty's Commissioners of Inquiry in Lower Canada," 17 July 1835 (no. 1), *BPP-C-C*, 7:180.

15 "Despatch from Lord Glenelg to His Majesty's Commissioners of Inquiry in Lower Canada," 17 July 1835 (no. 2), *BPP-C-C*, 7:207.

16 1 and 2 William 4, c. 23.

17 14 Geo. 3, c. 88.

18 André Garon has established this independence of the Councils after 1828; see Garon, "La fonction politique," 70, 77.

19 "Lord Aylmer's Despatch on 5th March 1834, addressed to the Right Honourable Edward Stanley," *BPP-C-C*, 7:326.

20 Morin's testimony before the House of Commons committee in May 1834 is reproduced in "Report from the Committee on Lower Canada," 3 July 1834, *BPP-C-C*, 1:102–6 (for the Legislative Council).

21 Garon, "La fonction politique."

22 This was one of the complaints included in the Ninety-Two Resolutions of 1834; see resolutions 51, 52, 75, and 77, *JHALC*, 1834, 323, 329–30.

23 "Copy of a Despatch from Lord Goderich," *JHALC*, 1831–32, 26.

24 "Despatch from Lord Glenelg to the Earl of Gosford," 17 July 1835, *BPP-C-C*, 7:212.

25 My calculations are based on the list of councillors provided in Desjardins, *Guide parlementaire*, 56–9.

26 Cited in Buckner, *The Transition*, 222. Burroughs paraphrases it in *The Canadian Crisis*, 87.

27 "Lord Aylmer's Despatch on 5th March 1834, addressed to the Right Honourable Edward Stanley," *BPP-C-C*, 7:327.

28 "Lord Aylmer's Despatch to the Right Honourable the Earl of Aberdeen," 18 March 1834, reproduced in *JHALC*, 1834, Appendix L.L.

29 *First Report on the State of the Representation*, 8, 14; Mackenzie, *Sketches of Canada*, 361–2; "Declaration," *The Constitution*, 2 August 1837.

30 Papineau, "Abolition du Conseil legislatif (Chambre d'Assemblée, 11 mars 1831)," in *Un demi-siècle de combats*, 164.

31 See resolutions 64–74, 84(8), *JHALC*, 1834, 327–9, 332.

32 According to Lord Glenelg, "the constitution of Lower Canada consists of various branches or members, to each of which Parliament has assigned such functions as were thought necessary to counterbalance the danger of abuse in the other organs of government" ("Despatch from Lord Glenelg to the Earl of Gosford, The Right Hon. Sir C.E. Grey and Sir G. Gipps, His Majesty's Commissioners of Inquiry in Lower Canada," 17 July 1835, *BPP-C-C*, 7:178).

33 Lord Gosford, Charles Grey, and George Gipps, "Second Report," 12 March 1836, *BPP-C-C*, 4:89.

34 Constitutional Association of Montreal, "[Address] to Men of British or Irish Descent," 20 November 1834, in Christie, *A History*, 4:40.

35 Thom (Camillus), *Anti-Gallic Letters*, 33, emphasis added.

36 Ibid., 204–5.

37 Ibid., 125.

38 Ibid., 208.

39 "The same law that gives the people representatives, without whose consent it cannot be asked for its money, not only gives it the right, but imposes upon it the obligation, to arm itself against kings, as well as those of the king's men who would attempt to rob it of the representative system" (Papineau, "Ouverture de la session parlementaire de 1837 [Chambre d'Assemblée, 19 août 1837]," in *Un demi-siècle de combats*, 477). The second resolution of the Assembly of Stanbridge (Missisquoi; held 4 July 1837) clearly affirmed that "[the people] possesses the inviolable right to amend, reform or change this government, whenever its security, its happiness or prosperity so dictate, or when public freedom is in peril, [and it may therefore] reassert its rights and act according to its own vigour, where its efforts to obtain justice elsewhere are ineffective" (*La Minerve*, 13 July 1837).

40 "Government is founded on the authority and is instituted for the benefit of a people; when, therefore, any government long and systematically ceases to answer the great ends of its foundation, the people have a natural right given them by their Creator to seek after and establish such institutions as will yield the greatest quantity of happiness to the greatest number" (Mackenzie, "Declaration"; *The Constitution*, 2 August 1837). See also the draft constitution published by Mackenzie in *The Constitution*, 15 November 1837.

41 *La Minerve*, 9 February 1832.

42 "I would earnestly recommend to the advisers of the crown, that they employ a leisure hour in comparing the history of the era preceding the revolution in North America, with events which are passing before the eyes on that interesting continent" (Mackenzie, *Sketches of Canada*, xxiv).

43 Mackenzie, *Sketches of Canada*, 14.

44 Papineau, "Assemblée de Saint-Laurent (Discours public, 15 mai 1837)," in *Un demi-siècle de combats*, 419.

45 Papineau, *Address*, 13.

46 Papineau, "Assemblée des comtés de l'Assomption et de Lachenaie (Discours public, 29 juillet 1837)," in *Un demi-siècle de combats*, 463.

47 "Adresse des Fils de la liberté de Montréal aux jeunes gens des colonies de l'Amérique du nord, 4 October 1837," in Bernard, comp., *Assemblées publiques*, 216.

48 Papineau, "Adresse de la Confédération des Six Comtés au peuple du Canada (Adresse publique, 24 octobre 1837)," in *Un demi-siècle de combats*, 496–7.

49 First resolution of the Assembly of the Six Counties, reproduced in *La Minerve*, 30 October 1837. Mackenzie forthrightly appeals to the "right [that] was conceded to the present United States at the close of a successful revolution, to form a constitution for themselves" (*The Constitution*, 2 August 1837).

50 Nelson is quoted in Dessaulles, *Papineau et Nelson*, 45. It should be said that the pamphlet was written to defend Papineau's conduct during the rebellions from Nelson's charges. It remains to be determined whether the quote is authentic. Gérard Filteau paraphrases, "the time has come to melt down our tin plates and spoons and make bullets out of them" (*Histoire des Patriotes*, 277).

51 Quoted in Filteau, *Histoire des Patriotes*, 277. Filteau asserts that this was all just an attempt to intimidate the authorities. At any rate, an unambiguous quote like this indicates that rebellion was clearly considered one way forward.

52 "I must say, that it is neither fear, nor scruple, which leads me to say that the hour has not yet struck ... Whoever is familiar with the history of the just and glorious revolution of the United States, sees such a unanimous concert of the most enlightened and the most virtuous men of all the countries of the world, who applaud the heroic and moral resistance put up by the Americans against the usurpation of the British Parliament, which sought to despoil them and appropriate their revenue, as they seek to do to ours today, that to follow successfully the path marked out by the patriots of 74 would be to ally oneself with the greatest and purest reputations of modern times" (Papineau, "Assemblée de Saint-Laurent [Discours public, 5 mai 1837]," in *Un demi-siècle de combats*, 432–3).

53 The Constitution, 26 July 1837.

54 Reprinted in Lindsey, *The Life and Times*, 2:358, Appendix F, and in *The Selected Writings*, 222–5, where its distribution is dated ca. 27 November 1837.

55 The quotes in this paragraph constitute only one paragraph of a speech by Papineau, "Abolition du Conseil législatif (Chambre d'Assemblée, 11 mars 1831)," in *Un demi-siècle de combats*, 156.

56 "The authority of a mother country over a colony can only exist as long as it may please the colonists who inhabit it; for, having been established and peopled by these colonists, the country belongs to them as of right, and consequently may be detached from any foreign connection whenever the nuisances resulting from a faraway executive power, which ceases to be in harmony with a local legislature, render such a step necessary to the inhabitants, in order to protect their life and their liberty or to acquire prosperity" ("Adresse des Fils de la liberté de Montréal," in Bernard, comp., *Assemblées publiques*, 215).

57 *La Minerve*, 5 June 1837.

58 Thom, *Anti-Gallic Letters*, 39.

59 "Great Loyal Meeting" (*Montreal Gazette*, 24 October 1837, 2, col. 5). The *Montreal Gazette* wrote in November, "It cannot be denied that those who have always been accustomed to wage political hostility against the Constitution and the supreme authority of ENGLAND, are now desirous of enforcing their arguments by physical prowess ... But it is fortunate for the peaceable members of society that, the courage of these revolutionary despots lacks much of the zeal of their ill-advised ambition. They have the audacity to project what they have neither the power, the strength, nor the hardihood to accomplish" (*Montreal Gazette*, 7 November 1837, 2, col. 4).

60 Blackstone, *Commentaries*, 1, 2 (1:157).

61 See Locke, "Second Treatise on Civil Government," ch. 11, sec. 134–6, in *Political Writings*, 328–31.

62 Blackstone, *Commentaries*, 1, 2 (1:157).

63 Ibid., 4, 6 (4:82).

64 For the discussion on the right to revolt, see Locke, "Second Treatise on Civil Government," 18, 199–210, in *Political Writings*, 363–9.

65 Thom (Anti-Bureaucrat), *Remarks*, 55. The Constitutional Association of Montreal stated, "it is this exclusive French Canadian spirit alone which has given rise to all the discontent existing in this Province ... No real oppression exists in the Province and no real grievance, consistent with the preservation of British supremacy, remains unredressed. The French Canadian leaders have endeavoured to excite the sympathy of the citizens of the United States, and of the professed republicans in Upper Canada ... as if their real views were republican, and as if that form of government were favoured by the French Canadian population" ("Address of the Constitutional Association of the City of Montreal to the Inhabitants of the Sister Colonies," [13 December 1837], in Christie, *A History*, 4:510).

66 Thom, *Letter*, 6–7.

67 Constitutional Association of Montreal, "Address of the Constitutional Association of the City of Montreal to the Inhabitants of the Sister Colonies" (13 December 1837), in Christie, *A History*, 4:508–9.

68 *Report from the Select Committee*, 12.

69 Thom, *Remarks*, 57.

70 Ibid., 58.

71 *Report from the Select Committee*, 17.

72 Quoted in Thom, *Anti-Gallic Letters*, 177–8. While Thom does not provide
the source of this quote, the statement is known to have been made on
8 April 1796; see *The Parliamentary Register*, 44:382.

73 *Montreal Gazette*, 14 January and 9 June 1836.

74 Thom, *Anti-Gallic Letters*, 40.

75 Ibid., 178.

76 Lord Gosford, Charles Grey, and George Gipps, "Second Report,"
12 March 1836, *BPP-C-C*, 4:90. Commissioner Gipps went further, declaring that London could not withdraw its armed forces from Lower Canada
since a civil war would ensue ("Extracts of the Minutes of Proceedings on
Monday 14 March 1836," *BPP-C-C*, 4:99).

77 Young, *The Politics of Codification*, 84–95; Carman Miller, "Day, Charles
Dewey," *DCB*, 11:237–9.

78 Lettre from Charles Dewey Day of 22 December 1837, published in the
Montreal Gazette on 17 February 1838.

79 *Le Canadien*, 17 January 1838.

80 Robinson, *Address*. On this issue, see also Jerry Bannister, "Canada as
Counter-Revolution: The Loyalist Order Framework in Canadian History,"
in *Liberalism and Hegemony*, ed. Constant and Ducharme, 112–27.

81 Robinson, *Charge*, 10.

82 This discussion on the difference between the preindustrial and industrial
states is directly derived from Greer, "The Birth of the Police in Canada,"
in Greer and Radforth, eds., *Colonial Leviathan*, 17–49 (18 for the quote).
On mob rule, see Greer, *The Patriots and the People*, 69–86.

83 Robinson, *Charge of the Honorable John B. Robinson*, 10. Robinson continued
along these lines on the occasion of his sentencing Lount and Matthews
to death. For him, the rebels' acts were wrong because there had been no
curtailment of liberty, property, or security (Robinson, *Address*).

84 Constitutional Association of Quebec, "Report [of the Executive
Committee]," 5 January 1836, in Christie, *A History*, 4:280.

85 British Rifle Corps to Gosford, in Christie, *A History*, 4:143.

86 Gosford to British Rifle Corps, 28 December 1834, in Christie, *A History*,
4:143.

87 Constitutional Association of Quebec, "Report [of the Executive
Committee]," 5 January 1836, in Christie, *A History*, 4:281.

88 Robert Baldwin Sullivan to Sir George Arthur, 1 June 1838, *The Arthur
Papers*, 1:172.

89 Fourth Russell Resolution, *BPP-C-C*, 9:15.

90 "Despatch from Lord Glenelg to the Earl of Gosford," 29 April 1837,
BPP-C-C, 9:18.

91 Fifth Russell Resolution, *BPP-C-C*, 9:15.
92 "Despatch from Lord Glenelg to the Earl of Gosford," 14 July 1837, *BPP-C-C*, 9:23.
93 *La Minerve*, 30 October 1837.
94 "Despatch from Lord Glenelg to the Earl of Gosford," 22 May 1837, *BPP-C-C*, 9:19.
95 I share the view of Allan Greer, for whom the rebellion of 1837 was the moment when Canada came closest to a revolution; see *The Patriots and the People*, 3–10.
96 On the repression of the rebellions, see Greenwood and Wright, eds., *Canadian State Trials*, vol. 2.
97 Second resolution adopted by the Constitutional Association of Quebec, 7 February 1838, in Christie, *A History*, 5:76. The abdication of James II was officially declared in the Bill of Rights of 1689.
98 For a good study of the Special Council, see Watt, "Authoritarianism."
99 Locke, "Second Treatise on Civil Government," 14:164, in *Political Writings*, 346; Montesquieu, *Spirit*, 11 (6:154).
100 "Lord John Russell to the Right Hon. C. Poulett Thomson," 7 September 1839, *BPP-C-C*, 13:10.
101 Durham, *Report on the Affairs*, 2:260.
102 *Montreal Gazette*, 31 March 1838.
103 *Le Canadien*, 21 March 1838.
104 Mill, "Considerations on Representative Government," in *On Liberty and Other Essays*, 243–4.
105 See John Stuart Mill, *Collected Works*, 6:405–35, 437–43, 445–64; Mill, *Autobiography*, 216–17.
106 Robinson, *Canada and the Canada Bill*, 138.
107 *Tables Relative to the Acts*, 92–124.

CONCLUSION

1 On this subject, see Ducharme, "Penser le Canada."
2 On the issue of Canadian parliamentary sovereignty, see Ajzenstat, *The Canadian Founding*; Resnick, *Parliament vs People*; Resnick, "Montesquieu Revisited," and "Burke or Rousseau? Parliament or People?," in *The Masks of Proteus*, chapters. 4–5. On the non-existence of a sovereign Canadian people, see Russell, *Constitutional Odyssey*.
3 McKay, "Liberal Order Framework," 624. On liberalism as defined by these three terms, see Roy, *Progrès, harmonie, liberté*, 49–53.

Bibliography

GOVERNMENT DOCUMENTS

British Parliamentary Papers - Colonies - Canada (BPP-C-C). Vols. 1–14 (1828–41). Shannon: Irish University Press, 1968–1971.
Hansard's Parliamentary Debates. 3rd series. London: Hansard, 1838.
Important Debate on the Adoption of the Report of the Select Committee on the Differences between His Excellency and the Late Executive Council in the House of Assembly, April 18th, 1836. Toronto: Jos. H. Lawrence, printer, Guardian Office, 1836.
Journals of the Continental Congress, 1774–1789. 34 vols. Edited by Worthington Chauncey Ford. Washington, DC: United States Government Printing Office, 1904-1937.
Journals of the House of Assembly of Lower Canada (JHALC) (1792–1837).
Journals of the House of Assembly of Upper Canada (JHAUC) (1828–40)
Journals of the Legislative Council of Lower Canada (JLCLC) (1792–1837).
The Parliamentary Register. London: J. Debrett, 1791.
Petition of the House of Assembly of Lower Canada to the King and the Two Houses of Parliament Adopted in Consequence of the Disclosure of the Instructions to the Governor and Commissioners. London: C. and W. Reynell, 1836.
Remontrances du Parlement de Paris au XVIIIe siècle. Published by Jean Flammermont and Maurice Tourneux. Vol. 2. Paris: Imprimerie nationale, 1889–1898.
Report of a Select Committee of the House of Assembly on the Political State of the Provinces of Upper Canada and Lower Canada. Toronto: R. Stanton, 1838.
Report of a Select Committee of the Legislative Council of Upper Canada, upon the Complaints Contained in an Address to the King, from the House of Assembly, passed 15th April, 1835, of the Rejection by the Legislative Council, of Bills Sent from the House of Assembly: and the Address of the Legislative Council to His Majesty, on that subject Upper Canada. Toronto: R. Stanton, 1836.
Report from the Select Committee of the Legislative Council of Upper Canada, on the State of the Province. [Toronto?]: R. Stanton, [1838].

Tables Relative to the Acts and Ordinances of Lower-Canada: Published by Order of His Excellency the Governor General, under the Superintendence of the Commissioners for Revising the said Statutes and Ordinances. Kingston: Printed by S. Derbyshire and G. Desbarats, 1843.

Upper Canada. Legislature. House of Assembly. Select Committee Appointed to Enquire into the State of the Representation of the People of Upper Canada. *First Report on the State of the Representation of the People of Upper Canada in the Legislature of that Province.* York [Toronto]: Office of the Colonial Advocate, 1831.

NEWSPAPERS

Le Canadien (1805–10, 1817–25, 1831–40).
Colonial Advocate (1824–34).
The Constitution (1834–37).
Gazette de Montréal/Montreal Gazette (1785–94).
Montreal Gazette (1836–40).
Quebec Gazette (1788–94).

SCHOLARLY SOURCES

Acomb, Frances. *Anglophobia in France, 1763–1789: An Essay in the History of Constitutionalism and Nationalism.* 1950. New York: Octagon Books, 1980.

Acton, Lord John Emerich Edward Dalberg. *The History of Freedom and other Essays.* London: Macmillan, 1907.

Adams, John. *A Defence of the Constitutions of Government of the United States of America.* 3 vols. London: Printed for John Stockdale, 1794.

Adelman, Jeremy. *Sovereignty and Revolution in the Iberian Atlantic.* Princeton: Princeton University Press, 2006.

Ajzenstat, Janet. "Canada's First Constitution: Pierre Bédard on Tolerance and Dissent." *Canadian Journal of Political Science* 23, no. 1 (1990): 39–57.

– *The Canadian Founding: Locke and Parliament.* Montreal and Kingston: McGill-Queen's University Press, 2007.

– "Durham and Robinson: Political Faction and Moderation." *Journal of Canadian Studies* 25, no. 1 (1990): 24–38.

– "Modern Mixed Government: A Liberal Defence of Inequality." *Canadian Journal of Political Science* 18, no. 1 (1985): 119–34.

– *The Once and Future Canadian Democracy: An Essay in Political Thought.* Montreal and Kingston: McGill-Queen's University Press, 2003.

– *The Political Thought of Lord Durham.* Montreal and Kingston: McGill-Queen's University Press, 1988.

Ajzenstat, Janet, and Peter J. Smith, eds. *Canada's Origins: Liberal, Tory or Republican?* Ottawa: Carleton University Press, 1995.

Albertone, Manuela. "Democratic Republicanism: Historical Reflections on the Idea of Republic in the Eighteenth Century." *History of European Ideas* 33, no. 1 (2007): 108–30.

Andrès, Bernard, and Marc-André Bernier, eds. *Portrait des arts, des lettres et de l'éloquence au Québec (1760–1840)*. Quebec: Presses de l'Université Laval, 2002.

Andrews, Stuart. *The Rediscovery of America: Transatlantic Crosscurrents in an Age of Revolution*. London: MacMillan Press, 1998.

Appleby, Joyce. *Liberalism and Republicanism in the Historical Imagination.* Cambridge, MA: Harvard University Press, 1992.

Applewhite, Harriet B., and Darline G. Levy, eds. *Women and Politics in the Age of the Democratic Revolution.* Ann Arbor: University of Michigan Press, 1990.

Arendt, Hannah. *On Revolution.* New York: Viking Press, 1965.

Armitage, David. *The Declaration of Independence: A Global History.* Cambridge, MA: Harvard University Press, 2007.

Armitage, David, and Michael J. Braddick, eds. *The British Atlantic World, 1500–1800.* New York: Palgrave Macmillan, 2002.

Arthur, Sir George. *The Arthur Papers: Being the Canadian Papers Mainly Confidential, Private, and Demi-Official of Sir George Arthur in the Manuscript Collection of the Toronto Public Libraries.* Edited by Charles R. Sanderson. Toronto: Toronto Public Libraries and University of Toronto Press, 1957–59.

Aughey, Arthur, Greta Jones, and W.T.M. Riches. *The Conservative Political Tradition in Britain and in the United States.* Rutherford, NJ: Fairleigh Dickinson University Press, 1992.

Baby, François. *Un Canadien et sa femme.* N.p., 1794.

Baechler, Jean. *Qu'est-ce qu'une idéologie?* Paris: Gallimard, 1976.

Bagehot, Walter. *The English Constitution.* 1867. Oxford: Oxford University Press, 2001.

Bailyn, Bernard. *Atlantic History: Concept and Contours.* Cambridge, MA: Harvard University Press, 2005.

– *The Ideological Origins of the American Revolution.* Cambridge, MA: Belknap Press of the Harvard University Press, 1967.

Baker, Keith Michael. *Inventing the French Revolution: Essays on French Political Culture in the Eighteenth Century.* Cambridge: Cambridge University Press, 1990.

– "Transformations of Classical Republicanism in Eighteenth-Century France." *Journal of Modern History* 73, no. 1 (2001): 32–53.

Banks, Kenneth. *Chasing Empire across the Sea: Communications and the State in the French Atlantic, 1713–1763.* Montreal and Kingston: McGill-Queen's University Press, 2003.

Banning, Lance. *Conceived in Liberty: The Struggle to Define the New Republic, 1789–1793.* Lanham, MD: Rowman and Littlefield, 2004.

– "Jeffersonian Ideology Revisited: Liberal and Classical Ideas in the New American Republic." *William and Mary Quarterly* 43, no. 1 (1986): 3–19.

– *The Jeffersonian Persuasion: Evolution of a Party Ideology.* Ithaca, NY: Cornell University Press, 1978.

– *The Sacred Fire of Liberty: James Madison and the Founding of the Federal Republic.* Ithaca, NY: Cornell University Press, 1995.

Barny, Roger. *Prélude idéologique à la Révolution française: Le Rousseauisme avant 1789.* Paris: Les Belles-Lettres, 1985.

Bartlett, Thomas, David Dickson, Daire Keogh, and Kevin Whelan, eds. *1798: A Bicentenary Perspective*. Dublin: Four Courts, 2003.

Bayley, Charles Calvert. "The Idea of Liberty in the Middle Ages." *Transactions of the Royal Society of Canada*, 56 (June 1962): 1–10.

Bélanger, Damien-Claude. "Les historiens révisionnistes et le rejet de la 'canadianité' du Québec: Réflexions en marge de la *Genèse des nations et cultures du nouveau monde* de Gérard Bouchard." *Revue d'histoire intellectuelle de l'Amérique française* 2, no. 1 (2001): 105–12.

Bélanger, Damien-Claude, Sophie Coupal, and Michel Ducharme, eds. *Les idées en mouvement: Perspectives en histoire intellectuelle et culturelle du Canada*. Quebec: Les Presses de l'Universite Laval, 2004.

Belchem, John. *Popular Radicalism in Nineteenth-Century Britain*. New York: St Martin's Press, 1996.

Bellavance, Marcel. *Le Québec au siècle des nationalités (1791–1918): Essai d'histoire comparée*. Montreal: VLB éditeur, 2004.

Benjamin, Thomas, Timothy D. Hall, and David Rutherford, eds. *The Atlantic World in the Age of Empire*. Boston: Houghton Mifflin, 2001.

Bentham, Jeremy. *An Introduction to the Principles of Morals and Legislation*. 1780, 1789. London: Athlone Press, 1970.

Berlin, Isaiah. *Two Concepts of Liberty*. Oxford: Clarendon Press, 1958.

Bernard, Jean-Paul, comp. *Assemblées publiques, résolutions et déclarations de 1837–1838*. Ville Saint-Laurent: VLB éditeur, 1988.

– *Les Rébellions de 1837–1838: Les Patriotes du Bas-Canada dans la mémoire collective et chez les historiens*. Montreal: Boréal express, 1983.

Bernard, Philippe. *Amury Girod: Un Suisse chez les Patriotes du Bas-Canada*. Sillery: Septentrion, 2001.

Bernier, Gérald, and Daniel Salée. "Les insurrections de 1837–1838 au Québec: Remarques critiques et théoriques en marge de l'historiographie." *Canadian Review of Studies in Nationalism* 13, no. 1 (1986): 13–29.

– *The Shaping of Québec Politics and Society: Colonialism, Power, and the Transition to Capitalism in the 19th Century*. Washington, DC: C. Russak, 1992.

Bevir, Mark. "Republicanism, Socialism, and Democracy in Britain: The Origins of the Radical Left." *Journal of Social History* 34, no. 2 (2000): 351–68.

Bidwell, Marshall Spring. *Mr. Bidwell's Speech on the Intestate Estate Bill in the Provincial Assembly of Upper Canada, January 24, 1831*. N.p., 1831.

– *Substance of Mr. Bidwell's Speech on the Second Reading of his Intestate Estate Bill, in the Session of 1832*. N.p., 1832.

Blackburn, Robin. "Haiti, Slavery, and the Age of the Democratic Revolution." *William and Mary Quarterly* 63, no. 4 (2006): 643–74.

Blackstone, Sir William. *Commentaries on the Laws of England*. 4 vols. Chicago: Chicago University Press, 1979 (1765–69).

Blanchet, François. *Appel au Parlement impérial et aux habitans des colonies angloises dans l'Amérique du Nord sur les prétentions exorbitantes du Gouvernement exécutif et du Conseil législatif de la province du Bas-Canada*. Québec: F. Vallerand, 1824.

Blom, Hans, John Christian Laursen, and Luisa Simonutti, eds. *Monarchisms in the Age of Enlightenment: Liberty, Patriotism, and the Common Good*. Toronto: University of Toronto Press, 2007.

Blum, Carol. *Rousseau and the Republic of Virtue: The Language of Politics in the French Revolution.* Ithaca, NY: Cornell University Press, 1986.

Bolingbroke, Henry St John, Viscount. *Bolingbroke Political Writing.* Edited by Isaac Kramnick. New York: Appleton-Century-Crofts, 1970.

Bouchard, Gérard. *The Making of the Nations and Cultures of the New World: An Essay in Comparative History.* Translated by Michelle Weinroth and Paul Leduc Browne. Montreal and Kingston: McGill-Queen's University Press, 2008.

– *Quelques arpents d'Amérique: Population, économie, famille au Saguenay, 1838-1971.* Montreal: Boréal, 1996.

Boulle, Pierre H., and Richard A. Lebrun, eds. *Le Canada et la Révolution française: actes du 6e Colloque du CIEE, 29, 30, 31 octobre 1987.* Montreal: Centre interuniversitaire d'études européennes, 1989.

Bourdages, Louis [Un habitant]. *Adresse à tous les électeurs du Bas-Canada sur le choix de leurs Représentans à l'élection prochaine.* Montreal: L. Duvernay, 1827.

Bourdin, Philippe, and Jean-Luc Chappey, eds. *Révoltes et révolutions en Europe et aux Amériques, 1773–1802.* Paris: A. Colin, 2004.

Bourque, Gilles. *Question nationale et classes sociales au Québec, 1760–1840.* Montreal: Parti Pris, 1970.

Bowsfield, Hartwell Walter. "Upper Canada: The Development of Political Consciousness in the 1820s." PhD diss. (History), University of Toronto, 1977.

Boyer, Jean-Pierre. "Le Québec à l'heure des révolutions atlantiques." Afterword to *Les Droits de l'homme,* by Thomas Paine, 355–424. Sillery, QC: Septentrion, 1998.

Brading, D.A. *Classical Republicanism and Creole Patriotism: Simon Bolivar (1783–1830) and the Spanish American Revolution.* Cambridge: Centre of Latin American Studies, University of Cambridge, 1983.

Bradshaw, Frederick. *Self-Government in Canada and How It Was Achieved: The Story of Lord Durham's Report.* London: P.S. King and Son, 1903.

Braud, Philippe. *Sociologie politique.* 2nd ed. Paris: Librairie générale de droit et de jurisprudence, 1994.

Brode, Patrick. *Sir John Beverley Robinson: Bone and Sinew of the Compact.* Toronto: University of Toronto Press, 1984.

Brown, G.P., ed. *Documents on the Confederation of British North America.* Toronto: McClelland and Stewart, 1969.

Brown, Wallace, and Hereward Senior. *Victorious in Defeat: The Loyalists in Canada.* Toronto: Methuen, 1984.

Brun, Henri. *La formation des institutions parlementaires québécoises, 1791–1838.* Quebec: Les Presses de l'Université Laval, 1970.

Brunet, Michel. "La Révolution française sur les rives du St-Laurent." *Revue d'histoire de l'Amérique française* 11, no. 2 (1957): 155–62.

Brymner, Douglas. *Report on Canadian Archives.* Ottawa: S.E. Dawson, 1893.

Buckner, Philip A. *The Transition to Responsible Government: British Policy in British North America, 1815–1850.* Westport, CT: Greenwood Press, 1985.

Buel Jr, Richard. *Securing the Revolution: Ideology in American Politics, 1789–1815.* Ithaca, NY: Cornell University Press, 1972.

Burdeau, Georges. *L'État.* Paris: Seuil, 1970.

Burke, Edmund. *Reflections on the Revolution in France.* 1790. London: Penguin Books, 1986.

– *The Writings and Speeches of Edmund Burke.* Vol. 3, *Party, Parliament, and the American War, 1774–1780.* Edited by Paul Langford. Oxford: Clarendon Press, 1996.

Burroughs, Peter. *The Canadian Crisis and the British Colonial Policy, 1828–1841.* London: Edward Arnold, 1972.

Burrow, J.W. *Whigs and Liberals: Continuity and Change in English Political Thought.* Oxford: Clarendon Press, 1988.

Canny, Nicholas, and Anthony Pagden, eds. *Colonial Identity in the Atlantic World, 1500–1800.* Princeton: Princeton University Press, 1987.

Careless, J.M.S. *The Union of the Canadas: The Growth of Canadian Institutions, 1841–1857.* Toronto: McClelland and Stewart, 1967.

Carlyle, A.J. *Political Liberty: A History of the Conception in the Middle Ages and Modern Times.* Oxford: Clarendon Press, 1941.

Cazzanigo, Gian Mario, and Yves Charles Zarka, eds. *Penser la souveraineté à l'époque moderne et contemporaine.* 2 vols. Paris: Librairie philosophique J. Vrin, 2001.

Chartier, Roger. *Au bord de la falaise: L'histoire entre certitudes et inquiétude.* Paris: Albin Michel, 1998.

Chisick, Harvey. "The Ambivalence of the Idea of Equality in the French Enlightenment." *History of European Ideas* 13, no. 3 (1991): 215–23.

Choquette, Leslie. *Frenchmen into Peasants: Modernity and Tradition in the Peopling of French Canada.* Cambridge: Cambridge University Press, 1997.

Christie, Nancy, ed. *Transatlantic Subjects: Ideas, Institutions, and Social Experience in Post-Revolutionary British North America.* Montreal and Kingston: McGill-Queen's University Press, 2008.

Christie, Robert. *A History of the Late Province of Lower Canada Parliamentary and Political from the Commencement to the Close of its Existence as a Separate Province.* 6 vols. Montreal: Richard Worthington, 1866.

Citizen of Quebec, A. *Observations on a Pamphlet Entitled A State of the Present Form of Government of the Province of Quebec; circulated in London, during the last Summer.* London: J.F. and C. Rivington, 1790.

Clark, J.C.D. *English Society, 1688–1832.* Cambridge: Cambridge University Press, 1985.

– *Revolution and Rebellion: State and Society in England in the Seventeenth and Eighteenth Centuries.* Cambridge: Cambridge University Press, 1986.

Clark, S.D. *The Movements of Political Protest in Canada.* Toronto: University of Toronto Press, 1959.

Coleman, Charly J. "The Value of Dispossession: Rethinking Discourses of Selfhood in Eighteenth-Century France." *Modern Intellectual History* 2, no. 3 (2005): 299–326.

Colley, Linda. *Britons: Forging the Nation, 1707–1837.* New Haven, CT: Yale University Press, 1992.

Condon, Ann Gorman. *The Envy of the American States: The Loyalist Dream for New Brunswick.* Fredericton, NB: New Ireland, 1984.

Condorcet, Antoine de. *Sur les élections et autres textes.* Edited by Olivier de Bernon. Paris: Fayard, 1986.

Constant, Benjamin. "The Liberty of the Ancients Compared with That of the Moderns: Speech Given at the Athénée Royal in Paris." In Benjamin Constant, *Political Writings,* edited and translated by Biancamaria Fontana, 307–28. New York: Cambridge University Press, 1988.

Constant, Jean-Francois, and Michel Ducharme, eds. *Liberalism and Hegemony: Debating the Canadian Liberal Revolution.* Toronto: University of Toronto Press, 2008.

Constitutional Association of Quebec. *First Annual Report of the Constitutional Association of Quebec, Presented 28th November, 1835.* Quebec: 1835.

Constitutional Association of the City of Montreal. *Representation on the Legislative Union of the Provinces of Upper and Lower Canada.* [N.p., 1837?].

Conway, Stephen. *The British Isles and the War of American Independence.* Oxford: Oxford University Press, 2000.

Cook, Terry. "John Beverly Robinson and the Conservative Blueprint for the Upper Canadian Community." *Ontario History* 64, no. 2 (1972): 79–94.

Cornu, Gérard. *Vocabulaire juridique.* Paris: Quadrige/Presses universitaires de France, 1987.

Cornu, Laurence. *Une autre république: 1791, l'occasion et le destin d'une initiative républicaine.* Paris: Harmattan, 2004.

Corrigan, Philip, and Bruce Curtis. "Education, Inspection and State Formation: A Preliminary Statement." *Historical Papers* (Canadian Historical Association) 20, no. 1 (1985): 156–71.

Coste, Brigitte. *Mably: Pour une utopie du bon sens.* Paris: C. Klincksiek, 1975.

Cott, Nancy F. *The Bonds of Womanhood: "Women's Sphere" in New England, 1780–1835.* New Haven, CT: Yale University Press, 1977.

Cottret, Bernard, ed. *Du patriotisme aux nationalismes (1700–1848): France, Grande-Bretagne, Amérique du Nord.* Paris: Éditions Créaphis, 2002.

Craig, Gérald. *Upper Canada: The Formative Years, 1784–1841.* Toronto: McClelland and Stewart, 1963.

Cranston, Maurice. "Jean-Jacques Rousseau and the Fusion of Democratic Sovereignty and Aristocratic Government." *History of European Ideas* 11 (1989): 417–25.

Creighton, Donald G. *The Commercial Empire of the St. Lawrence, 1760–1850.* 1937. Toronto: Macmillan.

– "The Economic Background of the Rebellions of Eighteen Thirty-Seven." *Canadian Journal of Economics and Political Science* 3, no. 3 (1937): 322–34.

– *The Road to Confederation: The Emergence of Canada, 1863–1867.* Toronto: Macmillan, 1964.

Cruikshank, E.A. "The Genesis of the Canada Act." *Papers and Records* (Ontario Historical Society) 28 (1932): 155–322.

Cunningham, Noble E. *Jefferson vs. Hamilton: Confrontations that Shaped a Nation.* Boston: Bedford/St Martin's, 2000.

Curtis, Bruce. "The Canada 'Blue Books' and the Administrative Capacity of the Canadian State, 1822–67." *Canadian Historical Review* 74, no. 4 (1993): 535–65.

- *The Politics of Population: State Formation, Statistics, and the Census of Canada, 1840–1875.* Toronto: University of Toronto Press, 2001.
- *Ruling by Schooling Quebec: Conquest to Liberal Governmentality: A Historical Sociology.* Toronto: University of Toronto Press, 2012.
- *True Government by Choice Men? Inspection, Education and State Formation in Canada West.* Toronto: University of Toronto Press, 1992.

D'Alembert, Jean Le Rond, ed. *Encyclopédie ou dictionnaire raisonné des sciences, des arts et des métiers.* 2 vols. Paris: Garnier-Flammarion, 1986.

Dagenais, Michèle. "S'interroger sur la 'nation': Une autre manière d'enseigner l'histoire du Canada." *Canadian Issues,* October-November 2001, 23–5.

Daire, Eugène, ed. *Physiocrates: Quesnay, Dupont de Nemours, Mercier de la Rivière, L'abbé Baudau, Le Trosne; avec une introd. sur la doctrine des Physiocrates, des commentaires et des notices historiques.* Geneva: Slatkine Reprints, 1971.

Dalton, Susan. *Engendering the Republic of Letters: Reconnecting Public and Private Spheres in Eighteenth-Century Europe.* Montreal and Kingston: McGill-Queen's University Press, 2003.

Darnton, Robert. "The Grub Street Style of Revolution: J.-P. Brissot, Police Spy." *Journal of Modern History* 40, no. 3 (1968): 301–27.

- "The High-Enlightenment and the Low-Life of Literature in Pre-Revolutionary France." *Past and Present* 51 (May 1971): 81–115.

David, Marcel. *La souveraineté du peuple.* Paris: Presses universitaires de France, 1996.

Davidoff, Leonore, and Catherine Hall. *Family Fortunes: Men and Women of the English Middle-Class, 1780–1850.* London: Hutchinson, 1987.

Davis, R.W., ed. *The Origins of Modern Freedom in the West.* Stanford: Stanford University Press, 1995.

De Brou, David. "Mass Political Behaviour in Upper-Town Quebec, 1792–1836." PhD diss. (History), University of Ottawa, 1989.

De Dijn, Annelien. "Aristocratic Liberalism in Post-Revolutionary France." *Historical Journal* 48, no. 3 (2005): 661–81.

De Lolme, Jean Louis. *The Constitution of England; Or an Account of the English Constitution.* London: Henry G. Bohn, 1853 (1771).

Delaporte, André. "Idée d'égalité, thème et mythe de l'âge d'or en France au XVIIIe siècle." *History of European Ideas* 14, no. 1 (1992): 115–36.

Desjardins, Joseph. *Guide parlementaire historique de la province de Québec, 1792–1903.* Quebec: N.p., 1902.

Dessaulles, Louis-Antoine. *Papineau et Nelson: Blanc et noir.* Montreal: Presses de l'Avenir, 1848.

Dessureault, Christian. "La crise sous Dalhousie: Conception de la milice et conscience élitaire des réformistes bas-canadiens, 1827–1828." *Revue d'histoire de l'Amérique française* 61, no. 2 (2007): 167–99.

- "L'élection de 1830 dans le comté de Saint-Hyacinthe: Identités élitaires et solidarités paroissiales, sociales ou familiales." *Social History* 36, no. 72 (2003): 281–310.

Dialogue sur l'Intérêt du Jour, entre plusieurs Candidats et un Électeur libre et indépen-dans de la Cité de Québec; Destiné pour être prononcé au Club Constitutionnel

Extraordinaire, Tenu le Samedi 19 mai 1792, par un Membre du dit Club, mais qu'un accident imprévu a empêch[é] d'être lû. Quebec: Herald, 1792.

Dickinson, H.T. *Liberty and Property: Political Ideology in Eighteenth-Century Britain.* 1977. London: Methuen, 1979.

Dickinson, H.T., ed. *Britain and the American Revolution.* London: Addison Wesley Longman, 1998.

Dictionary of Canadian Biography (DCB). Toronto: University of Toronto Press, 1966–.

Disraeli, Benjamin. *Selected Speeches of the Late Right Honourable Earl of Beaconsfield.* 2 vols. Edited by T.E. Kebbel. London: Longmans, Green, and Co., 1882.

– *Sybil: Or, The Two Nations.* 1845. Oxford: Oxford University Press, 1998.

– *Whigs and Whiggism, 1833–1853.* 2nd ed. Edited, with an introduction, by William Hutcheon; revised and expanded with a new introduction by Christopher B. Briggs. Washington, DC: Regnery, 2006.

Dorland, Michael, and Maurice Charland. *Law, Rhetoric and Irony in the Formation of Canadian Civil Culture.* Toronto: University of Toronto Press, 2002.

Doughty, Arthur G., and Norah Story, eds. *Documents Relating to the Constitutional History of Canada, 1819–1828.* Ottawa: J.O. Patenaude, 1935.

Du Calvet, Pierre. "Appel à la justice de l'État." In *Appel à la justice de l'État de Pierre du Calvet: Champion des droits démocratiques au Québec.* 1784. Sillery, QC: Septentrion, 2002.

Dubois, Laurent. *Avengers of the New World: The Story of the Haitian Revolution.* Cambridge, MA: Belknap Press of Harvard University Press, 2004.

– *A Colony of Citizens: Revolution and Slave Emancipation in the French Caribbean, 1787–1804.* Chapel Hill: University of North Carolina Press, 2004.

Ducharme, Michel. "Closing the Last Chapter of the Atlantic Revolution: The 1837–1838 Rebellions in Upper and Lower Canada." *Proceedings of the American Antiquarian Society* 116, no. 2 (2006): 411–28.

– "Penser le Canada: La mise en place des assises intellectuelles de l'État canadien moderne (1838–1840)." *Revue d'histoire de l'Amérique française* 56, no. 3 (2003): 357–86.

Duncombe, Charles. *Report upon the Subject of Education Made to the Parliament of Upper Canada, 25th February 1836.* East Ardsley, UK: S.R. Publishers Limited, 1966.

Dunham, Aileen. *Political Unrest in Upper Canada, 1815–1836.* Toronto: McClelland and Stewart, 1963.

Dunn, John. *The Political Thought of John Locke: An Historical Account of the Argument of the "Two Treatises of Government."* Cambridge: Cambridge University Press, 1969.

Dunn, Susan. *Sister Revolutions: French Lightning, American Light.* New York: Faber and Faber, 1999.

Durham, John George Lambton, Lord. *Report on the Affairs of British North America.* Edited by Sir Charles Lucas. Vol. 2, *The Report.* 1839. Oxford: Clarendon Press, 1912.

Eger, Elizabeth, Charlotte Grant, Clíona Ó Gallchoir, and Penny Warburton, eds. *Women, Writing and the Public Sphere, 1700–1830.* Cambridge: Cambridge University Press, 2001.

Egret, Jean. *La révolution des notables: Mounier et les Monarchiens, 1789.* Paris: Librairie Armand Colin, 1950.

Elkins, Stanley, and Eric McKitrick. *The Age of Federalism: The Early American Republic.* Oxford: Oxford University Press, 1993.

Epstein, James A. *Radical Expression: Political Language, Ritual, and Symbol in England, 1790–1850.* Oxford: Oxford University Press, 1994.

Errington, Jane. *The Lion, the Eagle, and Upper Canada: A Developing Colonial Ideology.* Montreal and Kingston: McGill-Queen's University Press, 1987.

Errington, Jane, and George Rawlyk. "The Loyalist-Federalist Alliance of Upper Canada." *American Review of Canadian Studies* 14, no. 2 (1984): 157–76.

Fahey, Curtis. *In His Name: The Anglican Experience in Upper Canada, 1791–1854.* Ottawa: Carleton University Press, 1991.

Faragher, John Mark. *A Great and Noble Scheme: The Tragic Story of the Expulsion of the French Acadians from their American Homeland.* New York: W.W. Norton, 2005.

Fecteau, Jean-Marie. "Lendemains de défaite: Les Rébellions comme histoire et mémoire." *Bulletin d'histoire politique* 7, no. 1 (1998): 19–28.

– *La liberté du pauvre: Sur la régulation du crime et de la pauvreté au XIXe siècle québécois.* Montreal: VLB éditeur, 2004.

Filteau, Gérard. *Histoire des Patriotes.* 1938. Montreal: L'Aurore/Univers, 1980.

Fink, Zera S. *The Classical Republicans: An Essay in the Recovery of a Pattern of Thought in Seventeenth-Century England.* Evanston, IL: Northwestern University, 1945.

Finlay, John L. "The State of a Reputation: Bédard as Constitutionalist." *Journal of Canadian Studies* 20, no. 4 (1985–86): 60–76.

Fischer, David Hackett. *Liberty and Freedom: A Visual History of America's Founding Ideas.* Oxford: Oxford University Press, 2005.

Fleming, Patricia, and Yvan Lamonde, eds. *History of the Book in Canada.* Vol. 1, *Beginnings to 1840.* Toronto: University of Toronto Press, 2004.

Flint, David. *William Lyon Mackenzie.* Toronto: Oxford University Press, 1971.

Foner, Eric. *The Story of American Freedom.* New York: W.W. Norton and Company, 1998.

Frye, Northrop. *Divisions on a Ground: Essays on Canadian Culture.* Toronto: Anansi, 1982.

Furet, François. *Interpreting the French Revolution.* Translated by Elborg Forster. New York: Cambridge University Press, 1981.

Furet, François, and Ran Halévi. *La monarchie républicaine: La constitution de 1791.* Paris: Fayard, 1996.

Furet, François, and Mona Ozouf, eds. *Le siècle de l'avènement républicain.* Paris: Gallimard, 1993.

Fyson, Donald. "Jurys, participation civique et représentation au Québec et au Bas-Canada: Les grands jurys du district de Montréal (1764–1832)." *Revue d'histoire de l'Amérique française* 55, no. 1 (2001): 85–120.

Galarneau, Claude. *La France devant l'opinion canadienne (1760–1815).* Quebec: Les Presses de l'Université Laval, 1970.

Gallichan, Gilles. "Pierre Bédard, *Le Canadien* et la notion de responsabilité ministérielle." *Bulletin d'histoire politique* 6, no. 3 (1998): 26–32.

Garner, John. *The Franchise and Politics in British North America 1755–1867.*
Toronto: University of Toronto Press, 1969.

Garon, André. "La fonction politique et sociale des chambres hautes canadiennes, 1791–1841." *Social History* 5 (April 1970): 66–87.

Gaspar, David Barry, David P. Geggus, and Darlene Clark Hine, eds. *A
Turbulent Time: The French Revolution and the Greater Caribbean.* Bloomington:
Indiana University Press, 2003.

Gates, Lillian F. "The Decided Policy of William Lyon Mackenzie." *Canadian
Historical Review* 40, no. 3 (1959): 185–208.

Gay, Peter. *The Party of Humanity: Essays in the French Enlightenment.* New York:
Albert A. Knopf, 1964.

Geggus, David Patrick. *Haitian Revolutionary Studies.* Bloomington: Indiana
University Press, 2002.

Geggus, David Patrick, ed. *The Impact of the Haitian Revolution in the Atlantic
World.* Columbia: University of South Carolina Press, 2001.

Gelderen, Martin van. *The Political Thought of the Dutch Revolt, 1555–1590.*
Cambridge: Cambridge University Press, 1992.

Gelderen, Martin van, and Quentin Skinner, eds. *Republicanism: A Shared
European Heritage.* 2 vols. Cambridge: Cambridge University Press, 2002.

Gentz, Friedrich von. *The Origin and Principles of the American Revolution
Compared with the Origin and Principles of the French Revolution.* Edited by
Richard Loss. Translated by John Quincy Adams. Delmar, NY: Scholars'
Facsimiles and Reprints, 1977.

Geyl, Pieter. *La révolution batave, 1783–1798.* Paris: Société des études robespi-
erristes, 1971.

Gilmour, Ian. *Inside Right: A Study of Conservatism.* London: Hutchinson, 1977.

Girod, Amury. *Notes diverses sur le Bas-Canada.* Village Debartzch [Quebec]:
J.P. Boucher-Belleville, 1835.

Godechot, Jacques Léon. *France and the Atlantic Revolution of the Eighteenth
Century, 1770–1799.* New York, Free Press [1965].

– "Revolutionary Contagion, 1770–1825." *Proceedings of the Annual Meeting of
the Western Society for French History* 4 (1977): 245–55.

Golay, Eric. *Quand le peuple devint roi: Mouvement populaire, politique et révolution
à Genève de 1789 à 1794.* Geneva: Slatkine, 2001.

Goubert, Pierre. *L'Ancien Régime.* 2 vols. Paris: Presses universitaires de France,
1969.

Gough, Hugh, and David Dickson, eds. *Ireland and the French Revolution.*
Dublin: Irish Academic Press, 1990.

Gould, Eliga H., and Peter S. Onuf, eds. *Empire and Nation: The American
Revolution in the Atlantic World.* Baltimore: Johns Hopkins University Press,
2005.

Gourlay, Robert. *General Introduction to Statistical Account of Upper Canada,
Compiled with a View to a Grand System of Emigration, in Connexion with a
Reform of the Poor Laws.* London: Simpkin and Marshall, 1822.

– *A Specific Plan for Organising the People, and for Obtaining Reform Independent of
Parliament, Addressed by Robert Gourlay, Esq., to the People of Fife – of Britain!*
London: J.M. Richardson, 1809.

- *Statistical Account of Upper Canada: Compiled with a View to a Grand System of Emigration.* 2 vols. London: Simpkin and Marshall, 1822.
- "To the Labouring Poor of England." [London?: n.p., 1822?] (London: Batchelar).

Goyard-Fabre, Simone. *La philosophie des Lumières en France.* Paris: Librairie C. Klincksieck, 1972.

Grayling, A.C. *Toward the Light of Liberty: The Struggles for Freedom and Rights that Made the Modern Western World.* New York: Walker and Company, 2007.

Greenfield, Robert S. "La Banque du Peuple, 1835–1871, and its Failure, 1895." MA thesis (History), McGill University, 1968.

Greenwood, F. Murray. *Legacies of Fear: Law and Politics in the Era of the French Revolution.* Toronto: University of Toronto Press, 1993.
- "Les patriotes et le gouvernement responsable dans les années 1830." *Revue d'histoire de l'Amérique française* 33, no. 1 (1979): 25–37.

Greenwood, F. Murray, and Barry Wright, eds. *Canadian State Trials.* 2 vols. Toronto: Osgoode Society for Canadian Legal History and University of Toronto Press, 1996–2002.

Greer, Allan. "1837–1838: Rebellion Reconsidered." *Canadian Historical Review* 76, no. 1 (1995): 1–18.
- "Historical Roots of Canadian Democracy." *Journal of Canadian Studies* 34, no. 1 (1999): 7–26.
- *The Patriots and the People.* 1993. Toronto: University of Toronto Press, 1996.
- *Peasant, Lord, and Merchant: Rural Society in Three Quebec Parishes, 1740–1840.* Toronto: University of Toronto Press, 1985.

Greer, Allan, and Ian Radforth, eds. *Colonial Leviathan.* Toronto: University of Toronto Press, 1992.

Grenon, Michel, ed. *L'image de la Révolution française au Québec, 1789–1989.* Ville LaSalle: Éditions Hurtubise HMH, 1989.

Grieder, Josephine. *Anglomania in France, 1740–1789: Fact, Fiction, and Political Discourse.* Geneva: Droz, 1985.

Gueniffey, Patrice. *La politique de la Terreur.* Paris: Gallimard, 2000.

Guerrier, W. *L'abbé de Mably, moraliste et politique. Étude sur la doctrine morale du jacobinisme puritain et sur le développement de l'esprit républicain au XVIIIe siècle.* Paris, 1886; reprinted in Geneva: Slatkine Reprints, 1971.

Gundersen, Joan R. *To Be Useful to the World: Women in Revolutionary America, 1740-1790.* New York: Prentice Hall International, 1996.

Hamilton, Alexander, James Madison, and John Jay. *The Federalist Papers.* 1788. Edited and with an introduction by Clinton Rossiter. [New York:] New American Library, [1961].

Hammond, Scott John. *Political Theory: An Encyclopedia of Contemporary and Classic Terms.* Westport, CT: Greenwood Press, 2009.

Harding, Alan. "Political Liberty in the Middle Ages." *Speculum* 55 (1980): 423–43.

Hare, John. *Aux origines du parlementarisme québécois, 1791–1793.* Sillery, QC: Septentrion, 1993.
- *La pensée socio-politique au Québec, 1784–1812.* Ottawa: Éditions de l'Université d'Ottawa, 1977.

Hare, John, and Jean-Pierre Wallot. "Les entreprises d'imprimerie et d'édition en Amérique du Nord britannique, 1751–1840." *Mens, Revue d'histoire intellectuelle de l'Amérique française* 5, no. 2 (2005): 307–44.

Harrington, James. *The Commonwealth of Oceana; and A System of Politics.* Edited by J.G.A. Pocock. Cambridge: Cambridge University Press, 1992.

Hartz, Louis. *The Liberal Tradition in America: An Interpretation of American Political Thought since the Revolution.* New York: Harcourt, Brace and World, Inc., 1955.

– *New Societies: Latin America, South Africa, Canada, and Australia.* New York: Harcourt, Brace and World, Inc., 1964.

Harvey, Louis-Georges. "Importing the Revolution: The Image of America in French-Canadian Political Discourse, 1805–1837." PhD diss. (History), University of Ottawa, 1990.

– *Le Printemps de l'Amérique française: Américanité, anticolonialisme et républicanisme dans le discours politique québécois, 1805–1837.* Montreal: Boréal, 2005.

Harvey, Louis-Georges, and Mark V. Olsen. "French Revolutionary Forms in French-Canadian Political Languages, 1805–1835." *Canadian Historical Review* 68, no. 3 (1987): 374–92.

Hayek, F.A. *The Constitution of Liberty.* 1960. Chicago: University of Chicago Press, 2011.

Hazard, Paul. *European Thought in the Eighteenth Century, from Montesquieu to Lessing.* Gloucester, MA: P. Smith, 1973.

Henderson, J.L. *John Strachan, 1778–1867.* Quebec: Presses de l'Université Laval, 1970.

Hexter, J.H. "The Birth of Modern Freedom." *Times Literary Supplement,* 21 January 1983, 51–4.

Hexter, J.H., ed. *Parliament and Liberty from the Reign of Elizabeth to the English Civil War.* Stanford: Stanford University Press, 1992.

Higonnet, Patrice. *Sister Republics: The Origins of French and American Republicanism.* Cambridge, MA: Harvard University Press, 1988.

Hobbes, Thomas. *The Leviathan.* 1651. London: Penguin, 1985.

Hobsbawm, Eric. *The Age of Revolution: 1789–1848.* Scarborough, ON: New American Library, 1962.

Hodgetts, J.E. *Pioneer Public Service: An Administrative History of the United Canadas, 1841–1867.* Toronto: University of Toronto Press, 1955.

Hoffman, John. *Sovereignty.* Minneapolis: University of Minnesota Press, 1998.

Hoffmann, Paul. *Théories et modèles de la liberté au XVIIIe siècle.* Paris: Presses universitaires de France, 1996.

Hufton, Olwen H. *Women and the Limits of Citizenship in the French Revolution.* Toronto: University of Toronto Press, 1992.

Hulliung, Mark. *Citizens and Citoyens: Republicans and Liberals in America and France.* Cambridge: Cambridge University Press, 2002.

Hume, Joseph. *The Celebrated Letter of Joseph Hume, Esq., M.P., to William Lyon Mackenzie, Esq., Mayor of Toronto, Declaratory of a Design to "Free these Provinces from the Baneful Domination of the Mother Country!": with the Comments of the Press of Upper Canada on the Pernicious and Treasonable Tendency of that Letter, and the Speeches, Resolutions and Amendments of the Common Council of this City,*

Which were the Result of a Motion of that Body to Disavow all Participation in the Sentiments of Mr. Hume. Toronto: G.P. Hull, 1834.

Hutson, James H. "Country, Court and Constitution: Antifederalism and the Historians." *William and Mary Quarterly* 38, no. 3 (1981): 337–68.

Jackson, Eric. "The Organization of Upper Canadian Reformers, 1818–1867." *Ontario History* 53, no. 2 (1961): 95–115.

Jackson, John Mills. *A View of the Political Situation of the Province of Upper Canada, in North America.* London: W. Earle, 1809.

Jacob, Margaret C., and Wijnand W. Mijnhardt, eds. *The Dutch Republic in the Eighteenth Century: Decline, Enlightenment, and Revolution.* Ithaca, NY: Cornell University Press, 1992.

Jainchill, Andrew. "The Constitution of the Year III and the Persistence of Classical Republicanism." *French Historical Studies* 26, no. 3 (2003): 399–435.

Jaucourt. "Natural Equality." In *Denis Diderot's The Encyclopedia: Selections,* edited and translated by Stephen J. Gendzier, 169–71. New York: Harper and Row, 1967.

Jefferson, Thomas. *The Life and Selected Writing of Thomas Jefferson.* Edited and with an introduction by Adrienne Koch and William Peden. New York: The Modern Library, 1998.

Johnson, J.K. *Becoming Prominent: Regional Leadership in Upper Canada, 1791–1841.* Montreal and Kingston: McGill-Queen's University Press, 1989.

Jones, Gareth Stedman, "Rethinking Chartism." In *Studies in English Working Class History (1832–1982),* 90–178. Cambridge: Cambridge University Press, 1983.

Jones, J.R., ed. *Liberty Secured? Britain before and after 1688.* Stanford: Stanford University Press, 1992.

Jourdan, Annie. *La Révolution, une exception française.* Paris: Flammarion, 2004.

Kaiser, Thomas E. "This Strange Offspring of Philosophie: Recent Historiographical Problems in Relating the Enlightenment to the French Revolution." *French Historical Studies* 15, no. 3 (1988): 549–62.

Kammen, Michael. *Sovereignty and Liberty: Constitutional Discourse in American Culture.* Madison: University of Wisconsin Press, 1989.

Kelly, Stéphane. *La petite loterie: Comment la Couronne a obtenu la collaboration du Canada français après 1837.* Montreal: Boréal, 1997.

– *Les fins du Canada selon Macdonald, Laurier, Mackenzie King et Trudeau.* Montreal: Boréal, 2001.

Kennedy, W.P.M., ed. *Documents of the Canadian Constitution, 1759–1915.* Toronto: Oxford University Press, 1918.

– ed. *Statutes, Treatises and Documents of the Canadian Constitution, 1713–1929.* Toronto: Oxford University Press, 1930.

Kerber, Linda K. *Women of the Republic: Intellect and Ideology in Revolutionary America.* Chapel Hill: University of North Carolina Press, 1980.

Kirk, Russell. *The Conservative Mind, from Burke to Santayana.* Chicago: H. Regnery Co., 1953.

Klooster, Wim. *Revolutions in the Atlantic World: A Comparative History.* New York: New York University Press, 2009.

Knowles, Norman. *Inventing the Loyalists: The Ontario Loyalist Tradition and the Creation of Usable Pasts.* Toronto: University of Toronto Press, 1997.

Koselleck, Reinhart. *Futures Past: On the Semantics of Historical Time.* New York: Columbia University Press, 2004.

Kramnick, Isaac. "Republican Revisionism Revisited." *American Historical Review* 87, no. 3 (1982): 629–64.

– *Republicanism and Bourgeois Radicalism: Political Ideology in Late Eighteenth-century England and America.* Ithaca, NY: Cornell University Press, 1990.

Kylmäkoski, Merja. *The Virtue of the Citizen: Jean-Jacques Rousseau's Republicanism in the Eighteenth-Century French Context.* New York: P. Lang, 2001.

La Fontaine, Louis-Hippolyte. *Les deux girouettes, ou l'hypocrisie démasquée.* Montreal: Imprimerie de La Minerve, 1834.

Lagrave, Jean-Paul. *Fleury Mesplet, 1734–1794: Diffuseur des Lumières au Québec.* Montreal: Patenaude, 1985.

Lamonde, Yvan. *Allégeances et dépendances: L'histoire d'une ambivalence identitaire.* [Quebec]: Éditions Nota Bene, 2001.

– "American Cultural Influence in Quebec: A One-Way Mirror." In *Problems and Opportunities in US–Quebec Relations,* edited by Alfred O. Hero, Jr. and Marcel Daneau, 106–26. Boulder, CO: Westview Press, 1984.

– "La vie culturelle et intellectuelle dans le Québec des XVIIIe et XIXe siecles: Quelques pistes de recherche." *Revue d'histoire de l'Amérique française* 54, no. 2 (2000): 269–79.

– *Ni avec eux ni sans eux: Le Québec et les États-Unis.* [Quebec]: Nuit Blanche, 1996.

– *The Social History of Ideas in Quebec.* Translated by Phyllis Aronoff and Howard Scott. Montreal and Kingston: McGill-Queen's University Press, 2013.

– *Territoires de la culture québécoise.* Quebec: Presses de l'Université Laval, 1991.

Lamonde, Yvan, and Gérard Bouchard, eds. *Québécois et Américains: La culture québécoise aux XIXe et XXe siècles.* Montreal: Fides, 1995.

Lanctôt, Gustave. *Canada and the American Revolution, 1774–1783.* Translated by Margaret M. Cameron. Toronto: Clarke Irwin, 1967.

Landes, Joan B. *Women and the Public Sphere in the Age of the French Revolution.* Ithaca, NY: Cornell University Press, 1988.

Langley, Lester D. *The Americas in the Age of Revolution, 1750–1850.* New Haven, CT: Yale University Press, 1996.

Larue, Richard. "Allégeance et origine: Contribution à l'analyse de la crise politique au Bas-Canada." *Revue d'histoire de l'Amérique française* 44, no. 4 (1991): 529–48.

– "La crainte de l'égalité: Essai sur un fondement symbolique de l'État au Canada, 1791–1867." PhD diss. (History), Université Laval, 1990.

Lawson, Philip. *The Imperial Challenge: Quebec and Britain in the Age of the American Revolution.* Montreal and Kingston: McGill-Queen's University Press, 1989.

Leeb, I. Leonard. *The Ideological Origins of the Batavian Revolution: History and Politics in the Dutch Republic, 1747–1800.* The Hague: Nijhoff, 1973.

Lefebvre, André. *La* Montreal Gazette *et le nationalisme canadien (1835–1842).* Montreal: Guérin, 1970.

Leith, James A. *Space and Revolution: Projects for Monuments, Squares and Public Buildings in France, 1789–1799*. Montreal and Kingston: McGill-Queen's University Press, 1991.

Lemarchand, Guy. "À propos des révoltes et des révolutions de la fin du XVIIIe siècle: Essai d'un bilan d'historiographie." *Annales historiques de la Révolution française* 340 (2005): 145–74.

Lerner, Ralph. *The Thinking Revolutionary: Principle and Practice in the New Republic*. Ithaca, NY: Cornell University Press, 1987.

Létourneau, Jocelyn. "L'avenir du Canada: Par rapport à quelle histoire?" *Canadian Historical Review* 81, no. 2 (2000): 230–59.

– *A History for the Future: Rewriting Memory and Identity in Quebec*. Translated by Phyllis Aronoff and Howard Scott. Montreal: McGill-Queen's University Press, 2004.

Library of Congress. *The Impact of the American Revolution Abroad: Papers Presented at the Fourth Symposium, May 8 and 9, 1975*. Washington: Library of Congress, 1976.

Lindsey, Charles. *The Life and Times of William Lyon Mackenzie*. 2 vols. Toronto: P.R. Randall, 1862.

Lipset, Seymour Martin. *Continental Divide: The Values and Institutions of the United States and Canada*. New York: Routledge, 1990.

– *North American Cultures: Values and Institutions in Canada and the United States*. [Orono, ME]: Borderlands, 1990.

– *Revolution and Counterrevolution: Change and Persistence in Social Structures*. New York: Basic Books, 1968.

Lively, Jack, ed. *The Enlightenment*. London: Longmans, 1966.

Locke, John. *Political Writings*. London: Penguin Classics, 1993.

Loft, Leonore. "J.P. Brissot and the Evolution of Pamphlet Literature in the Early 1780s." *History of European Ideas* 17, no. 2–3 (1993): 265–87.

Lynch, John. *Simón Bolívar and the Age of Revolution*. London: University of London Institute of Latin American Studies, 1983.

Mably, Gabriel Bonnot, abbé de. *De la législation, ou, Principes des loix*. Amsterdam: [n.p.], 1777.

– *Phocion's Conversations, or The Relation between Morality and Politics*. London: Printed for the author, and sold by Mr. Dodsley, 1769.

– *Principes de morale*. Paris: A. Jombert, 1784.

– *Sur la théorie du pouvoir politique*. Edited by Peter Friedmann. Paris: Éditions sociales, 1975.

Mackenzie, William Lyon. *The Selected Writings of William Lyon Mackenzie*. Edited by Margaret Fairley. Toronto: Oxford University Press, 1960.

– *Sketches of Canada and the United States*. London: E. Wilson, 1833.

– *To the Honorable the Commons of the United Kingdom of Great Britain and Ireland in Parliament Assembled: The Humble Petition of William L. Mackenzie, Printer, Member Representing the County of York in the Legislative Assembly of Upper Canada*. London: Bridgewater, 1833.

MacKinnon, Neil. *This Unfriendly Soil: The Loyalist Experience in Nova Scotia, 1783–1791*. Montreal and Kingston: McGill-Queen's University Press, 1986.

Mackintosh, Sir James. *The Miscellaneous Works of the Right Honourable Sir James Mackintosh.* Philadelphia: Carey and Hart, 1846.

MacMahon, Darrin M. "The Counter-Enlightenment and the Low-Life of Literature in Pre-Revolutionary France." *Past and Present* 159 (May 1998): 77–112.

Macpherson, C.B. *The Political Theory of Possessive Individualism: Hobbes to Locke.* Oxford: Clarendon Press, 1964.

Mairet, Gérard. *Le principe de souveraineté: Histoire et fondement du pouvoir moderne.* Paris: Gallimard, 1997.

Malia, Martin. *History's Locomotives: Revolutions and the Making of the Modern World.* New Haven: Yale University Press, 2006.

Mancke, Elizabeth. "Early Modern Imperial Governance and the Origins of Canadian Political Culture." *Canadian Journal of Political Science* 32, no. 1 (1999): 3–20.

– *The Fault Lines of Empire: Political Differentiation in Massachusetts and Nova Scotia, ca. 1760–1830.* New York: Routledge, 2005.

Mandeville, Bernard. *The Fable of the Bees, or, Private Vices, Publick Benefits.* 1714. Edited by F.B. Kaye. Indianapolis: Liberty Classics, 1988.

Manning, Helen Taft. *The Revolt of French Canada, 1800–1835: A Chapter in the History of the British Commonwealth.* Toronto: Macmillan, 1962.

Marat, Jean-Paul. *Les chaînes de l'esclavage.* 1774. Brussels: Complexe, 1988.

Mason, H.T., and W. Doyle. *The Impact of the French Revolution on European Consciousness.* Gloucester, UK: A. Sutton, 1989.

McCoy, Drew R. *The Elusive Republic: Political Economy in Jeffersonian America.* 1980. Chapel Hill: University of North Carolina Press, 2002.

McCulloch, Michael. "The Death of Whiggery: Lower-Canadian British Constitutionalism and the *tentation de l'histoire parallèle.*" *Journal of the Canadian Historical Association* 2, no. 1 (1991): 195–213.

McKay, Ian. "The Liberal Order Framework: A Prospectus for a Reconnaissance of Canadian History." *Canadian Historical Review* 81, no. 4 (2000): 617–45.

McLaren, John, A.R. Buck, and Nancy E. Wright, eds. *Despotic Dominion: Property Rights in British Settler Societies.* Vancouver: UBC Press, 2005.

McMillan, James F. *France and Women, 1789–1914: Gender, Society and Politics.* London: Routledge, 2000.

McNairn, Jeffrey L. *The Capacity to Judge: Public Opinion and Deliberative Democracy in Upper Canada, 1791–1854.* Toronto: University of Toronto Press, 2000.

McRae, K.D. "An Upper Canada Letter of 1829 on Responsible Government." *Canadian Historical Review* 31, no. 3 (1950): 288–96.

Mellor, Anne K. *Mother of the Nation: Women's Political Writing in England.* Bloomington: Indiana University Press, 2000.

Melzer, Sara E., and Leslie W. Rabine, eds. *Rebel Daughters: Women and the French Revolution.* Oxford: Oxford University Press, 1992.

Milani, Lois Darroch. *Robert Gourlay, Gadfly: Forerunner of the Rebellion of Upper Canada 1837.* [Thornhill, ON]: Ampersand Press, 1971.

Mill, John Stuart. *Autobiography.* London: Longmans, Green, Reader, and Dyer, 1882.

- *Collected Works of John Stuart Mill.* Edited by John M. Robson. Vol. 4, *Essays on England, Ireland, and the Empire.* Toronto: University of Toronto Press, 1982.
- *On Liberty and Other Essays.* Oxford: Oxford University Press, 1998.
Miller, David, ed. *The Blackwell Encyclopaedia of Political Thought.* Oxford: Basil Blackwell, 1987.
- ed. *Liberty.* New York: Oxford University Press, 1991.
Mills, David. *The Idea of Loyalty in Upper Canada, 1784–1850.* Montreal and Kingston: McGill-Queen's University Press, 1988.
Milobar, David. "The Origins of British-Quebec Merchant Ideology: New France, the British Atlantic and the Constitutional Periphery, 1720–1770." *Journal of Imperial and Commonwealth History* 24, no. 3 (1996): 364–90.
- "Quebec Reform, the British Constitution and the Atlantic Empire, 1774–1775." *Parliamentary History* 14, no. 1 (1995): 65–88.
Milton, John. *Aeropagitica and other Political Writings of John Milton.* 1644–60. Edited by John Alvis. Indianapolis: Liberty Fund, 1999.
Mitchell, L.G. *Charles James Fox.* Oxford: Oxford University Press, 1992.
Mondelet, Dominique [Un avocat]. *Traité sur la politique coloniale du Bas-Canada: Réflexion sur l'état actuel du pays.* N.p.: D. Mondelet, 1835.
Monette, Pierre. *Rendez-vous manqué avec la révolution américaine.* Montreal: Québec Amérique, 2007.
Monnier, Raymonde. "Républicanisme et révolution française." *French Historical Studies* 26, no. 1 (2003): 87–118.
Montesquieu, Charles de Secondat, baron de. *The Spirit of the Laws.* Translated by Thomas Nugent. New York: Hafner, 1949.
Moore, Christopher. *The Loyalists: Revolution, Exile, and Settlement.* Toronto: Macmillan, 1984.
Morgan, Cecilia. *Public Men and Virtuous Women: The Gendered Languages of Religion and Politics in Upper Canada, 1791–1850.* Toronto: University of Toronto Press, 1996.
Morgan, Edmund S. *Inventing the People: The Rise of Popular Sovereignty in England and America.* New York: W.W. Norton and Co., 1988.
Morley, Vincent. *Irish Opinion and the American Revolution, 1760–1783.* Cambridge: Cambridge University Press, 2002.
Morrison, Michael A., and Melinda Zook, eds. *Revolutionary Currents: Nation Building in the Transatlantic World.* Oxford: Rowman and Littlefield, 2004.
Mossé, Claude. *L'Antiquité dans la Révolution française.* Paris: Albin Michel, 1989.
Muzzo, Johanne. "Les mouvements réformiste et constitutionnel à Montréal, 1834–1837." MA thesis (History), UQAM, 1990.
Neatby, Hilda. *Quebec: The Revolutionary Age, 1760–1791.* Toronto: McClelland and Stewart, 1966.
Needham, Marchamont. *The Case of the Commonwealth of England, Stated.* 1650. Edited by Philip A. Knachel. Charlottesville: University Press of Virginia, 1969.
Nelson, Robert. *Déclaration d'indépendance et autres écrits.* Edited and annotated by Georges Aubin. Montreal: Comeau et Nadeau, 1998.
Nemo, Philippe. *Histoire des idées politiques aux temps modernes et contemporains.* Paris: Presses universitaires de France, 2002.

Neville, Henry. *Plato Redivivus or, A Dialogue Concerning Government.* 1681. In *Two English Republican Tracts,* edited by Caroline Robbins, 61–200. London: Cambridge University Press, 1969.

Newman, Gerald. *The Rise of English Nationalism: A Cultural History, 1740– 1830.* New York: St Martin's Press, 1987.

Newman, Simon P., ed. *Europe's American Revolution.* Houndmills, Basingstoke: Palgrave Macmillan, 2006.

Nicolet, Claude. *L'idée républicaine en France (1798–1924): Essai d'histoire critique.* Paris: Gallimard, 1982.

Noel, S.J.R. *Patrons, Clients, Brokers: Ontario Society and Politics, 1791–1896.* Toronto: University of Toronto Press, 1990.

Norbrook, David. *Writing the English Republic: Poetry, Rhetoric and Politics, 1627– 1660.* Cambridge: Cambridge University Press, 2000.

Norton, Mary Beth. *Liberty's Daughters: The Revolutionary Experience of American Women, 1750–1800.* Boston: Little, Brown, 1980.

Ouellet, Fernand. *Economic and Social History of Quebec, 1760–1850.* Translated under the auspices of the Institute of Canadian Studies. [Ottawa]: Macmillan of Canada; Institute of Canadian Studies at Carleton University, 1980.

– "Les insurrections de 1837–38: Un phénomène social." *Social History* 1, no. 2 (1968): 54–82.

– *Lower Canada, 1791–1840: Social Change and Nationalism.* Translated by Patricia Claxton. Toronto: McClelland and Stewart, 1980.

– "La tradition révolutionnaire au Canada: À propos de l'historiographie des insurrections de 1837–38 dans le Bas-Canada." *Revue de l'Université d'Ottawa* 55, no. 2 (1985): 91–124.

Paine, Thomas. *Common Sense.* 1776. Edited with an introduction by Isaac Kramnick. Harmondsworth, Middlesex: Penguin Books, 1986.

– *Rights of Man.* 1791. Ware (Hertfordshire): Wordsworth Editions, 1996.

Palmer, Robert R. *The Age of the Democratic Revolution: A Political History of Europe and America, 1760–1800.* 2 vols. Princeton: Princeton University Press, 1959–1964.

– "American Historians Remember Jacques Godechot." *French Historical Studies* 61 (1990): 879–92.

– "Notes on the Use of the Word 'Democracy,' 1789–1799." *Political Science Quarterly* 68, no. 2 (1953): 203–26.

Palmer, Robert R., and Jacques Godechot. "Le problème de l'Atlantique du XVIIIe au XXe siècle." In *Storia Contemporanea,* vol. 5 of *Relazioni del X Congresso Internazionale di Scienze Storiche,* 173–239. Florence: G.C. Sansoni Editore, [1955].

Pangle, Thomas. *The Spirit of Modern Republicanism: The Moral Vision of the American Founders and the Philosophy of Locke.* Chicago: Chicago University Press, 1988.

Papineau, Louis-Joseph. *Address of the Hon. L.J. Papineau to the Electors of the West Ward of Montreal.* [Montreal?]: n.p., 1834.

– *Un demi-siècle de combats: Interventions publiques.* Edited by Yvan Lamonde and Claude Larin. Montreal: Fides, 1998.

– *Lettres à Julie*. Edited by George Aubin and Renée Blanchet. Sillery, QC: Septentrion, 2000.
– *Papineau*. Edited by Fernand Ouellet. Quebec: Presses de l'Université Laval, 1959.
Paquette, Gabriel. *Imperial Portugal in the Age of Atlantic Revolutions: The Luso-Brazilian World, c. 1770–1850*. Cambridge: Cambridge University Press, 2013.
Pateman, Carole. *The Disorder of Women: Democracy, Feminism and Political Theory*. Cambridge: Polity Press, 1989.
– *The Problem of Political Obligation: A Critical Analysis of Liberal Theory*. New York: John Wiley and Sons, 1979.
Patterson, Graeme. "An Enduring Canadian Myth: Responsible Government and Family Compact." *Journal of Canadian Studies* 12, no. 2 (1977): 3–16.
– "Whiggery, Nationality, and the Upper Canadian Reform Tradition." *Canadian Historical Review* 56, no. 1 (1975): 25–44.
Peerce, Rod. "The Anglo-Saxon Conservative Tradition." *Canadian Journal of Political Science* 13, no. 1 (1980): 3–32.
– "The Myth of the Red Tory." *Canadian Journal of Political and Social Theory* 1 (Spring-Summer 1977): 3–28.
Peltonen, Markku. *Classical Humanism and Republicanism in English Political Thought, 1570–1640*. Cambridge: Cambridge University Press, 1995.
Pentland, Gordon. "Patriotism, Universalism and the Scottish Conventions, 1792–1794." *History* 89, no. 295 (2004): 340–60.
Petitions from the Old and New Subjects, Inhabitants of the Province of Quebec, to the Right Honourable the Lords Spiritual and Temporal. London: n.p., 1791.
Pettit, Philip. *Republicanism: A Theory of Freedom and Government*. New York: Oxford University Press, 1997.
Philpott, Daniel. *Revolutions in Sovereignty: How Ideas Shaped Modern International Relations*. Princeton: Princeton University Press, 2001.
Picard, Nathalie. "Les femmes et le vote au Bas-Canada de 1792–1848." MA thesis (History), Université de Montréal, 1992.
Pitkin, Hanna Fenichel. "Are Freedom and Liberty Twins?" *Political Theory* 16, no. 4 (1988): 523–35.
– *Fortune Is a Woman: Gender and Politics in the Thought of Niccolo Machiavelli*. Chicago: University of Chicago Press, 1999.
Piva, Michael J. "Debts, Salaries and Civil Service Reform in Pre-Confederation Canada." *National History* 1 (1997): 127–37.
– "Getting Hired: The Civil Service Act of 1857." *Journal of the Canadian Historical Association* 3, no. 1 (1992): 95–127.
Pocock, J.G.A. *The Machiavellian Moment: Florentine Political Thought and the Atlantic Republican Tradition*. Princeton: Princeton University Press, 1975.
– *Politics, Language and Time: Essays on Political Thought and History*. New York: Atheneum, 1971.
– *Virtue, Commerce and History: Essays on Political Thought and History, Chiefly in the Eighteenth Century*. Cambridge: Cambridge University Press, 1985.
Pocock, J.G.A., ed. *Three British Revolutions: 1641, 1688, 1776*. Princeton: Princeton University Press, 1980.

Pocock, J.G.A., and Richard Ashcraft. *John Locke: Papers Read at a Clark Library Seminar, 10 December 1977*. Los Angeles: William Andrews Clark Memorial Library, University of California, 1980.

Polasky, Janet. *Revolution in Brussels, 1787–1793*. Hanover: New England University Press, 1987.

Porter, Roy. *Enlightenment: Britain and the Creation of the Modern World*. London: Allen Lane, Penguin Press, 2000.

Prévost, Jean-Guy. "Espace public, action collective et savoir social: Robert Gourlay et le *Statistical Account of Upper Canada*." *Social History* 35, no. 69 (2002): 109–39.

Price, Richard. *Political Writings*. Edited by D.O. Thomas. Cambridge: Cambridge University Press, 1991.

Priestley, Joseph. *Political Writings*. Edited by Peter N. Miller. Cambridge: Cambridge University Press, 1993.

Pritchard, James. *In Search of Empire: The French in the Americas, 1670–1730*. Cambridge: Cambridge University Press, 2004.

Rahe, Paul A. *Republics Ancient and Modern: Classical Republicanism and the American Revolution*. 3 vols. Chapel Hill: University of North Carolina Press, 1994.

Rahe, Paul A., ed. *Machiavelli's Liberal Republican Legacy*. Cambridge: Cambridge University Press, 2006.

Raynal, abbé (Guillaume-Thomas-François). *The Revolution of America by the Abbé Raynal, Author of the Philosophical and Political History of the Establishments and Commerce of the Europeans in Both the Indies*. Edinburgh: n.p., 1782.

Rea, J.E. "William Lyon Mackenzie – Jacksonian?" *Mid-America: An History Quarterly* 50, no. 3 (1968): 223–35.

Read, Colin. *The Rebellion of 1837 in Upper Canada*. Ottawa: Canadian Historical Association, 1988.

Reid, John Phillip. *The Concept of Liberty in the Age of the American Revolution*. Chicago: University of Chicago Press, 1988.

Reid, Philippe. "L'émergence du nationalisme canadien-français: L'idéologie du *Canadien* (1806–1842)." *Recherches sociographiques* 21, nos. 1–2 (1980): 11–53.

Resnick, Philip. *The Masks of Proteus: Canadian Reflections on the State*. Montreal and Kingston: McGill-Queen's University Press, 1990.

– *Parliament vs. People: An Essay on Democracy and Canadian Political Culture*. Vancouver: New Star Books, 1984.

Reynolds, Siân, ed. *Women, State and Revolution: Essays on Power and Gender in Europe since 1789*. Amherst: University of Massachusetts Press, 1987.

Richard, Carl J. *The Founders and the Classics: Greece, Rome, and the American Enlightenment*. Cambridge MA: Harvard University Press, 1994.

Robbins, Caroline. *The Eighteenth-century Commonwealthman: Studies in the Transmission, Development, and Circumstance of English Liberal Thought from the Restoration of Charles II until the War with the Thirteen Colonies*. Cambridge, MA: Harvard University Press, 1959.

Robespierre, Maximilien. *Oeuvres de Maximilien Robespierre*. Compiled and annotated by Auguste Vermorel. Paris: F. Coursol, 1866.

– *Virtue and Terror.* Edited by Jean Ducange. Translated by John Howe.
  New York: Verso, 2007.
Robinson, John Beverley. *Address of the Honourable Chief Justice Robinson, on
  Passing Sentence of Death upon Samuel Lount and Peter Matthews.* [Toronto:]
  Guardian Office, [1838].
– *Canada and the Canada Bill.* London: J. Hatchard and Son, 1840.
– *Charge of the Honorable John B. Robinson, Chief Justice of Upper Canada to the
  Grand Jury at Toronto (Thursday, 8th March, 1838,) on Opening the Court
  Appointed by Special Commission to Try Prisoners in Custody on Charges of Treason.*
  Toronto: R. Stanton, 1838.
– *A Letter to the Right Hon. Earl Bathurst, K.C., on the Policy of Uniting the British
  North-American Colonies.* London: W. Clowes, 1825.
Rodgers, Daniel T. "Republicanism: The Career of a Concept." *Journal of
  American History* 79, no. 1 (1992): 11–38.
Rodriguez O., Jaime E. *The Independence of Spanish America.* New York:
  Cambridge University Press, 1998.
Rodriguez O., Jaime E., ed. *Mexico in the Age of Democratic Revolutions: 1750–
  1850.* Boulder, CO: Lynne Rienner, 1994.
Roebuck, John Arthur. *The Canadas and their Grievances.* N.p., 1835.
– *Existing Difficulties in the Government of the Canadas.* London: E. and W.
  Reynell, 1836.
Ross, Dorothy. "The Liberal Tradition Revisited and the Republican Tradition
  Addressed." In *New Directions in American Intellectual History,* edited by John
  Higham and Paul K. Conkin, 116–31. Baltimore: Johns Hopkins University
  Press, 1979.
Rossiter, Clinton Lawrence. *Seedtime of the Republic: The Origin of the American
  Tradition of Political Liberty.* New York: Harcourt, Brace, 1953.
Rousseau, Guildo. *L'image des États-Unis dans la littérature québécoise, 1775–1930.*
  Sherbrooke: Editions Naaman, 1981.
Rousseau, Jean-Jacques. "Considerations on the Government of Poland and
  on Its Planned Reformation." In *The Plan for Perpetual Peace, On the
  Government of Poland, and Other Writings on History and Politics,* edited by
  Christopher Kelly, translated by Christopher Kelly and Judith Bush, 167–
  240. Vol. 11 of *The Collected Writings of Rousseau,* edited by Roger D. Masters
  and Christopher Kelly. Hanover, NH: Published for Dartmouth College by
  University Press of New England, 2005.
– *Discourse on Political Economy.* In *The Social Contract and Other Later Political
  Writings,* edited and translated by Victor Gourevitch, 3–38. New York:
  Cambridge University Press, 1997.
– *Discourse on the Origin and Foundations of Inequality among Men (Second Discourse).*
  In *The Discourses and Other Early Political Writings,* edited and translated by
  Victor Gourevitch, 111–222. New York: Cambridge University Press, 1997.
– *Émile.* 1762. Translated by Barbara Foxley. London: J.M. Dent, 1911.
– *Julie, or, The New Heloise: Letters of Two Lovers Who Live in a Small Town at the
  Foot of the Alps.* 1761. Translated by Philip Stewart and Jean Vaché.
  Hanover: Dartmouth College: University Press of New England, 1997.
– "Plan for a Constitution for Corsica." In *The Plan for Perpetual Peace, On the
  Government of Poland, and Other Writings on History and Politics,* edited by

Christopher Kelly, translated by Christopher Kelly and Judith Bush, 121–
65. Vol. 11 of *The Collected Writings of Rousseau*, edited by Roger D. Masters
and Christopher Kelly. Hanover, NH: Published for Dartmouth College by
University Press of New England, 2005.

- *Politics and the Arts: Letter to M. d'Alembert on the Theatre*. Edited and translated by Allan Bloom. Ithaca, NY: Cornell University Press, 1968.

- *The Social Contract*. In *The Social Contract and Other Later Political Writings*, edited and translated by Victor Gourevitch, 39–152. New York: Cambridge
University Press, 1997.

Roy, Fernande. *Progrès, Harmonie, Liberté: Le libéralisme des milieux d'affaires francophones à Montréal au tournant du siècle*. Montreal: Boréal, 1988.

Russell, Lord John. *An Essay on the History of the English Government and
Constitution from the Reign of Henry VII to the Present Time*. London: Longman,
Hurst, Rees, Orme, and Brown, 1823.

Russell, Peter A. *Attitudes to Social Structure and Mobility in Upper Canada, 1815–
1840*. Lewiston, NY: Edwin Mellen Press, 1990.

Russell, Peter H. *Constitutional Odyssey: Can Canadians Be a Sovereign People?*
Toronto: University of Toronto Press, 1992.

Rutherford, Paul. *The Making of the Canadian Media*. Toronto: McGraw-Hill
Ryerson, 1978.

Ryan, Alan, ed. *The Idea of Freedom: Essays in Honour of Isaiah Berlin*. Oxford:
Oxford University Press, 1979.

Ryan, Mary P. *Women in Public: Between Banners and Ballots, 1825–1880*.
Baltimore: Johns Hopkins University Press, 1990.

Ryerson, Egerton [A Canadian]. *The Affairs of the Canadas in a Series of Letters*.
London: J. King College Hill, 1837.

Ryerson, Stanley Bréhaut. *Unequal Union: Roots of Crisis in the Canadas, 1815–
1873*. 2nd ed. Toronto: Progress Books, 1983.

Sabrevois de Bleury, Charles Clément. *Réfutation de l'écrit de Louis Joseph
Papineau: Ex-orateur de la Chambre d'assemblée du Bas-Canada, intitulé Histoire
de l'insurrection du Canada, publiée dans le recueil hebdomadaire La Revue du
progrès, imprimée à Paris*. Montreal: J. Lovell, 1839.

Saint-Victor, Jacques de. *Les racines de la liberté: Le débat français oublié, 1689–1789*.
Paris: Perrin, 2007.

Schama, Simon. *Patriots and Liberators: Revolution in the Netherlands, 1780–1813*.
New York: Knopf, 1977.

Schulte Nordholt, Jan Willem. *The Dutch Republic and American Independence*.
Chapel Hill: University of North Carolina Press, 1982.

Scott, Jonathan. *Commonwealth Principles: Republican Writing of the English
Revolution*. Cambridge: Cambridge University Press, 2004.

Scruton, Roger. *The Meaning of Conservatism*. Harmondsworth: Penguin Books,
1980.

Séguin, Maurice. *L'idée d'indépendance au Québec: Génèse et historique*. Trois-
Rivières, QC: Boréal Express, 1967.

Sellers, M.N.S. *American Republicanism: Roman Ideology in the U.S. Constitution*.
New York: New York University Press, 1994.

- *The Sacred Fire of Liberty: Republicanism, Liberalism and the Law*. New York: New
York University Press, 1998.

Sewell, Jonathan, and John Beverley Robinson. *Plan for a General Legislative Union of the British Provinces in North America.* London: W. Clowes, 1824.

Shalhope, Robert E. "Republicanism and Early American Historiography." *William and Mary Quarterly* 39, no. 2 (1982): 334–56.

– "Toward a Republican Synthesis: The Emergence of an Understanding of Republicanism in American Historiography." *William and Mary Quarterly* 29, no. 1 (1972): 49–80.

Sheldon, Garrett Ward. *Encyclopedia of Political Thought.* New York: Facts on File, 2001.

Shortt, Adam, and Arthur G. Doughty, eds. *Documents relating to the Constitutional History of Canada, 1759–1791.* 2 vols. 2nd ed., rev. by the Historical Documents Publication Board. Ottawa: Printed by J. de L. Taché, 1918.

Sidney, Algernon. *Discourses Concerning Government.* 1698. Edited by Thomas G. West. Indianapolis: Liberty Classics, 1990.

Sieyès, Emmanuel Joseph. *What is the Third Estate?* 1789. Edited by S.E. Finer. Translated by M. Blondel. London: Pall Mall Press, [1963].

Simard, Sylvain, ed. *La Révolution française au Canada français.* Ottawa: Presses de l'Université d'Ottawa, 1989.

Skinner, Quentin. "The Idea of Negative Liberty: Philosophical and Historical Perspectives." In *Philosophy in History: Essays on the Historiography of Philosophy,* edited by Richard Rorty, J.B. Schneewind, and Quentin Skinner, 193–221. Cambridge: Cambridge University Press, 1984.

– *Liberty before Liberalism.* Cambridge: Cambridge University Press, 1998.

– "The Republican Ideal of Political Liberty." In *Machiavelli and Republicanism,* edited by Gisela Bock, Quentin Skinner, and Maurizio Viroli, 293–309. Cambridge: Cambridge University Press, 1990.

Small, Stephen. *Political Thought in Ireland, 1776–1798: Republicanism, Patriotism and Radicalism.* Oxford: Oxford University Press, 2002.

Smith, Adam. *An Inquiry into the Nature and Causes of the Wealth of Nations.* 1776. Edinburgh: Adam and Charles Black, 1850.

Smith, Allan. *Canada: An American Nation? Essays on Continentalism, Identity, and the Canadian Frame of Mind.* Montreal and Kingston: McGill-Queen's University Press, 1994.

Smith, David E. *The Republican Option in Canada, Past and Present.* Toronto: University of Toronto Press, 1999.

Smith, Lawrence A.H. "*Le Canadien* and the British Constitution, 1806–1810." *Canadian Historical Review* 38, no. 2 (1957): 93–108.

Smyth, Jim, ed. *Revolution, Counter-Revolution, and Union: Ireland in the 1790s.* Cambridge: Cambridge University Press, 2000.

Solé, Jacques. *Les Révolutions de la fin du XVIIIe siècle aux Amériques et en Europe.* Paris: Éditions du Seuil, 2005.

Staël, Madame de. *Des circonstances actuelles qui peuvent terminer la Révolution et les principes qui doivent fonder la république en France.* 1798. Edited by Lucia Omacini. Genève: Droz, 1979.

Stewart, Gordon T. *The Origins of Canadian Politics: A Comparative Approach.* Vancouver: UBC Press, 1986.

Stewart, Walter. *True Blue: The Loyalist Legend.* Toronto: Collins, 1985.

Story, Joseph. *Commentaries on the Constitution of the United States, with a Preliminary Review of the Constitutional History of the Colonies and States before the Adoption of the Constitution.* 2 vols. 1833. Boston: Little, Brown, and Co., 1891.

Strachan, John. *A Discourse on the Character of King George the Third: Addresses to the Inhabitants of British America.* Montreal: Nahum Mower, 1810.

– *The John Strachan Letter Book: 1812–1834.* Edited by George W. Spragge. Toronto: Ontario Historical Society, 1946.

– *A Letter to the Right Honorable Thomas Frankland Lewis, M.P.* York [Toronto]: R. Stanton, 1830.

– *Observations on a "Bill for Uniting the Legislative Councils and Assemblies of the Provinces of Lower Canada and Upper Canada in one Legislature and to Make Further Provision for the Government of the said Provinces."* London: W. Clowes, 1825.

Sullivan, Vickie B. *Machiavelli, Hobbes, and the Formation of a Liberal Republicanism in England.* Cambridge: Cambridge University Press, 2004.

Swords, Liam. *The Green Cockade: The Irish in the French Revolution, 1789–1815.* Dublin: Glendale, 1989.

Tackett, Timothy. "Conspiracy Obsession in a Time of Revolution: French Elites and the Origins of the Terror, 1789–1792." *American Historical Review* 105, no. 3 (2000): 691–713.

Talmon, Jacob Leib. *The Origins of Totalitarian Democracy.* London: Secker and Warburg, 1952.

Taylor, Charles. *Sources of the Self: The Making of the Modern Identity.* Cambridge, MA: Harvard University Press, 1989.

– "What's Wrong with Negative Liberty?" In *Philosophy and the Human Sciences.* New York: Cambridge University Press, 1985.

Terrel, Jean. *Les théories du pacte social: Droit naturel, souveraineté et contrat de Bodin à Rousseau.* Paris: Seuil, 2001.

Thom, Adam (Anti-Bureaucrat). *Remarks on the Petition of the Convention and on the Petition of the Constitutionalists.* Montreal: Herald, 1835.

Thom, Adam (Camillus). *Anti-Gallic Letters; Addressed to His Excellency The Earl of Gosford, Governor-in-Chief of the Canadas.* Montreal: Herald Office, 1836.

Thom, Adam (An Emigrant). *Letter to the Right Hon. E.G. Stanley, His Majesty's Principal Secretary of State for the Colonies.* Montreal: N.p., 1834.

Thompson, E.P. *The Making of the English Working Class.* New York: Pantheon Books, 1963.

Tousignant, Pierre. "La genèse et l'avènement de la constitution de 1791." PhD diss., Université de Montréal, 1971.

Trudel, Marcel. *Louis XVI, le Congrès américain et le Canada, 1774–1789.* Quebec: Éditions du Quartier latin, 1949.

Turgot, Anne-Robert-Jacques. *The Formation and Distribution of Wealth: Reflections on Capitalism.* Translated and edited by Kenneth Jupp. London: Othila, 1999.

Underhill, Frank. *In Search of Canadian Liberalism.* Toronto: Macmillan, 1961.

Uribe-Uran, Victor M., ed. *State and Society in Spanish America during the Age of Revolution.* Wilmington, DE: SR Books, 2001.

Van Kley, Dale, ed. *The French Idea of Freedom: The Old Regime and the Declaration of Rights of 1789.* Stanford: Stanford University Press, 1994.

Verney, Jack. *O'Callaghan: The Making and Unmaking of a Rebel.* Ottawa: Carleton University Press, 1994.

Viger, Denis-Benjamin. *Analyse de l'entretien sur la conservation des établissements du Bas-Canada, des lois, des usages, etc. de ses habitants.* Montreal: James Lane, 1826.

– *Considérations sur les effets qu'ont produit en Canada, la conservation des établissements du pays, les moeurs, l'éducation, etc. de ses habitants et leurs conséquences qu'entraîneraient leur décadence par rapport aux intérêts de la Grande-Bretagne.* Montreal: James Brown, 1809.

– *Considérations relatives à la dernière révolution de la Belgique.* 1831. Montreal: F. Cinq-mars, 1842.

– *Observations de l'hon. D.B. Viger contre la proposition faite dans le Conseil législatif, le 4 mars 1835, de rejeter le Bill de l'assemblée pour la nomination d'un agent de la Province.* Montreal: Ludger Duvernay, 1835.

Vile, M.J.C. *Constitutionalism and the Separation of Powers.* Indianapolis: Liberty Fund, 1998.

Viroli, Maurizio. *For the Love of Country: An Essay on Patriotism and Nationalism.* Oxford: Clarendon Press, 1995.

Voltaire. *Essai sur les moeurs et l'esprit des nations et sur les principaux faits de l'histoire depuis Charlemagne jusqu'à Louis XIII.* 2 vol. 1748–75. Paris: Garnier Frères, 1963.

Wade, Mason. "Quebec and the French Revolution of 1789: The Mission of Henri Mezière." *Canadian Historical Review* 31, no. 4 (1950): 345–68.

Wallot, Jean-Pierre. "En guise de conclusion." *Annales historiques de la Révolution française* 45, no. 3 (1973): 428–35.

– "Frontière ou fragment du système atlantique: Des idées étrangères dans l'identité bas-canadienne au début du XIXe siècle." *CHA Historical Papers* 18, no. 1 (1983): 1–29.

– *Un Québec qui bougeait: Trame socio-politique au tournant du XIXe siècle.* Montreal: Boréal Express, 1973.

– "Religion and French-Canadian Mores in the Early Nineteenth Century." *Canadian Historical Review* 52, no. 1 (1971): 51–94.

– "Révolution et réformisme dans le Bas-Canada (1773–1815)." *Annales historiques de la Révolution française* 45, no. 213 (1973): 344–406.

Ward, Lee. *The Politics of Liberty in England and Revolutionary America.* Cambridge: Cambridge University Press, 2004.

Watt, Steven. "Authoritarianism, Constitutionalism and the Special Council of Lower Canada, 1838–1841." MA thesis (History), McGill University, 1997.

Webking, Robert H. *The American Revolution and the Politics of Liberty.* Baton Rouge: Louisiana State University Press, 1988.

Whitfield, Ernest A. *Gabriel Bonnot de Mably.* London: G. Routledge, 1930.

Wilson, Alan. *The Clergy Reserves of Upper Canada: A Canadian Mortmain.* [Toronto]: University of Toronto Press, [1968].

Wilson, David A. *Paine and Cobbett: The Transatlantic Connection.* Montreal and Kingston: McGill-Queen's University Press, 1988.

Wilton, Carol. *Popular Politics and Political Culture in Upper Canada, 1800–1850.* Montreal and Kingston: McGill-Queen's University Press, 2000.

Wollstonecraft, Mary. *A Vindication of the Rights of Men; with, A Vindication of the Rights of Woman, and Hints.* 1790–92. Edited by Sylvana Tomaselli. Cambridge: Cambridge University Press, 1995.

– *A Vindication of the Rights of Woman.* 1792. London: Penguin Books, 1985.

Wood, Gordon S. *The Creation of the American Republic, 1776–1789.* Chapel Hill: University of North Carolina Press, 1998.

– "Ideology and the Origins of Liberal America." *William and Mary Quarterly* 44, no. 3 (1987): 628–40.

– *The Radicalism of the American Revolution.* New York: A.A. Knopf, 1992.

Wootton, David, ed. *Republicanism and Commercial Society, 1649–1776.* Stanford: Stanford University Press, 1994.

Wright, Johnson Kent. *A Classical Republican in Eighteenth-Century France: The Political Thought of Mably.* Stanford: Stanford University Press, 1997.

Yarbrough, Jean M. *American Virtues: Thomas Jefferson on the Character of a Free People.* Lawrence: University Press of Kansas, 1998.

Young, Andrew James. "American-Upper Canadian Contributions to the Development of Early Colonial Political Opposition, 1805–1828." MA thesis (History), Queen's University, 1999.

Young, Brian. *The Politics of Codification: The Lower Canadian Civil Code of 1866.* Montreal and Kingston: Osgoode Society for Canadian Legal History and McGill-Queen's University Press, 1994.

Zeller, Suzanne. *Inventing Canada: Early Victorian Science and the Idea of a Transcontinental Nation.* Toronto: University of Toronto Press, 1987.

Index

Jackson, John Mills, 80, 207n83
Jacobins, 22, 29, 190n24, 219n135.
   See also Robespierre, Maximilien
James II, 199n81, 212n14
Jarvis, Samuel, 88
Jarvis, William, 80
Jaucourt, Louis de, 24–6
Jautard, Valentin, 38–9, 42
Jefferson, Thomas, 24, 99, 104, 171,
   190n23, 194n21, 211n7
judicial branch, 51, 55, 68, 143; for
   the American federalists, 31; in
   Great Britain, 31; moderns' view
   of, 31, 137, 51; and impeachment
   of judges, 66–7; republicans' view
   of, 51, 112; in Upper Canada, 80

Kelly, Stéphane, 18
Kempt, James, 92–3, 163
Kimber, René-Joseph, 107
Koselleck, Reinhart, 4
Kramnick, Isaac, 19

La Fontaine, Louis-Hippolyte, 18, 96,
   215n86
Lacombe, Claire, 119
Lake St Pierre, 184
Lally-Tolendal, Trophime-Gérard de,
   24
Lamonde, Yvan, 122
Larue, Richard, 160
Latin America, 16–17, 20, 54
legislative assemblies (colonial), 47–
   9, 54, 61; and Constitutional Act,
   59–60; and control of subsidies,
   67–8, 91, 93; as creatures of
   Parliament, 60, 168; constitutionalists view of, 141–50; granted to
   the Canadas, 41–4, 48, 50–1; lacking impeachment power, 66; and
   ministerial responsibility, 61; reformers' view of, 55–6; republicans' view of, 107–8; role in

colonial government, 60; speaker's
   role in, 74–5; taxation power of,
   57, 139. *See also* Legislative
   Assembly of Lower Canada;
   Legislative Assembly of Upper
   Canada
Legislative Assembly of Lower
   Canada, 11, 50–2, 54, 56, 92;
   agent in London, 100; conflict
   with other government bodies,
   93–4; and control of subsidies, 67–
   72, 91, 93, 166, 179–80; French
   Canadian domination of, 72, 91,
   108, 131, 156, 162; and impeachment, 58, 66–7; judges sitting in,
   143; and Legislative Council, 55;
   and ministerial responsibility, 63,
   68; and proposed Canadian union,
   72–4; republican interpretation of,
   76, 108; taxation power of, 139;
   and women's suffrage, 118–22
Legislative Assembly of Upper
   Canada, 52, 86, 94; and control of
   subsidies, 80, 91, 93, 112, 166;
   Gourlay's critique of, 85; and ministerial responsibility, 87
legislative branch: in absolute monarchy, 30; constitutionalists' view of,
   50, 144; moderns' view of, 31–2;
   reformers' view of, 56; relationship
   to executive branch, 44, 47–8, 54–
   5, 58–63, 65, 68, 116; republicans'
   view of, 5, 28–31, 49, 70, 116. *See
   also* Special Council; separation of
   powers
legislative councils, 44, 46, 48, 75,
   142–3; accepted by reformers, 70;
   and assemblies, 70; compared with
   House of Lords, 48; and constitutionalists, 131, 148, 162, 178; in
   Lower Canada, 50, 55–6, 65, 67,
   103, 149–50, 156; and proposed
   Canadian union, 72, 131; as

provincial ministry. *See* ministerial
responsibility
public assemblies of 1837, 97, 123,
170, 172–3, 180; Malbaie, 108;
Saint-Constant, 105; Saint-
François, 211n4; Saint-Marc, 106,
216n88; Saint-Scholastique, 122–
3, 173; Six Counties, 170–1, 179;
Stanbridge, 232n39

Quebec Act (1774), 42, 66, 73, 104
Quebec City, 77
Quebec Conference of 1864, 57
Quebec Gazette (Gazette de Quebec), 37,
39–40, 49, 132. *See also* Neilson,
Samuel; Neilson, John
Quebec Mercury, 55
Quesnay, François, 24

Radicals (English), 23, 25, 82, 89–
90, 96–7, 161; elitism of, 117; inspired by American Revolution,
15; relationship with Canadian republicans, 100. *See also* Price,
Richard; Priestly, Joseph
radicals (Upper Canada), 9, 13, 162–
3, 166, 168; accused of disloyalty,
98; and control of Assembly, 94–5,
108–9; distinguished from liberals,
102; espouse republicanism, 160;
Gourlay identifies with, 82–6; and
Legislative Council, 110–11;
Mackenzie and, 90; and
Rebellions, 180–1. *See also* Gourlay,
Robert; Mackenzie, William Lyon;
republicanism
Rahe, Paul A., 19
Raynal, Guillaume-Thomas François,
103
Rebellions (Canada), 3, 7, 18, 77,
127, 170–6, 180–1; as final chapter of Atlantic Revolutions, 95; impact on constitutionalists, 154–5

Red River Colony, 132
Reflections on the Revolution in France,
43
Reform Bill (United Kingdom,
1832), 92
reformers, 9, 18, 43–4, 54–5, 128–9,
161; election victory of 1828, 94;
in Lower Canada, 54–77, 91, 112,
166; and primogeniture, 103–4;
radicalization of, 70–7, 86, 91–2,
95, 163, 166; in Upper Canada,
77–91, 112–13, 133. *See also*
Bédard, Pierre-Stanislas; Gourlay,
Robert
Reid, John Phillip, 21
relationship between civil liberties
and political freedom, 32–6
religious tolerance, 10, 36, 38, 41,
134–5
removal of public servants. *See*
impeachment
representation, 29, 31–2, 107, 109,
146; Gourlay on, 82–3, 85; committee of inquiry on, 94, 108–9
republicanism, 8, 17, 30–1, 50, 122;
and corruption, 27, 75, 82, 89,
106–8; and ethnic nationalism,
156–7; as ideology, 19, 24, 161;
and individual rights, 19; and
mixed government, 75–7; and patriotism, 27, 105; and popular sovereignty, 28–9, 34, 50; as
subversive force, 34, 36, 43, 75,
161; and virtue, 24, 26–7, 105–6
republicanism in the Atlantic world,
16–17, 19, 23–24, 30, 34, 106;
ethnic inclusivity of, 123; as inspiration for Patriotes and radicals,
99–102. *See also* republican liberty
republicanism in Canada, 9, 23, 38–
40, 92, 95–8, 102–28, 160–1; appeal to Atlantic republicans, 19;
Constitutional Act as antidote to,